Your Own Pigs
You May Not Eat

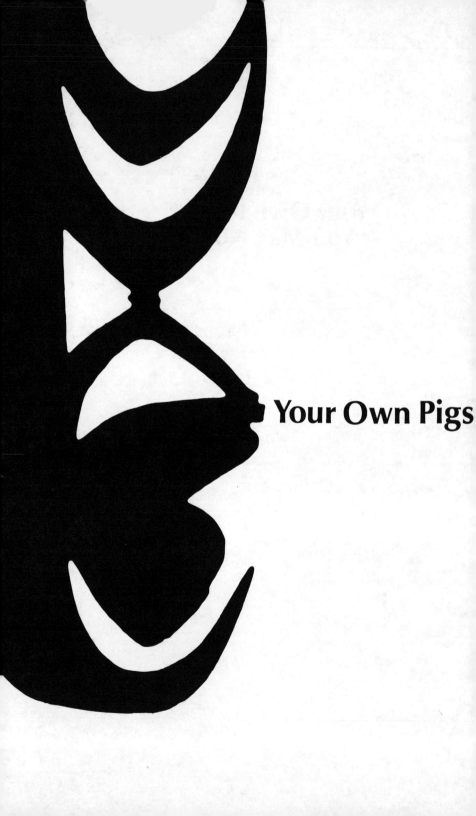

Your Own Pigs

Paula G. Rubel
Abraham Rosman

You May Not Eat

A Comparative Study
of New Guinea Societies

The University of Chicago Press
Chicago and London

0823073

Paula G. Rubel and Abraham Rosman are
professors of anthropology at Barnard College
and Columbia University. They are the authors
of *Feasting with Mine Enemy*.

The University of Chicago Press, Chicago 60637
The University of Chicago Press, Ltd., London

©1978 by The University of Chicago
All rights reserved. Published 1978
Printed in the United States of America
82 81 80 79 78   54321

Library of Congress Cataloging in Publication Data

Rubel, Paula G.
    Your own pigs you may not eat

Bibliography: p.
    Includes index.
    1.   Ethnology—New Guinea.   2.   Commerce, Primitive—
New Guinea.   3.   Rites and ceremonies—New Guinea.
I.   Rosman, Abraham, joint author.   II.   Title.
GN671.N5R8   301.29'95   78-7544
ISBN 0-226-73082-4

To Daniel, David, Erika, and Lewis

Howard: "Give him some tobacco." (Dobbs gives the Indian his tobacco pouch. The Indian takes it and offers his own.)

Howard: "Gracias."

Dobbs: "We give them our tobacco. They give us theirs. I don't get it. Why doesn't everybody smoke his own?"

From the screenplay of *The Treasure of the Sierra Madre*

Contents

Figures

Acknowledgments

This book is a comparative study of a number of New Guinea societies. It involves the analysis of ethnographic data gathered by many anthropologists. Without their original research, we could not have done our comparative analysis.

We first began to work on this project during our sabbatical year, 1972–73, which we spent at the University of Cambridge. We would like to thank the Department of Anthropology and King's College for the hospitality they extended to us during that year, and especially to thank Professors Edmund Leach and Meyer Fortes for intellectual stimulation as well as thoughtful assistance. During that year we also had an opportunity to present some of our ideas, subsequently incorporated into this book, at the Colloquium on "Ecology and Society in Melanesia" in Paris. We would like to thank Jacques Barrau and Maurice Godelier for having invited us to participate in this Colloquium.

In the summer of 1974, we did field work in New Guinea to supplement our library research. In addition to gathering information from informants, we were able to observe exchange ceremonies in several areas. This field research was sponsored by the National Science Foundation (GS-42952) and we would like to extend our thanks to them for their generous support. We would also like to thank Andrew and Marilyn Strathern, our colleagues at the New Guinea Research Unit, Dan and Shelby Harrison of S.I.L., and Mr. and Mrs. Malcolm McKellar for their help and hospitality while we were in New Guinea. We are particularly grateful to the many people in the various communities we visited who took the time to talk to us and assist us in gathering information.

We are in debt to Barnard College for providing us with a Faculty Research Grant and a Shell Assist Grant to aid us in carrying out this research. Professor Edwin Cook was particularly helpful in providing us with unpublished materials.

For their comments and suggestions on the manuscript, we would like to thank Harvey Pitkin, Sally McLendon, George C. Bond, and Rena Lederman. However, we take all responsibility for whatever appears in this book. The ideas in this book have been presented to our students in several seminars over the past few years, and we have appreciated their stimulating responses. Finally, we are grateful to Constance Budelis and Marisa Bolognese, who typed the manuscript.

Your Own Pigs
You May Not Eat

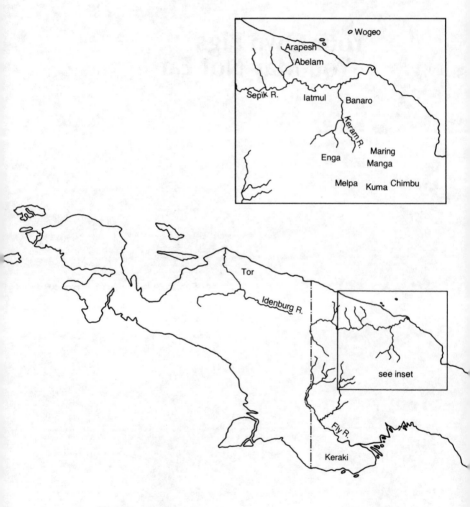

Map of New Guinea

1 Introduction

"Why doesn't everybody smoke his own tobacco?" In New Guinea, one might well ask: why doesn't everyone eat his own pigs; why doesn't everyone eat his own yams?

One of the most striking characteristics of New Guinea societies is the presence of large-scale ceremonial distributions, at which great quantities of raw and cooked foodstuffs are distributed. These will usually be returned in kind at a later date. When groups live in different ecological zones and exchange goods which are not directly available to the other group, the economic utility of such exchanges is apparent. But F. E. Williams has posed the question of why groups living in the same environment exchange like for like. The latter forms of exchange must have a significance that is not utilitarian. Such ceremonial distributions are total social phenomena, in the sense of the term used by Marcel Mauss. As total social phenomena they manifest the interplay between the kinship and marriage structure, the nature of political leadership, the economic structure, and the religious and symbolic systems. The focus in this book is on these ceremonial distributions as a starting point in understanding the relationship between exchange and these social and cultural domains.

The theoretical framework utilized in our analysis relies on both structuralism and exchange theory. We feel that it is necessary to present our interpretation of the essential characteristics of structuralist theory. Structuralism begins with a basic distinction between the observational or surface level of phenomena and the underlying structure.

In contrast to other theoretical approaches, structuralism places greatest emphasis upon the relationship between elements, rather than upon the nature of those elements themselves. When one focuses upon relationships, then the elements that are in a relationship will have certain general characteristics. Elements must be bounded so that they are distinct and separate from one another. Elements in relationship may be identical to one another, or different from one another. Elements are themselves analytical constructs.

Though relationship is the most important aspect of structure, structure is more than mere relationship. A structure is a system and a relationship is only a part of a system. The systemic nature of a structure is such that all the elements in relationships are interrelated. All the elements in relationship must be specified, and by specifying the elements the system is bounded. Those things not relevant as elements are outside the structure and excluded from the analysis. Since structures are systems, it follows that a change in one element will result in changes in the other elements and in the structure. Structural laws describe the covariation of elements in a structure.

Another characteristic of structures is that they may be ordered into hierarchies. There is a connection between hierarchies and the relative boundedness of structures. What is external to a structure at a lower level is internal to the structure that encompasses it at a higher level. The structures at each level of a hierarchy retain their systemic characteristics. A taxonomy, or hierarchically ordered classification, in and of itself, is not a structure. The structure of a taxonomy is the statement of the principles describing the relationships between the elements, not merely the hierarchical arrangement of the elements themselves.

Finally, the concept of transformation is a necessary part of the definition of a structure. Transformation refers to the nature of the relationship between different structures. In a single society, if the structure of each cultural domain can be mapped isomorphically one upon the other, then it can be said that a single structure underlies these different cultural domains. In some societies, the mapping process does not result in a single structure. Instead, there may be two homologous structures, not immediately reducible one to the other. The transformational relationship between these two homologous structures is more complex in that it is underlaid by a single structure at a more general level in the hierarchy of structures. Lévi-Strauss's use of the concept of transformation can be seen in his reference to the three levels of communication distinguished by sets of rules which govern the circulation of women, goods and services, and messages. "These three forms of communication are also forms of exchange which are obviously interrelated (because marriage relations are associated with economic prestations, and language comes into play at all levels). It is therefore legitimate to seek homologies between them and define the formal characteristics of each type considered independently and of the transformations which make the transition possible from one to another" (Lévi-Strauss 1963: 83).

The transformational relationship between homologous structures in a single society is a synchronic one. The differences between homologous structures in the same society, which lead these structures to be viewed as transformations of one another at a single point in time, may be used as clues for the exploration of diachrony. Jakobson has pointed this out for linguistics, noting, "The start and finish of any mutational process coexist in the synchrony and belong to two different subcodes of one and the same language" (Jakobson 1970: 22–23). The concept of transformation is also involved in diachronic analysis. Structures representing two different time periods for the same society may be compared. Continuity may be maintained and the structures remain identical, or the later structure may be related to the earlier structure through a transformation. Another approach to transformation involves the comparison of a structure or structures of a single society with the structures of one or more other societies within a geographic area, with the assumption of a more or less remote genetic relationship between them. As one moves in the analysis from one society to another, the structures of the second are shown to be a transformation of the first.

The ideas presented above represent our view of the central concepts in structuralism. They draw upon the theoretical writings of Lévi-Strauss (1963, 1969), Leach (1961, 1976), and Jakobson (1970). Cultural anthropologists who have used a structuralist approach in their work have been criticized because it is said that their models are synchronic and static and unable to deal with change and process. In the work that follows we have sought to apply Jakobson's linguistic approach regarding the relationship between synchrony and diachrony to cultural data, and to deal with the ways in which structures are transformed through time.

There is a direct relationship between structuralism and exchange. The defining characteristic of exchange is the giving and receiving of women, goods and services between groups. Exchange links groups and these linkages constitute relationships. An investigation of exchange is therefore an investigation of relationships between groups. Because of this focus upon relationships, the analysis of exchange inevitably is structuralist in character.

Structuralist models of social relations between groups have been based upon rules concerning the exchange of women between those groups. The three types of structural models based on such rules advanced initially by Lévi-Strauss are restricted exchange, based on bilateral cross-cousin marriage; generalized exchange, based on patrilateral cross-cousin marriage; and generalized exchange, based upon matrilateral cross-cousin marriage. For each of these models, a particular marriage rule spells out how groups are linked to one another through the exchange of women. Each of these models represents a different type of structure, in which groups as elements are combined in a different way.

Affinal exchanges of goods, so common in all societies, naturally follow along the same lines as the exchange of women for these structural models. They are expressions of the same structure. Affines also exchange services with one another, such as burial services. These exchanges of services by affines are still another expression of the same structure.

The three types of structural models originally derived from rules governing the exchange of women represent a family of models related through a series of transformations. The restricted exchange model, based upon bilateral cross-cousin marriage, represents the basic form of which the other two are transformations. Both forms of generalized exchange arise from a prohibition on one or the other cross-cousin. Lévi-Strauss (1969) has spelled these transformations out in detail, as well as the means by which the structure can be undermined if the rules of prohibition are ignored.

Any form of exchange creates relationships between groups. Therefore exchanges of goods and services can be the basis for structures, even when exchanges of women between these groups are prohibited. Where this is present, there are rules that govern the exchange of goods and services with one set of groups, and a different set of rules that govern the exchange of women with another set of groups. Goods and services exchanged with affines in this case will be different from goods and services exchanged with exchange partners. Rules may even be present which parallel the incest taboo and compel individuals to exchange goods that they are forbidden to consume themselves. Some of the societies which we shall consider forbid individuals from eating the pigs and yams which they themselves have raised.

Exchanges not only link groups in relationships, but also serve to separate them. Exchange may be the means by which opposition and competition are expressed. In the New Guinea societies to be discussed, exchanges are always controlled by men. Though women may produce the things that are exchanged, it is the men who do the exchanging. Male-female relations are therefore illuminated by examining exchange. When men exchange with other men, the structure of leadership and political organization is brought into play.

Detailed descriptive ethnographic accounts of New Guinea societies date from the first decade of the twentieth century, with the appearance of Malinowski's study of *Mailu* (1915), and Seligman's description of the *Melanesians of British New Guinea* (1910). These early studies concentrated on coastal peoples or offshore island peoples. Thurnwald's account of the Banaro, published in 1916, which we utilize in our analysis, is one of the earliest accounts of a Lowland people. Ethnographic research in the twenties and early thirties continued to concentrate on the Lowlands. A number of theoretical interests informed this research, including an interest in the relationship between culture and psychology, male and female differences, the holistic integration of cultures, as well as straightforward ethnographic description. Ethnographic research in the New Guinea Highlands began in the latter part of the thirties, but it was not until after World War II that extensive field research was carried out in this area. The theoretical approaches adopted by field workers after the war represented an expansion of interests which included the ecological approach. Some of the more recent work in Highland and Lowland New Guinea has emphasized the theories of structuralism, exchange and symbolic anthropology. There is also a long tradition of ethnographic research in West Irian, formerly Dutch New Guinea, which continues up to the present. Despite this large corpus of ethnographic material, there has been relatively little comparative research done on New Guinea societies. While there have been a number of books bringing together articles on religion, marriage, politics, and male-female relations in New Guinea societies, only their introductions attempt to make comparative generalizations on those topics (Lawrence and Meggitt 1965; Glasse and Meggitt 1969; Berndt and Lawrence 1971; Brown and Buchbinder 1976). Allen's (1967) comparative study of male cults and initiation does attempt to make generalizations about this specific phenomenon.

The comparative method we have adopted involves a selection of thirteen New Guinea societies. These have not been selected randomly. The societies examined are those whose ethnographic descriptions provide detailed information on the operation of the variables under consideration. We are aware that the units that we are referring to as "societies" above, which are also the descriptive units of analysis of the ethnographers, are in many respects artificial units. In his description and analysis, the ethnographer bounds these units. With our emphasis on exchange and our interest in external relationships created and maintained by exchanges, there are no longer clear-cut, bounded entities called societies. Linguistic boundaries and differences in cultural meanings are bridged by exchanges of women and goods, creating a larger field of exchange, often with a single underlying structure.

The methodology employed in this study derives from the theoretical framework that we have outlined above. The study is comparative, and involves a multiplicity of variables that are examined in a particular sample of societies.

The variables of the study are rules regarding the nature of descent and descent-group formation, rules regarding post-marital residence, rules regarding exchange of women and goods with affines, rules regarding ceremonial exchange, rules regarding exchange of goods with spirits, the structure of the spirit world, the organization of leadership, and kinship terminology. We are concerned with rules and with normative statements since these are what we use to build structural models. We are equally concerned with behavior and actual events, especially those involving exchanges. Both the rules presented by the native informants and their actual behavior represent surface phenomena. From these two areas of surface phenomena we, the analysts, construct structural models. This distinction between surface phenomena and structural model is analogous to de Saussure's distinction between *parole* and *langue* (de Saussure 1966). The variables of the study outline a set of cultural domains. Verification of structural models for a single society comes about through the demonstration that a single structure underlies cultural material thought to be unrelated. A single society may have one underlying structure or a number of underlying structures that are in homologous relationships to one another. The demonstration of homology is another form of verification of the underlying structure.

Whether a society has a single underlying structure, or a number of underlying structures in homologous relationship to one another, the dominant structure, as our analysis of these societies will reveal, is that most clearly expressed in the ritual involved in exchange ceremonies. We consider these structures to be dominant because they are the embodiment of the cognitive themes of the society, they serve to

organize behavior in different areas of life, including exploi-
tation of the environment. The prohibition upon eating one's
own pigs, and the need to exchange them, is an illustration
of this.

Chapters 2–11 of this book consist of the analysis of thirteen different societies, in terms of the variables presented
above. Each chapter concludes with a structural model, or
models, arrived at as the result of the analysis.

Each of the next six chapters takes a related group of the
variables and treats it comparatively in all of the societies in
our sample.

Chapter 18, the conclusion, demonstrates the way in
which the underlying structures of the societies in our sample may be related to one another by a series of transformations.

2

Tor, Keraki, and Banaro

The simplest type of exchange structure is that created by direct reciprocal exchange, which Lévi-Strauss refers to as "restricted exchange." This kind of exchange creates a two-sided structure, which may take the form of moieties or other varieties of dual organization. Groups may reciprocally exchange women, goods and services. With respect to the exchange of women, the most direct expression of reciprocal exchange is sister exchange.

The societies to be examined in this chapter share a rule of marriage through the exchange of sisters. They therefore all share a common structure of duality, which is expressed in various ways in the three societies.

Tor

Since there is a certain degree of cultural unity in the Tor area, the various groupings of this river basin have been described in a single monograph. The population of the area is about one thousand. Many of the languages spoken by the people of the Tor belong to the Berrik language group, and this language is the lingua franca of the district.

Thirteen different tribal groups are identified in this area. The largest numbers eighty-five individuals and several include less than fifty individuals. Each tribe is an autonomous group occupying its own territory, and its boundaries are fixed and known to all. Members of the tribe have collective rights to that territory which are inalienable as long as there is one surviving member of the tribe. The economy is primarily one of sago collection.

Members of different tribal units may intermarry, have ceremonial relations with one another, or war upon one another. Basically their relationship is a rivalrous one. However, some tribes maintain an elder brother–younger brother relationship with one another which entails the right to utilize each other's territory. Such "brother tribes" may not wage war against each other or practice sorcery against one another. Between other pairs of tribes, there may be a perpetual state of war.

Each tribe has one major semipermanent village that is the center of social and religious activity. In addition, there are subsidiary hamlets temporarily occupied primarily for sago collection. Other hamlets may be used for security purposes.

There are no formal positions of leadership among the people of the Tor area. Success in economic endeavors such as hunting, gardening, house building and canoe building gives men a certain degree of prestige. Extensive knowledge of myths may also be a factor in leadership. In addition, men with organizational ability will assume authority in certain situations. Active leaders tend to be younger rather than older men, since only the former possess the physical strength necessary to the economic endeavors that gain them renown. When these men become older, they still retain the prestige but not the influence they had earlier (Oosterwal 1961: 96–97). However, Oosterwal also recounts instances when, in the absence of individuals to assume positions of leadership, communal activity such as building a bachelor's house or communal hunt was stalled.

Most marriages take place within the tribe or village. Sometimes marriages take place between individuals of two tribes when there is a shortage of women due to the low population of the villages. The ideal marriage pattern is sister exchange. Oosterwal notes, "In principle, a man can only contract a marriage when he can offer a younger sister or another female relative to his wife's brother in exchange. This obligation of exchange is expressed by the people of the Tor as: 'When you have no sister, you cannot marry' " (Oosterwal 1961: 101). "However, serious objections may be raised to a certain marriage by the girl's brother as well as by her father and her mother's brother, especially when the latter is not yet married. For then, he himself has the right to give his Si Da in exchange for a wife for himself" (Oosterwal 1961: 103). It is clear in this instance that the mother's brother has not received a wife in exchange for his sister. Occasionally the return of a woman for a woman is delayed for some time. There is variation in marriage preferences and prohibitions among these thirteen tribes. All of these tribes allow marriage with an actual cross-cousin. Some tribes allow marriage with one or both parallel cousins while others forbid it. Shortages of women as potential wives may result in the overriding of even these prohibitions. The use of brideprice to obtain a wife, instead of sister exchange, seems a recent introduction and is performed secretly. A sacred flute may on rare occasions also be exchanged for a wife (Oosterwal 1961: 110). The combination of sister exchange and bilateral cross-cousin marriage is presented in a diagram by Oosterwal and would seem to be the pattern followed, if appropriate women are present (Oosterwal 1961: 106). If this is the case, then it would seem that sister exchange continues to occur over generations between two family lines.

A man wishing to negotiate a marriage first engages in discussion with his future brother-in-law regarding the proposed sister exchange. He offers him small presents including fish. The father and mother's brother of the future bride are also consulted. If the parties agree, the bride prepares sago mash for her husband-to-be and feeds him the first mouthful. His public eating of it signifies their marriage. "Food and sexual intercourse are closely associated in the Tor district and regarded as almost synonymous in married life" (Oosterwal 1961: 100). Most marriages do not involve simultaneous exchange of sisters, but rather the return of a woman is promised in due course. Until the return takes place and the exchange is completed, the bridegroom is considered to be in debt to his wife's elder brother. The husband regularly presents fish and other food gifts or trade goods to his wife's elder brother as long as he remains a debtor (Oosterwal 1961: 108).

After a child is born to the marriage, that child's mother's brother plays an important supportive role. Mother's brother will plant trees, lay out fields, and help his sisters's son build a house, as well as play an important ritual role. The sister's son has obligations in return, including giving the mother's brother a share of the returns of his hunting and the blowing of his mother's brother's flutes (Oosterwal 1961: 66, 86, 168).

The mother's brother plays a central role in the initiation of a boy, which is held in a special house deep in the forest. After puberty, boys are seized and sequestered there for more than two months. The food for each boy is cooked and fed to him by his mother's brother. At the start of the ceremony, the initiates are anointed with snake fat by their mothers' brothers, who tell them myths extending over many days which explain the significance of the ceremonies. Special songs are imparted to the sisters' sons which are essential for successful capture of specific animals, birds, and fish. At the conclusion of the initiation, each boy receives new arm and leg bands woven for him by his mother's brother. The boys then wash in the river, and return to their village, where a large dance feast is held, to which members of other tribes are invited. Henceforth the boy will sleep in the bachelor's house and will be bound by a number of food taboos (Oosterwal 1961: 239–47). These taboos are removed after the *mengan* ceremony four to six years later. At this ceremony, the youths are fed *mengan* fruit pulp by their fathers, followed by a dance. They may now marry.

In one context a sister's son is identified with his mother's brother. This is in what Oosterwal calls the flute-owning group. The flutes are the sacred ceremonial symbols of life which are kept in the men's house and used in a variety of ceremonies. The men who own flutes as a group are connected to one another by matrilineal kin ties. The flutes bear the same name and are said to personify this matrilineal kin group. A boy's first flute is made by his father and given to him. Oosterwal presents the following picture linking the exchanges of women and flutes. In a marriage exchange, two men exchange sisters. In the next generation, each gives his son a flute which then becomes the property of the matrilineal kin group linking the boy and his mother's brother. Oosterwal notes, "Thus a marriage by exchange always implies a double exchange. The bride-giver yields one woman and receives another in return. But for a giver of life who has been relinquished—the woman produces the food and bears children, both of which maintain the group—the bride-giver also receives a flute, which also is a giver of life" (1961: 235).

Though the people of the Tor do not have domesticated pigs, the pig constitutes an important object in the ceremonial distribution system and is their favorite food. The hunter who has killed a boar must divide it amongst the villagers, but he is not allowed to eat any of it (Oosterwal 1961: 65). Men may also catch piglets in the forest and raise them to maturity. These pigs are named, described, and addressed by kinship terms and are fed sago, which creates a special kinship relationship between the pig and the woman who feeds it and her family. The pig is killed at a feast by a distant relative of the owner and all in the tribe partake of the meat except the owner and his family. "The boar, however, is not kept to serve as food. The owner uses the meat as a medium of exchange. Moreover, it is also used for the fulfilling of his social obligations, such as food gifts to certain (affinal) relatives" (Oosterwal 1961: 72). Boars may be raised not by their owners but by people in other tribes. In these circumstances, the owner may eat the meat of that pig since he has not raised it, but the one who has given it food may not. The keeper receives fish, vegetable food, or material goods in exchange. Tribes that keep one another's pigs are thereby linked in pig-feeding alliances.

Feasting and the distribution of food are an integral part of all social occasions and define the essentially rivalrous nature of the relationship between groups. At least an equal return must be presented, or there is a loss in prestige. The building of the men's ceremonial house that is the focal point of the village is accompanied at each stage by feasts. The inaugural feast for the new men's house requires many months of gathering and preparing foodstuffs. This feast is also associated with the theme of fertility. Sago is prepared by the

women, and men constantly hunt pigs. The prestige of the
community is linked to the size of the feast that they make,
since people from other tribes are invited and it is considered
a great religious occasion (Oosterwal 1961: 214). Oosterwal
compares this feast to a potlatch. He says, "The food distributions . . . also play an important part in the everlasting
rivalry of the tribes. The more food is offered to the guests,
the higher the hosts are held in respect. Those food distributions make the other tribes envious, who in their turn
will try to offer their guests still more food. The duration of
the *faareh* feast—and the longer the feast lasts, the greater the
prestige the host acquires—primarily depends on the
amount of food, which a tribe is able to collect" (Oosterwal
1961: 238). The jaws of the pigs that have been killed and
cooked for the feast are hung from the roof of the men's
house and displayed to the guests. Subsequently other feasts
are held in the men's house which resemble this inaugural
feast. The flute feast, a feast which only men attend, is held
in the men's house. A special flute pig is hunted, killed,
cooked, and, together with sago, ceremonially fed to the
flutes. During the period before the flute feast, as well as
before the *faareh* feast, men are not allowed to have sexual
intercourse (Oosterwal 1961: 231).

When a conflict between men in the same village is resolved, the last stage is an exchange of goods between the
two parties.

Keraki

West of the Fly River, in the Morehead District, an area of
swampy marshland and sparse population, live a congeries
of people, including the Keraki who are the subject of *Papuans of the Trans-Fly* by F. E. Williams. In 1926, the total
Keraki population numbered between seven and eight
hundred. The Keraki are divided into nine tribes, each of
which is made up of three or four permanent villages. Each
tribe has its own territory. The villages that make up a tribe
usually act as a unit in feasting, initiation, and warfare (Williams 1936: 51, 55).

There are both permanent and temporary villages. The

Keraki repair to the latter, which are located along river banks, during the dry season. Only the permanent villages on higher ground contain coconut groves, and the *mongovivi*, the permanent houses whose interiors are used for storing yams and sweet potatoes while people sleep on the verandas (Williams 1936: 15, 17). One or more major tracts of land are associated with each village.

A moiety structure is found among the Keraki. "The moiety is called *widama* (literally 'side', or 'half')" (Williams 1936: 64).

> The whole of the Morehead district, comprising the Keraki, Gambadi and Semariji peoples, is divided into three groups, of which membership is determined by patrilineal descent. They are called Bangu, Maiawa, and Sangara, and will be referred to as sections. Everywhere, however, it is found that the first two, Bangu and Maiawa, are closely associated to the exclusion of the third, Sangara. The population is in fact divided into exogamous moieties; Bangu and Maiawa may not intermarry, but either may marry with Sangara. Since Maiawa is in all respects so closely bound up with Bangu, and since in numbers it constitutes a very small minority, it may be treated virtually as part of Bangu. When it is necessary therefore to distinguish between moieties, I shall speak of the Bangu Moiety and the Sangara Moiety, the first being understood to include Maiawa (Williams 1936: 57).

Other names which are used to refer to Bangu, Maiawa, and Sangara have the meaning of "front", "middle", and "rear", respectively. "Front" and "middle" are grouped together and opposed to "rear." The two moieties are associated with different sets of hawks as their totems. Bangu is associated with the sun, sago, bananas, "female" drum, and certain kinds of yam and sweet potatoes; Sangara with the moon, other yams and sweet potatoes, sugar cane, taro, coconut, tobacco, dog, bull roarer, and sacred bamboo flutes.

In most cases, the men of a village belong to a single section. When men of two sections live in the same village, each section occupies its own area. Postmarital residence is virilocal. Williams uses the term "local group" to refer to the men of the same section who live together. "In all kinds of concerted endeavor it seems to take the foremost place. Its members are united by kinship, by common interest, and by a strong sentiment of fellowship" (Williams 1936: 66). Since the moiety (or section) is exogamous, the local group, which belongs to a particular section, is also exogamous. The local group acts as a unit in hunting, gardening, and making sago, in holding feasts and attending feasts in other villages, in boys' initiation ceremonies, in mourning rites, in rites of fertility at harvest time, in the ownership of bull roarers, and in carrying out negotiations for a marriage.

Williams presents an extended discussion of totems, as they relate to groups of differing magnitude. Moieties, as we have noted, are identified with totems. Totems are also associated with single tribes or groups of tribes. Specific totems are also associated with patrilineal exogamous local groups which Williams calls *tuarar* (Williams 1936: 96). *Tuarar* carry out activities aimed at the magical control of their totemic species and other forms of magic which their group controls. This is in contrast to the paucity of ceremonial activities associated with the totems of groups of other magnitudes. The *tuarar* does not seem to coincide with the local group discussed above (Williams 1936: 98).

There is a position of headman, which Williams discusses at some length.

> We have already seen that there are no well established "chiefs" in the Morehead district. To the individuals who by more or less general consent hold the leadership of the local groups I have given the name "headman", though it may well be that even such a noncommittal word is too pretentious. There is at times, in fact, some doubt among the villagers themselves as to who their headman actually is. . . . It may certainly be said that the headman's status is at best very vaguely defined; his authority varies in different groups with his personal character; and it often merges imperceptively with that of others of the old men (Williams 1936: 236).

The activities of the Keraki headman are the same as those of the Big Man in other New Guinea societies. "The headmen are expected to stand above others as foodproducers and feast-makers" (Williams 1936: 235). The headman is expected to be a man of wealth and generosity. Though not necessarily involved in sorcery or rain making, which, among the Keraki, are primarily individual rather than group activities, he does take a leading role in public rites of magic and in initiation ceremonies. He is caretaker of the group's ceremonial bull roarer. He acts on behalf of his group in extending and in receiving invitations to feasts. Though the headman initiates group activities such as preparations for feasts, hunts, and sago making, this reflects a consensus reached by his group after much discussion and does not constitute orders given by the headman to members of his group.

In one respect, the Keraki headsman appears to differ from the typical Big Man in other New Guinea societies—succession is said to be hereditary. Williams indicates, "The headman's position is hereditary, passing from elder brother to younger brother and eventually back to the son of the elder. . . . The succession, however, may pass for the time being out of the immediate family to a classificatory brother who happens to be senior or dominant in the village. . . . Insofar as the local group remains a close-knit patrilineal kin it is normally the eldest among them, provided he is able-bodied and has the requisite strength of personality, who will be the headman" (Williams 1936: 242–43). The Keraki term *warasari* is said to refer to the headman. "The word *warasari*, on the other hand, might be given to several individuals in the group, to any in fact who stood out above the others as notabilities or as men of substance" (Williams 1936: 242). In attempting to reconcile the various pieces of information on succession to headmanship provided by Williams, one is forced to conclude that formal hereditary succession, as that concept is utilized in anthropology, does not apply. The position of headman is not clearly delineated, either by chiefly insignia or by ceremonial installation to the position. Personal qualities play an important role in acquiring and maintaining the position, though seniority in birth order confers an initial advantage.

The majority of marriages take place between members of the same tribe or between neighboring tribes. Though one may marry within one's own tribe, the spouse must be of the opposite moiety, of a different *tuarar*, and of another local group, since these units are exogamous. Exchange is the principle underlying marriage among the Keraki. Williams observes, "The rule that marriage should be negotiated by exchange is observed almost without exception . . . it may be said that in the ideal instance two men give one another their true younger sisters (*nungan*); but when a man has no true sister to dispose of he will be furnished with a classificatory sister from among his kin; and failing this he will procure a woman of the same moiety from another locality, not as a wife but as a 'sister' to exchange for a wife" (Williams 1936: 134–35). Several of Williams's informants mentioned direct wife purchase as a possibility; however, since no cases could be cited, Williams dismisses this as an idea introduced to some Keraki from elsewhere. In contrast, numerous cases of the purchase of a sister to exchange for a wife are cited (Williams 1936: 139). If a man without a true sister receives a classificatory sister from a kinsman in order to exchange her for a wife, he is under obligation to return a woman to that kinsman in the future. Exchange of sisters, true or classificatory, may be simultaneous or deferred, but a woman must eventually be returned for a woman given.

Though the marriage negotiations are handled by the immediate families involved, "the local group also feels the responsibility as a whole; that it acts as a unit in the ceremonies; and that it enforces the keeping of the contract as one between itself and another group of the same status" (Williams 1936: 114). Villages, made up of one or more local groups, also seem to be units involved in the exchange of women. Williams indicates that there is continuing reciprocity in the exchange of women between particular pairs of villages (Williams 1936: 135).

If exchange of sisters, true and classificatory, is carried out by the same two groups over generations, then individuals will in effect be marrying their bilateral cross-cousins. Williams notes, "As far as kinship regulation is concerned it is seen that a man usually marries his *mwitei* (classificatory cross cousin) and less frequently, his *bava* (classificatory sister's daughter). Marriage with a girl standing in any other relation may be regarded as theoretically banned" (Williams 1936:

131). This cross-generational marriage is a deferred return for a sister given.

After marriage a woman goes to live with her husband's group and is incorporated into it. Her former relationship to her natal group has been transformed into an affinal relationship between the two families (Williams 1936: 112).

Men who exchange sisters with one another are *tambera* ("exchange-fellow") to each other. Each stands as mother's brother to his *tambera*'s child. The mother's brother performs ritual services for his sister's child. Williams observes that "since there are two mother's brothers viz. the *tambera* or exchange-fellows, who perform the ritual services to each other's children, the duties of the *bava* (MoBr) are part of the reciprocal obligations in the exchange" (Williams 1936: 115). A certain degree of ambivalence, even hostility, exists in the affinal relationship and affines practice name avoidance.

At various rites de passage, affines carry out important ceremonial roles. The first occasion for the mother's brother to carry out ritual services is when the child's ears are pierced at about the age of five. The child sits on the knee of one *bava*, and has his ears punctured by two other *bava*. In this act, the child's true *bava* is assisted by his classificatory brothers. "The *bava* makes a present of his first bow and arrows to his small nephew, and receives a large gift of food from the parents. It is understood, of course, that both the services and the gifts are to be returned in kind when the operating *tambera* has a child of his own ready for ear-piercing" (Williams 1936: 178). A single boy may have his ears pierced, or several boys may have their ears pierced at one time. In either case, ear piercing may be the occasion for a large feast, the guests being the entire group of the *bava* who do the ear piercing. It would appear that, when several boys are having their ears pierced at the same time, the *bava* involved all come from one group, which has had a series of exchange marriages with the host group over time.

About three years later, the boy's nasal septum is pierced by his *bava*. The *bava* gives his sister's son a bow, arrows, and a drum, and once again is given food in return.

A boy's initiation is clearly the most important of the rites de passage. The several villages comprising a tribe hold a single initiation ceremony, at which boys from both moieties are initiated at the same time. The initiates are taken to the place of seclusion, introduced to the bull roarers, beaten, and after a ceremonial meal they are paraded through the village where they run the gauntlet before the women. They are then led back into the place of seclusion where they are sodomized, henceforth to be at the disposal of the senior males of the opposite moiety for this purpose. Sodomy continues for their several months of seclusion. They reappear at the large ceremonial feast and food distribution which conclude the initiation, and they are then given penis sheaths. The sodomy continues for another year, but ends when the boy receives a second penis sheath after a lime-eating ceremony.

The participating individuals carry out a number of distinctive roles. The individuals carrying out these roles fall into two categories—members of their own local group and affines (cross-cousins and mother's brothers). These categories of individuals are in opposite moieties. Members of the opposite moiety introduce the initiate into manhood by beating him, showing him the bull roarer, sodomizing him, and finally giving him his penis sheath. Members of his own moiety feed him, protect him, and succor him. Since boys of both moieties are initiated at the same time, both moieties are simultaneously providing the service of initiating the boys of the opposite moiety into manhood.

When a man dies, his mother's brother's people dig the grave for their deceased sister's son, for which service they are given a burial feast by the fellow villagers of the deceased. Some time later a ceremonial burning of the deceased's belongings is carried out by the mother's brother's group, and they are feasted once again. Male and female members of the deceased's local group go into mourning, observing a number of taboos including a taboo on village coconuts. A year or so later, the mourning taboos are lifted, and this is the occasion for a large feast. At this feast, the coconuts and yams which have been accumulated are distributed to the brothers of the women mourners and the mother's brother's group of the deceased. The recipients at the mortuary feast and at the other funerary feasts are therefore affines, representing villages with which the deceased's village exchanges women.

Williams observes, "It would be hard to overestimate the importance of feasts in Keraki culture. There is no question that they provide one of the main interests in the native's life, with the long preparations involved, the general stir and sociability of the actual event, and especially the satisfaction of making a good 'show.' There is no question either that they provide a stimulus for food-production. . . . the general effect of a decision to make a feast is that those responsible cultivate a greater area of land and work doubly hard" (Williams 1936: 234). A ritual justification is necessary for every feast held, and the rites de passage discussed above provide the majority of these occasions. Sometimes several events may be held simultaneously, in conjunction with a single feast. Since the occasion for feasting is typically a rite de passage, the majority of the guests fall into the category of affines (Williams 1936: 230–31). Feasts are always group events. Larger feasts are hosted by single villages, or by the combined villages of a tribe as in the initiation feasts.

The distribution of pork is an important component of feasts. The Keraki do not breed pigs. They capture them as piglets in the bush, and confine them in sties where they are fed until they reach enormous size. The individual who captures a piglet customarily gives it to someone else, who raises it and becomes its "owner." Because of his sentimental attachment to the pig, the "owner" cannot kill it, and at a feast it is killed by someone else. The "owner" then formally presents the pig to another man. (From Williams's account it seems likely that this is the man who originally captured the piglet.) "In the distribution of the flesh, tally is taken of the amounts dispersed so that the repayments made in due course may be compared with the original" (Williams 1936: 225). It seems, from the Williams account, that several men may kill pigs simultaneously at a large feast. Cooked meat and vegetables, as well as uncooked pork, are distributed, with exact measures made of the distributions in order to compare with past and future distributions (Williams 1936: 24).

Yams, which are also distributed at feasts, are displayed on huge food racks after the harvest. The size of the display is indicated by a patrol officer's report cited by Williams which estimates the amount of small yams displayed at between twenty-five and thirty tons. This display was exhibited in a structure which was 130 yards long, six feet high at either end, and thirty feet high at the center. Tallies are kept of size of yam heaps, length and circumference of individual yams of record size, length of fence covered by the displayed yams, and numbers of yams given. These tallies record the achievement of the distributors and are a continuing source of prestige. Williams notes, "for in no wise is a man's measure more surely taken than by the amount of food he can produce and give away" (Williams 1936: 23).

When a dispute breaks out between groups, one may challenge the other to a competitive display and exchange of small yams. Subsequently, there is a return feast and exchange at which the losers must make up their deficiency, in order to maintain the balance of reciprocity (Williams 1936: 234–35).

In the course of his discussion of exchange-marriage, Williams raises a point that relates to a central theme of our book, discussed in chapter 1. In considering the function of exchange in general, he notes, "But the reciprocity is not the point here. Why is the exchange made in the first place? Economically it is senseless. For the people of the district live in a uniform environment and climate, and they produce food by uniform methods. Each group could eat its own garden produce and pigs. Why do they insist on giving some of their food away, merely receiving a like quality in return?" (Williams 1936: 166–67).

Williams's answer is that exchange fosters friendly social relationships, but Williams's own material demonstrates that exchange also involves competition and rivalry. Both of these elements, as discussed earlier, are inherent in all exchanges.

Banaro

The Banaro, located on the Keram River, the lowest tributary of the Sepik, have four villages, each composed of from three to six hamlets. Each hamlet consists of a single gens with its own ceremonial men's house or so-called "goblin hall." (We are using Thurnwald's terminology—gens, sib, and goblin hall. A gens is a patriclan; a sib is one-half of the moiety division into which each patriclan is divided; a goblin hall is the ceremonial men's house or *house tamberan*.) Each gens is exogamous and is divided into two halves, which Thurnwald refers to as sibs. These sibs consist of patrilineally related males. The sib is the landowning unit, with rights to named sago places, and hunting and gardening areas with known boundaries (Thurnwald 1916: 278). Postmarital residence is virilocal. The goblin hall of each hamlet is divided longitudinally into two halves to correspond to the two sibs of its gens. "The sibs themselves have no special names other than 'the left', *bon,* and 'the right', *tan,* drawn from their place in the goblin hall" (Thurnwald 1916: 257). Two rows of fireplaces line each side, while the sacred flutes and ceremonial regalia occupy one end. Thurnwald observes, "The external form of the settlement reflects precisely the internal organization of the tribe; for the goblin hall, with adjacent houses in the same clearing mirrors the social unit, the gens, just as the symmetric partition of the goblin hall into two parts, the division of the gens into halves. The symmetry in the arrangement of the goblin hall is the expression in space terms of the principle of social reciprocity or the 'retaliation of like for like' " (Thurnwald 1916: 258).

Among the Banaro there are no chiefs, and the Big Men are not even mentioned. Thurnwald instead refers to "gerontocracy." He emphasizes that the old men control younger men by their knowledge, especially of magic, which they pass on in exchange for deference and allegiance. "They exercise their power, not by command, but by advice" (Thurnwald 1916: 283).

The marriage pattern is one of sister exchange, as strictly observed as possible, to the point where Thurnwald reports infanticide of the second born child until the appropriately sexed child to match the first is born (Thurnwald 1916: 272). If a death should take place in infancy or in childhood, a cousin may be substituted for a brother or sister (Thurnwald 1916: 273). The exchange of women takes place between the sib of one gens, in one hamlet, and a corresponding sib in another gens, in another hamlet. "Accordingly a bridegroom of the right side (*tan*) must take his bride from the same side of the other gens: a bridegroom of the left side (*bon*) takes his bride from a left sib" (Thurnwald 1916: 259). When a pair of marriages is negotiated, the second sib in each gens concerned will immediately also negotiate such a marriage exchange (see figure 1).

The two sibs in a gens within a single hamlet, the "left" and the "right" sides, never intermarry and instead are linked in a special, named friendship relationship called the *mundu*. Thurnwald notes, "These two sibs are united by a bond of friendship for mutual protection and pleasure, as well as for purposes of revenge against outsiders. The two sibs are considered to be the best of friends. They 'can never fight' against each other" (Thurnwald 1916: 259). The two sibs in a gens do not intermarry but instead are involved in the initiation rites of one another, as well as each other's marriage and death rites. Within the sib, the *mundu* relationship is inherited, so that the sons of men who are *mundus* are themselves *mundu* to each other (Thurnwald 1916: 263). Thus we have two sets of cross-cutting divisions, encompassing two hamlets. A particular sib (*bon* or *tan*) must marry into its corresponding sib in another gens, so that the sibs of gens A are linked to the sibs of gen B in marriage. The two sibs in each gens, the "left" and the "right" are linked through reciprocal ceremonial rights and obligations at each other's rites de passage, rather than being linked in marriage. According to Thurnwald's discussion of various ceremonies and his diagrams, there is continuity of the *mundu* relationship between sibs of the same gens and apparently continuity of the marriage relationship as well. He indicates that gens do intermarry over several generations but that this is not required (Thurnwald 1916: 384).

The relationship between *mundu* is one that involves the exchange of services at a series of rites de passage. One of these services is copulation in a ceremonial context with women who have married into the sib of one's *mundu*. Marriage does not mean exclusive sexual access. Quite the contrary, a woman will have regulated sexual relations with a

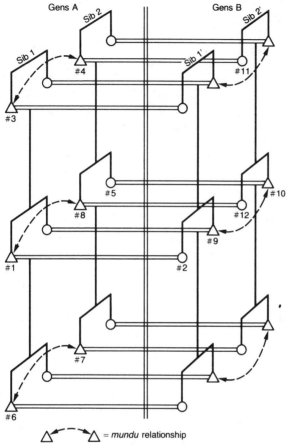

Fig. 1.   Dual Organization among the Banaro

number of specified males in the sib which is *mundu* to the
one into which she has married.

When a girl (#2, see figure 1) reaches puberty her initiation rites lead directly into marriage and the two are not
differentiated (Thurnwald 1916: 267). The girl is secluded for
nine months, after which a ceremony is held in which the
girl's bridegroom's father (#3) leads her to the goblin hall,
where his *mundu* (#4) copulates with her in front of the bam-

boo flutes, which represent the gods. Then it is the turn of the bridegroom's father (#3) to go to the goblin hall, where he impregnates the future daughter-in-law (#12) of his *mundu*. "The bridegroom [#1] is not allowed to touch her until she gives birth to a child [#6]. This child is called the Goblin's child" (Thurnwald 1916: 262). After the child is born, the husband with his new wife and the child move into a new house, which he has built in the interim. "On solemn occasions the goblin father [#4] continues to exercise his 'spiritual' function in the goblin hall" (Thurnwald 1916: 262).

Boys of the two sibs (#6 and #7) are initiated at the same time. The paternal grandfathers (#3 and #4) who acted reciprocally as goblin fathers of the first born and the mother's brothers of the initiates (#9 and #10) hunt pigs. "Later on, the two mother's brothers and the two legal fathers [#1 and #8] eat the head of the pig" (Thurnwald 1916: 263). Examination of figure 1 will show that this involves individuals of all four groups in the structure. At this point in the ceremony, the young male initiate (#6) moves into a different age grade, at the same time that the boy's father's father's *mundu* (#4), his goblin father who sired him, is transferring his *mundu* rights to his own son (#8), thereby moving himself into a higher grade that is outside the *mundu* system. From this point on, #8 will have ritual intercourse with #2. This indicates the presence of a series of generational grades. Subsequently, the boys are shown the sacred flutes and they go through a painful initiation rite, involving the insertion and extraction of blades of barbed grass into the urinary tract. Thurnwald notes the importance of the mother's brother as "the boy's protector who takes part in all initiation ceremonies" (Thurnwald 1916: 333). Though never stated by Thurnwald, it would seem that the person performing the initiation is the *mundu* of the boys' father (#8). At the rite's conclusion five months later, the boys' fathers and mothers' brothers slaughter pigs which, with other food, are prepared and then eaten during the final ceremonies. The boy's mother's brother shaves his temple and the back of his head. After the father presents a love charm to his son, the son (#6) has his first sexual experience with the wife (#11) of his mother's goblin initiator (the man who sired him), i.e.

father's father's sibfriend or *mundu*. She is the wife of the man who was involved in the early stages of his initiation but who gave up his *mundu* rights to his son when the initiate's status changed. After the completion of these rights, the boy is allowed to associate with women.

The death of a man (#1) is the occasion for further exchanges of sexual services between *mundu*-linked sibs. After the ashes of the corpse are returned to the house of the deceased, "Intercourse takes place between the dead man's brother and the wife (#5) of the widow's brother's sibfriend, or the wife (#5 again) of his sister's husband's sibfriend; that is he takes the wife of the *mundu* in the corresponding sib in the gens from which the deceased's wife originated" (1916: 267). An examination of figure 1 will reveal that if the deceased man (#1) is in left sib, gens A, his brother will have intercourse with a woman born into right sib, gens A. When the pot with the ashes is buried, the deceased's sibfriend's son (#7) exercises marital rights over the widow in the deceased man's house and thereafter he is responsible for the care of the widow. The final ceremony of the mortuary rites also takes place in the goblin hall. "The next evening the deceased's brother enters into his deceased brother's right and exchanges wives with his deceased brother's sibfriend (#8)" (Thurnwald 1916: 269).

The exchange of wives also takes place at the dedication of a new goblin hall. "The festivities in this case are again concluded with the exchange of women of both sibs among the *mundus*. On this occasion four pigs are slaughtered, two for each (longitudinal) half of the hall" (Thurnwald 1916: 270).

The Banaro kinship terminology reflects many aspects of the structure of sister exchange and the *mundu* relationship. In terms of typologizing based on cousin terminology, the Banaro have been categorized as having Hawaiian cousin terminology. However, in Thurnwald's presentation of the material, there is seemingly conflicting data on cousin terms. Thurnwald presents two sets of cousin terms. The first, which is identical to the set of terms for brother and sister, *ma-aia*, elder cousin or brother or sister, and *me-nein*, younger cousin or brother or sister, would make the system Hawaiian (Thurnwald 1916: 318). The second set of terms, *ma-aitji,* elder cousin, and *me-tiana,* younger cousin, are identified as being in the opposite gens to ego (Thurnwald 1916: 335). If the second set of terms are the only cousin terms applied to cross-cousins, then the system is Iroquois. In the first ascending generation, the same term, *mi-nio,* is used for all males, consanguineals, and affines except for mother's brother, who is called *mu-api.* The term for mother, *mu-maia,* is extended to all women except for mother's brother's wife who is called *mu-mana.* Father's sister is called by the same term as mother unless she is exchanged in marriage for mother, in which case she is called by the same term as mother's brother's wife.

This last point is an exemplification of one of the major features of the Banaro terminology, that is, the presence of alternative terms used if women have been exchanged in marriage. In addition, separate terms exist relating to the goblin father/goblin child relationship. The terminology always distinguishes first born, who is the goblin child, whether male or female, from subsequent siblings both as speaker and referrent. Special terms are also present which relate to the *mundu* relationship of the particular ego. These features combine to give a distinctive appearance to the Banaro terminology.

There is a structure underlying the seemingly random pattern of ceremonial sexual intercourse among the Banaro. From the female point of view, a woman has ritual intercourse with three generations of men of her husband's *mundu*-linked sib: she is first inpregnated by the *mundu* of her husband's father, she later has intercourse with her husband's *mundu,* and finally she initiates a young boy who is her husband's *mundu's* son into manhood by having intercourse with him. As Thurnwald points out, "Thus the three men of the other sib with whom the woman has to deal . . . are a father and his son, and eventually this latter person's grandson" (Thurnwald 1916: 270). Referring to figure 1, woman #2, in left sib, gens B, has sexual intercourse respectively with males #4, #8, and #7, all of them in right sib, gens A. Right sib, gens A is in a *mundu* relationship with left sib, gens A—her husband's sib.

The structure of Banaro society is one of reciprocal exchange, involving two forms of dual organization. There are two kinds of exchange links. Marriages join gens A to gens B through sister exchange. Gens are split into two parts and each part has its paired opposite in the other gens into which it marries, resulting in two pairs of intermarrying groups (Ax and Bx, Ay and By, figure 2). The two parts of a gens do not intermarry but instead perform a variety of sacred ceremonial services for one another during the course of rites de passage. Men from sibs that have *mundu* relations with one another (Ax and Ay, Bx and By) have sexual intercourse on three ceremonial occasions with the wives of their *mundus*. The cross-cutting moieties create four quadrants. Men in one quadrant (Ax) have *mundu* relationships with a second quadrant Ay), take wives from a third quadrant (Bx), and have ceremonial sexual intercourse with the women of the fourth quadrant (By).

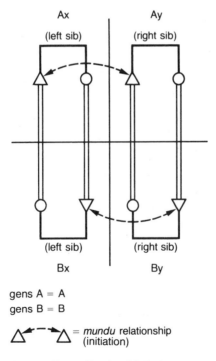

gens A = A
gens B = B

△ ⟵ - - ⟶ △ = *mundu* relationship
               (initiation)

Fig. 2.   Banaro Cross-Cutting Moieties

Conclusion

The three societies considered in this chapter are geographically remote from one another. All three are characterized
by sparse population, low population density, and small autonomous social units, and they are located in areas of linguistic diversity.

However, they represent variations of a single-structure
dual organization that is based upon sister exchange. In each
of these societies, a man can marry only if he has a sister to
exchange.

If sister exchange is continued from one generation to the
next, then the resulting pattern is one in which two groups
are linked over time through the continuing exchange of sisters. An implication of such a continuing structure is bilateral cross-cousin marriage. Of these three societies, the
Keraki explicitly state that they usually marry their cross-
cousins. Though the ethnographers of the Tor and the Banaro
do not report a preference for marriage with bilateral cross-
cousins, the diagrams that accompany their analyses imply
its presence.

Sister exchange represents but one manifestation of dual
organization in these societies. Other manifestations are the
various moiety structures that are also present.

In two of the three societies, Keraki and Tor, exchanges of
pigs parallel exchanges of women in that, as you cannot
marry your own sister, you cannot kill and eat a pig you have
raised. You give your sister to a man in another group who
remains in debt until he returns his sister to you. If you raise
a pig you must also give it to be eaten by someone else, who
remains in debt to you until he returns an equivalent. This
kind of pig exchange is congruent with a dual structure in the
same manner as sister exchange. As we shall see later on, this
need not be the case. Exchange of women may represent one
structure and exchange of pigs another and different kind of
exchange structure.

Elements involved in exchange shared by the three
societies considered in this chapter are characteristic of many
other New Guinea societies, as will be shown in the subsequent chapters of this book. The presence of competitive

exchanges, the resolution of conflict by means of exchange, the importance of achieving exact reciprocity, the linking of prestige and giving, and the relationship between giving and political leadership will be reoccurring themes in our analysis of other New Guinea societies. With respect to political leadership, the three societies discussed in this chapter exhibit rudimentary forms of Big Man structure.

These three societies, Tor, Keraki, and Banaro, represent structural variations on the common theme of dual organization. Each of them has something beyond simple moieties. In the case of the Keraki, a three-part division is contained within the moiety organization that controls marriage. Though there are no explicit moieties among the Tor, the marriage structure creates a patrilocally based dual division, which is cross-cut by the matrilocal flute-owning groups. This resembles the structure of patrilocal descent groups cross-cut by matrilocal moieties as found in Wogeo, to be examined later in greater detail. The cross-cutting moieties of the Banaro are of a different type. The distinction between sides that exchange women and sides that exchange goods and services foreshadows the structure of Abelam and Arapesh societies.

3 Iatmul

The Iatmul live along a stretch of 100 miles on both banks of the Sepik River. Iatmul territory begins about 150 miles from the mouth of the Sepik. The area is quite swampy and the Iatmul are dependent upon the seasonal flooding and recession of the river waters in their practice of sago cultivation. The river provides fish, plant food, and driftwood, which are important to the Iatmul economy. Pigs used in exchanges are raised by women (Bateson 1936: 53, 70).

The Iatmul settlement pattern is one of large, compact villages. Villages are politically independent units. Some villages are allied to one another while others are enemies. The village ideally is divided transversely by a ceremonial dance ground into two living areas each of which is occupied by a patrilineal moiety. The ceremonial houses of the two moieties stand on the dance ground. Each moiety consists of a large number of patrilineal kin groups called *ngaiva*. The residential area of each moiety is divided into sections each occupied by a different *ngaiva* (Bateson 1931–32: 257). *Ngaiva* are not ranked with respect to one another. The *ngaiva*, which Bateson refers to as "clans," own sacred totemic objects, and myths. Clans also own names, and membership in a clan is based on possession of a name. "Marriages are often arranged in order to gain names. Reincarnation and succession are based upon the naming system. Land tenure is based on clan membership and clan membership is vouched for by names" (Bateson 1936: 228). The structure of kin groups and the nature of their relationship to one another is not discussed in detail by Bateson. Postmartial residence is virilocal. Households are composed of two or three nuclear families living together in one big house with no partition separating the individual families. The heads of these families are related to one another as brothers or classificatory brothers.

A distinctive characteristic of Iatmul social structure is the identification of alternate generations in several different spheres. There is an Iatmul term, *mbapma,* meaning line. "In any patrilineal lineage there are two *mbapma,* one containing the members of ego's generation, his grandfather generation and his son's son generation; the other contains members of his father's generation and his son's generation" (Bateson 1936: 283). Further, "A man takes his father's names and applies them to his own son, similarly, he takes his father's sister's names and applies them to his daughter"—this was repeatedly reiterated to Bateson by his informants. Bateson also notes, "Theoretically, a man is reincarnated in his son's son; and a woman in her brother's daughter" (Bateson 1936: 18n; see also 233, 42). Similarly, "in the case of shamanism there is a vague belief that on the death of a shaman the shamanistic spirit is most likely to pass to his son's son" (Bateson 1931–32: 258). The identification of alternative generations is a structural principle underlying the kinship terminology (see figure 3).

Several different marriage rules are presented by Bateson, and he recognizes that they conflict with one another. (Bateson [1936: 88] refers to these statements as "formulations which would regulate marriage in a positive way if they were consistently obeyed." We treat them as rules that can be used to build models.) These rules are:

1. "A woman should climb the same ladder that her father's father's sister climbed, i.e. she should enter as bride the house which her father's father's sister entered, she should marry her father's father's sister's son's son (or re-

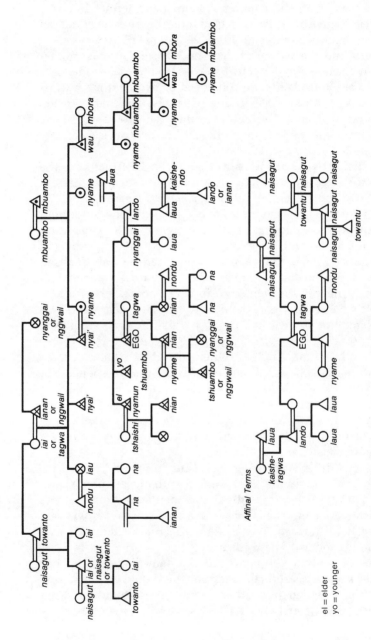

el = elder
yo = younger

Fig. 3. Iatmul Kinship Terminology (from *Naven*, Gregory Bateson, 1936; from diagram, p. 380, and glossary)

ciprocally a man should marry his father's mother's brother's son's daughter or *iai*)" (Bateson 1936: 88). Another formulation of this rule was presented earlier by Bateson as follows: "First, there is the system by which a man marries a woman of the group into which his father's father had married, the woman who is called *iai* before marriage. After marriage she is called *tagwa* (woman, wife) or more exactly *iairagwa*. I have reason to believe that this wife should be treated quite differently from wives acquired in other ways. Thus, I was told in Tambunum (where I spent three days) that a man's *iai* may enter his house and become his wife of her own volition and that he cannot say her nay. Further that he could not divorce his *iairagwa*, and I observed a definite avoidance of her name" (1931–32: 279–80). Bateson also notes, "There is a second cliche which defines *iai* marriage: '*Laua's* son will marry *wau's* daughter'. This refers to marriage of a man with his father's mother's brother's daughter, a relative who is also called *iai*" (Bateson 1936: 89). This is a cross-generation marriage. However, it is equivalent to *iai* marriage since the woman is from the same clan as father's mother and father's mother's brother's son's daughter. The man is taking a wife from the clan which should be wife giver to him but she is of the wrong generation (see figure 4).

2. " 'The daughter goes as payment for the mother'. This is a way of stating that a man marries his father's sister's daughter" (Bateson 1936: 89).

3. " 'Women should be exchanged'. This is more usually stated by the natives in reference to sister exchange—a man giving his sister as wife to the man whose sister he himself marries" (Bateson 1936: 90). "Marriages with women other than *iai* are usually accompanied by exchange of sisters. Thus a man's sister will marry his wife's brother" (Bateson 1931–32: 264). Bateson specifically notes that sister exchange is not permitted when *iai* marriage takes place (Bateson 1932: 264). The exchange of women need not involve real sisters but may involve women of the same clan or women of the same village who are considered classificatory sisters for the purposes of the exchange (Bateson 1931–32: 285).

When we began our analysis of Iatmul marriage structure, we hypothesized that the basic structure was that of father's

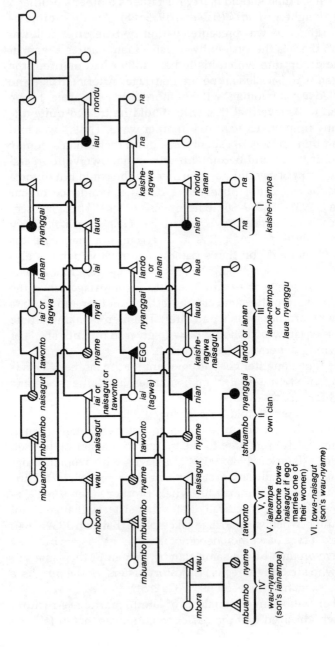

Fig. 4. Iatmul Marriage Structure

sister's daughter marriage, with an alternative of sister exchange. As noted above, Bateson had presented father's sister's daughter marriage as one of the Iatmul marriage rules. Further, when we charted the pattern of *iai* marriage (rule 1 above), given patrilineal descent, what seemed to emerge was an overall structure of patrilineages, related to each other by a pattern of father's sister's daughter marriage. Bateson himself saw a relationship between the two marriage rules that he noted were generically connected in a curious way (Bateson 1936: 89). This hypothesis had to be discarded for the following reasons. Iatmul informants indicated to us that marriage with real first cross-cousin, either father's sister's daughter (*na*) or mother's brother's daughter (*nyame*), is prohibited. The only preferences mentioned were *iai* marriage or sister exchange (Rosman and Rubel 1974: 3, 8, 9, 12, 16, 19, 25, 30). In addition, collapsing the structure of *iai* marriage into FaSiDa marriage resulted in the merging of mother's brother's lineage and sister's children's lineage, a distinction that is of critical importance terminologically as well as in the Naven ceremony. It would seem that real father's sister's daughter is not acceptable as a spouse. What can one therefore make of the rule that the daughter goes as payment for the mother? Classificatory father's sister's daughter marriage might be considered as a possibility but it seems unlikely since that marriage preference would set up the same kind of structure as real father's sister's daughter marriage. We would therefore interpret the statement as referring to a delay of one generation in the return of a woman and linked, as Bateson notes, to the formulation that women should be exchanged.

Iai marriage, in which an ego marries his FaMoBrSoDa creates a structure of generalized exchange. Father's mother's name is carried by *iai* whom ego marries. Iai marriage seems to be the pattern that is reflected in the kinship terminology. In figure 4 it can be seen that each group requires two wife-taker and two wife-giver groups, necessitating a minimum of eight groups for the total system to operate. In the first generation, ego's group C receives a woman from B and gives a woman to D. In the second generation, group C receives from A and gives to E. The third generation recapitulates the first. In her analysis of Iatmul marriage structure, Korn presents a diagram depicting the way in which a group relates to its two wife-giving and two wife-taking groups (Korn 1971: 116). Bateson long ago pointed out that ego's group was related to four other groups each of which was named (Bateson 1936: 280). As noted in figure 4, the kinship terminology sorts according to these particular lineages. The principle of the identification of alternate generations is operative in the kinship terminology, particularly with reference to terms for males.

The third formulation presented by Bateson is that women should be exchanged. The structural implications of this marriage rule—restricted exchange between pairs of groups—are diametrically opposite to those resulting from the generalized exchange of *iai* marriage. In the latter, wife givers and wife takers are always separate and no return is ever made for a woman received. In the former, wife givers and wife takers are not separate but constitute a single group. These two structures therefore cannot be collapsed into a single structure. Bateson notes that if *iai* marriage takes place there can be no exchange of sisters (Bateson 1931–32: 264). Our informants uniformly indicate the same thing—*iai* marriage cannot be accompanied by sister exchange. Sister exchange involves two groups in an ongoing relationship. As Bateson notes, "This is the relationship between certain pairs of clans which regard each other reciprocally as *lanoa nampa* or *laua nyanggu*—both terms are used—and who do a great deal of work for each other. This relationship is reciprocal between clans and apparently depends not upon any particular present or past marriage, but upon a tradition that the women of the one clan often marry men of the other and vice versa. The relationship finds ritual expression on various occasions, especially in mortuary feasts, but is never, I think, marked by the *naven* system" (Bateson 1936: 96, n. 2). When a sister exchange occurs, overlapping categories of kinship terminology result. The prohibition against marriage with first cousin prevents the continuation of the tie through bilateral cross-cousin marriage. Entities that maintain an exchange of women may be as large as villages. In such cases women of different clans may be considered classificatory sisters in the exchanges.

Related to sister exchange is the relationship called *tambinien*, which is passed on from father to son. "*Tambinien* are partners and help each other. . . . *Tambinien's* children should marry *tambinien's* children, with brother-sister exchange, and that *tambinien* would be cross if such marriages were not arranged" (Bateson 1931–32: 264–65). Pairs of clans would seem to be in a *tambinien* relationship with one another (Bateson 1931–32: 413). In *Naven*, Bateson glosses *tambinien* as "A partner in the opposite moiety, who is of the same generation group as the speaker, e.g. members of initiatory groups Ax3 are tambinyanggu of Ay3" (Bateson 1936: 285). "There is a second term *kaishi-kaishi* apparently synonomous with *tambinien*. . . . *Tambinien* are partners and their children ought to marry with brother-sister exchange. *Kaishi-kaishi* are persons whose children are married or betrothed with brother-sister exchange, the reduplicated form of the word and the absence of avoidance being correlated with the mutual equality resulting from the exchange. *Kaishendo* are persons whose children marry according to the *iai* system; the avoidance of *kaishendo* being correlated with the assymetry of the system in which brother-sister exchange is forbidden" (Bateson 1931–32: 264–66). Thus there are two sets of terms used by the parents of children who have married one another. These two sets of terms clearly refer to the two different marriage patterns. Since either one or the other of the marriage patterns may be followed, but not both at the same time, one would expect these alternative sets of affinal terms.

In addition to prohibition of marriage with one's own sister, there is a ban on marriage with any relatives called *naisagut* such as wife's mother (Bateson 1936: 91). In his earlier discussion on marriage prohibitions Bateson singles out wife's brother's wife as a prohibited mate (Bateson 1931–32: 288). In terms of the structure of *iai* marriage, this prevents an ego from taking a wife from the wife giver of his wife giver.

The nature of the articulation of the two marriage structures, *iai* marriage and sister exchange, cannot be ascertained from the ethnographic material. The direct exchange of sisters would short-circuit the *iai* marriage structure, as would marriage with FaSiDa. The Iatmul see them in complementary relationship, either there is *iai* marriage or sister exchange.

With respect to rank differences and political leadership, Bateson says there is no hereditary rank though wealth can be inherited. Thus, the son of an influential man has greater initial advantages. A man may become important and a Big Man through the acquisition of wealth—by magical power, through the force of his character, by prestige in war, by the possession of mythical knowledge, by intrigue, and by shamanism (Bateson 1931–32: 257–58). At the death of a Big Man, "A figure is set up by the members of his initiatory moiety to represent him and is decorated with symbols of all his achievements. Spears are set up to the number of his kills and baskets are suspended from the shoulder of the figure to the number of his wives" (Bateson 1936: 48). An influential man may have as many as eight or ten wives who come from different clans (Bateson 1931–32: 286).

Since Bateson's analysis of the Iatmul focuses almost entirely upon the *naven* ceremony, we do not have extensive material dealing with exchange behavior. The statements on marriage preference imply continuing relationships between kin groups. Thus marriage tends not to set up a new relationship between groups but rather to reaffirm an existing relationship with affines. Marriage is accompanied by the payment of a bride price consisting of shells and other valuables. "The natives say quite articulately that the purpose of the bride price is to prevent the wife's relatives from using sorcery against the husband" (Bateson 1936: 79).

A marriage creates a relationship between brothers-in-law. The separation of the two types of brother-in-law which is present in the kinship terminology is confirmed in the behavioral picture. In characterizing the relationship between a man and his wife's brothers (*tawontu*), Bateson states, "The sense of indebtedness therefore remains and the wife's relatives have always the right to call on the husband for any task, like housebuilding, for which a crowd of manual labour is necessary" (Bateson 1936: 79). Other tasks which his wife's relatives may call upon him to perform include repairing of ceremonial houses, repairing gardens, and pulling canoe logs. As Bateson notes, this labor is unreciprocated in kind or in equivalents of any sort, and therefore the relationship is an asymmetrical one. Of course, a man, in turn, can call upon the labor of his sister's husband (*lando*). Brothers-in-law both compete and cooperate with one another. As Bateson notes, "The chief characteristic of the brother-in-law relationship among the Iatmul is a mutual ambivalence about the fact that one man has given his sister to be the wife of the other" (Bateson 1936: 79). When sister exchange occurs there is symmetry in the relationship rather than asymmetry, and opposition is reduced to a minimum (Bateson 1936: 80).

With the birth of a child, to the relationship between brothers-in-law is now added the relationship between mother's brother and sister's son. Mother's brother and sister's son are seen as having a connection in blood: "In the native theory of conception, blood and flesh are believed to be products of the mother, while the bones of the child are contributed by the father" (Bateson 1936: 209, n. 1; see also 42). Soon after the birth, the mother's brother (*wau*) goes to present the child with a coconut and "a personal name which refers to the totemic ancestors of the *wau's* clan" (Bateson 1936: 9). The suffixes on the names from mother's clan, -*awan*, refer to masks and are probably connected with the dancing of the sister's son in the totemic ancestor masks of his maternal clan (Bateson 1936: 42). The child, of course, gets names from his father's clan which define membership in that patrilineal group, as well as access to land.

The relationship between mother's brother and sister's son is at the heart of the *naven* ceremony. The analysis of this ceremony was the focus of Bateson's book on the Iatmul. Whenever a *laua*—sister's son or daughter—boy or girl, man or woman, performs some standard cultural act, especially for the first time in his life, the occasion may be celebrated by his *wau*—mother's brother—by the performance of the *naven*. The *naven* ceremony is also performed after rites de passage of the *laua* such as boring the ears, boring of the nasal septum, initiation, marriage, and possession by the shaman's spirit (Bateson 1936: 8). For sister's son a *naven* is held after his marriage but not at the birth of his child; for sister's daughter a *naven* is held at birth of her child but not at her marriage (Bateson 1936: 48). Mortuary rites do not include the performance of a *naven* ceremony.

Bateson's focus was upon interpreting the symbolism of the *naven*. We are also interested in the exchanges that take place, to which Bateson gives only brief attention. After a long description of the ceremonial behavior of all the participants in the *naven*, Bateson then presents the data on the exchanges that occur at the close of the ceremony. In the course of the *naven* ceremony described in detail, the small girl, the *laua*, in whose honor the *naven* is being given, presents an adze decorated with shell which her father has given her to give to her *wau*, mother's brother. This marks the end of the ceremony (Bateson 1936: 17).

A general distribution of food and valuables then takes place. The pigs that are distributed all go from mother's brother's lineage to the lineage of sister's child (Bateson 1936: 18). Pigs go from members of the *wau* lineage to members of the *laua* lineage, except for the anomalous eighth pig, which seems to be given by the *wau* lineage to its own *wau* lineage. However, if sister exchange has taken place in the previous generation, then the anomalous pig given to a mother's brother's son is really being given from one bilateral cross-cousin to another. It is also at the same time a *wau* to *laua* distribution. As part of the *naven*, there is a return present of shell valuables from the *laua* lineage to the *wau* lineage.

There are other exchanges between *wau* and *laua* which mirror the *naven*. Bateson does not indicate what the context of these exchanges is, but observes, "We saw above that the *wau* makes considerable presentations of food—especially pigs and fowls—to the sister's son. But these gifts—unlike the corresponding food gift of the mother—prompt the boy to a sense of indebtedness, and he makes in return presentations of shell valuables to his *wau*" (Bateson 1936: 81). If a *wau* feels his *laua* is in need he will kill a pig and be subsequently recompensed for it with shells (Bateson 1931–32: 266). A man may also impart clan secrets and spells to his sister's son in exchange for shell valuables though these may not be inherited by the sister's son's son (Bateson 1936: 36). In all of these exchanges, the direction of particular kinds of valuables is always the same. The *laua* always receives pigs or fowl or food from the *wau*, and the *wau* always receives shell valuables as a continuation of the bride price paid for his sister.

The *laua* performs a number of services for his *wau* and has ritual obligations to his wau's clan. The *laua* carves the ceremonial posts for the *wau's* ceremonial clan house and the ancestral heads adorning the masks of his *wau*. He aids his *wau* in house building and in formal debating in the ceremonial house. He performs the unpleasant task of eating a preparation made from scrapings of the totemic relics of his maternal clan at the *pwivu* ceremony. At the *tshuggykepma* ceremony, "the *lauas* exhibit the totemic ancestors" (Bateson 1936: 10). The *laua* blows the ancestral flutes of the *wau*, may ornament his body with plants that are the totemic ancestors of his *wau*, and eats the pork when his *wau* sacrifices a pig to clan ancestors (Bateson 1936: 45; 1931–32: 420, n. 57).

When a man dies, both his *wau* and *laua* lineages take part in the mortuary ceremony called *mintshanngguu*. There are two parts to the ceremony. In the first part, the men of the dead man's clan sing name songs all night, while the *laua* of the deceased play the flutes of his clan while hidden under a suspended platform. The next morning, the *wau* of the deceased come with their clan flutes. While the dead man's clan play these flutes in their position as *laua*, the *wau* sing their name songs. Three lineages are involved in the ceremony, the lineage of the deceased, the *wau* lineage, from which his mother came, the *laua* lineage to which he gave his sister. Noticeably absent is a death payment to the deceased's maternal clan, a payment that is common in so many other New Guinea societies. Its absence seems to us to be linked to the preference for marriage with FaMoBrSoDa which sets up continuing affinal relations of wife giver to wife taker with mother's clan. The death payment in other societies usually marks the termination of the affinal relationship.

The pattern of *iai* marriage is characterized by asymmetrical affinal relationships. The *wau-laua* relationship is also characterized by asymmetry, that is, pigs going in one direction and shell valuables in the other, one kind of service performed by *laua* and another kind of service performed by *wau*. Sister exchange, the alternate form of marriage, is symmetrical. A sister is exchanged for a sister, bride price goes in both directions as do services, and competition between brothers-in-law is minimized. When children are born of two such marriages, then each man stands as *wau* to the other's children, equalizing the exchanges. There are other symmetrical relationships among the Iatmul. *Tambinien*, discussed above in connection with sister exchange, is one such relationship. Our field material indicates that *tambinien* help each other. They give one another sago, small yams, and fish.

The *tambinien* relationship contrasts with another paired relationship—that of *tshambela*. Bateson notes, "There is a term *tshambela* which is primarily used in a classificatory sense, and is only secondarily specialized, enabling a man to speak of one *tshambela* as especially his. [The term *tshambela* is clearly a cognate to the Abelam term *tshambəra*, referring to exchange partners who give each other pigs and large yams.] Certain clans are *tshambela* to certain other clans. The relationship between the clans is a mutual one, the clans being in this way paired off" (Bateson 1931–32: 270). Clans that are *tshambela* to each other are obliged to behave in certain ways when their *tshambela* is in an embarrassing situation. "If he (the *tshambela*) fell down they would all fall down in turn on the spot where he fell. Or if he dropped his lime gourd and broke it, they would all fling their gourds on the ground in the identical spot. This would be followed by a feast" given by the shamed *tshambela* to his partner (Bateson 1931–32: 270–71). Furthermore, "It is also the duty of *tshambela* to assist each other in certain ways at initiation ceremonies, and the *tshambela* of a successful homicide has the task of cleaning the captured skull" (Bateson 1931–32: 271). Clans that are *tshambela* to one another also live in different parts of the same village (Bateson 1931–32: 270). In his description of initiation, Bateson notes that the *tshambela* helps the initiate to carry out the food taboos since the initiate must not touch the food with his hand. Like the initiator, the boy's *tshambela* is said to present him with a series of gifts at the close of the initiation (Bateson 1931–32: 438, 439). The *tshambela* also plays a role in the *naven*. He kills a fowl and presents the prepared feathers as a headdress to the *iau* (father's sister, dressed as a man) of the child being honored (Bateson 1931–32: 277).

Additional material on the *tshambela* relationship was gathered in the field. Informants reiterated that the *tshambela* relationship is a clan-to-clan relationship, one entire *ngaiva* standing as *tshambela* to another. The *tshambela* relationship is inherited from father to son. In both Timbunke and Mindimbit villages, informants stated that the children of *tshambela* cannot marry. In Tambunum, they stated that children could marry. *Tshambela* must belong to different house *tamberans* (ceremonial houses). A man cannot build his own house or house *tamberan*. This service is performed for him by his *tshambela*. In exchange he gives pigs, big yams, bananas, shells, and cassowary to his *tshambela*. He does not give his *tshambela* fish. One cannot eat one's own pig, or cassowary and wild pig caught in the bush. These must be given to the *tshambela* (or sister's son). When the *tshambela* asks for food or for help, it must be provided. The *tshambela* can place a taboo on a man's coconuts, which cannot be picked until the taboo is removed. Should *tshambela* fight, the relationship cannot be terminated, even if one partner breaks the ceremonial food bowl in the plaza. They must mend the breach by exchanging pigs, chicken, and betel nuts. The items which *tshambela* exchange—big yams, shells, wild pigs, cassowary, and pigs—are in contrast to what is exchanged by *tambinien*—sago, small yams, and fish.

The sequence of initiation ceremonies is one in which the structure of relationship is an exchange of services between groups. Initiation advances boys to manhood through a series of rites, scarification, and seclusion so that they may be admitted to the men's house or ceremonial house from which they have hitherto been excluded. The ceremonial house or *ngaigo* is the focus of activity for the climactic stages of the initiation. Within its walls, the scarification of the initiate's back, breast, and navel area takes place and the sacred objects shown to the boys are kept. There seem to be two kinds of *ngaigo*. Bateson notes, "In the biggest *ngaigo*, all the clans of the village have their fires and platforms, while smaller *ngaigo* are usually owned by pairs of clans, each clan owning one end of the building" (Bateson 1931–32: 259). It is interesting to note that in the plan for the large ceremonial house provided by Bateson, there are sitting platforms for eight clans (four on each side). Each has its own slit gong and hearth (see diagram, Bateson 1931–32: 260). No floor plan is provided for the small *ngaigo* used by only two clans.

The model for initiation presented by Bateson in the *Naven* book is in terms of two pairs of cross-cutting moieties, divided into age grades (see figure 5). This analytical structure of Bateson's presents certain problems. The totemic moiety division, variously called Sun-Moon or Kishit-Miwot would appear to provide the basis for the A-B moiety division. Informants in the field identified the initiatory moieties with Kishit and Miwot and sorted clans according to this moiety division (Rosman and Rubel 1974: 13, 20, 23). Bateson also identifies Kishit and Miwot as the initiatory moieties (Bateson 1931–32: 256, 434). The individual who scarifies the novice comes from the opposite moiety. The two quadrants on the A side in Bateson's model are initiated by the two quadrants on the B side at the same time. The sides of the ceremonial house are divided into Kishit and Miwot and clans are lined up on either side according to whether they are Kishit or Miwot (Rosman and Rubel 1974: 20, 21). Kishit and Miwot also feast each other and exchange big yams, sago, live pigs, chickens, ducks, and coconuts (Rosman and Rubel 1974: 2, 6, 7). The important point to note here is that clans are sorting themselves in the initiatory moiety structure. The basis for the moiety division x and y is initially difficult to comprehend since no labels are attached to these divisions. The understanding of the x-y division lies in the information about the *tambinien* relationship. As earlier noted, Bateson states that members of initiatory groups Ax3 are *tambinien* of members of initiatory group Ay3. Individuals or clans that are *tambinien* to one another are both in either A or B. The *tambinien* relationship does not cross this moiety division. This was clarified still further by informants in the field who told us that boys who were scarified at the same time stood as *tambinien* to one another (Rosman and

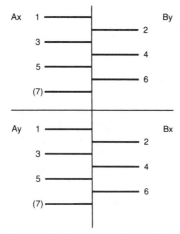

Fig. 5.   Bateson's Diagram of Iatmul Initiation

Rubel 1974: 2, 7, 23, 28). We noted earlier that the term *tambinien* also related to sister exchange. The children of *tambinien*, it was said, should marry in sister exchange. *Tambinien* was said to be synonomous with *kaishi-kaishi,* the parents of children who marry in symmetrical sister exchange, as contrasted with people whose children marry in asymmetrical *iai* marriage. Since clans stand in a *tambinien* relationship to one another, the x-y moiety division also sorts clans, just as the A-B moiety division sorts them.

In regard to the age grades, there are certain unstated assumptions underlying the model proposed by Bateson. The facts he presents are as follows: he states that 1 are the fathers of 3 who are the fathers of 5 and, likewise, 2 are the fathers of 4 who are the fathers of 6. These would appear to be real genealogical strata. The relationship between 2 and 3, 4, and 5, etc., is said to be between elder brother and younger brother, that is, a half generation interval (Bateson 1936: 245–46). "Younger brother" is said to be initiated by "older brother", that is, 2 initiates 3, 3 initiates 4, and so on. This kinship usage is obviously metaphoric since the two parties are in different moieties. The initiators are also, at a certain

stage in the initiation, referred to as the "mothers" of the
novices (Bateson 1936: 76, n. 1). Though Bateson does not
state the following points, it would seem to be the case that
initiation ceremonies commence every seven to ten years. At
that time, the boys of A would be initiated by B or vice versa.
The initiation ceremonies for boys in either moiety would
commence therefore once every fourteen to twenty years
(once a generation). The age grade terms collected from
Palimbai by Bateson refer to the boys initiated at the same
time. Thus Ax3 and Ay3 are *mbandi* and By4 and Bx4 are
kamberail (Bateson 1936: 244, 245). The boys live in a small
ceremonial house apart from the village and its main ceremonial houses. The term *mbwole* refers to the boys' ceremonial house occupied by the two groups of boys of moiety A,
Ax5, and Ay5, which are being initiated at the same time,
while the term *tagail* refers to the ceremonial house used by
Bx4 and By4 boys when they are initiated.

There are a number of contrasting roles discernible in the
activity of the initiation. A group of initiators forces the boys
to go through a series of ordeals and subjects them to bully-
ing. "While group Ax3 is initiating By4, Ay3 is initiating Bx4
on the opposite side of the ceremonial house and between
these two initiating groups there is constant bickering and
rivalry in the manner of their performance" (Bateson 1936:
134). The fathers of the initiates try to protect them against
extreme cruelty. During the scarification, the mother's
brother, the *wau*, holds the initiate on his knee and later puts
soothing oil on the boy's cuts. The crucial question is: who
are the initiators? As we have noted above, Bateson states
quite explicitly that boys are initiated and scarified by men of
the opposite moiety. Therefore, members of a boy's own
lineage cannot be the initiators. Furthermore, the fathers are
said to protect the boys from the extremes of the initiators.
Though mother's lineage may be in the appropriate moiety,
we noted from Bateson that the *wau*, mother's brother, also
plays a soothing role during initiation. Furthermore, the *wau*
holds a *naven* for his *lau* in honor of the latter's initiation. We
have previously indicated that *tshambela* also play a role in
initiation, in assisting initiates to carry out food taboos after
scarification ceremonies, and in giving the initiate a series of

utilitarian gifts at the close of initiation. In contrast to the role of initiator, the role of *tshambela* is one of assistance and succor. It would seem that the *tshambela* is not the initiator. If an initiate is in quadrant Ax, his father would also be in Ax (see figure 6). As a result of sister exchange through the *tambinien* relationship, his MoBr would be in quadrant Ay. The two clans exchanging women, represented by these two quadrants, are in the A moiety. The *tshambela* of the boy's father would be in the Bx quadrant, with By as the quadrant of the initiator.

The structure underlying initiation would seem to be based on the intersection of two dual organizations—one deriving from sister-exchange marriage between groups, the other based on the paired *tshambela* relationship between clans. We must return now to the question of alternative marriage forms among the Iatmul. *Iai* marriage, which is complementary to sister-exchange marriage, is closely re-

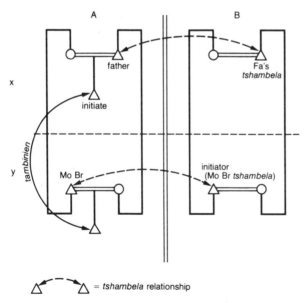

= *tshambela* relationship

Fig. 6.   The Structure of Iatmul Initiation

lated to the *naven* ceremony and to Iatmul kinship terminology and produces a structure of generalized exchange with which moieties are incompatible. This structure does not seem to be related to the structure of initiation.

The structure of dual organization which characterizes the three societies discussed in the previous chapter is evident once again in the case of the Iatmul. The cross-cutting moiety structure of the Banaro is recapitulated in the structure of Iatmul initiation. The *tshambela* relationship is like the *mundu* relationship of the Banaro in that both involve an exchange of ritual service but no intermarriage. The Iatmul are different from the Tor, Keraki, and Banaro in that they also have a complementary marriage pattern, that of *iai* marriage. Marriage with FaMoBrSoDa involves a unidirectional movement of women between groups, and thus creates a structure of generalized exchange. The Iatmul prohibition on marriage with any first cousin means that each group will be involved with two wife-giving and two wife-taking groups. This prohibition also prevents sister exchange in successive generations, so that the Tor-Keraki-Banaro structure is not recapitulated exactly. Affinal exchanges, which were important in the previous chapter and were symmetrical, continue to be important, especially in the *naven*, but are no longer symmetrical among the Iatmul when the asymmetrical *iai* marriage pattern occurs.

The *naven* ceremony, as interpreted by Bateson, serves to express the linkage over time between two clans, one the wife givers, the other the wife takers. In Bateson's analysis of *naven* symbolism *wau* is identified as a male mother, as well as brother-in-law. From the *naven* description, *laua* and his clan, particularly his father's sister, are identified as males. The *naven* symbolizes the marriage relationship between wife givers, who are identified in the ceremony with the females whom they give, and wife takers, who are identified with the males who take wives.

4 Northern Abelam

The Northern Abelam live near the Sepik River, adjacent to the Arapesh and not far from the Iatmul. The Abelam and the Iatmul speak related languages of the Ndu family (Laycock 1973: 24–25). The basic residential unit is a hamlet, several of which form a village. Each hamlet has its own ceremonial house or *house tamberan*. Hamlets may be composed of a single clan or of named sections each of which is associated with a different clan or subclan (Kaberry 1940–41: 241–42; 1966: 342). "Patrilineal descent is the ideal and there is a patrilineal bias to clan membership" (Kaberry 1966: 357). However, according to the figures which Kaberry gives, "If we consider the composition of clans in terms of full corporate membership, we find that they comprise only 59.2% agnates" (Kaberry 1966: 357). There is considerable shifting of residence and individuals affiliate with and participate in the activities of groups with which they reside. People may also be in an intermediate status operating with more than one group. These residential groups, which are called clans and are conceived of ideologically as patrilineal though the basis for an individual's membership in the group may vary, are the units with which we are concerned. Such groups have continuity over time and the structure of their relationships to one another is not affected by the shifting nature of the affiliation of individuals with these groups.

The clan is a corporate entity. Names are clan property. "Personal names are handed down within the clan from generation to generation. There is no belief in reincarnation, but through this mechanism, the link with the clan ancestors is preserved: 'men are lost, but the names remain' " (Kaberry 1940–41: 94). The name of an ancestor is bestowed on the child by the father or father's father. A girl receives the name of father's sister (Kaberry 1940–41: 246). "The clan has its own name, its totem, plant emblems, songs and affiliation with one of the *ngwalndu* (ritual carvings) in the *house tamberan*" (Kaberry 1940–41: 94). The clan totem is a bird, but there is no belief in descent from the totem, nor is it taboo as food. A person also inherits a relationship to the ritual carvings (*ngwalndu*) of his mother's clan as well as to her clan totem, which is forbidden to him as food. Kaberry does not indicate what the implications of this inheritance are for the Abelam.

Title to land descends in the male line. If a family starts a new hamlet, it still retains the right to the property in the ancestral hamlet for a time. Regarding usufruct, Kaberry notes,

> An area of bush, however is used by a number of individuals: firstly, the members of the lineage who inherit it and who will hand it on to their children. Secondly, cross cousins and sister's children, who have the right to cut timber and draw on the water supply. Within the lineage, the head man decides on the portions to be cleared for gardens, marks out the plots and distributes them among his wives, his sons and his brothers. He may also give plots to his sister's children, his cross cousins and affinal relatives, who in the following year will lend him a section of their land. Once the division is made, the temporary owner has rights of entry and full control over any crop he may grow. Land is plentiful and fertile and disputes over ownership are rare (Kaberry 1941–42: 345).

If a more permanent shift of residence occurs, and shift of clan affiliation takes place, the nonagnates involved become incorporated into the clan with which they reside. This would account for the high proportion of nonagnates in the clan as quoted above.

Quarrels within a clan are strongly disapproved. Quarrels

among men of different clans or hamlets within a village arise over adultery and accusations of sorcery (Kaberry 1966: 349). If the wronged party cannot prove his accusations of adultery he challenges the defendant to an exchange of long yams. The disputants are thus converted into ceremonial exchange partners (Kaberry 1966: 349).

The village with its component hamlets is an independent entity vis-à-vis other villages. Each village has its categories of enemy villages (*mama*) and friendly villages. Quarrels with enemy villages arise over rights to sago palms. Kaberry cites the Abelam as stating, " 'Over women we fight not; over food we fight not; over sorcery not. Only over sago' " (Kaberry 1966: 365). Land acquisition is not a cause of fighting. However, if an enemy is routed, gardens might then be taken over by the victors.

A dual division also exists among the Northern Abelam. "Members of the village are divided into two groups (*ara*) for purposes of initiation and the ceremonial exchange of pigs and yams" (Kaberry 1940–41: 239). She also remarks that the *ara* "are not totemic and they do not regulate marriage. A man of one *ara* has his ceremonial partner in the opposite *ara*, whom he addresses as *wuna tshambəra*. This relationship is often handed down between lineages, and hence has some affinity with the clan system. It is not possible to obtain a consistent list of *tshambəra* in terms of the latter. The general practice is for a man and his sons to be *tsbambəra* to another man and his sons" (Kaberry 1940–41: 256). Kaberry has more recently made a further statement about the *ara*. She notes, "*Ara* are not localized, nor are they kin groups. . . . Ideally, the clans of a hamlet should belong to the same *ara* and have ceremonial exchange relations with an adjacent hamlet" (Kaberry 1966: 341). In addition, hamlets in opposite *ara* are linked in pairs.

The information provided by Kaberry on the *ara* would seem to support a structure of dual organization based on ceremonial exchange partnerships. The exchange partners of one hamlet are paired with men in another hamlet, in the opposite *ara*. The two sides of this dual organization are not named. One side refers to itself as *nanara* (meaning "us" or "same"), and to the other side as *dera* (meaning "opposite") (Rosman and Rubel 1974: 11). Though several men in one hamlet may have *tshambəra* in their paired hamlet, the focus of the ceremonial exchanges is in the hands of the Big Men of the respective hamlets. A son inherits his father's *tshambǝra,* so that the relationship between two hamlets is perpetuated over time. Frequently a hamlet will be a single-clan community, thus placing clans in opposite sides of the dual division. However, the processes of fission and fusion of clans sometimes result in two segments of the same clan being in opposite *ara.* This is the reason that, as Kaberry points out, it is impossible to range clans on one side or the other. If an individual shifts his residence to another hamlet, then he may also shift his *ara* affiliation so that it is consistent with the hamlet where he is now residing. The exchange aspects of the *tshambǝra* relationship will be discussed below.

Various activities are organized by the Big Man of a clan. Large yams, which are grown for ceremonial purposes, are under the control of the Big Man though planted on individually cultivated plots. Female labor cannot be used for ritual reasons in the growing and harvesting of the large yams that are used in the ceremonial exchange with *tshambǝra.* Rather, the labor of young men is important for this activity. Acting on behalf of his clan, the *nǝma:ndu* (senior male or Big Man) who has performed the ritual magic over the yams, has mobilized the labor for the large yam gardens, and has observed the food and sex taboos, assumes titular ownership of the yams of his kinsmen in the clan at the display (Kaberry 1941–42: 95). Though affinal and cross-relatives may use the land of the clan, the production and display of the large yams is in the hands of the clan, including its nonagnatic members, under the leadership of the *nǝma:ndu.*

The Big Man also acts as the organizer of communal labor for various large-scale activities such as the organization of work teams to carve a slit gong, and the construction of a new *house tamberan.* In the latter case he may call on other villages for help with timber (Kaberry 1941: 355; 1966: 341, 355). These services are later reciprocated.

"There is no system of hereditary chieftainship, but each clan has its important men *nǝma:ndu* who as elders exercise much influence over the younger members" (Kaberry 1940: 240). Kaberry further notes, "The elder who excels as 'a yam grower' is a big man or *nǝmandu.* He is the entrepreneur in activities involving the collaboration of his own clan and group in its relations with other clans, both within and outside the hamlet. The status of *nəmandu* has two components: that of seniority in age (the same term is used for elder sibling) and that of outstanding achievement" (Kaberry 1966: 360–61).

Though a man's status in the community could be increased by his prowess as a fighter, or his ability as a carver or painter of designs, he must also be a great yam grower. Kaberry points out the case of Kilegwanbab, who had a reputation as a fighter: "But he was considered less important than a number of his contemporaries, because he had had affairs with women and therefore was not to be trusted with the responsibility of performing the rites and magic for the yams of others. Another clan brother assumed this office together with the titular ownership of the yams of the clan" (Kaberry 1941–42: 336n). Though Kaberry notes that Big Men and their sons are *tshambəra* to other Big Men and their sons in clans in the opposite *ara*, the characteristics that are deemed desirable in a Big Man are mostly achieved characteristics. Thus a son may or may not play an important role in affairs of a clan, though his father might have in the past. Since leadership positions are not inherited there is no formal succession. Young men within a lineage regardless of their kinship position are evaluated in terms of the qualities desirable in a Big Man. "The young man who grows a large yam and is an energetic gardener increases his status and is pointed out as one likely to be an important man in the future" (Kaberry 1941–42: 95). Forge reiterates all of these points in his description of the Eastern Abelam. He notes, "Even to be the son of a big man gives virtually no advantage in the unending battle for prestige" (Forge 1970b: 270). The career of a rising young man does not place him in competition with his elders but rather with his age mates. "Competition for prestige occurs between men of the same generation who belong to different clans and ideally different hamlets" (Kaberry 1966: 361).

Though the labor of women is not used in the growing of yams for ceremonial purposes, female labor is still of great importance to Big Men. It is important for a Big Man to have more than one wife in order to be able to raise sufficient food for feasts. Since pigs are in the care of women, a Big Man will need the labor of more than one wife to care for the pigs which he requires for exchanges with trading partners and the valuable shell rings which are used in exchanges with affines.

In order to maintain his role as an entrepreneur, the Big Man must attract and hold on to people who will assist him in his endeavours. There is competition between Big Men to attract new people and to hold on to the labor of younger brothers and sons—junior members of the lineage—who may be tempted to branch off on their own. A young man is dependent upon a Big Man to whom he is subordinate. A young man who is ambitious and dissatisfied with his position in his own clan may leave and attach himself to a leader of another subsection of that clan where he sees more opportunities. The Big Man gives direct assistance to young members of his clan with gifts of long yams, pigs, and rings, which are used to make various ceremonial payments. He will also give young men opportunities to develop the qualities necessary for future leadership. The Big Man also gives his knowledge of spells. By his abstention from sexual intercourse with his wives, he places himself in a state of ritual purity for the whole group, to insure their success in yam growing and in the ceremonial exchange with their *tshambara*. Thus, the Big Man must maintain sexual abstinence in order for the group to grow truly magnificent yams.

The Big Man of the founding clan of the hamlet is known as the Big Man of the hamlet. Kaberry notes, "There is no big man for the whole village and no ranking of hamlet heads. Some enjoy more reknown as yam growers and artists and have a larger following but in terms of formal status they are equivalent. Collectively, they are the big men of the village; as individuals, their relations with one another are mediated through hamlet and dual organization in *ara*. Big men of both *ara* collaborate in activities which affect the village as a unit" (Kaberry 1966: 355). The *ara* organization is internal to the village—the biggest men represent the village in opposition to other villages.

From the dual structure discussed above one might expect that some form of exchange marriage was present. Marriage within the clan is forbidden. "Marriage between full cross-cousins is regarded as equivalent to a marriage between siblings and is incestuous; but marriage into mother's clan is permitted, and occurred in 6.2% of the unions recorded" (Kaberry 1966: 349). Sister exchange is also mentioned as occurring. Kaberry notes, "Exchanges of women between clans is favored and of the 207, 14.9% were of this type. In a further 13.5%, the exchange was completed in the next generation" (Kaberry 1966: 349). This exchange of women between clans is a more generalized form of sister exchange. Though true cross-cousins may not intermarry, the marriage of their children is said to promote cooperation between the two clans (Kaberry 1966: 349). Most marriages occur within the village (73.4 percent in the case of the village studied by Kaberry). Marriages occur both within and between hamlets. Marriages outside of the village take place primarily with friendly villages (68 percent), although it is interesting to note that 32 percent of the extravillage marriages are with traditional enemy or *mama* villages. Kaberry reports that 15 percent of the marriages among the Abelam are polygynous. Each wife has her own residence and garden. Both wives may live in the hamlet, but more frequently the second wife continues to reside in the hamlet of her parents, though the products of her labor go to her husband. There is a certain amount of regional variation in marriage patterns among the Abelam. Kaberry notes that for the Western Abelam, father's sisters's daughter marriage was preferred and therefore union with a cross-cousin was permitted. The kinship terminology of the Northern Abelam village that Kaberry studied resembled that of the terminology for the Western Abelam (1940–41: 250, n. 14; 1941: 210).

These statements about marriage among the Northern Abelam are interesting in their juxtaposition. Though exchange of women is favored, bilateral cross-cousin marriage is forbidden. Similarly, the completion of the exchange of women between clans in the following generation takes place, though the Northern Abelam do not permit father's sisters's daughter marriage. Marriage between the children of cross-cousins is favored, thus serving to maintain the exchange ties between kin groups through women. These statements suggest a pattern in which there is sister-exchange between two kin groups, no marriage between the cross-cousins in those groups in the following generation, and the possibility of sister-exchange between their children in the third generation.

The kinship terminology for the Northern Abelam presented by Kaberry is of the bifurcate merging type. There is one term for father and father's brother, *yaba;* there is one term for mother and mother's sister, *nua.* Parallel cousins have the same terms as siblings. The term for mother's brother is *wau;* for sister's son it is *rauwa.* The term for father's sister is *yau.* Matrilateral and patrilateral cross-cousins, both male and female, are termed *mbandu.* There is a separate and complete set of terms for affinal relatives which differs from the terms for consanguines. The same term is used for wife's brother and sister's husband.

We turn now to an analysis of the exchanges among the Abelam. The first category of exchanges which we will examine is between affines. As will be seen below, exchanges between affines always involve shell rings. These rings are obtained from the Arapesh in exchange for pigs, and are made from giant white clam shells. They vary in value depending on size and lightness. Some are given the name of the owner's totem. Rings are presented at rites de passage and are not interchangeable with any other form of valuable except for pigs. Rings are never presented to individuals within one's patrilineage.

The first exchange between affines occurs at a marriage. A marriage is formalized by the presentation of from three to five rings by the groom to the family of the bride. In addition, he contributes ten yams for distribution and the greater part of the feast that is held (Kaberry 1940–41: 361). In this, the groom is assisted by his patrilineal relatives. The prestige which comes from giving a large number of rings accrues to the groom and his relatives who have assisted him. This is the formal sanction of the marriage and by the acceptance of the rings the bride's family relinquishes rights to her labor. If the marriage is within a hamlet no rings are given since this is a single kin group. In the case of a marriage with a classificatory sister, Kaberry notes that the brother of the wife in explaining why he did not receive rings said, " 'My younger brother cannot. If she stays with another man he will give me valuables. My younger brother cannot' " (Kaberry 1941–42: 212).

When a child is born a ring is given to the mother's brother of the child. "If a ring is not handed over the mother's brother or mother's mother may curse the child and cause it to sicken and die" (Kaberry 1940–41: 245). Elsewhere, Kaberry cites mother's brother as someone who might practice black magic against his sister's son, though mother's brother is also seen as protector (Kaberry 1941–42: 218, 353).

The description of male initiation among the Northern Abelam as presented by Kaberry is similar to the description provided by Forge for the Eastern Abelam, though the social structures of the two groups differ. Though Kaberry does not mention the role of the mother's brother in initiation, Forge notes that the mother's brother has, "the right to perform ceremonial services for the sister's son particularly during initiation services which have to be paid for in the highly valued shell rings" (Forge 1970a: 274).

At death there is also a distribution of rings. After a man dies the deceased's mother's brother and the mother's brother's son dig the grave. Rings are handed over to the mother's brother of the deceased and to his children. This is done so that the spirits of his mother's clan will protect the deceased's spirit until it is strong enough to join its paternal ancestors (Kaberry 1940–41: 362). "Besides a mother's relatives, a person's father's sister's son might also receive a ring in return for a ring given previously. Recipients lose the right to cut timber from the bush of the dead man and his descendants. It will be remembered that cross-cousins have a reciprocal right to cut timber on one another's property; hence the mourning exchanges are one means by which the rights of the clan over land are reasserted" (Kaberry 1940–41: 362). From the inception of a marriage, rings go in one direction—from the receivers of the woman to her own lineage. At the birth of the child of that marriage and at the death of that child, rings will go to the clan that gives the woman. The giving of a ring at marriage creates a brother-in-law relationship. Brothers-in-law must not quarrel; "they exchanged hospitality, offered gifts of betel nut and tobacco, and worked together in the garden " (Kaberry 1941–42: 213). The brother-in-law relationship is perpetuated between the sons of those brothers-in-law. The relationship has the same qualities. "A man would say, 'there is my cross-cousin (mbandu); we cut bush together; we plant yams together; cross-cousins must not quarrel' " (Kaberry 1941–42: 85).

> Good will between them [cross-cousins] is particularly stressed, and if a quarrel arises, their relatives intervene and try to persuade them to make peace and exchange rings. The same practice also occurs if brothers-in-law

have a dispute. I could receive no explicit reason why this ceremonial exchange of rings was limited to these two relationships, but my informants always said emphatically: "Cross-cousins must not quarrel; brothers-in-law must not quarrel. If they do, they exchange rings." It seems as though the method of resolving differences between affinal relatives is carried down to the next generation. That is, between cross-cousins (Kaberry 1940–41: 248).

A man would often address his brother-in-law affectionately as *wuna yu:a*, "my ring," that is, an object of value (Kaberry 1941–42: 213). From the description of how both matrilateral and patrilateral cross-cousins are treated it is clear that they are conceptualized as affines, since they are given rings. Though rivalry and disputation may occur between brothers, rings are never exchanged, for they are members of one clan (Kaberry 1941–42: 213). This parallels the point that rings are never exchanged if marriage is within the clan, as in the case of the marriage with a classificatory sister.

Since the Abelam do not allow marriage between cross-cousins, it can be seen that marriage establishes an affinal relationship between groups which lasts for two generations and then may be renewed. (Forge, who worked among the Eastern Abelam, refers to the relationship set up by each marriage which lasts for three generations. He remarks that numerous exchanges persist between the two groups for about one hundred years [Forge 1971: 137]. The material presented by Forge on the Eastern Abelam indicates that there are differences in kinship terminology and social structure between them and the Northern Abelam.) The presentation of rings to the wife givers establishes the relationship and the giving of rings to the cross-cousins of the deceased terminates the relationship with the wife-giving group. The giving of a ring at a death to the father's sister's son terminates the relationship between the father's sister's group and the deceased's lineage who had been wife givers to them and thus the recipients of rings from them at rites de passage. It would appear that the giving of rings defines the affinal relationship.

Pigs used in exchanges between trade partners may be purchased with rings. Portions of the pig are claimed by members of the group according to the size and number of rings they have contributed to its purchase (Kaberry 1941–42:

347). Alternatively people who need rings may purchase them with pigs. Forge notes that rings displayed at the completion of a *house tamberan* are a symbol of peace and participation (Forge 1970a: 277).

The ambivalence of the affinal relationship is exemplified by the view of mother's brother as both protector and a source of refuge, and as source of harmful magic. The relationship with cross-cousin and brother-in-law seems also to be fraught with the possibility of dispute. The giving of rings to these various categories of affine would appear to symbolize the desire for harmony.

The exchanges between *tshambara*, ceremonial exchange partners, constitute another important sector of Abelam exchange. A man cannot eat the pigs he himself has raised, nor can he eat wild pigs or cassowary he has killed in the bush. The meat of these animals must be given to one's *tshambara* (Rosman and Rubel 1974: 43, 46, 50, 56, 59, 61; this information was elicited by the authors in response to direct questions on this topic).

The focus of the relationship between *tshambara* involves the exchange of large yams. The Abelam "possess a yam cult which is also linked with other forms of ritual and magic, with prestige and political control, with the organization of labour in kinship groups, with the differentiation between the sexes, marital relationships, and with the settlement of disputes" (Kaberry 1941–42: 357). The yam cult culminates in the ceremonial display and subsequent exchange of large yams, between *tshambara*. "The exchanges constitute one of the main interests in the life of the men; they are the means by which status and prestige are secured both within and without the village" (Kaberry 1941–42: 349). The yams utilized in the ceremonial exchange are grown in separate plots.

> There is a close identification between a man and his finest yam; it is a symbol of his manhood and industry. Many of the longest yams (five to ten feet in length) are not eaten: they are displayed at harvest, stored, distributed, stored again and eventually planted, except for a few unsuitable portions which are handed over rather grudgingly to the women for soup. After the harvest ceremonies, some are given away at girls' puberty ceremonies, male initiation, marriage and death; the finest are normally reserved for

presentation to a ceremonial partner once or twice a year; and one or two may be handed over to men in another village with which there is a relationship of traditional hostility (Kaberry 1966: 340).

Women are taboo to the yams. They are not allowed to participate in any of the activities associated with these yams, nor are the men involved in the work with the yams allowed to have sexual intercourse during the period of cultivation. The Big Man under whose supervision the gardening takes place is responsible for performing the various spells associated with yam cultivation, and observing all the necessary taboos from planting to harvesting. He arranges the dates for the harvest, the elaborate decoration of the yams with masks and headdresses, and their subsequent display on the piazza in front of the *house tamberan* of his clan. (Kaberry 1941–42: 95, 354, 348). A good harvest will be the occasion for a dance that is attended by the whole village and visitors from other villages. A feast is held and on that occasion the yam songs are sung and the clan of the hamlet is glorified and the reputation of its leader enhanced. These yam songs disparage the yams belonging to rivals in other clans in the opposite *ara*.

The exchange of the large yams is between *tshambara*, each of whom represents his clan, which has worked as a group from the time of planting until the time of the exchange of the yams. These two groups are in opposite halves of the dual organization—in different *ara*—and they also represent two different hamlets within the village. Kaberry makes mention of the association of yams and the institutionalized rivalry between members of the dual organization (*ara*) (Kaberry 1941–42: 338). After the display and feast, the yams to be ceremonially exchanged are "Then carried down to the hamlet of the partner" (Kaberry 1941–42: 348). All of the leaders of a hamlet who are of the same *ara* arrange to transfer the ceremonial yams to their respective partners on the same day (Kaberry 1966: 353). Tallies are made of the length and thickness of the yams and the return that occurs subsequently during the year is expected to be an exact equivalent. However, each side attempts to return more than it has received. "This is not an act of generosity; it is further means of asserting superiority and of belittling the efforts of the rival and his group. The latter, if they feel they cannot make a suitable return later, refuse to accept all the yams, and make the excuse that they are a small clan and have no 'big man' to perform the magic. They may then be taunted with being afraid, and they either accept the challenge to produce bigger ones in the next season or, if they realize that this is impossible, insist on the rule that exchanges should be equivalent and compel the donors to take back the surplus" (Kaberry 1941–42: 348).

Kaberry indicates that, when there is a complete failure to observe the rules relating to the ceremonial exchange relationship, the wronged partner will ceremonially break the bowl in which soup is served to his partner, and state that the relationship is finished (Kaberry 1941–42: 348). However, even under these circumstances, the wronged partner, after a time, will begin exchanging again (Rosman and Rubel 1974: 41). Since the *tshambɔra* relationship is one of competition and rivalry, disputes do occur between *tshambɔra*. When this happens, the initiator of the dispute gives yams and pigs to his partner, and the exchange relationship continues (Rosman and Rubel 1974: 10, 33, 36). The emphasis is on the continuity of the relationship.

Other kinds of quarrels between men of different hamlets in the same village may be ended by the two becoming permanent ceremonial exchange partners who are in rivalry with one another.

Exchanges between *ara* also occur at initiation into the tamberan cult. "During boyhood, adolescence and later manhood, a man is initiated into the various stages of the Tamberan cult" (Kaberry 1940–41: 361). The men of one *ara* perform the service of initiating the males of the opposite *ara*. At the first stage, the initiates are secluded in the *house tamberan* for one or two months and are fed only white soup made by their *tshambɔra*. The boy's penis is incised by his *tshambɔra*. In exchange for these services, "Pigs and yams are paid to the *tshambɔra*" (Kaberry 1940–41: 357, 361). Initiation ceremonies take place in a village usually every year. Hamlets associated with one *ara* hold initiation ceremonies in alternate years in their hamlet and the following year perform the same services for their opposites.

In describing initiation among the Eastern Abelam, Forge's account parallels what has been presented above. The *tshambɔra* incises the boy's penis, instructing him on how to do this himself in the future in order to cleanse himself from sexual contact with women. Forge points out that the *ara* are divided into age grades. He notes also that the mother's brother of the initiate plays an active role in that he carries and shields the initiate while the initiate is undergoing punishment in various ordeals at the hands of the initiators. The mother's brother is paid for these services with valued shell rings (Forge 1970a: 274–75). Initiators and mothers' brothers play opposing roles in initiation. During one of the eight stages of the initiation cycle the initiate is shown the *ngwalndu,* the sacred carved figures of his clan. Passing through the stages enables the initiate to use the spirits inhering in the *ngwalndu* as part of the yam magic (Kaberry 1940–41: 355, 357). The yams are said to have the same spirit as the spirits in the *ngwalndu* in the *house tamberan* which represents the clan (Kaberry 1940–41: 356). "On the facade of the *house tamberan* are represented the *ngwalndu* associated with the clans of the hamlet and in addition those of the clans which stand in a ceremonial exchange with them" (Kaberry 1966: 347). Forge notes the same identification and indicates that it is reinforced by a stylistic unity in the artistic representations of the ritual carvings, the decorated wicker masks of the yams, and the painted faces of the boy initiates (Forge 1970a: 280).

From this description of the *tshambəra* relationship between men of different *ara,* we can draw the following structural picture. In the competition and rivalry of the yam cult, clans are ranged against their rivalrous counterparts in the opposing *ara* of the village. The focal point of the competition is the *tshambəra* relationship between the Big Men of each lineage, who direct the activities concerning the yams through every stage of the sequence. These same *tshambəra,* who competitively exchange yams with one another, also perform the service of initiating their partner's sons, for which they receive pigs and yams.

Exchange relationships may exist between villages that are traditional enemies to one another. Truces were sometimes arranged by neutral Big Men and involved the exchange of pigs, long yams, and hostages. "It is significant that allies and neutral villages who are regarded as friends do not exchange yams" (Kaberry 1941–42: 344). Traditional enemies who are exchanging long yams during a truce period are not referred to as *tshambəra*. In addition to yams, traditional enemies also exchange pigs.

Intermarriage is said to be another means of establishing cooperation between hostile villages, and in fact one-third of the marriages outside the villages are with traditional enemy villages. Intervillage relationships may cross cultural boundaries. The Northern Abelam are in close contact with Arapesh villages. Kaberry's village included an Arapesh village among its friendly villages (Kaberry 1966: 363). There is a category of trade friends, *pətə*, who assist travelers in long trade expeditions to the coast (Kaberry 1966: 371, n. 11).

For the Abelam, the structure of initiation and the structure of ceremonial exchange partners, *tshambəra*, is the same—that is, the dual organization of the *ara*. Ceremonial exchange partner and affine are distinguished by the difference in categories of goods exchanged with each. With affines, one always exchanges rings; with exchange partners, one always exchanges yams. Yams and shells are never interchangeable. While shells symbolize peace, yams symbolize competition and conflict. Pigs may be purchased with rings but pigs are given to exchange partners rather than to affines. Though exchange partners and affines who are in the opposite *ara* seem to be separate, the mechanism that keeps them apart over time is unclear from the data available.

Another kind of relationship can be seen between the structure of exchange of women, and the structure of exchange of long yams between exchange partners. Groups of men exchange women in order to reproduce those groups. Reproduction is achieved through sexual intercourse with and impregnation of the women exchanged. In the structure of exchange of long yams, men reproduce long yams, which are their symbolic equivalent, by means that demand the exclusion of women. Women are excluded from every phase of the production of long yams, for it is felt that they will contaminate the long yams by contact. The Big Man in charge of growing the long yams to be exchanged must observe sexual abstinence throughout the entire growing period. The yams are painted, given masks, and decorated as though they were men, for the ceremonial exchange. What is produced by male fertility is an emblem of maleness which is dressed up like a man. The yam cult is a statement that men are able to reproduce a metaphoric male society, without the aid of, and indeed through the exclusion of, women.

The structure of yam exchange represents an inversion of the structure of exchange of women, both structures in different ways relating to sexuality and reproductiveness.

The relationship between the dual organization of the Abelam and that found among the previously discussed societies will be deferred until after our description of the Arapesh.

5 Arapesh

The Arapesh occupy a coastal strip of land, an inland range of hills, and a portion of the plains beyond those hills in the Sepik area of New Guinea. The material to be used in this analysis refers primarily to the Mountain Arapesh, although Fortune indicates that the entire Arapesh area shares a common culture. The largest political unit is a locality. The locality is made up of a number of hamlets each of which is ideally a single-clan community. The patrilineal clans are individually named. Garden lands, trees, and sago patches are individually owned and those belonging to the men of a clan are contiguous. The clan as a group has rights to particular hunting areas in uncleared forest. Though this is ideally the case, in actuality there is a considerable fluctuation in residence. Individuals may affiliate with and garden on the land of their cognatic and affinal kinsmen. Each clan has associated with it a supernatural creature called a *marsalai*, which is said to inhabit a dangerous spot on clan land around which gather the ghosts of the clan dead and their wives (Mead 1947: 181). When individuals from the clan desire to use the land, they must inform the *marsalai* (Mead 1935: 17). There are no clan-associated totems. However, there is one account of an initiation ceremony in which the house posts were carved to represent *marsalai*. When a clan becomes reduced in numbers it may adopt a boy from another clan to increase its numbers: several rings will be paid for that child (Mead 1947: 190). In this way the patrilineal clan perpetuates itself as an entity, maintaining its agnatic ideology as it absorbs nonagnates or nonrelatives.

Within the locality, one hamlet may serve as the chief ceremonial center. This hamlet will be occupied by people from several clans. It will have one or more tamberan houses, the male ceremonial houses.

Clans within a locality are grouped into moieties. Mead's picture of the ideal village is as follows:

> . . . the locality is really an enlargement of the ideal village, around which cluster a number of small hamlets, with all ceremonial life centered in the village. Such an ideal locality would be divided into two parts; one half would contain a number of gentes classified as *iwhul*, tabooing the *kuman* (hawk) and the other a number of gentes classified as *ginyau*, tabooing the *kwain* (black and red cockatoo). The feasting village would have a large tamberan house with two ends exactly alike, each door surmounted by the enlarged gable called a *map*. . . . Each moiety would have a portion of the residence ground of the village and an *agehu*, or feasting plaza, within the village where ancestral stones would be arranged. Meanwhile, outside the village, each gens would have a hamlet where its members built their dwelling houses and stored their yams, planted fallow garden lands, sago patches, and hunting land on which the gens members hunted (Mead 1947: 179).

The separation into *iwhul* and *ginyau* is the most prominent feature of the moiety division. Mead states, "Every group of people consisting of two or more gentes should be divided for feasting purposes into an *iwhul* and a *ginyau*" (Mead 1947: 194). The moiety organization seems not to be related to the prohibition or control of marriage. The operation of the moiety organization and its relationship to exchange will be discussed below.

The unity of the locality comes into play in warfare that is carried out between localities. Mead indicates, "But although actual warfare—organized expeditions to plunder, conquer, kill or attain glory—is absent, brawls and clashes between villages do occur, mainly over women" (Mead 1935: 23).

From Fortune's description of incidents between Arapesh localities which resulted in several deaths and followed certain patterns including the use of a battlefield, particular weapons—spears and bows and arrows—and some strategy including ambush, one would conclude that these encounters were not "brawls" but rather conformed to the type of warfare which occurs elsewhere in New Guinea (Fortune 1939). This is very clearly distinct from the feuding between clan hamlets in a community in which no lives are taken and settlement is by the exchange of rings. The sole cause of warfare between localities is the abduction of women, and the acquisition of territory is never involved. The strategy of abduction involves the use of a go-between who sounds out the willingness of the woman to leave her husband. The aggrieved husband need not lead the attack. The old men and the war leaders immediately take charge and the clans are mobilized (Fortune 1939: 29).

During the course of the relations between localities, there are abductions, clashes, and intermarriages. Mead describes such a sequence of events in the relations between the localities of Alitoa and Wihun, and Alitoa and Liwo (Mead 1947: 273). Mead also provides an example of a peace settlement that involved the sending of two women in marriage from one village to the other (Mead 1947: 265). Fortune also reports the payment of a pig for a man killed (Fortune 1939: 24).

There is no concept of inherited rank, authority, or organized leadership among the Arapesh. However, the political role of the Big Man emerges very clearly from the data on exchange, as will be demonstrated below. The "bigness" of a man relates to the number of exchange events in which he has played a principal part. For example, Mead notes, "Ombomb had several pigs and therefore was vulnerable, for he was preparing to make the first of a series of feasts that would lead to his being a big man" (Mead 1935: 118). Mead indicates that it seems more likely that the son of a Big Man will also be a Big Man, though this is not the result of any inheritance of accumulated goods coming from his father (Mead 1947: 221). The eldest son is given the largest postinitiatory feast (*balagasi*). It marks the retirement of his father. An important man may on this occasion build a larger house and give it to his son as well as betroth two wives to this son.

However, the son must use his own abilities to capitalize on these initial advantages. All the teenage boys in a village are evaluated on their potentialities to be future Big Men and a likely candidate is assigned a *buanyin* (exchange partner) from among the young men in a clan in which one of his elder male relatives has *buanyin* (Mead 1935: 28). The *buanyin* relationship will be described more fully below.

At his death, the Big Man is accorded special attention. A feast is held to end the mourning for a Big Man. The bones of a Big Man are seen as having special magical power. "The bones of a man who has been a successful yam planter, a successful hunter, a feast maker, strong in leadership and speech making, have this intrinsic quality" (Mead 1940: 433). Big Men will make more elaborate feasts at the rites de passage of their children than will ordinary men.

There is a category of men, referred to by the term *alomato'in*, which may be translated as male wastrel or male woman (Mead 1940: 352). This term does not connote homosexuality but instead refers to failure to maintain obligations involving food distribution and the observance of the necessary taboos concerned with food. Thus it may be seen as the contradiction or obverse of the Big Man.

The only statement regarding marriage rules is that "Formally, the children of parents who use brother and sister, cross-cousin, or two generations-apart-child-of-cross-cousin terms to each other are not allowed to marry, nor may a man marry a woman whom he calls either aunt, daughter, or niece, nor may a woman marry a man whom she calls father, or mother's brother, or nephew" (Mead 1947: 199). Mead phrases the marriage rule in terms of kinship terminology. Since Arapesh kinship terminology is of the Omaha type (see figure 7), so that the criterion of generation is not employed to differentiate terms, the marriage rules must be translated into Arapesh terms from the English terms given by Mead, in order for its operation to be understood. The terms may be sorted according to lineages (see figure 8). In addition to ego's own lineage, six other lineages are delineated by the terminology. In the three ascending generations from ego, three of these lineages have given a woman to ego's lineage, and three other lineages have received a woman. For ego's mother's lineage, the two terms are *wau'en* for males (MoBr and MoBrSo) and *ama'e'u* for females (MoSi and MoBrDa).

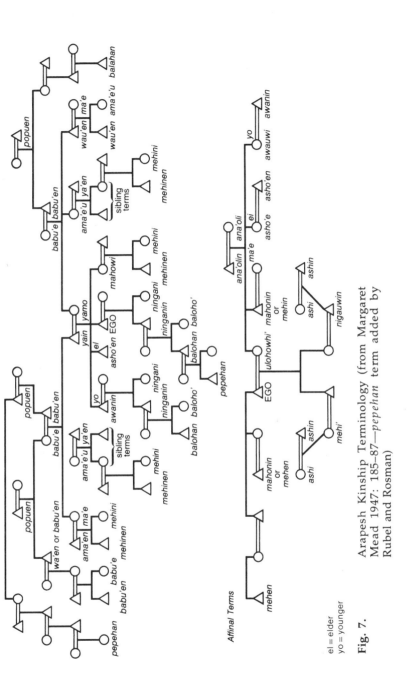

Fig. 7. Arapesh Kinship Terminology (from Margaret Mead 1947: 185–87—*pepehan* term added by Rubel and Rosman)

Affinal Terms

el = elder
yo = younger

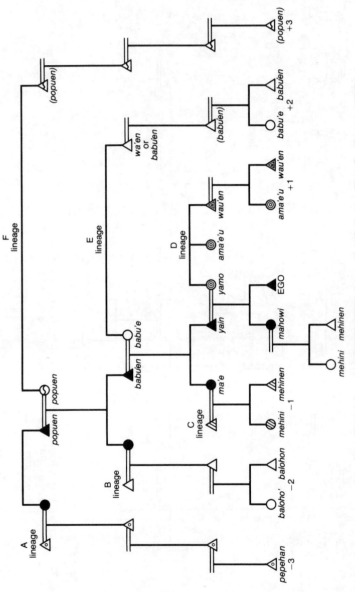

Fig. 8. Arapesh Kinship Terminology Sorted into Lineages. Plotted in terms of lineages giving women to (D,E,F) and taking women from (A,B,C), ego's lineage (terms in parentheses are hypothesized).

For the lineage that gave a woman to ego's father's father, the term *babu'e* is used for females and *babuen* for males. (Mead gives *wa'en* as an alternative term to *babuen* for FaMoBr. We are assuming that this is the same term as *wau'en* [Mead 1947: 404], the term for MoBr, and that ego will use this term because he acts as a surrogate for his father when his lineage treats that lineage as a mother's brother's lineage.) For the lineage that gave a woman to ego's FaFaFa, the term *popuen* is used. Since this is a lineage terminology, the terms for the different degrees of matrilateral collateral relatives on ego's own generation reflect the generation in which a woman was given to ego's lineage. Thus matrilateral third cousins have the same term as great-grandparents; second cousins have the same term as grandparents; first cousins have the same term as maternal aunt and uncle. In ego's own generation, the three degrees of patrilateral cross-cousins are the descendants of the three lineages each of which have taken a woman from ego's lineage, in the previous three generations. Descendants of a lineage that took a woman three generations back are called *pepehan*; descendants of a lineage that took a woman two generations back are called *baloho'* and *balohon*; descendants of a lineage that took a woman one generation back are called *mehini* and *mehinen*. (The terms *mehini* and *mehinen* are also used for sister's children, who cannot be of the same lineage as FaSi children. This usage reflects the fact that *wau'en* and *mehinen* are reciprocal terms.) These are the terms used respectively for great-grandchild, grandchild, and sister's child. They represent the reciprocals of the three previous sets of terms. Because ego is referred to by each of these matrilateral cross-cousins as *popuen, babuen,* and *wau'en,* he refers to them by the reciprocal term *pepehan, balohon,* and *mehinen.*

Mead's statement regarding the marriage rule becomes much clearer when examined in light of the discussion of the kinship terminology sorted in terms of a lineage structure. According to that rule ego cannot marry a woman from any of the six lineages represented in the terminology given in figure 8. There appears to be some variation on this point, since informants reported to us that they could marry women in the *popuen* and *pepehan* categories three generations after a previous marriage (Rosman and Rubel 1974: 37, 42, 48, 58, 64, 70). The sequence of payments to mother's lineage which will be discussed below seems to support the possibility of a renewal of marriage ties in the third generation, after the payments cease.

In terms of a positive preference in marriage, sister exchange is mentioned in a number of instances. Mead comments, "It is good that brother and sister should marry brother and sister, that if one clan gives two of its girls to the other, the other clan should reciprocate two of its daughters. This is no hard and fast rule" (Mead 1935: 81–82). She notes further,

> Members of a gens are sometimes regarded collectively when there is question of sister exchange or near sister exchange in marriage, but here the same practice also leads to equating all the members of a large village or of an entire locality, . . . true sister exchange occurs rather seldom, and there is more of a desire to find some way in which a return can be claimed to have been made than there is a desire for an actual return. The most elaborate legal fictions are continually resorted to so that members of different gentes or different villages can claim that one marriage may properly be regarded as a return for another (Mead 1947: 182–83).

An analysis of the data from the village of Alitoa reveals that at least four real sister exchanges occurred. Other cases are present in the ethnographic material where the Arapesh present the case as a return of a woman for a woman previously received (Mead 1935: 155). Sister exchange is not reflected at all in the kinship terminology. After a marriage between lines, the marriage prohibition quoted above would prevent renewal of this tie between those family lines for several generations. However, Mead remarks, "The menfolk of the two clans already bound together by several ties will urge a further tie" (Mead 1935: 82). There is a continuing relationship between sets of clans within the locality of Alitoa, and between Alitoa and other localities, particularly with Liwo and Wihun. These relationships between clans and between localities are viewed and presented in terms of exchanges of women. It would seem, therefore, that the marriage prohibitions, which ideally prevent marriages between families for three generations, refer to lineages and do not extend to entire clans. This marriage prohibition would imply that the Arapesh remember their genealogical pedigrees for many generations. This is, in fact, the case for the Arapesh according to Fortune (personal communication).

Among the Arapesh, infant betrothal is the norm. At the age of seven or eight, the betrothed girl will go to live in her future husband's house. She becomes a part of her husband's clan and it said that "they grew her." She may ultimately marry a man in that clan other than the one to whom she was originally betrothed.

Polygamy exists but it is frequently the result of the levirate operating within a clan so that if a woman's husband dies, she is inherited by his brother or other male clan relative. Though it is convenient to have two wives, Mead states that a man is not enriched by the additional labor of a second wife (Mead 1935: 109).

We turn now to an analysis of Arapesh exchange. The Arapesh are very explicit about the identity in meaning of the exchange of women and the exchange of pigs and yams. It is summed up in the famous Arapesh aphorism quoted by Lévi-Strauss.

> Other people's mothers
> Other people's sisters
> Other people's pigs
> Other people's yams which they
>   have piled up
> You may eat,
> Your own mother
> Your own sister
> Your own pigs
> Your own yams which you have piled up
> You may not eat.
>
> (Mead 1940: 352)[1]

Mead observes that the attitude toward one who eats his own yams is analogous to attitudes toward incest. The pigs that a person raises are considered to be his children; the owner of a pig is referred to as its father (Mead 1940: 361). Mead also notes, "The ideal distribution of food is for each person to eat food grown by another. . . . Under the guid-

---

1. In a legend, a man who has seen a *marsalai* is cursed by the *marsalai* before it destroys him. The curse is: "Go, copulate with your sister, go and copulate with your mother, go and eat your own pig, go and eat the yams which you have made into a ceremonial pile. In the night you will go to pieces completely" (Mead 1933–34: 42).

ance of this idea, an Arapesh man hunts only to send most of his kill to his mother's brother, his cousin, or his father-in-law. The lowest man in the community, the man who is believed to be so far outside the moral pale that there is no use reasoning with him, is the man who eats his own kill—even though that kill be a tiny bird, hardly a mouthful at all (Mead 1935: 28–29).

The relationship between a mother's brother and sister's son is the focal point for a whole series of exchanges. In the case of the Arapesh, the mother's brother is always the recipient. Fear of brother's curse that will make sister barren or mother's brother's curse upon the child hovers over the relationship (Mead 1947: 199; 1940: 414). The relationship is begun in the previous generation in which a betrothal sets up the link between the two families. There is no exchange of goods at the time of betrothal, which occurs when the girl is seven or eight years old. The girl goes to live in the boy's household, and she is incorporated into that household. At her first menstruation, after a period of seclusion and fasting, the girl's shoulder and buttocks are scarified by her mother's brother. Then she is ceremonially fed by her future husband. This is followed by a presentation of gifts by her brothers to the couple which consist of knives, spears, baskets, net bags, and bows and arrows. Subsequently, the young husband hunts for meat, which is then used for a feast given to all those who have helped, including the girl's mother's brother who made the scarifications (Mead 1940: 420–21).

Some time after puberty, during a feast, shell rings are presented by the husband's family to the family of the wife. Rings are the most important item presented to affines, and symbolize the affinal relationship. Some dozen rings are given and in addition sometimes strings of dog's teeth as well. Only three or four rings are kept permanently. For the remainder, exact equivalents are returned by the wife's family to that of the husband. This exchange of rings comes subsequent to the first sexual intercourse of the couple. A marriage establishes a relationship between brothers-in-law. "With a brother-in-law, one hunts, one gardens, one travels, one sleeps" (Mead 1947: 198).

The birth of a child continues the affinal relationship into the next generation, and the father of that child acts towards his brother-in-law as the mother's brother of his child. The mother's brother relationship is consistently one-sided; mother's brother is always the recipient. This begins at birth. Mead notes, "The father buys the child from the mother's brother, he 'pays for the blood'. The child then becomes his, and if a girl, he can control any bride price which is paid for her" (Mead 1947: 195). The payment at birth is two to three rings. The child's blood is still conceptualized as belonging to the mother's lineage. Ear and nose piercing is done by mother or mother's sister; a wounded man pays his mother's brother for blood spilled.

When he reaches adolescence a boy goes through the rites of initiation. The initiatory rites serve to introduce him to the mysteries of the tamberan cult. The rites involve isolation from females, the observance of a series of taboos, and the incision of the boy's penis. The boy learns that the tamberan spirit is only the beating of the tamberan drum and the noise from the flute or bull roarer. When a Big Man makes a rite de passage ceremony he may invite the presence of the tamberan with all the additional ceremony and feasting that goes with it (Mead 1940: 228).

Mead notes the connection between initiation and the dual division in the following statements: "At initiation, *kuman* belong to one line and *kwain* to another. . . . In initiatory ceremonies, *kuman* and *kwain* groups are seated separately" (Mead 1947: 184). This would seem to indicate that both initiates and audience are divided into moiety groups, but the functions of these groups are not indicated.

"Curiously enough, in the ritual shedding of blood at incision, the importance of the mother's brother disappears, although in so many parts of the area, it is he or his surrogate who does the cutting, or dresses the wounds of the novice (Tchambuli, Iatmul, Mundugumor). Here in Arapesh, he performs no such function; the old men all contribute blood for the novices to drink, i.e. they become mothers and give birth to the child, and the Cassowary who is the surrogate of the entire male group performs the operation. But afterwards, the Arapesh youth must make a feast and pay his mother's brother for the shed blood" (Mead 1947: 195). The position of Cassowary, who actually performs the incision of the boys' penises, is the hereditary right of a single clan in any locality (Mead 1940: 427; 1947: 182). Mead notes elsewhere that the mother's brother plays a role in the initiation ceremonies for a single youth at which the mother's brother beats the initiate, but there is no role mentioned for him in the large interlocality initiation ceremonies that take place every six or seven years and at which thirty or forty boys are initiated at one time. The role of the sponsor is also mentioned in connection with initiation. The sponsor performs a variety of services for the initiate, such as accompanying him to the bathing pool and weaving arm bands for him. In one of her accounts of initiation, Mead mentions that feasts are made for the sponsors. There is no information on the nature of the relationship between sponsor and initiate or initiate's father; however, she notes that sponsors are feasted at the feast for mother's brother after the initiation. On the basis of our field material, it seems likely that the boy's sponsor is his father's *buanyin*. After the initiation ceremonies are over and before the feast for mother's brother, the initiate is taken, dressed in regalia, on a tour of his father's trade partners. He receives a gift in each home he visits.

The feast given for the mother's brother after initiation is known as *balagasi*. Mead indicates that the mother's brother may publicly challenge the father of a sister's son to give him a large *balagasi* in the boy's name (Mead 1940: 425). A feast of some kind is obligatory; its magnitude may vary. At the close of the *balagasi,* the boy's father gives the mother's brother's group of the boy a bunch of leaves which marks the giving of the feast and serves as a demand that the mother's brother's group now guard the boy's health (Mead 1940: 426).

Since one's blood is said to be the property of one's maternal clan, when a man is wounded either in an accident or by an enemy, the injured man must make a payment of shell rings to his mother's brother; the same type of payment to mother's brother is made when a man is placed in a shameful situation. In the case of the shaming of a Big Man, his mother's brother (or cross-cousin) can invoke the tamberan so that the whole male community becomes involved and the Big Man must feast the tamberan. It is the mother's brother who has the right to shed the blood of his sister's child. He opens boils for sister's child and scarifies the adolescent girl at her initiation.

At the death of a man, payments of rings are also made by members of the man's lineage, his brothers or sons, to the natal lineage of his mother. This is in the same category of payments made to mother's brother (*wau'en*). Since the deceased's true mother's brother is probably dead, his son (also termed *wau'en*) will be the recipient. The deceased man and his son, who is giving the rings, both stand as *mehinen* to the recipient lineage. A relationship was established when the deceased's father married his mother and was continued through his birth and initiation until it was finally ended at his death.

Mead indicates that *mehinen* (FaSiSo) can also be present as recipients of rings at a death. However, she states, "There is no rubric under which a *mehinen* has any rights to receive property at such a time" (Mead 1947: 198). One explanation for death payments to *mehinen* offered by Mead, which seems most in accord with the structure of affinal relationships, is that it is a result of a previous sister exchange. "Note that with brother and sister exchange, which happens not infrequently among the Arapesh, the two kinds of cross-cousins will be in the same place; in a large death feast, where the emphasis tends to be upon payment to a *place,* this tends further to confuse the proper distinctions between mother's brother's son and father's sister's son" (Mead 1947: 404–5, n. 1). In this quote, Mead is referring to actual death payments made to a *wau'en* and a *mehinen* of the deceased man who are both from the same place. As was pointed out in the discussion of a sister exchange above, reference is being made here to clan sisters rather than true sisters. Elsewhere, in a discussion of rites de passage, *mehinen* are not listed as recipients at any of the occasions (Mead 1947: 228).

A second major category of exchange is that which takes place between *buanyin,* men who are ceremonial exchange partners to one another and are in opposite moieties. Theoretically every Arapesh male may have a *buanyin* but, in fact, usually the Big Men of the two clans are *buanyin* to one another and serve as the focus of exchanges between their groups. "The 'big men' stand in a continuous exchange relation with exchange partners, theoretically members of the opposite moiety and always members of a different clan. These exchange partners call each other *buanyin,* are hereditary, usually in the male line, but not necessarily in the direct line" (Mead 1937: 32). Informants stressed that when a man dies, his son inherits his father's *buanyin* relationship. In the absence of a son, a man will adopt someone to take his place (Rosman and Rubel 1974: 4, 5, 10, 20, 28, 36, 38, 56, 59). The son of a Big Man will inherit his father's *buanyin* relationships but, given the flexibility of leadership in the Big Man structure, that son may not represent his group in future exchanges with *buanyin*. There is some question as to whether the children of *buanyin* can marry. This will be discussed more fully below when we consider the relationship between marriage structure and the structure of exchange.

The *buanyin* relationship is a competitive one, and quarrels between *buanyin* may occur. Such quarrels are settled by the exchange of pigs and yams. If a man is unable to hold up his end of the *buanyin* relationship and finds that he is not able to continue to match his rival in returning the equivalent of what has been given, he can sever the relationship. He does this by placing a large wooden bowl surrounded by twigs on the public plaza. It is interesting to note that other ways of expressing the termination of relationships, including kin relationships, involve the cessation of food exchanges (Mead 1940: 438, 354). However, informants emphasized the continuity of the *buanyin* relationship. Even after the symbolic termination of the relationship, exchanges are again initiated which allow the relationship to continue.

The aphorism quoted above states the Arapesh rule that people may not eat their own yams and pigs. These things constitute the major items of exchange between *buanyin* who are in opposite moieties. Products of the hunt, such as wild pigs, cassowaries, and tree kangaroos must also be presented to one's *buanyin*. (In coastal Arapesh villages large fish, such as sharks, must also be given to one's *buanyin*.) An exact return is expected and can be demanded if it is not forthcoming. Though the basis of the *buanyin* relationship involves the exchange of food items, *buanyin* do not seem to feed each other directly. When one man makes a formal presentation of pigs or game to his *buanyin*, the latter immediately redistributes what he has received. "*Buanyin* give each other feasts at which neither *buanyin* eats, but each distributes food to his helping friends and relatives" (Mead 1937: 33).

Both short, hairy yams and long yams are grown by the Arapesh. The small yams may be eaten by the grower; the long yams must be given to one's *buanyin*. The yam cult as practiced among the Abelam is not present among the Arapesh. However, some of the elements linking sex and yam growing are present. Yam gardening is considered men's work; menstruating women and sexual intercourse must be kept separate from yam growing (Mead 1940: 449). "If he observes the proper rules his yams will grow; if he fails, if he encounters menstrual blood, or goes near the yams while his wife is menstruating or too soon after intercourse, then they will take offense, they will not grow, but will sulk and run away" (Mead 1940: 353). To improve the growing of yams, a man will abstain from sex with his wife for the growing period (Mead 1940: 421). Hunting is also affected by sexual activity and contact with menstrual blood. If a man has not observed the proper rules, he will not see the game. Sexual abstention is also necessary prior to carrying pigs to a feast, and when performing the ritual for success of pig exchanges (Mead 1940: 350, 353).

When a man has a particularly good harvest of long yams, he announces his intention to make an *abullu* and to present them to his *buanyin* (Mead 1938: 183; Rosman and Rubel 1974: 2, 8, 14, 15, 35, 36, 38, 46, 55, 59, 68). After harvest, the yams are painted in particular patterns and arranged in piles of ninety-six, after being measured with a long vine. If more than one man is involved, each has his own yam pile. Meat must be collected for the accompanying feast. A man is assisted by his relatives and by a sponsor whom he selects. Members of other hamlets in the locality are invited. Special *abullu* songs are sung and dances are performed. The maker of the *abullu* goes through a rite carried out by his sponsor which ensures the repetition of a good harvest. The guests are feasted and then leave presents of meat, plates, pots, or net bags, and carry away with them net bags filled with yams for seed. The maker of the *abullu* is not supposed to eat the progeny of those yams for up to ten generations and individuals are said to keep a genealogical record of yams. Some time later, a final feast is held to release the holder of the *abullu* and his wife from the remaining taboos. After this feast, the sponsors are given rings. Throughout her accounts, Mead never states what is the nature of the relationship between the giver of an *abullu* and his sponsor. However, the giving of a ring to the sponsor in exchange for assistance at a ritual leads us to believe that the sponsor is an affine of some kind. The recipients of yams are *buanyin*. The vine used to measure the quantity of yams that have been distributed "is kept and fastened up on the outside of the house and may be referred to in ceremonial boasting between hereditary exchange partners (*buanyin*)" (Mead 1938: 337). The vine, which measures the circumference of the pile of yams, as well as the stick which measures its height, is important in the challenge aspect of the *abullu* and the rivalry between *buanyin*, since the recipient must return an equivalent pile of yams at some future date. If one can give an even larger amount than what was received the previous time, one's prestige is enhanced. A man can demonstrate in this way that he is a Big Man.

The *buanyin* relationship refers to a relationship between men within a single locality. It is characterized by challenge and rivalry; one gives to one's *buanyin*, and then one challenges him to return what has been given. However, in relations between localities which involve large-scale exchanges it is expected that a man will help his *buanyin* if the *buanyin* is a principal in such an interlocality exchange. If such help is not forthcoming, there will be recriminations by the *buanyin* who needed assistance. Mead describes an incident between two *buanyin*, Aden and Balidu, where the recriminations took place after Balidu had made a *balagasi* feast and had not received aid from his *buanyin*, Aden (Mead 1947: 305–6).

A particular type of feast is made in connection with a formal request for help in accumulating property for the large interlocality feasts. A man will establish "formal ties with a group of members of the opposite dual division (ideally), who will formally undertake to help him, and who will formally participate in the honors of the feast, while his close relatives who help him informally will participate only informally. The principal of such a feast is called the trunk (*bauwanag*), and the men whose help he formally requests and secures are called the 'dogs' (*nubag*)" (Mead 1947: 225). The two sides of the dual division referred to here are the *iwhul* and *ginyau* divisions of the moiety organization. The "dogs" are on the opposite side of the moiety division to the trunk. Though Mead does not make the direct connection, it is apparent that the "dogs" are the *buanyin* of the trunk (see Mead's description of a dog feast [1947: 298, 305–6]; Rosman and Rubel 1974: 39, 60). Mead further notes, "Each important man in one half of the village would have an hereditary feasting partner, a *buanyin*, in the other half" (Mead 1947: 179). "*Buanyin* . . . should be members of gentes which are ranged on opposite sides of the dual organization, *ginyau* and *iwhul* (feasting divisions)" (Mead 1947: 204). A man planning a large feast in the future assumes the role of "trunk." He selects several men on the opposite side of the moiety organization who either are Big Men, or who are on the way to becoming Big Men (Mead 1937: 33). He gives a series of three feasts to the dogs. The dogs return what they have received at these feasts shortly before the trunk is to make his large feast. The return made by the dogs is referred to as vomit (*gogwilis*). It is interesting that the term vomit is used, since in other contexts feeding is considered the basis of a relationship. Dogs, of course, feed their young by vomiting. If the dogs in turn redistribute what they have received from the trunk—pigs and uncooked food along with feast food—to other people and thereby spread the obligation, pigs will move back along the same lines of the distribution. Mead refers to this as a chain feast (Mead 1947: 225). The culmination of the dog feasts and the chain feasts are the large interlocality feasts and rite de passage feasts.

There is a separate term, *gabunyan*, which refers to ceremonial exchange partners in an intervillage exchange. These *gabunyan* are usually involved in exchange of ceremonial complexes and sacred flutes and in the performance of interlocality initiations (Mead 1947: 229). Interlocality feasts are organized so that "for each locality there is a principal, who acts as 'trunk', as organizer of the preliminary feasts in his own locality, and contracts with the other principal, his *gabunyan*, to make the necessary payments" (Mead 1947: 229). Housebuilding is a part of any large ceremonial undertaking. A "trunk" usually builds a new house to hold his yams (Mead 1938: 245). Yam storage houses are larger than dwelling houses.

There is another category called *ano'in*, which the Arapesh see as related to *buanyin*. This is a competitive and rivalrous relationship that does not involve exchange. People born on the same day can be *ano'in*, or people who have quarreled may become *ano'in* to one another. In quarrels over the stealing of women, the wronged party "if he already stands in no

ceremonial relationship to the leader of the other party may
say, 'From now on, he and I are *ano'in*. He may stay in his
place and I will stay in mine. I will plant yams. He can plant
yams. I will raise pigs. He can raise pigs. I will give feasts.
He can give feasts. We will each watch the other,' setting up
a lifetime of long distance rivalry" (Mead 1947: 206). The
ano'in relationship may be inherited. Children of *ano'in*
should marry. There is no further information to clarify the
implications of the last two points.

There is a last category of exchange partners which Mead
refers to as hereditary trade partners, without providing an
Arapesh equivalent. A series of dyadic relationships between ego and his hereditary trade partners in other villages
forms a path leading from the mountain Arapesh to the
plains Arapesh in one direction and to the beach Arapesh in
the opposite direction. Individuals have their own trade
partners and their own "roads," and people from the same
village tend to go through the same localities. The summation of individual paths is a "road" of a locality or hamlet.
There is a belief that these trade friendships were initiated
through intermarriage. It is said to be a good idea if the
children of trade friends marry. As we noted above, an integral part of a boy's intiation involves the introductory visits
that he makes to each of his father's trade partners. This
"ancestral road" becomes his as he reaches manhood. In addition to visits to his father's trade partners, he also makes
visits to the houses of his father's sisters and other women of
his lineage who have married out, along the same "road,"
indicating that women have married into the same localities
where there are trade friends. The goods involved in such
exchanges include shells from the coast, which are exchanged for tobacco, plumes, net bags, and other goods from
inland. No accounting is kept of exact equivalences in these
exchanges between trade partners. Dance complexes and the
paraphernalia associated with them also travel along these
roads. They may also be the paths by which bodily sub-
stances to be used for sorcery are carried from the mountains
to the plains, where the sorcerers dwell.

Among the Arapesh there seem to be two kinds of structures of exchange—one structure involving the exchange of
women between groups, the second involving the exchange
of pigs and yams between *buanyin* in a two-sided moiety

structure. The marriage structure combines the following elements. Once a marriage is contracted between two families, further marriages cannot take place for the next two generations. After this point, the marriage tie may be renewed. The link between two families established by a marriage is continued in the form of affinal exchanges. In exchange for a woman going in one direction, bride wealth is the first in a series of presentations made to the group giving the woman, which continues for two more generations. Such presentations include birth and initiation payments to mother's brother, and the final payment at the death of the child of this marriage, which is made by the son of the deceased to the dead man's mother's lineage. These presentations are unidirectional, and their most important component is shell rings. Looking at the larger units, clans and localities exchange sisters, real and classificatory, with one another and keep an accounting of the state of the exchange. Since they emphasize roughly equal exchanges of women between groups, affinal relationships would appear to be balanced, for each group would be a wife giver to the other. Between families affinal exchanges are unequal, but between localities emphasizing equivalence in the exchange of women, the affinal exchanges tend to be in balance.

The moiety division of the Arapesh involves feasting, in which *buanyin* exchange with their partners in the opposite moiety. The structure of exchange between *buanyin* is thus the moiety structure. The *buanyin* relationship is hereditary so that links between opposite sides are maintained over generations. *Buanyin* exchange primarily pigs and yams, in contrast to affines, who exchange shells.

Buanyin are exchange partners on opposite sides of the moiety division in a village and *gabunyan* are ceremonial exchange partners in exchanges between villages. In such an exchange *gabunyan* act as the "trunks" of their respective villages.

Finally, we must consider the relationship between these two structures. Though Mead emphasizes the great similarity between the affinal relationship and the *buanyin* relationship, they differ in important respects. The exchange of goods after a marriage is unidirectional, whereas the *buanyin* relationship emphasizes exact equivalence. The things exchanged are different: affines receive shell rings; *buanyin* exchange pigs and yams. The *buanyin* relationship is characterized by competition and rivalry, in contrast to the affinal relationship. In light of the above, one would expect a complete separation between the two relationships, such that *buanyin* are not connected in an affinal relationship and that their children do not marry. The ethnographic information on this point is equivocal. Mead notes, "There is the native statement that the children of *buanyin* (ceremonial exchange partners) should marry" (Mead 1940: 329). Fortune indicates that when *buanyin* become affines, the *buanyin* relationship must cease since *buanyin* compete and affines do not (Fortune, personal communication). Analysis of our own data on the point of whether children of *buanyin* can marry also reveals equivocation (Rosman and Rubel 1974: 3, 9, 11, 22, 30, 36, 38, 45, 56, 59, 67). In some villages the people said yes; in others they said no. When the children of *buanyin* marry, it may be necessary for the *buanyin* relationship to cease, though the relationships between their respective groups may be maintained by other men who assume the roles of *buanyin*. In the exchange of women between clans and between localities equivalence is desired. In the exchanges between *buanyin* representing two clans, and *gabunyan* representing two localities, exact equivalence is also the ideal.

In the case of the Arapesh as well as the Abelam, we see, once again, two structures of exchange, one dealing with women and the other dealing with the exchange of pigs and yams between exchange partners. Like the Abelam, the Arapesh have sister exchange but it takes place between units of larger magnitude like localities. The Arapesh have extended the Abelam prohibition against marriage with first cross-cousins to all second cross-cousins. The structure of exchange of women sets up the affinal relationship, which is defined by the exchange of shell rings. This is in contrast to the structure of exchange between exchange partners which is defined by the exchange of yams and pigs among the Arapesh. The separation of women from yam cultivation, hunting, and the exchange of yams and pigs is present among the Arapesh. It is the reproductive aspect of women, menstruation and sexual intercourse, which necessitates that they be kept apart from these activities. The Arapesh would seem therefore to have a somewhat weakened version of the Abelam yam cult, but the same type of transformational relationship between the two structures of exchange is present. The exchange of women is necessary to ensure the reproduction of the group through sexual intercourse between men and women, and the exchange of yams and pigs is necessary to ensure the reproduction of these things, which is achieved through the exclusion of women. While the Abelam emphasize the potency of the grower in growing a few very long yams, the Arapesh measure the circumference of the pile of yams and its height. The Arapesh grower may not eat these yams but is compelled to exchange them. Though the grower may not eat these yams for ten generations, the recipient may. Like women, yams must be exchanged. The reproduction of human society and yams and pigs therefore depends upon exchange, and both structures of exchange deal with fertility and reproduction though they are symbolic inversions of one another.

The dual structure that was the theme of chapters 2 and 3 is clearly evident among the Abelam and Arapesh. However, it characterizes only the structure of exchange of goods and the exchange of services during initiation rites. In regard to marriage, the Abelam and Arapesh have a series of prohibitions on future marriage after a marriage has taken place. Among the Arapesh, the prohibitions produce a Crow-Omaha marriage system as Lévi-Strauss has defined it. However, continuing sister exchange, which characterized the societies in chapter 2 and underlay their structure of dual organization, is present among both Abelam and Arapesh, though with reference to localities (Arapesh) and clans (Abelam) rather than to lineages.

6 Wogeo

The island of Wogeo is one of the Schouten Islands and lies thirty miles off the north coast of New Guinea, near the mouth of the Sepik River. At the time of Hogbin's first study in 1934 the population of the island was 929.

The minimal social unit is the household. After marriage a man will build a new house next to the house of his father, for his wife and future children. The nuclear family comprises the household. The residential pattern is predominately virilocal. The residential unit is thus a core of agnatically related males. These men have also inherited plots of garden land from their fathers. The garden plots of closely related males lie next to one another. Such a cluster of households of agnatically related men has a single headman or *kokwal*. The group is identified as the followers of that headman. The staple crop is taro, with bananas, sugar cane, and greens as subsidiary crops. Coconuts, almonds, and Tahitian chestnuts are also important.

Though the typical land inheritance pattern is one in which the sons of a man will inherit his land, with the largest number of plots going to the eldest son, a headman or important man will also give land as part of the dowry of his eldest daughter. This land is always referred to as dowry land in succeeding generations. The couple may live uxorilocally but this is not necessarily the case. This land is not under control of the husband, though he may farm it since women do not do agricultural work. If the couple live virilocally, the brother of the girl will hold the land for her. In the next generation, this land passes to the woman's sons who would, if the couple lived uxorilocally, be living in that village. In the succeeding generation, that land should be returned to its original owners in the form of dowry land given with a girl who is married back into the original group. This is a form of second cross-cousin marriage where a boy marries his father's father's sister's son's daughter (Hogbin 1944–45: 329). As the result of the passage of dowry land, there may be nonagnates living in a village and farming its land. The emphasis however, seems to be on eventually re-turning dower land to its original agnatic owners. In the Wogeo conceptualization, the rights to farming land derive from the rights to tie down particular roof rafters when the men's house of the village is constructed. Each beam repre-sents a certain series of plots of land. A man inherits the right to tie down a particular roof beam from his father and the right to use the lands associated with that beam. The two headmen or *kokwal* in a village have the right to tie down the beams over the central doorways (Hogbin 1939–40: 161). The roof of the men's house "is thus a sort of diagram of the utilization of all the agricultural land in the neighborhood" (Hogbin 1939–40: 161).

In earlier publications, Hogbin referred to the residential unit as a patrilineal clan or lineage and indicated that the native term *dan,* meaning water, a euphemism for semen, was used to refer to this grouping (Hogbin 1934–35a: 314; 1944–45: 324). In these publications, he emphasized that pat-rilineal inheritance of land was the basis of recruitment for this patrilineal group, though nonagnates were sometimes included. The presence of a few nonagnates in the residential unit or cluster, as he referred to it, seems to have led Hogbin to modify his earlier position. In his latest work he no longer uses the term patrilineal clan with reference to this group. Rather, he notes, "The criterion for membership is filiation—being the child of a particular parent, usually father, occasionally mother—and hence inheriting that parent's land rights" (Hogbin 1970a: 25). Hogbin finally falls back on the following: "There appears to be no alternative to my speaking of the occupants of a housing cluster or of a headman and his followers" (Hogbin 1970b: 308).

We have decided to call these residential clusters patrilineages for the following reasons. They do not conform to the pattern of cognatic descent groups or ambilineages where there is an option to reside with and utilize the resources of either father or mother. Affiliation and residence with mother's group occurs only under certain circumstances, as we have noted. The emphasis upon returning dowry land to its original group via a later marriage would appear to stress the corporateness of the patrilineage and its relationship to its own land. The core of the residential group whose dwellings cluster around that of their headman or *kokwal* and whose garden plots surround their section of the village is a group of male agnates and therefore a patrilineage. Hogbin has also indicated that this unit is exogamous (Hogbin 1938: 224). Each patrilineage has its own system of magic (Hogbin 1934–35b: 378).

Each village has a pair of *kokwals,* and their groups. The headmen occupy houses on either side of the clubhouse with the houses of their patrilineages in the immediate vicinity. Hogbin notes, "The plan of the average settlement thus shows two clusters of houses with a meeting place in between" (Hogbin 1970a: 19). Though each *kokwal* commands only the members of his own patrilineage, there are occasions when the two *kokwals* act in consort in tabooing a particular food crop in preparation for a feast.

Several villages are grouped into a district, which acts as an entity vis-à-vis other districts. No one village seems to have primacy within the district. There are five districts on the island. Hogbin notes, "Each district is linked in an alliance with one of the rest and opposed to two others" (1970b: 305). From a map of Wogeo it is clear that enemy districts are adjacent to each other and friendly districts and and those considered neutral are further away. Relations between districts that are enemies to one another involve raiding, theft, adultery, and armed conflict as well as intermarriage and food exchanges. Hogbin observes that "Jealousy between the districts is keen, and the most trifling incidents such as theft of a pig or a case of adultery have several times led to battles. Yet very little blood is shed, and no ground has ever changed hands afterwards—indeed, it is not so much as mentioned'' (Hogbin 1939–40: 137).

In addition to the patrilineages there are also exogamous matrilineal moieties present on Wageo. They are named after the bat and the hawk. The word for this unit is *tina,* which is also the word for mother. These units cross-cut the district, village, and patrilineage. Since moieties are matrilineal and exogamous, a father and his son would be in opposite moieties, However, ego and his father's father are in the same moiety. People who are members of the same moiety consider themselves of one blood, but only when a genealogical connection can be traced do they consider themselves one kin (Hogbin 1970a: 17). However, they do not act in concert as a group at any time. Moieties function ceremonially. Individuals of one moiety are chosen to intiate the boys of the opposite moiety and the individuals from one moiety bury people from the opposite moiety. A number of significant relationships involve individuals of opposite moieties. These include the relationship of blood brothers or bond friends which is established during one of the rites of initiation and which is useful in arranging assignations or elopements, and the relationship of exchange partners, or *bag,* who are always of opposite moieties and from different districts.

The Wogeo *kokwal,* head of the patrilineage, is different from the Big Man in other New Guinea societies. His position is institutionalized and there is a formal mode of succession. The *kokwal* has more land than any of his followers. For example, Marigum, a *kokwal* of Dap village, has three acres of land while his followers have approximately one-half acre each. He also has more trees than they do. Hogbin notes, ''More important however, is the fact that he received tribute in the form, not of gifts, but of labor, from his fellow clansmen. They are expected to work for him without any return, save their meals, whenever he undertook any important work such as clearing land, fencing, nutting, housebuilding and canoe construction, and in the course of five months I found that everyone in Dap labored for Marigum on an average only a little less than one day per week" (Hogbin 1938–39: 299). With respect to harvesting of food, "The whole clan as well as relatives living elsewhere assist the *kokwal* with his harvest. Gifts are not made in return but the people are given the usual meal by his household at the end of the day" (Hogbin 1938–39: 311). Each patrilineage has special taro gardens under the *kokwal's* control in which food is grown exclusively for exchange in interdistrict festivals (Hogbin 1935–36: 3). *Kokwals* also lead all activities that are associated with the building of canoes for overseas trade expeditions (Hogbin 1934–35b: 377). *Kokwals* have the responsibility for the maintenance of law and order within their own group (Hogbin 1935–36: 3). The position of the *kokwal* is associated with a particular insignia, boars' tusks (Hobgin 1934–35a: 318). The privilege of wearing boars' tusks is passed on by a headman to both sons and daughters (Hobgin 1940–41: 25). The wearing of boars' tusks would appear to mark off a category of individuals. There is no indication of what happens to the boars' tusks inherited by younger sons and daughters. However, aside from the headman and his immediate family there does not seem to be a group of individuals set apart as the descendants of former headmen.

The *kokwal* is in control of ritual and magic. There are two spirit monsters: the *lewa* personified by masks which are associated with intradistrict food distributions, *walage,* and the *nibek* personified by flutes which are associated with interdistrict and more elaborate food distribution, *warabwa.* Hogbin notes, "A headman, on reaching a decision about the organization of a food distribution, performs the ceremony to conjure up the monsters appropriate to the importance of the distribution" (Hogbin 1970a: 58). Every *kokwal* owns a pair of male-*lewa* names, one for each of his two masks, and several pairs of flutes, each with a particular name. Further, "He has the right to order flutes or masks for family celebrations, such as those at the first menstruation of one of his daughters" (Hogbin 1970a: 59). Before the house of each *kokwal* there is a columnar block of basalt surrounded by flat stones. Each of these is associated with a particular culture hero with whom the *kokwal* has a special relationship. This relationship gives the *kokwal* the right to his building site (Hogbin 1970a: 14–15). The myths about the culture heroes concern the origins of Wogeo institutions, and include magical spells. The myths are known to all, but the details of the magic are the sole property of headmen, who perform the rites for the benefit of others. Examples of this are the beauty magic performed for the members of an overseas trading expedition, and weather magic. In addition to the magic used for the benefit of the group and carried out by the *kokwal*, there is another body of magical lore distinct from this which is concerned with the affairs of individuals such as increasing the fertility of a garden and promoting health. This category of magic also derives from the culture heroes but is available to any individual. The presence of illness and disease is usually attributed to sorcery, or *yabou*. The vast majority of sorcerers are headmen and all headmen are said to be sorcerers. One's own leader is not considered to be a sorcerer but rather a person who, because of his knowledge and power, can protect the group against sorcery (Hogbin 1970a: 153; 1970b: 326). The inquest to ascertain whether a death is the result of sorcery and to decide if a death is to be avenged is always conducted by a *kokwal* (Hogbin 1970a: 154).

There is a formal mode of succession to the office of headman or *kokwal*. The rule is: "Headmen . . . have the right to choose who shall follow them, though a number of conditions have to be satisfied before a man is eligible for appointment. He must possess certain qualifications of character and be the offspring of a headman and his mother's firstborn son; moreover, it is essential that at the time he takes up the duties of leader he shall be old enough to command respect and obedience. . . . As one would expect, the headman always prefers to be succeeded by a son, but most important men are polygamous, and there are thus two or three sons from whom to choose. Only when these are all too young does the title pass out of the family to a half brother or nephew" (Hogbin 1940:24). A *kokwal* will often have a favorite son from among the several first-born sons of his wives. The nature of his favorite emerges in a variety of ways as illustrated in "The Father Chooses His Heir." However, the formal act of nomination, which takes place during the lifetime of the present holder, is publically proclaimed before a multitude of assembled guests at a large interdistrict food distribution, the *warabwa*. The chosen heir then receives instruction in the corpus of magic systems particular to the office which are known to his father (Hogbin 1970b: 190). Therefore, there is a fixed rule of succession, but it is not one of primogeniture. Succession is not the result or the outcome of the competition between claimants. However, disputes are common within the patrilineage concerning succession. An eldest son who does not appear to be the one to be selected may have acrimonious relations with his father. Ill feeling between brothers is common.

Both patrilineage and matrilineal moieties are exogamous. In addition, there is a prohibition against marriage with any first cross-cousin. In the folk conceptualization any woman a man eats with is considered to be a sister and therefore not suitable as either a sexual partner or a mate. First cousins are viewed in this way. There is a marriage preference in which the ideal marriage is between the children of cross-cousins. In particular, an eldest son should marry his father's father's eldest sister's eldest son's eldest daughter (Hogbin 1970a: 26). Recalling our discussion of land inheritance, this marriage is a means by which dowry land is returned to its original owners two generations later. Five out of thirty marriages recorded at random by Hogbin were between the children of cross-cousins (Hogbin 1939–40: 139). Occasionally sister exchange occurs if the women have no objection (Hogbin 1934–35a: 323). A man may also marry his daughter into the village of her mother and this is seen as a fitting return for his own wife (Hogbin 1940–41: 20). The two patrilineages that make up a village work their lands separately. People of these patrilineages do not view one another as siblings. Consequently, marriages can and do occur between them. Marriages between the children of the *kokwals* are favored. Marriages also occur, as noted above, between enemy districts. The headman of Dap and the headman of Falala village, who compete in intervillage exchanges, are also affines. Intermarriage also occurs with women from other islands with whom the men from Wogeo trade (Hogbin 1934–35b: 397).

The presence of a preference for marriage with second cross-cousin taken together with localized patrilineages and nonlocal matrilineal moieties, both exogamous, suggest the possibility that Wogeo can be seen as an eight-class section system like that of the Aranda. We have considered this possibility. However, there are no named or identifiable marriage classes, or categories. If one systematically plots the Wogeo preference for marriage with father's father's sister's son's daughter, eight classes of intermarrying people emerge.

Polygyny is quite common. Hogbin presents a figure of thirteen out of thirty-six marriages as polygynous. Most of the men in the polygynous marriages are important men. The reasons given for such marriages are the desire for many offspring and the desire for labor for agricultural purposes provided by an additional wife. Divorce is not frequent and never occurs after the birth of a child, since the father has absolute control over the children. If a divorce occurs he keeps the children; hence wives never leave their husbands after a child is born.

Wogeo kinship terminology has Iroquois cousin terms. In the first ascending generation there are three terms. Mother, mother's sister, father's sister, and mother's brother's wife are all called *tina*. Father, father's brother, mother's sister's husband, and father's sister's husband are all called *tama*. Mother's brother has a distinct set of terms, *kalawa* and *nigwa* (Hogbin gives no explanation for two terms). The same terms are also applied to sister's child. The most interesting feature is in the affinal terminology. A male speaking ego calls his wife's sister and his brother's wife *tina*. A female speaking ego calls her husband's brother and sister's husband *natu*, the same term used for her own children. *Natu* is used for own children, children of same-sex siblings, and children of same-sex parallel cousins and cross-cousins.

We turn now to an analysis of the various categories of exchange. Exchanges between kin occur at marriages. The eldest child of an important man will usually be betrothed a

year or two before the suitable age for marriage. A betrothed
girl is always furnished with dowry land, as has been discussed before. A headman may furnish his daughter with
sacred flutes he has carved as part of her dowry to be held in
trust for her eldest son. The ceremonies after the first
menstruation of a girl are more elaborate if she has been
previously betrothed. Hogbin notes, "The relatives of the
future bridegroom considering that their honor is involved,
make lavish contributions towards the accompanying feast"
(Hogbin 1944–45: 330). After this ceremony she goes to live
with her bridegroom in a trial marriage situation. Either
partner can refuse to accept the match. After a few months, if
the couple agree to remain together, the girl's father gives
several pigs to the boy's family. This is known as "the ladder," which ratifies her right to "go up into their house"
(Hogbin 1944–45: 332–33). This presentation constitutes the
wedding. The bride's parents and their kin are given a quantity of dried fish in return.

When dowry land is given and is exploited by the husband, though title to it continues to reside in the wife, the
husband makes presentations of some of the produce from
the land to the wife's father or eldest brother. In general, one
has the obligation to help one's brother-in-law even to the
point of taking part in the expedition for revenge if he is
murdered, as one would for a brother (Hogbin 1970a: 22).

After a child is born, there is a naming ceremony. Senior
maternal and paternal relatives each choose one name for a
child, but the name chosen by the paternal relative is much
more significant. A ceremony takes place at which the senior
paternal relative repeats the names of his forebears until he
reaches the one selected for the child. In the case of the first
born son or daughter of a headman, there is then a distribution of food. Hogbin does not indicate the relationship of
donors to recipients but merely notes that relatives assemble
(Hogbin 1970a: 139; 1942–43: 293).

The girl's first menstruation rite, the only important initiation ceremony for a woman, also involves kin primarily.
There is a series of ceremonies which involves only the
women of the village. Invitations come from paternal and
maternal aunts and for the daughter of a *kokwal* from other

villages as well. Male relatives play a relatively minor role, weaving the rattan bands on the girl which are her decoration. For the daughter of a *kokwal*, the flutes may be called out to play in her honor. The daughter of a *kokwal* is decorated with boars' tusks. The celebration is broken up by the men, and the women come down and prepare the final feast. There are no other specifically kin exchanges and, as can be seen, mother's brother does not play a distinctive role in any of these ceremonies. From that time on, a menstruating woman remains in seclusion.

At the various initiation rites for boys, it is the matrilineal moiety structure that is significant. Ear piercing, the first rite for a boy, takes place sometime after weaning. A headman organizes an ear piercing for his own son. Sons from other households in the village as well as sons brought by their fathers from other villages may have their ears pierced at the same time as part of a large single ceremony. Each father chooses a man from his own moiety, which is opposite to that of the son whose ears are being pierced, to perform the operation. Each father of an initiate provides at least one pig and the villagers contribute additional food. Headmen of other villages come with their flutes to honor the host, and their women bring food. A ritual fight between men of opposite moieties takes place. Such ritual fights are the only circumstances when the rules against showing any form of verbal or physical aggression to one of the opposite moiety are suspended. The piercing of the ears follows and then comes the feast and distribution of food, most of which is taken home by the guests to be shared with other men in their own village (Hogbin 1970a: 105–7).

In mid-childhood, a boy is ceremonially separated from his mother when he is formally admitted to the men's house. When the son of a headman reaches the appropriate age his father arranges for the ceremony. Other boys from other villages within the district are also included. Pigs are provided by the fathers of the boys, and as a compliment to the headman a pig may be provided by a headman of a village in another district. The father of each boy chooses a sponsor or guardian, who ought to be of the moiety opposite to that of the boy. The boys are brought down to the beach by their

sponsors and told the secret of the flutes, which represent the
nibek spirits. The boys are taken back to the men's house and
then adorned for the remainder of the day. The next day,
there is a ceremonial procession around the village led by the
son of the man who sponsored the rite, his guardian, and his
slightly older brothers and cousins and followed by a boy of
the opposite moiety and his guardian and relatives, with
boys of the opposite moieties alternating in the rest of the
procession. The final ceremony involves a trip to a mountain
brook where the boys arrange themselves in pairs, one from
each moiety, and immerse their faces in water, simultaneously becoming blood brothers from that moment on
(Hogbin 1970a: 106, 113).

Some time later the rite of scarifying the boy's tongue takes
place in order to let out the pollution received from his
mother's milk and from contact with women. In this case the
specialist who performs it and his assistants, who are the
guardians of the boy, can be of either moiety. No feast or
distribution is involved. When the boy is about eighteen, his
father arranges for a person of the moiety opposite to the boy
to instruct him on the incising of his penis. This purificatory
rite is then carried out periodically. It is done on an individual basis. After the first instruction, a man will periodically
incise his own penis to allow the blood to flow profusely.
This is done to allow accumulated "bad blood" to escape.
This procedure is referred to as male menstruation. Hogbin
notes, "females regain their purity by natural menstruation,
and men regain theirs by artificial menstruation." (Hogbin
1970a: 88). Purification through menstruation is necessary as
a result of contamination. Sexual intercourse is considered to
be contaminating to both sexes. The other means by which
individuals can become contaminated is through contact
with the spirit world, which takes place when men are involved in initiation, erecting a new men's house, and burial
of a body, especially when there is contact with the corpse.
After each of these events, a man should incise his penis.
People who are in a contaminated state are considered to be
chilled. Illness, death, and contact with the spirit world are
associated with the cold. "Heat is essential for living, and
without it impotence and loss of vitality are inevitable"

(Hogbin 1970a: 84). An individual who is ritually cold becomes warm again by fasting, bathing, being rubbed with ginger, and finally being fed hot vegetable curry (Hogbin 1934–35a: 331–32; 1970a: 84–85).

The final initiatory rite is the assumption of adult headdress. The arrangements are in the hands of *kokwals,* since pigs are required for the final feast. The senior paternal uncle who is of the opposite moiety to the boy acts as sponsor and weaves the successively larger hair cones that are required while the hair grows. During this time, the boy does little work but is invited to visit relatives in other villages who present him with food. His mother's senior brother may even kill a pig in his honor. When the hair is long enough, it is trimmed by the sponsor and a feast is prepared for the men of the village. This signifies that the boy is ready to marry (Hogbin 1970a: 121–24).

The final rite involving the moiety structure occurs after a death. Male members of the opposite moiety dig the grave beneath the house. When a *kokwal* dies, other *kokwals* of the appropriate moiety come forward to help dig the grave. During the course of burial, Hogbin notes, "One of the close affines or a cross cousin, again belonging to the opposite moiety, drives the spirit out of the land of the living" (Hogbin 1970a: 162). All those who have had contact with the corpse, close kin as well as members of the opposite moiety, become contaminated and are made ritually cold by this contact. After the mourning taboos have been observed for a few days to a month, mourners in the dead man's village decorate those who live elsewhere and the latter return to their homes with food. A headman who has participated in the digging of the grave gets from one to four pigs as payment. Those who have had contact with the corpse must subsequently undergo ritual purification.

Though all of the rites de passage for males and funerals, as discussed above, require the participation of individuals of the two moieties, the members of the moieties do not form groups ceremonially opposed to one another. The moieties are nonlocalized categories of individuals who perform ceremonial services for each other. Since the ceremonial service is provided on an individual basis by the members of the opposite moiety, there are no large-scale distributions from one moiety to the other as an integral part of these rites.

Food has a multiplicity of meanings in Wogeo society. According to Hogbin, "Food is the principle object of wealth. Without ample gardens and pigs a man cannot hope to become distinguished" (Hogbin 1935–36: 17). People derive great pleasure from seeing and handling large quantities of food which are displayed at the big food distributions. As a Wogeo informant stated, " 'We display our food like this to do honour to our *kokwals*. Their reputation is made greater by the amount of food. Visitors come and say, 'The *kokwal* of this place must be a great man to have so much.' When people do not like their *kokwal* they contribute in meager fashion to his distribution.' " (Hogbin 1938–39: 324). The act of eating, and with whom you eat, also have multiple meanings beyond mere ingestion. Hogbin provides a case of brothers who have quarreled and whose reconciliation takes the form of eating a meal together in the center of the village, indicating that they were "brothers once more" (Hogbin 1939–40: 136). We noted in our discussion on marriage that men and women who regularly eat together cannot conceive of having sexual relations or being married to one another. The incest rule is stated in the metaphor of eating together. One must not eat meat from a pig that one has raised and fed. In food distribution great care is taken to see to it that no one gets meat from the pig he has contributed. According to Hogbin, "If he or any member of the family ate it, even unwittingly, they [sic] would inevitably become seriously ill" (Hogbin 1970b: 323).

The basic unit in large-scale food distributions that occur in Wogeo consists of the *kokwal* and his patrilineage. The *kokwal* initiates and organizes the *walage*, which involves villages within a single district, and the *warabwe*, which involves villages of different districts. We shall first describe the *walage*.

Hogbin says the *kokwal* "arranges a *walage* as a good will gesture to reward those who have laboured for him at some family celebration, perhaps the first menstruation of his daughter or the lifting of a food taboo declared when a distant but highly respected relative has died" (Hogbin 1970b: 304).

The *kokwal* who is to hold a *walage* places a taboo on a bush or tree crop by summoning the spirits known as *lewa*. If the crop to be tabooed is coconuts, the village *lewa*, embodied in masks and represented by masked dancers, is called forth at dusk. If the crop is chestnuts, or another bush crop, then bush *lewa*, embodied in bull roarers are summoned. When the village *lewa* is summoned, she arrives by canoe and, inpersonated by a young man in skirts, procedes—obviously pregnant—to the men's house. Steaming bowls of vegetable curry, food given to those in ritual danger, are brought as an offering to the *lewa* and are consumed by the men. There is an interval of time, before the *lewa* delivers her children. During this time their garments are made. "The different parts of the costumes are . . . associated with the club (men's house), and land, rafter, and *lewa* ornaments all go together. The householders who till the soil we may call A not only have to lash rafter A1, but also furnish skirt fringe A2 or possibly a pair of sleeves" (Hogbin 1970a: 62). The mother *lewa* produces male twins, who are represented by the costumed masks owned by the headman. After this the collection of ripe coconuts is banned. Several months later, when a sufficient number of coconuts has been accumulated, the *lewa* are sent back to the spirit world and the *walage* distribution of coconuts is held.

Hogbin gives details of a particular *walage* given by Marigum, the headman of Dap. Marigum, in this case, banned chestnuts, a bush crop, for one month's time by summoning the bush *lewa* personified by the bull roarer. This *walage* marked his youngest son's admission to the men's house, an event described in the section on rites de passage. Invitations were sent to all of the *kokwals* in the other villages in Wonevaro district. Boys from these four villages (Job, Mwarok, Kinaba and Baria) had participated in the initiation along with Marigum's son. Several days before the *walage* the taboo was lifted and the crop picked. On the day the *walage* was to take place, each household in Dap village brought its contribution to the cleared area before

Marigum's house. The chestnuts were then put into three
large baskets with piles of fifty coconuts next to each basket.
The guests from three villages arrived in the early evening
bringing with them baskets of chestnuts and coconuts. One
village, Baria, did not send people because of an internal
quarrel. The contributions from the guests were kept separate and then redistributed, making sure that they did not go
back to the original giver. Chestnuts and coconuts were carried the next day to Baria, whose headman three days later
sent a return basket and coconuts to Marigum. Though the
walage distribution is not overtly competitive in comparison
with the *warabwa*, there is a relationship between what
people give and receive and their prestige. All the villages in
the district must be involved, whether they wish to or not, as
demonstrated by what happened to the village that did not
appear.

The larger and more elaborate interdistrict food distribution is the *warabwa*. According to Hogbin, "The *warabwa*
may be considered as a form of political aggression;
moreover, it usually commemorates an event of significance
to a wider section of the community, such as the headman's
appointing one of his sons as official heir, the construction of
a brand new dwelling for himself or a clubhouse for his fellow villagers, or the settlement of a serious dispute" (Hogbin
1970b: 304). (In what follows, we shall be using Hogbin's
account of the *warabwa* as given in his article, "Food Festivals and Politics in Wogeo" [1970b]. His account of the
warabwa in *The Island of Menstruating Men* [1970a] diverges
from this in that he separates the *warabwa* that involves the
humiliation of a rival from the *warabwa* that is in celebration
of an important event like the building of a men's house; he
calls the former a potlatch festival. Our interpretation follows
the position in Hogbin's article.) As mentioned earlier, individuals have exchange partners or *bag* who are members of
the opposite moiety. The *bag* relationship is inherited from
father to son, with a reversal of moieties in the succeeding
generation. Those exchange partners of *kokwals* who are in
enemy or neutral districts are the principal recipients of a
warabwa. Since a *warabwa* is indispensable after the events
noted above, the potential recipients of a *warabwa* are alerted

when their exchange partners in enemy districts have observed such an event. The *kokwal* planning the *warabwa* has to plant extensive gardens well in advance. The *kokwal* who is holder of a *warabwa* is also assisted by the *kokwal* who is his *bag* in a friendly district. The latter may also plant special gardens, the crop of which is presented as a contribution to his friend's *warabwa* (Hogbin 1938–39: 300).

The next stage is the public notification that a particular *kokwal* has been selected as the recipient of a *warabwa*. This must take place in the house of the giver of the *warabwa*, which therefore necessitates the giver luring to his house in some way the potential recipient who is said to be his traditional enemy. This public notification is called a *warupo*, of which Hogbin gives several examples. Marigum, the headman of the Wonevaro village of Dap, has completed a new house. Marigum persuades his father-in-law to pretend that he is dying in order to induce the *kokwal* from the neutral village of Ga to visit and pay his final respects to his old friend. While passing through Dap on the way back he is invited into Marigum's house and the ritual challenge is thrown down in the form of a coconut. The tricked *kokwal* responds with alarm. According to Hogbin, "but Marigum, calmed him down, or perhaps reminded him of his manners, by pointing out that this was a shot not with a spear but with a nut and soon there would be plenty of pork to eat" (Hogbin 1970b: 310). A week or two after the formal challenge, the *kokwal* who is giving the *warabwa* summons the *nibek* spirits, which are embodied in the sacred flutes, in a ceremony marking the ban on the slaughtering of pigs. The ceremony summoning the *nibek* is performed at dawn, and the *nibek* arrive by canoe from across the sea. The flutes represent the voices of the *nibek* monsters. "They symbolize masculinity and hence play a vital role in a male cult." (Hogbin 1970a: 82). Though they are symbols of masculinity, flutes occur in pairs. The longer of the pair is called male, and the shorter female. A headman owns several pairs, each of which is named (Hogbin 1970a: 73). "Flautists . . . receive regular magical potions from the headman to maintain their strength, but after even a single day's performance they must refrain from contact with the opposite sex and from smoking until the next new moon" (Hogbin 1970a: 75). For the next year or so pigs are fattened and many extra gardens are cleared and planted. During this time the flutes are periodically played. If the *warabwa* is to commemorate the building of a headman's house or a men's house, the actual building may take place during this time.

After the necessary quantity of food has been accumulated, the donors and their wives and all their helpers, including the *kokwals* from other allied villages who as exchange partners or *bag* are contributing, visit the two villages in the district who are to be the recipients of the *warabwa*. They tie coconuts on the houses of those who are to receive pigs. The visitors are feasted and receive presents of utilitarian objects, but not gifts of food. Then the final preparations are made. A large platform in the shape of a dugout canoe with outrigger some fifty feet long is constructed for the display of food. The women from the recipient villages come and dance in the donor village and receive gifts of utilitarian objects. Then the men of the recipient villages come and dance with the men of the donor village. On entering the village they perform purification rites driving away evil spirits with torches and spears. On the final day, all the food is arranged on the platform early in the morning. The pigs are fastened and attached to the outrigger. The *kokwal* performs magic so that the guests will eat little and the joints will go far. The arrival of the visitors on this final day is marked by a brawl. Hogbin states, "The rules of kinship behavior are suspended, and persons who ordinarily are expected to treat one another with formal respect, such as certain affines and members of opposite moieties, are allowed to indulge in the foulest abuse and to exchange blows" (Hogbin 1970b: 318). The brawl is not between guests and recipients but is a free-for-all. Then a period of formal dancing takes place, followed by a magic rite to preserve the peace of the village and give it protection from attack. The final stage is the distribution of all the pigs and food. The scope of what is distributed is indicated in the data provided by Hogbin for one of the two *warabwas* he actually observed. "At the Gol *warabwa*, there were seventeen pigs, five tons of taro, three tons of husked dried almonds, two hundred ropes of bananas (at least two and a half thousand pieces), five thousand green drinking coconuts, and hundreds of bunches of areca nut and betel pepper" (Hogbin 1970b: 317). The distribution itself is completely informal. Hogbin states, "Immediately the recipients come forward and without further ceremony strip the platform. The donors and their families . . . each indicates the pig he has provided and who is to take it. The almonds, coconuts, and other products are divided into equal quantities for each pig. Those who are to bear the burdens, men and women, take up their loads, and within an hour the hosts are alone, often with only the barest scraps to eat" (Hogbin 1970b: 320). The next day there is a ceremony to send the *nibek* back to the spirit world. Hogbin states, "They [the *nibek*] have eaten the pigs from the village and must wait for another invitation" (Hogbin 1970a: 80).

The *kokwal* and the other recipients of the *warabwa* must now make a return exactly equivalent to what they were given. The group that has not made the return must refrain from attacking the donors or their helpers until the return is made. This return can take place immediately if the receiver is a very rich man. The return is made without any ceremonies and does not constitute a *warabwa*. The original donors conceive of the pigs they have given as "alive" until they receive a return, at which point the pig "dies." The one counteroffering described by Hogbin is the one made by Kaman to Marigum fifteen months after the *warabwa*. After Kaman's village have accumulated the necessary supplies, Marigum is notified. The next day he and his followers go to Kaman's village to collect the fifteen pigs and bags of almonds, coconuts, and other foods. There is no ceremony at all and the food offerings are covered and the pigs kept under the house to avoid display. On returning to their village, Marigum's followers complain about what they consider to be the meagerness of the return, which is customary in such a situation. The next day, the pigs are butchered and cooked. Most of the meat is set aside in portions to be given to *kokwals* who are trading partners in villages in the allied district of Bukdi who helped in the *warabwa*. These are large chunks, weighing about ten pounds each. By the third day of distribution, pork begins to return to Marigum's village of Dap in greater quantities than it is being sent out. As much as eighty to one-hundred pounds of meat reaches Kaman's village of Falala, which presented the counteroffering. Great care is taken to see to it that the people who gave particular pigs do not receive from their own pig, since it would cause illness. Kaman receives no portions and after all the distributions Marigum has only a tiny portion left for himself, according to Hogbin, "Thereby confirming that leaders prefer to think of their followers, and hence to confine their feasting to sucking the bones" (Hogbin 1970b: 324).

The final exchange relationship we will discuss involves the exchange that takes place between Wogeo and villages on the coast of New Guinea and on the other Schouten Islands. This occurs between long-distance exchange partners, who are also called *bag*. A man from Wogeo who goes on an expedition will have a partner in every one of the villages visited. *Kokwals* will have other *kokwals* or their equivalents as their *bag* (Hogbin 1934–35b: 398). Partnerships are usually handed down from father to son but a man may also form a new relationship if he wishes. Building a canoe for overseas voyages requires magical spells and a series of ceremonies. Since the *kokwal* of one of the clans of Dap controls the magic to commence canoe building, such work begins only with his approval. Only two of the five districts of Wogeo build canoes to engage in such overseas exchanges. People in non-canoe-building districts will use a connection through marriage with a trading district to thus participate in the exchanges.

The picture that emerges from an analysis of the exchanges is one in which the *kokwal* and his followers (patrilineage) are the predominant structure. In the two large-scale food exchanges, the *walage* and the *warabwa*, the exchanges take place between sets of *kokwals* and their followers. A *walage*, which involves *kokwals* and their groups within a district, is held after the conclusion of a rite de passage ceremony of some type which the *kokwal* has sponsored for someone in his family. The prestige of the *kokwal* who is sponsoring a *walage* is enhanced by all the events that constitute a *walage*. The invitation to a *walage*, extended by the *kokwal* who is the sponsor, is phrased in terms of "coming to receive nuts."

This is despite the fact that guests themselves bring nuts when they come to the *walage*. The food is not cooked or transformed. The redistribution is immediate—chestnuts for chestnuts and coconuts for coconuts—yet the prestige goes to the sponsor and is reflected upon his followers.

The *warabwa* occurs on the occasion of an event which is of political significance. The formal announcement of the succession of an heir is one such occasion. The widest possible circle of witnesses from other districts, including enemy and friendly districts, is assembled to hear the public declaration of the heir (Hogbin 1970a: 78). The building of a new men's house and the completion of a house for the *kokwal* are also events that signal the *kokwal's* political importance. The settlement of a dispute is obviously a political event. Hogbin sees the *warabwa* as a form of political aggression. The *warupo* or invitation is indeed a challenge, but even here the challenge is not to fight with weapons but with food, which ultimately will be distributed and eaten by large numbers of people. The other events of the *warabwa* do not emphasize competition. The ritual brawl that takes place is not hosts versus guests and is also a concomitant of other kinds of ceremonies. Though the *kokwal* to whom the *warabwa* is directed is a *kokwal* in the opposite moiety and a *bag* or exchange partner in an enemy district, he may also be an affine as well as a cross-cousin, as is the case with Marigum and Kaman. Their relationship, as well as their separation, is symbolized by the *warabwa*. The *warabwa* sets apart *kokwals* in enemy districts who are the recipients of *warabwas* and *kokwals* in friendly districts who, as *bag* or exchange partners, help the sponsor when he gives a *warabwa*. The *warabwa* is one of the several kinds of events involving districts that are enemies to one another. Youths from one district in an expedition may entice women from any enemy district into adulterous liaisons. The men from the enemy district respond in violent anger and this results in fighting, nowadays in a football match and brawl. Friendly relations are restored and a *warabwa* to settle a dispute will be held. Between the *warabwa* and counteroffering the village from the district which is the recipient of the *warabwa*, and in debt, may not attack the village that is the host or its allies in the *warabwa*. After the countergift, another amorous expedition may be launched, starting the cycle again (Hogbin 1938: 228).

It is clear from the discussion above that the patrilineages and their *kokwals* are the interacting groups in these smaller and larger-scale food distributions. The importance of the patrilineage as a unit in these exchanges is a reflection of the solidarity of the lineage as a residential group and a land-holding unit. The two *kokwals* who are guest and host at a *warabwa* must be in opposite moieties since they are exchange partners to one another. However, the followers of each *kokwal* are members of both moieties so that opposition of *kokwals* and their patrilineages is not paralleled by opposition of moieties. The matrilineal moieties are categories, not groups, and have no residential unity. A father and son, though members of the same patrilineage, must be members of opposite moieties. However, a grandfather and his grandson are in the same moiety. The matrimoiety division thus serves to divide every patrilineage into two parts composed of individuals of alternate generations, such that generations 1, 3, and 5 are members of one moiety and generations 2, 4, and 6 are members of the opposite moiety within a patrilineage. There are two kinds of relationship which a man can have with someone from the opposite moiety. The first is the blood-brother relationship. This has its origin in the initiation ceremony in which two boys from opposite moieties are ceremonially immersed in water at the same time. Since initiation involves boys from villages within the district, the blood-brotherhood relationship is between men of the same district. The second type of cross-moiety relationship is the exchange partnership or *bag*. This is between men of opposite moieties in different districts. Exchange partnerships are inherited from father to son, so that in the succeeding generation the moieties of the individuals are reversed. The moiety categories are the organizing basis for activities at the major rites de passage including death. Even in those activities that stress one patrilineage as opposed to other patrilineages, such as the *warabwa*, the categorization of matrimoieties comes into play since a *kokwal* directs the *warabwa* to his *bag* in the opposite moiety. The ritual brawl at a *warabwa* opposes people in opposite moieties who otherwise must never show violence toward one another. In Wogeo, in contrast to other New Guinea societies, the mother's brother does not play a prominent role. Rather it is the people of the opposite matrimoieties who perform the equivalent services. Since mother's brother is of ego's moiety he cannot fulfill those functions. Another interesting contrast is that in other New Guinea societies, mother's brother and mother's father are always receivers of goods, especially rings, beginning with the marriage of mother and father, whereas in Wogeo, at marriage the bride's father is giver of pigs and sometimes land and does not receive. Further, at rites de passage ego's mother's brother is usually a giver, not a receiver. In general, if wife givers are involved in exchanges it is as givers rather than receivers.

The question must be posed: what are the structural implications of the combining of patrilineages and crosscutting matrimoieties? Though functionally similar to the moieties of Banaro and Iatmul in that they carry out initiation, the matrimoieties of Wogeo are structurally very different. The combination of matrimoieties and patrilineages, both of which are exogamous, has the effect of dividing every patrilineage into two alternate generation groups, which may be likened to the Iatmul *mbapma*. However, Wogeo and Iatmul have different marriage patterns. Iatmul has a pattern of father's mother's brother's son's daughter marriage whereas Wogeo instead has a preferred marriage with father's father's sister's son's daughter. The structure created by such a marriage pattern with patrilineages and matrimoieties requires eight groups to operate. The information on Wogeo is insufficient and does not permit us to conclude as to the presence or absence there of such an overall structure. The combination of marriage with father's father's sister's son's daughter and sister exchange is found among the Manga and Maring of the New Guinea Highlands, who will be discussed in the next chapter.

Wogeo is also like Highland societies in that exchange partners or *bag* are also affines. This is in contrast to Arapesh, Abelam, Iatmul, and Banaro, where affines and exchange partners are separate, creating two structures of exchange.

The two structures of exchange, which in Abelam and Arapesh are associated with different aspects of fertility and reproduction, are not apparent in Wogeo. However, Wogeo does share with Arapesh and Abelam the separation of male and female. Hogbin points out that "each sex is perfectly alright in its own way, but contact is fraught with danger for both" (Hogbin 1934–35a: 330). The male and female spheres of activity are culturally separate. "The people sum up the situation in the saying, 'Men play flutes, women bear infants' " (Hogbin 1970a: 101). In the myth of the origin of the *nibek* flutes women originally owned the flutes, which played by themselves, but they were stolen by a man and from that time on boys had to learn the difficult task of blowing them in order to become men (Hogbin 1970a: 100). In actual life, men and women are in continual contact, most dangerously in the sexual intercourse that is necessary for women to bear the children in order to reproduce the society. Both males and females must periodically menstruate in order to cleanse themselves of the contaminated blood. As noted above, contamination can also come about as a result of contact with the spirit world, and the same kinds of purification procedures are used. In Wogeo as in Abelam and Arapesh, men also periodically incise the penis.

7 Maring and Manga

The two societies discussed in this chapter are considered jointly because they are structurally identical.

The Maring are a population of about seven thousand speaking a common language, Maring, and occupying areas in the middle Simbai and Jimi valleys. The Jimi and Simbai valleys, which are in the Bismark Mountain range, lie immediately to the north of the Sepik-Wahgi divide, which is also north of the more densely populated central Highland area. They are geographically contiguous to and linguistically related to the Middle Wahgi peoples such as the Kuma. The Maring comprise some twenty localized groups. The Tsembaga group in the Simbai Valley studied by Rappaport and the Fungai group in the Simbai studied by Vayda and Lowman-Vayda are two such groups. Although Rappaport writes only about the Tsembaga, Lowman-Vayda treats the Maring-speaking population by and large as a single entity, and so shall we in this chapter.

There are several levels of social grouping among the Maring. Since postmarital residence is virilocal, patrilineally related males tend to remain together. Men and women live apart, the men in men's houses, which range in size from two to fourteen males (Rappaport 1968: 13), and each married woman with her unmarried daughters, small sons, and pigs in a separate house. Women are concerned with planting tubers and greens, and men with bananas, sugar cane, and pitpit (Rappaport 1968: 43). It is not clear to which level in the segmentary structure the men's house corresponds. The men's house unit is the minimal unit and would seem typically to be the subclan unit, but as Lowman-Vayda points out, the minimal unit may be a clan, subclan, or sub-subclan (Lowman-Vayda 1971: 325). "The subclan is the basic ritual and economic unit in Maring society. Subclan members are expected to garden together, to share food, and to make sacrifices to common ancestor spirits in the subclan's sacred grove" (Lowman-Vayda 1971: 322). The subclan is also the unit that negotiates for wives with subclans of other clans.

The next more inclusive level of the segmentary structure is the clan. A clan is usually associated with a particular contiguous territory, which also includes forest land. Among the Tsembaga, analyzed by Rappaport, there are five clans, of which three contain subclans, and the other two clans— smaller in size—are themselves the minimal units. The clan is the unit that putatively claims common patrilineal descent and has a body of ancestor spirits in common. The Fight Ancestor Spirits protect clan territory and the fighters of the clan, and control Fight Magic belonging to the clan. Each clan has its own Fight Magic House and Fight Medicine Man. The Ordinary Ancestor Spirits are responsible for imparting knowledge about those other aspects of Maring life not controlled by Fight Ancestor Spirits, such as "with which clans one should exchange wives, food and trade items" (Lowman-Vayda 1971: 328). Ideally, clans are considered to be the largest exogamous units within which individuals may not intermarry. Rappaport's material on the Tsembaga indicates that three clans, two with very small populations which occupy a single area, do not intermarry and comprise an exogamic unit. The core of the clan is a group of males who claim to be related agnatically, though they need not demonstrate it. Affines and nonagnates may also reside with a clan. Within one or two generations their descendants become regular members of the clan (Lowman-Vayda 1971: 322).

Finally there is the clan cluster, equivalent to the phratry in other Highland societies, which is the most inclusive named level of the segmentary hierarchy. Clans in the same cluster occupy territories that are immediately adjacent to one another. They may or may not be patrilineally related. The several clans that make up a cluster have a higher frequency of marriage with one another than with clans outside the cluster. They also coordinate their warfare activities (Rappaport 1968: 28). They jointly organize ritual activities and sponsor the *kaiko,* the large-scale pig ceremony. A clan cluster would seem to have a single dance ground. When clan clusters are quite large, subclusters with separate dance grounds may exist within such a clan cluster (Lowman-Vayda 1971: 324).

Fusion and fission of segments on the different levels of the hierarchy occur as populations expand and contract. Examples of each type are provided by both Rappaport and Lowman-Vayda (Rappaport 1968: 18, 25, 113, 116; Lowman-Vayda 1971: 324).

Among the Maring, political leadership involves access to ancestor spirits. Two kinds of ancestor spirits exist—Fight Ancestor Spirits, who are the spirits of agnatic relatives slain in battle, and Ordinary Ancestor Spirits, the spirits of all others who have died. Fight Ancestor Spirits, also known as Red Spirits, inhabit the upper part of a territory, are inherent in fire and lightning, thus providing the conceptual basis for fire taboos that prohibit the eating of food cooked over the same fire with food of an enemy. Ordinary Ancestor Spirits inhabit the low ground and are associated with coldness, wetness, and the cycle of fertility, growth and decay. They control certain natural phenomena, such as epidemics and earthquakes (Lowman-Vayda 1971: 327–28). According to Rappaport, other nonhuman spirits called *koipa maŋgiaŋ* also inhabit the low ground in addition to the Ordinary Ancestor Spirits (Rappaport 1968: 38–39).

Men in contact with these two categories of ancestor spirits carry out activities on behalf of their kin group. Rappaport and Lowman-Vayda both present data that, on the one hand, indicate a separation of the man associated with Fight Ancestor Spirits, known as Fight Magic Man, from the man associated with Ordinary Ancestor Spirits, known as Ancestor

Spirit Man (*rauwa yu*); and, on the other hand, indicate that there is usually only one man who performs both roles—referred to as Fight Medicine Man. On this Rappaport notes, "In the morning spells are said by 'fight magic man' (*bampkunda yu*), of whom there are one to three in each clan, and who are usually but not necessarily shamans as well" (Rappaport 1968: 120). Further, Rappaport uses the term shaman (*kun kaze yu*) in connection with activities associated with Fight Ancestor Spirits (Rappaport 1968: 129, 132). Lowman-Vayda indicates, "Ancestor Spirit Men, in the cases known to me, occupy also the position 'Fight Magic Man'. . . . The positions of Fight Magic Man and Ancestor Spirit Man appear to be merged in the position of Fight Medicine Man (*aram ku yu*)" (Lowman-Vayda 1971: 340). The term *aram ku yu* is glossed by Rappaport as the Fight Magic Men who keep the magic stones (Rappaport 1968: 125). Most of the activities of the ritual and political leader—the Fight Medicine Man—are concerned with warfare and sacrifice of pigs to the ancestors. Since decisions made by the Fight Medicine Man have political implications, his ritual knowledge becomes the basis for his political leadership. There is usually one Fight Medicine Man for each clan. He is in charge of the sacred Fight Magic Stones, which are housed in the Fight Magic House. In time of war, he plays the role of military strategist determining through divination which of the enemy should be killed and also whether to resume war (Lowman-Vayda 1971: 341, 344). He remains in the rear of battle, heavily protected by the men close to him, for injury to him fortells the death of a man in his group and the Fight Medicine Man's death means the routing of his group (Rappaport 1968: 138; Lowman-Vayda 1971: 348). The behavior of the Fight Medicine Man is hedged in by many taboos, particularly in time of war (Rappaport 1968: 125). "These taboos may involve proscriptions on sharing the same fire with women, on consuming certain crops and animals and on travel within as well as outside of the territory" (Lowman-Vayda 1971: 347).

The other area in which the Fight Medicine Man, through his contact with the ancestors, makes decisions that affect the entire clan is in regard to the sacrifice of pigs on various ritual occasions. He determines how many pigs will be slaughtered, and which pigs (color, size, and sex) (Lowman-Vayda 1971: 343). On this point Rappaport notes, "As in the case of all important rituals, shamans first sought the ancestors' approval for the matter at hand, and asked them to designate those pigs they wanted to receive, to specify the *raku* or pig-killing places, at which they wanted to receive them, and to appoint the day on which the killing should take place" (Rappaport 1968: 166).

The Fight Medicine Man also has oratorical ability, which he demonstrates at seances when he is in contact with ancestral spirits, and at various stages of the *kaiko* or pig festival. He may use seances to publicly rebuke and to try to control the behavior of fellow-clansmen, through his contact with the ancestral spirits (Lowman-Vayda 1971: 338). He also represents his own clan vis-à-vis other clans.

According to Lowman-Vayda, "Maring speakers apply the term Big Man (*yu ruo-yondoi*) to at least the following types of men: Unvanquished Men, who have been marked for assassination by an enemy, but nonetheless survive; Ancestor Spirit Men, who are able to 'hear the talk' of clan ancestor spirits; and Fight Medicine Men, who are in charge of sacred fight objects and the care of young warriors in times of war" (Lowman-Vayda 1971: 336). As we have noted above, Lowman-Vayda merges Ancestor Spirit Men and Fight Medicine Men into a single category. The Unvanquished Man, merely because he has survived attempted assassination, does not seem to be able to act as a political leader. Having been favored by ancestor spirits who protected his life, he is now in a position to attempt further contact with those spirits and thus to become a Fight Medicine Man (Lowman-Vayda 1971: 340). The Unvanquished Man is a possible step in becoming a political leader as a Fight Medicine Man.

In several respects the Maring Fight Medicine Man or Big Man seems to differ from Big Men in other Highland Societies. There is no indication that the Maring Big Man directly acts as a central node in production or coordinator of a productive unit involving either yam or pig production, though he has a central role in decisions regarding pig slaughter for the whole clan. Big Men are more likely to have several wives and therefore have more material assets because of the productive capacities of their wives (Lowman-Vayda 1971: 348). However, in contrast to other societies, there is no mention of nonagnatic followers being attracted to the Big Man by the promise to them of a wife from among the women he controls, though nonagnates are present in the group. Nor are there accounts of Big Men contributing to the bride price of distant agnates or nonagnates in return for their support. The constituency of the Big Man is the clan, whose ancestor spirits he can contact.

The Big Man, having more wives, has more affines. He therefore maintains a more extensive affinal exchange network than the ordinary man. This affinal network can be the source of useful information about manpower of other groups which can be used by the Fight Medicine Man in military strategy.

Generosity is a value and is strengthened by fear of witchcraft leveled at the miserly man who does not give (Rappaport 1968: 131). However, distribution of material wealth does not make one a Big Man (Lowman-Vayda 1971: 326). Rappaport notes, however, "Big Men tend to be wealthy, tend to be shamans, and tend to be in possession of the rituals concerned with fighting" (Rappaport 1968: 29).

Ideally, the position of Fight Medicine Man should be passed on to a biological son, or a paternal nephew, so that the position will be kept within the subclan. However, there is flexibility in succession. Lowman-Vayda describes a ritual involving several assembled candidates who smoke tobacco. The Unvanquished Man, mentioned earlier, may be one of these candidates. The first to choke on the smoke becomes the successor. This ritual seems to be associated with the transmission of access to Ordinary Ancestor Spirits. A son usually inherits fight magic and the guardianship of fight magic stones from his father. If the ritual knowledge has not been transmitted to a successor, preferably a son, during the lifetime of the Big Man, as he nears death he waits for his son to kill a pig and offer him pork. If the son does not do this because he does not want the position, the knowledge and position are passed on to the closest classificatory son in the subclan who does offer pork and is willing to assume the position.

The introduction of the Kunagage cult, particularly among the Tsembaga, has opened up access to ancestor spirits for more men. There are therefore more men operating in a ritual leadership context among the Tsembaga than in other Maring groups. According to Lowman-Vayda, "This would, for instance, explain the differences in our interpretations [Rappaport and Lowman-Vayda] on the inheritance of political offices, on the number of Big Men in each clan, and on the degree of influence that Big Men exact" (Lowman-Vayda 1971: 354).

As has been mentioned earlier, the clan is ideally the exogamic unit, but Rappaport notes that three of the five Tsembaga clans form a group within which marriages are not allowed. The stated preference is for Tsembaga men to marry Tsembaga women. This occurred in 44 percent of the recorded Tsembaga marriages. Another 22 percent of Tsembaga wives are from the neighboring Tuguma, and the remaining 34 percent come from nine other local groups (Rappaport 1968: 18–19).

Tsembaga marriage prohibitions prevent a man from marrying women from the following groups, in addition to women of his own clan: mother's clan, clans of the mothers of clan brothers, MoSiHu clan, FaSiHu clan, clans of FaSiHus of clan brothers. Also prohibited are sisters of a deceased wife (Rappaport 1969: 125).

Rappaport says that "According to informants, sister exchange is the ideal way to obtain a wife" (Rappaport 1969: 127). When this occurs, the exchange is usually simultaneous; occasionally the return may be delayed for as long as a decade. A man without sons may attract a young man of his subclan by offering that young man a wife obtained in exchange for the older man's daughter (Rappaport 1969: 122).

The Maring are also said to have a prescriptive marriage rule. "This rule states that one of a woman's granddaughters (a son's daughter) should marry into her natal subclan. This is called returning the planting material" (Rappaport 1969: 126; see also 1968: 102). The rule requires a man to marry his FaFaSiSoDa. This is a form of delayed exchange, the return being made two generations later. A return cannot be made in the generation following the first marriage, since marriage with a first cross-cousin is prohibited. The prescriptive rule brings about a renewal of ties between clans in alternative generations, and "Moreover, they do recognize a special relationship between two clans that have renewed their marriage ties, saying that they form a 'pig-woman road' " (Rappaport 1969: 126).

A woman may also be obtained in exchange for valuables, rather than for another woman. A woman may be given as a wife to a man from an ally group as payment to that man for having avenged a homicide. As part of peace-making rituals, the two former enemies exchange women. "These women are explicitly regarded as 'wump' (planting material) through which the slain can be replaced, and the children they bear are named after those whom their brothers, fathers, or grandfathers have killed" (Rappaport 1968: 220).

Rights in women and their disposition in marriage exchanges reside in the minimal agnatic unit, the subclan or clan (Rappaport 1969: 122; Lowman-Vayda 1971: 325).

According to Rappaport, "Kin terms are Iroquois on ego's generational level and bifurcate merging in the first ascending generation, but generational in the first descending and the second ascending generations" (Rappaport 1968: 24).

The structure of exchange for the Maring is one in which groups are linked to one another as affines. The major arena for such affinal exchanges is the *kaiko,* or pig festival. The first of these affinal exchanges is the payment of bride wealth. Substantial payments of valuables including shell ornaments, steel axes, and bush knives (which have replaced ceremonial stone axes) are made by the groom to those having financial interest in the girl. Most men are helped to amass valuables for these payments by members of their subclans. These payments are accompanied by cooked pork. This first payment, also known as "woman wealth," is generally made after the bride and groom have harvested their first garden. This payment may be delayed for years until the next *kaiko* (Rappaport 1969: 130). Subsequent payments are made by the husband after the birth of children and are sometimes referred to as "child price" (Rappaport 1968: 103;

1969: 131). If child price is not paid for a girl, the girl's mother's agnates retain financial interest in her and receive a portion of her bride price when she later marries (Rappaport 1969: 122–23). The wife receiver continues to stand in a generalized debt relation to his affines and some men may make five or more affinal payments (Rappaport 1969: 131). If sister exchange has taken place, identical amounts of valuables are exchanged between both sides. Such exchanges are particularly large and involve the contributions of many men to assist the groom. When the wife dies and is buried on her husband's land, the husband or his son will make a death payment to the wife's natal group which is reciprocated (Rappaport 1969: 131). When a man dies, payment is made to his mother's group (Rappaport 1968: 103, 215). These death payments are usually made at the *kaiko* immediately following the death.

An aspect of the exchange relationship between affines is the granting of rights to land—which we are calling dowry land—by the bride's agnates to her husband. Land is not granted by the groom's family to the family of the bride. The grant of dowry land goes in the direction opposite to that of bride wealth. Such dowry land consists of usufructory rights to a particular garden plot. Rappaport is unclear regarding the duration of these rights, but notes, "Affinal land grants are said to be made in perpetuity, but it is not surprising that they often revert to the donor or his heirs after one generation" (Rappaport 1969: 135; see also 1968: 22). Rappaport further notes that a son may continue to use dowry land received by his father. Dowry land must be considered not by itself but with reference to the whole range of affinal exchanges and to the prescriptive marriage rule. A wife is supplied and she is considered "planting material" (Rappaport 1969: 122). The dowry land that her husband is granted is "planting material" of a different sort. According to the marriage rule, the granddaughter of this woman is returned two generations later and the Tsembaga call this "returning the planting material." It is probable that the dowry land is also returned along with the girl at this time. Rather than a comingling of groups and land as depicted by Rappaport, the flow of dowry land back and forth would seem to be part of the larger exchange structure of women and goods between linked groups.

Maring local groups like the Tsembaga usually share at least one border with an enemy group (Rappaport 1968: 100). At any point in time, relations with an enemy group will involve open hostility or truce. Other neighboring groups are allies, who assist in the fights against one's enemies. Allies and enemies may both be affines. Periods of open hostility alternate with periods of truce, ending with the *kaiko,* a year-long pig festival at which allies and ancestors are repaid for their assistance in the previous period of warfare. Hostilities are forbidden during the truce and the *kaiko.* After the end of the *kaiko,* at which allies and ancestors are repaid, hostilities may be resumed. Former allies may become enemies, just as enemies may become allies. We will now examine warfare, truce, and *kaiko* rituals in terms of exchanges with allies and with ancestors.

The "nothing" fight is the first stage of more serious warfare. On the night before the fight, the minimal social unit, clan or subclan, seeks the support of both Fight Ancestor Spirits and Ordinary Ancestor Spirits through the shaman (*kun kaze yu*). (Shaman is the term Rappaport uses to refer to Fight Medicine Men [Rappaport 1968: 120].) Pigs are promised to the ancestor spirits in the future if the outcome of the fight is successful (Rappaport 1968: 119).

Before the serious stage of warfare, the "ax fight," fighting stones, which are stone mortars and pestles, are hung in the Fight Magic House (*ringi yin*) of each landholding group or clan. "By hanging up the fighting stones, a group places itself in a position of debt to both allies and ancestors for their assistance in the forthcoming ax fight" (Rappaport 1968: 126). Hanging the fighting stones institutes a series of taboos, such as: the prohibition on the trapping of marsupials, eating eels, or eating marsupials and pandanus fruit together, for all members of the group. Drums may not be beaten. The enemy group is formally designated, and one can no longer eat food cooked on their fires, or raised by them. Two pigs are sacrificed, a male—the "Head Pig"—to the Fight Ancestor Spirits, and a male or female to the ordinary Ancestor Spirits. Before the slaughter of the male pig dedicated to the

Fight Ancestor Spirits, the names of immediate ancestors who have been killed in battle are called out, and their help is solicited in the upcoming fight. The Ordinary Ancestors are also addressed as their pig is killed. The two pigs are cooked in separate ovens. While the pigs are cooking, the Fight Ancestor Spirits inform the shaman which of the enemy are to be killed. When the pigs are removed from their respective ovens, the salted fat belly of the pig offered to the Ordinary Ancestor Spirits is given to the allies who have come to aid in the fight. The salted fat belly of the pig sacrificed to the Fight Ancestor Spirits is consumed by the warriors of the host group, after they have blackened themselves with ritual ash from the fire made inside the Fight Magic House with wood from *kawit,* a species of tree said to house the Red Spirit. The warriors must now assume extensive food taboos on marsupials, snakes, and eels and on greens and other vegetables which may extinguish their 'fire' (Rappaport 1968: 135). They cannot have sexual intercourse, nor eat food cooked by a woman or from the same fire used to cook food for a woman.

When the battle is concluded, each side holds its separate truce ceremony. This ceremony is accompanied by a pig sacrifice at the *raku,* a sacred ancestral burial ground. The Tsembaga have several *raku* in their territory, each associated with a separate subclan. Allies and affines attend their ceremony. All the adult and adolescent pigs of the host group are killed at this time (Rappaport 1967: 24). Some pigs are killed for the Fight Ancestor Spirits, but most are killed for the Ordinary Ancestor Spirits. The belly fat of the Fight Ancestor Spirit pigs is cooked with all varieties of wild animals and greens in a special oven. Both groups of spirits are thanked in addresses for their help in the fighting (Rappaport 1968: 147). Most of the pork dedicated to the Ordinary Ancestor Spirits is presented to allies, and the salted belly fat is presented to them on the following day in a separate ceremony. The warriors now remove the sacred ash that they have worn in battle, ending most of the taboos instituted just before the battle. The *rumbim* plant is planted in the middle of the special oven where food has been prepared and a Fight Magic Man makes a speech to the ancestors thanking them for help in the fight and promising them many more pigs at the future *kaiko*. All male members of the group place a hand on the *rumbim* as it is planted, and this action publicly signifies that a man is to be identified with that group. As long as the *rumbim* remains planted, the group may not fight. However the taboo against sexual intercourse has been lifted with the removal of the sacred ash. The planting and growth of the *rumbim* is connected with fertility, since the Fight Magic Man tells the group that intercourse with their wives will now result in children who will be strong and grow quickly (Rappaport 1968: 148–49).

In contrast to the male symbolism associated with the planting of the *rumbim*, the *amame*, which is planted at this time by the Fight Magic Man around the oven where the *rumbim* stands, is associated with females. "While planting it the taboo man asks that the spirits of the low ground care well for the *amame*, that the pigs grow fat, that the women be fertile, and that gardens flourish" (Rappaport 1968: 149). Both *rumbim* and *amame* are also planted over graves. These two plants represent the symbolic relationship between death and fertility, since the dead are called upon to make the living multiply. This is a time of truce, even though the fighting stones remain hanging (Rappaport 1968: 150).

There is an interval of five to ten years between the planting of the *rumbim* and the *kaiko*. This is to permit the pig herds to grow to sufficient size after the slaughter of all adult pigs at the planting ritual. It will take as little as five years if the group is in a good place, and much longer if it is not. Throughout the period that the *rumbim* is in the ground, the group remains in debt to both allies and ancestors for their past help. Some of the previous taboos, such as taboos against trapping marsupials, the pigs of the Fight Ancestor Spirits, and eels, the pigs of the Ordinary Ancestor Spirits, remain in effect until the debt to the ancestors has been paid at the *kaiko*. Marsupials may be eaten, but not with pandanus, the latter being associated with Ordinary Ancestor Spirits (Rappaport 1968: 151). Similarly, men of the group may not eat pigs given to them when they attend the *kaikos* of other groups, presumably their allies, until their debt to allies and ancestors is repaid at their *kaiko*.

The first stage of the *kaiko* involves planting of stakes at the boundaries of the group's territory. The allied groups are invited to participate in the first stage of this ceremony. Pigs are sacrificed, one for each clan at its own *raku*, and the ancestors are thanked and informed that there are now enough pigs for the *kaiko*. Rappaport states that normally three pigs are sacrificed by the Tsembaga as a whole, corresponding to the three "subterritorial" groups. The bodies of these pigs are cooked and the meat distributed to each local population. The heads, hearts, and lungs are carried to the various *ringi* or ceremonial houses where they are cooked while the stakes are formally planted by the whole Tsembaga group at the boundary of the territory of one of the groups after the whole territory is rid of the spirits of slain enemies. On the way, they sing fight songs. If the enemy was routed during the warfare and they have not returned to plant their *rumbim*, enemy territory is annexed by the planting of stakes so as to incorporate all or part of this land. Otherwise the stakes are planted at old boundaries. They return to open the ovens at the *ringi* house at which time the taboo on trapping marsupials is abrogated. At about the time of the stake planting, special gardens are cleared and planted by the Tsembaga as a whole for the purpose of feeding the visitors at the forthcoming *kaiko*.

At this time, all of the Tsembaga move to houses or build new houses around a single traditional dance ground, forming a nucleated settlement or ceremonial village. Two large houses to accommodate visitors are built at the edge of the dance ground. After the fencing in of the dance ground, a ceremony is performed to induce the ancestors to see to it that the men's dancing will be strong and keep unmarried local girls from succumbing to the attractions of visiting men and eloping with them.

Two months after stake planting, *marita pandanus* (yambi-yellow-fruited variety), associated with the low ground and Ordinary Ancestor Spirits, is eaten once and then tabooed. It is now time to trap marsupials—*ma*—the "pigs" of the Fight Ancestor Spirits. Subclans trap marsupials on their own "high" territories. The trappers are subject to the same taboos as in warfare, including taboos against sexual intercourse, eating food prepared by women, or entering—or eating food grown in—the lower region of the territory. The older men smoke the marsupials in the smoke houses belonging to the clans.

After a month of trapping marsupials, the people are now ready to uproot the *rumbim*. On the day preceding the uprooting, pigs are sacrificed separately at the *raku* to both groups of spirits. Cassowaries are also sacrificed to the Fight Ancestor Spirits at this time (Rappaport 1968: 176). The Fight Ancestor Spirits are told that they will be given pigs in exchange for marsupials and for help in warfare (Rappaport 1968: 176). In the 1962 *kaiko*, thirty pigs were slaughtered. The smaller animals were killed for the Fight Ancestor Spirits, cooked in ovens above the ground, and consumed by members of the host group. The pork from the bodies of the other pigs killed for the Ordinary Ancestors and cooked in separate below-ground ovens was distributed to allies. "For the most part, this flesh was given unceremoniously by each man to those men among the allies, usually his own affines or non-agnatic cognates, who assisted in the fight because of their ties to him" (Rappaport 1968: 180). A number of taboos are nullified, including the taboo against eating *marita pandanus*, while marsupials are trapped. The *marita pandanus* (red variety) is harvested with care from groves planted by now-deceased ancestors, and carried in a ritual procession to the *raku*. There, after chanting and sobbing, the *pandanus* fruit is stabbed with a cassowary bone dagger. "Among some Maring local populations cassowaries are also commonly sacrificed to the red spirits" (Rappaport 1968: 176). Legs and buttocks of the entire group are rubbed with pandanus oil to give them strength, and bellies of females are rubbed to make them fertile. The last ritual act involves eating *marita pandanus* and marsupials, which are cooked together. Rappaport interprets the eating as a means of integrating those things that have been previously segregated, including the two types of spirits, the living and the dead, and warfare and peaceful activities. In terms of the entire ritual cycle, we see the eating as a transformation. During the period of hostilities, the warriors were imbued with the spirits of the Fight Ancestors. Their influence has gradually been diminishing as taboos, such as that against sexual intercourse, have consecutively been removed. The act of eating the pandanus represents the taking into oneself of the spirits of the Ordinary Ancestors, and the expulsion of the Fight Ancestor Spirits (Rappaport 1968: 179–80). This act marks the point in the transition to peaceful activities, to courtship, sex, marriage, children, and relations with affines as marriage partners rather than allies. These activities are associated with cold, the low ground, spirits of Ordinary Ancestors, fertility, growth, and decay.

The *rumbim* is then uprooted and carried in a procession to the boundary, where it is disposed of and stakes planted. The procession returns to the dance ground, where drumming and singing continue all night. The *kaiko*, meaning dance, has now begun. The first stage of the *kaiko* is called the *wobar*, referring to songs sung at this time which are also sung for a "nothing" fight. This stage lasts for six months as the yams ripen in the garden and the dance ground is prepared. The second stage, *de*, refers to songs sung on the way to the ax fight. "The two stages of the *kaiko*, informants say, recapitulate the two stages of warfare" (Rappaport 1968: 182). At inauguration of the *de*, five pigs are killed, and the meat is consumed by the Tsembaga themselves. A ceremony cleansing the dance ground of enemy spirits takes place at this time. The fighting stones are lowered from the center post of the Fight Magic House. Contact with the enemy is still forbidden. It is now possible to trap eels.

Neighboring groups are invited by the Tsembaga to come to dance. Individual Tsembaga men extend invitations to their affines, kinsmen, or trading partners in other local populations (clan clusters), but these are, in effect, invitations to the entire group. The inviters are responsible for accumulating food for their guests, but others of their group usually help. The visitors, decorated with elaborate feathers, come charging onto the dance ground, singing war songs. After the dancing, vegetable foods are piled up on the dance ground. One of the hosts, in a formal speech, "recounts the relations of the two groups; their mutual assistance in fighting, their exchange of women and wealth, their hospitality to each other in times of defeat" (Rappaport 1968: 188). Each pile of food is presented to a guest who has been formally invited. He in turn redistributes it to the men and women who have come with him. Dancing continues through the night. The following morning, two types of trading activities take place. On the dance ground, trade in plumes, shells, marsupial furs, axes, and salt, is carried out impersonally via immediate exchange, which is completed on the spot. In the men's house, trading partners and kinsmen give members of the local group the same kinds of valuables—plumes, axes, and shells—but return is delayed until a future *kaiko* or visit when the Tsembaga will go as guests (Rappaport 1968: 189–90). At the 1962 *kaiko*, thirteen different visiting groups came to dance at the Tsembaga dance ground.

The climax of the *kaiko* is the large-scale slaughter of pigs, the *konj kaiko*, which takes place approximately one year after the *rumbim* has been uprooted. This begins with the trapping of eels, the "pigs" of the Ordinary Ancestor Spirits. Subclans trap eels in their own territories. At this time, men must avoid the high ground. The ceremonial fence is built on a slope above one end of the dance ground. It has a window through which the distributions of pork will be made. Separate *raku* will be used as pig slaughtering grounds for each of the two kins of spirits, individual subclans using their own *rakus*. At the *rakus* for Ordinary Ancestor Spirits *timbi* houses are erected. A brief ritual accompanies the raising of the center pole. The pole is set on a sleeping mat upon which valuables are placed. It is scraped of moss, which falls on the valuables, and an eel is etched along its length. A song is sung to entice trading partners to bring valuables (Rappaport 1968: 200). Direct ancestors are addressed by name, thanked for the eels, offered valuables, and requested to look after the women and children of the group. The spirits of the ancestors who have died in battle are also addressed, so that they will not become jealous. The foci of this ceremony, however, are the Ordinary Ancestor Spirits.

At the 1962 *kaiko*, five young Tsembaga men went through a ritual dedication to the Fight Ancestor Spirits. This form of initiation did not involve any ordeals, but various food taboos and taboos on sexual intercourse and visiting the high ground were placed upon them. They were secluded in the men's house, and their hair was woven into an elaborate headdress. It is not clear whether all young men go through this ritual, but all young men destined to become Fight Magic Men must go through it (Rappaport 1968: 204).

On the day before the big pig slaughter, "taboo pigs" (in 1962, they numbered fourteen) are killed, and cooked in above-ground ovens. The taboos to be abrogated by this sacrifice are associated in general with the Fight Ancestor Spirits, although both categories of ancestor spirits are addressed before the killing. These taboos had been instituted in connection with mourning, relations with enemies after warfare, and antagonisms arising within the group (Rappaport 1968: 206–7). Those of the local group who are participating in this ritual and whose taboos are now terminated eat the pigs that have been sacrificed.

The large-scale pig sacrifice takes place on the following day, most of the pigs being sacrificed to the Ordinary Ancestor Spirits. For the *kaiko* that Rappaport observed, a total of eighty-two pigs were killed at a number of *raku*, sixty-eight for the Ordinary Ancestor Spirits and fourteen for the Fight Ancestor Spirits, one for each man killed in the last fight. The eels that have been trapped earlier and represent the "pigs" of the Ordinary Ancestor Spirits, are ceremonially brought to the *raku*. They are used to flail the one or two special pigs dedicated to particular immediate ancestors among the Ordinary Ancestor Spirits. "The eels were then hung, along with shell valuables and beads, on the center post of the *timbi* houses so that wealth might increase" (Rappaport 1968: 212). The eels and pigs are cooked together in the *timbi* house, and eaten on the following day after the concerned ancestors are requested to insure the fertility of people, pigs, and crops. This ends the taboo on eating eels.

The meat from pigs dedicated to the Fight Ancestor Spirits is kept for consumption by the Tsembaga themselves, along with the entrails, heads, and sometimes other parts of other pigs dedicated to the Ordinary Ancestor Spirits. The remainder of the pork is distributed to visitors from other groups. In the 1963 *kaiko*, members of seventeen different visiting groups received pork in 163 separate presentations, ranging from several pounds of flesh or fat to entire animals.

It would appear that the 163 presentations were made to affines, allies, and trading partners of the Tsembaga men, and "the Tuguma, Aundagai, Kauwasi and Manambaut received much the greatest part of this pork" (Rappaport 1968: 214). The primary recipients then "redistributed their portions to members of their own and other groups" (Rappaport 1968: 214). Those visiting affines who received entire pigs butchered and cooked these pigs themselves at the *raku* after the ceremony, but affines who were allies in the last fight returned the pig bellies to their hosts. No ceremonies accompany this, but the recipients make a return gift of an ax, a bush knife, or a shell before butchering their pigs (Rappaport 1968: 211). All others receive their meat cooked, on the following day.

Nineteen prestations of valuables to affines were also made as part of the final stage of this *kaiko*. These included bride wealth, child payments, and death payments (Rappaport 1968: 215; 1969: 132).

The culmination of the *kaiko* on the next day, witnessed by the greatest number of people from all groups friendly to the Tsembaga, is the presentation of packages of salted pork belly to those key men of other groups through whom allies had been mobilized. These amounted to twenty-five or thirty men at the 1963 *kaiko*, and included all men of other groups who had been wounded in the earlier fighting and sons of those slain. This presentation is made through the window of the ceremonial fence, after the recipient-to-be has charged up to the fence, swinging his ax, followed by his supporters shouting battle cries. His mouth is stuffed with fat, and the remainder of what he receives is redistributed by him to his followers (Rappaport 1968: 217). As the visitors dance, the Tsembaga knock down the fence and join the dancing. The *rumbim* planted when the dance ground was built is uprooted and thrown in the direction of the enemy. The *kaiko* is now over. Warfare can now begin again, and usually did in former times.

The structure of exchange for the *kaiko* emphasizes a number of distinctions. In the nature of the giving, ancestors are distinct from the living, Ordinary Ancestor Spirits from Fight Ancestor Spirits, agnates from affines, and within the affinal category allies from nonallies. The Tsembaga exchange with all of these categories, but not with enemies. Their only contact with enemies involves fighting—all other contact is taboo. They may not eat food prepared over the same fire as that of an enemy—nor can they eat with someone who has eaten with an enemy.

The Tsembaga exchange pigs with their ancestors. They give their ancestors live pigs and get the "pigs" of their ancestors—eels and marsupials—in exchange. The latter are preserved—live in the case of eels and smoked in the case of marsupials—until the taboos surrounding them have been lifted. Live pigs are given by the Tsembaga to the Fight Ancestor Spirits at the Stake Planting Ceremony to enable them to trap marsupials, and at the ceremony connected with *rumbim* uprooting to enable them to eat the preserved marsupial meat, which has been smoked. This constitutes an exchange. The trapping of eels commences after pigs are given to the Ordinary Ancestor Spirits in connection with the lowering of the fight stones and at the eel flaying ceremony, where pigs are dedicated to Ordinary Ancestor Spirits, after which the eels can be eaten.

Though eels and marsupials are both preserved before they are consumed, the methods of preservation are contrastive. The smoking of marsupials is through fire and smoke, elements that embody the Fight Ancestor Spirits, and preservation is through heat and dryness, which also characterize the Fight Ancestor Spirits. Eels are kept alive in water, and wetness and coldness are associated with Ordinary Ancestor Spirits. The process of smoking, which could just as well be applied to eels and pork, is applied only to marsupials because it is an element in a contrastive set that is in turn part of a larger structure.

Live pigs are presented to both categories of ancestors, while pork or dead pigs are given to affines who never receive live pigs (Rappaport 1968: 103; 1969: 132). Thus deceased ancestors must be given live pigs, and live affines and allies must be given dead pigs. Pigs given to affines are cooked at the *raku*, though the cooking may be done by the affines themselves. Pigs dedicated to Fight Ancestor Spirits are always eaten by agnatic members of the group, while pigs dedicated to the Oridinary Ancestor Spirits are eaten by affines and allies. Salted pig belly from pigs dedicated to the Ordinary Ancestor Spirits is eaten only by allies, a subcategory of affines, at the *kaiko* ceremonies, thereby setting them apart as a category. Pigs are given spiritually to ancestors and actually to allies and affines. Pigs to the Fight Ancestor Spirits are exchanged for help in warfare as well as for their "pigs," the marsupials. The pigs in actuality are eaten by the agnatic group itself—not by affines. Pigs to the Ordinary Ancestor Spirits are exchanged for growth, strength, and fertility of the group and for their "pigs," the eels. These pigs in actuality always go to affines who have ensured the fertility and procreation of the group by the giving of their women.

Allies are recruited from affines. But allies and affines can become enemies and vice versa. The Kundagai, who were enemies of the Tsembaga in 1963, having routed them in the fifties, had formerly been their affines (Rappaport 1969: 130). Conversely, after a long period of enmity, a truce may become permanent and hostile relations may be ended by the exchange of women as wives. Ideally, each of the men slain in battle should be replaced by a woman given by the former enemy, and the Tsembaga, in 1963, were planning such an exchange of women with their former bitter enemy, the Kundagai (Rappaport 1969: 128).

The Manga speak Narak, a language closely related to Maring. The Narak-speaking peoples occupy the valleys of the Tasau and Jimi rivers and the area in between. They are immediately north of the Waghi-Sepik divide, which separates them from Middle Waghi peoples like the Kuma. In the Jimi Valley, the Narak people have a common border with Maring peoples with whom they interact.

Though the Manga and Maring differ linguistically, they are neighboring peoples with an underlying structure in common. The segmentary structure in the two societies is very similar. In both, the subclan is the unit that gardens together, makes affinal payments as a unit, and maintains its own cemetery for its ancestors. The subclan may contain more than one men's house, each with its own Big Man.

Subclans combine into clans, which are territorially defined
and which are the exogamic units. Clans make up a phratry
or clan cluster, which operates as a unit in war and in the pig
festival. These are the largest entities that operate as units
vis-à-vis other like units with whom they fight or whom they
invite as guests to their pig festival. These are the units of
study for the ethnographers—the Manga and Tsembaga are
respectively a phratry and a clan cluster—but these units
must be seen as part of a larger structure of relationship. The
Manga and Maring have been seen as separate systems by
the ethnographers because of the linguistic differentiation;
however, phratries from both linguistic groups form part of
the same larger structure. For instance, the Manga, a Narak-
speaking phratry, intermarry frequently with the Yuomban,
a Maring-speaking phratry, with whom they share a common border. The point of difference in the segmentary structure of Manga and Maring is the presence in the Manga of
clan moieties between the subclan and clan levels. The clan
moiety represents a division of the clan into two parts that
represent the two parts of the ceremonial village, each with
their own set of sacred stones.

Leadership in the two societies is divided into two components, one of which is concerned with warfare and magic
associated with warfare. These may be combined in a single
individual or held by two men. These leadership positions
are on the clan level in the Maring and on the clan-moiety
level among the Manga. Leaders at this level cooperate to
make decisions affecting the highest-level groupings, since
there is no single leader to represent these levels of segmentation.

The structure of marriage is identical for the two societies.
Both have sister exchange as an ideal, as well as a prescriptive marriage rule for marriage with FaFaSiSoDa. This prescriptive marriage rule, in both cases, is seen as a way in
which a man returns his daughter as payment for his mother.
In the Maring case, the mother has come with dowry land,
which is returned to her patrilineage with her granddaughter. No transfer of dowry land among the Manga is
mentioned, and a man may make a payment for his mother
in lieu of his daughter. Sister exchange and FaFaSiSoDa mar-

riage are complementary marriage patterns. The clan as the unit of exogamy is related to other clans by these patterns of exchange of women. These links in both groups are referred to as "roads." Marriages link clans in the same phratry as well as clans belonging to different phratries.

The overall structure of the pig festival is essentially the same for the two societies, as is the cosmology that underlies it. In both groups, spirits of deceased ancestors are divided into two groups associated with a series of binary oppositions. Fight Ancestor Spirits or Warrior Spirits are the spirits of agnates killed in battle and are associated with the high ground, fire, hot things, dryness, and warfare, while the Ordinary Ancestor Spirits or Lesser Spirits are associated with the low ground, river valleys, coldness, wetness, and vegetable, animal, and human fertility. This set of binary oppositions is the framework for sorting territory, animal types, and natural phenomena. In the pig festival, activities, the location of events, the ways in which objects are used, and the sorting of people is in line with this framework of oppositions. The pig festival occurs after a war and in anticipation of future wars. The pig festival has as its purpose to make a return to allies and ancestors in exchange for their assistance in previous warfare. In addition to warfare, fertility is a concurrent and equally important theme. Success in warfare and fertility are dependent upon both allies, who are at the same time affines, and ancestors—the Fight Ancestor Spirits who help you to be successful and preserve your group when at war and the Ordinary Ancestor Spirits who promote human fertility.

Chart 1 is a schematic representation of the temporal sequence of events of the pig festival in the two societies. It is evident that groups on the different levels of the segmentary structure carry out equivalent activities in the two societies. The Manga have clan moieties as an intermediate level between subclan and clan and most of the activities performed at the clan-moiety level among the Manga are the activities carried out by the Maring clan.

A comparison of the ceremonies in the two groups reveals the following. The Maring ceremonies highlight the contrastive position of marsupials and eels who are, respectively, pigs of the Fight Ancestor Spirits and pigs of the Ordinary Ancestor Spirits. Among the Manga, eels are important, though they are not referred to as the pigs of the ancestors, nor is there indication that they are tabooed for trapping or eating at any point during the ceremonial cycle. However, the eels are killed and cooked at the same time in the cycle in both societies. Marsupials are not mentioned as having any role to play during the Manga pig festival. At the equivalent point in the ceremony where the Maring cook smoked marsupial with pandanus and eat them together, the Manga substitute pork. In both societies, at this ceremony, the pandanus is treated with reverence, is picked from a tree associated with a deceased ancestor and, in the Manga case, the pandanus fruit is said to represent that ancestor. In both societies, cassowaries are associated with war and in both are sacrificed during the pig festival as an offering to the spirits of war.

Table 1	Comparison of Maring and Manga Pig Festivals (material in parentheses refers to the Manga [from Cook 1967])	
	Maring	Manga
War Ritual	Hang Fight (War) Stones; done by clan (clan moiety); intersex taboos; pig sacrificed to both types of ancestor spirits (warrior spirits).	
Truce	Subclans sacrifice pigs to both groups of ancestors. Plant *rumbim,* by clan. Fight Stones still up, no drumming.	Manga truce rituals are not an integral part of the pig festival.
Pig Festival	5-10 years later. Clan cluster plants stakes at boundary. Makes gardens for guests.	1 year plus to pig killing. Clan moiety plants *om.* Plants garden for guests. Play flutes, no drumming. Sing war songs, Fight Stones still up.

Lift taboo against   . . .
hunting marsupials.
Smoke marsupial meat.

Pandanus and marsupial eaten (pandanus and pork). Subclan sacrifice at cemeteries, pandanus ceremony, move to clan (clan-moiety) ceremonial area and uproot *rumbim* (*om*), dispose of *rumbim* (*om*) at boundary, (clan cluster, phratry) stakes planted; pig festival formally begins.

Fight Stones lowered; pigs killed for Ordinary Ancestor Spirits; trap eels.	Shift from one set of sacred stones to the other; no more war songs, only fertility-ancestor songs; pigs killed for Red Spirit, ancestors asked for fertility.

Bamboo torch ceremony on danceground to dispel spirits of enemies.

Affinally linked clan clusters (phratries) who have been allies come to dance and trade.

Trapping of eels by subclan members.

Wigs constructed for young men dedicated to the ancestors.

	Killing of pigs to cover the "bananas" by individual families.
Killing of taboo pigs by subclan members; taboos lifted.	Subclan kills pigs of "mature" taboos, eels and female pigs cooked together, taboo on sex lifted.
	Cassowary and pig killed, former decorated.
Large-scale pig killing; eels and pigs cooked together.	Pigs to be given killed and cooked and added to pork from pigs of mature taboos.

Large-scale distribution to allies through gate in ceremonial fence at ceremonial village danceground.

Though eels, marsupials, and cassowaries are important in the pig festival, the most important sacrificial animal is the pig. Pigs are domesticated animals directly associated with human beings. The structure of exchange of pigs involves the sacrificing and giving of live pigs to dead ancestors and giving of pork, dead pig, to live affines and allies. The dead receive live gifts which, after they are killed and cooked, are given to live affines and allies. Ancestors and allies have given help in the previous hostilities and they receive a return in the pig festival. In addition, among the Maring, marsupials and eels are conceptualized as the pigs of the Fight Ancestor Spirits and Ordinary Ancestor Spirits, and these spirits receive pigs in return for their "pigs," which they give to men. The domesticated pigs of men are here contrasted with the "pigs" of the ancestors from the two zones of the wild—the high and the low. Among the Maring, pigs sacrificed to the two kinds of ancestors are always separated in that the meat of the pigs sacrificed to the Fight Ancestor Spirits is always eaten by the agnatic group, while pigs sacrificed to the Ordinary Ancestor Spirits are given to the affines. This distinction is not made by the Manga, but affines are not present to receive pork except at the last two pig-killing ceremonies of the pig festival, in contrast to the Maring where affines are present on several occasions during the festival.

The Maring and Manga are like Wogeo, in that the affinal relationship is the basis for the exchange relationship at large-scale ceremonial distributions rather than being contrastive with it as is the case in Abelam, Arapesh, Iatmul, and Banaro. The Maring-Manga have a prescriptive marriage rule for marriage with FaFaSiSoDa, and a complementary pattern of sister exchange, which is identical to that of Wogeo. In the case of the Maring, though not among the Manga, dowry land is given with women, as is also the case in Wogeo. Two separate exchange structures are therefore not present in Maring-Manga. Unlike those Lowland societies where exchange of shell rings defines the affinal relationship and that of pigs and yams defines the exchange-partner relationship, shells, pigs, and other valuables are given to allies and exchange partners who are at the same time affines.

The Maring-Manga, in their large-scale ceremonial pig festival, make presentations to both the living and the dead (ancestor spirits). Similarly, in Wogeo the *walage* and *warabwa* ceremonial distributions involve the invoking of appropriate spirits, the *lewa* and the *nibek*. The *lewa* are fed vegetable curry at the *walage*, and the *nibek* are fed pigs at the *warabwa*. The two kinds of ancestor spirits of the Maring-Manga are not distinct in terms of payments made to them in that both get live pigs. The contrast is between the live pigs given to spirits and dead pigs given to affines and allies. Warfare and fertility are the central themes of the Maring-Manga pig festival. These themes represent a set of binary oppositions which is manifested in the distinction between the two kinds of spirits, the two characteristics of affines as wife givers and allies and the various symbolic oppositions discussed above.

Separation of the sexes is also an important theme in Maring-Manga as evidenced by the taboos against sexual intercourse and eating with women during times of warfare and rituals associated with warfare. For the Manga, the entire period of the pig festival is a time of abstinence. In the case of the Maring, sexual abstinence is necessary during the period of the rituals associated with the Fight Ancestor Spirits. This is because men in contact with the Fight Ancestor Spirits are considered to be hot. Their contact with women, who have the capacity for reproduction and are thus associated with the spirits of the low ground, the Ordinary Ancestor Spirits, and with the cold, is dangerous at this time. The hot-cold opposition is one of the set of binary oppositions discussed above. This represents an inversion and transformation from Wogeo, where heat is associated with health and fertility and coldness with sickness and death. Unlike Maring and Manga, contact with all spirits in Wogeo places an individual in a cold state, which requires that he be purified and made warm ritually and with hot food. Among the Maring and Manga, involvement in warfare demands a ritual separation of men from women which is analagous to the separation of men and women associated with the yam cult of the Abelam and Arapesh. In several respects the yam cult of the Lowland societies seems ritually equivalent to warfare in Highland societies. The Wogeo *warabwa* is directed toward exchange partners in enemy or neutral districts, not toward allies. Goods are prominently displayed and competitiveness and challenge are important elements of the *warabwa*. This makes it structurally similar to warfare. In contrast, the Maring-Manga pig festival is not competitive. Warfare is intimately connected with the pig festival, but the distribution itself is to allies, not to enemies.

8   Kuma

The people we will describe are referred to by Reay as the Kuma. They are part of a large grouping of peoples whom Reay calls Nangamp, and whom are also referred to as the people of the Middle Waghi since they inhabit the area of the Waghi Valley west of the Chimbu River. Luzbetak, whose material we will also use, describes another group of Middle Waghi people centered around Nondugl. We refer to these two groups collectively as Kuma. The Middle Waghi people number some twenty-five thousand.

The settlement pattern is such that men and women have separate houses. Each wife has a house close to the gardens where she raises sweet potatoes. Men live alone in their own houses, or with one or two close agnates. Their plantations of sugar cane and bananas are close by. These houses are located on the crests of hills for defensive reasons (Reay 1959b: 80). The family's pigs live in stalls in the wife's house. If the wife has few pigs, she may share her husband's house. A wife usually brings meals to her husband's house.

Land is plentiful, and therefore not a source of dispute or warfare. Clearing and cultivating unused land gives title to the land to the man who performs the labor and his descendants. After this, the former owner has no claim. If a group is routed in a war and driven from its land, that land will remain unoccupied since the victors fear to use it because of sorcery traps and vengeful ghosts. The vanquished will seek other land from some other group which it will get in exchange for women promised in marriage (Reay 1959a: 7). Land is owned by males and inherited equally by sons. Bush land, which is used for collecting firewood and grazing pigs, is owned by the subclan or sub-subclan. A man may reside uxorilocally and receive land from his father-in-law. In such a case, he does not participate in all of the group activities but only indirectly through his sponsor. His contributions to group exchanges are channeled through his sponsor. The son of such a man, born in his mother's kin group, participates fully in group activities such as courting parties and in exchanges, but in terms of marriage he is considered a member of his father's original group and is expected to take a bride from his mother's group. The grandson of the in-marrying son-in-law is fully incorporated into the group and must marry outside his group. A man may also reside with his brother-in-law temporarily or for a longer period of time. Such a man gains a multiplicity of contacts and his host gains additional labor for himself and for his group. Though land is plentiful, labor is not. Pressure from their natal group may be exerted upon men not residing with that group to return.

The Kuma view their system as a segmentary lineage structure with an ideology of patrilineal descent. The ideal mechanisms for group formation are the branching off of groups descended from brothers; however, the actual mechanisms for group formation are different and not discussed by the Kuma, who insist that present-day groups are based upon agnatic descent from a common ancestor. Genealogical reckoning is not significant and elicited genealogies go back no further than four generations. As is characteristic of segmentary lineage structures, the groups at successively more inclusive levels, which make up the Kuma system, are potentially subject to change, especially on the lower levels. Growth in size leads to segmentation; decline in size to disappearance as a separate entity.

The smallest named group in the segmentary system is referred to by Reay as the sub-subclan. It is said that genealogical links could be traced between members of this group. Sub-subclans are invariably said to have been founded by brothers. Their father's name is never known. The corporate activities of the sub-subclan include gardening, house building, and providing marriage payments.

Segmentation is present below the level of the sub-subclan. This segmentation may take one of two possible forms. In one instance, there may be a separation on a genealogical basis; Reay refers to these as sublineages founded by brothers. In addition to traceable genealogical connection between the members, the sublineage is associated with a definite locality. In sub-subclans in which people assume but cannot demonstrate genealogical relationship, subdivisions may take the form of factions composed of followers of different leaders. Minimal divisions of both types may coexist in the same sub-subclan and Reay provides an example of this (Reay 1959a: 42). Ideally, since brothers should remain together, the sublineage form should be the most frequent, but it is not. The relation between brothers is an ambivalent one. The ideal is that they should stand together. But they tend to quarrel and eventually not to remain together in the same minimal residence unit. The younger brother frequently moves off in order to become independent of his older brother, who would have authority over him if he remained. A younger brother who moves off may try to attract followers and directly compete with his older brother for influence (Reay 1959a: 74). The followers he attracts are usually from outside the group. In order for a younger brother to assume a recognized position of leadership, he must form a separate domestic group.

The sub-subclan tends to be a localized unit though members of related sub-subclans may live somewhat interspersed so that each subclan is not a distinct and separate entity. There is a Kuma term for group which is applied to all groupings, from the level of the sub-subclan up. It is the term *doogum*. The term small *doogum* refers to the sub-subclan or subclan. The term big *doogum* refers to the clan or its localized equivalent.

The subclan, which comprises several sub-subclans, has a distinct territory and is named. It is the unit of warfare, its members acting together in the decision to go to war assisted by other subclans of the clan. It is the unit that exchanges women. The subclan is also traditionally associated with a single burial place.

The clan is a named group associated with a distinct territory. It is the exogamic unit. Clans vary greatly in size of population. Smaller clans, numbering from one hundred to three hundred, are subdivided simply into subclans. Intermediate-sized clans, numbering two hundred to nine hundred, have two levels of segmentation, the subclan and the sub-subclan. Large clans, from seven hundred to seventeen hundred, have three levels: clan segments, subclans, and sub-subclans. The clan is the widest political unit within which there is some kind of law and order (Reay 1964: 242). Disputes are adjudicated by subclan leaders. Though decision to go to war is made on the subclan level, approval of the other subclans within a clan is necessary, since subclans within a clan are bound to assist one another in the event that they face defeat. Therefore, nominally, it is the whole clan that goes to war. Causes of warfare are failure to meet obligations in exchange of women and exchange of valuables (Reay 1959a: 55). Some clans stand as permanent traditional enemies to one another, while others are friendly clans who intermarry, but do not form a single larger political community since they do not have to support one another in warfare. Still other clans are potential enemies as well as potential affines (Reay 1964: 242). Sorcery is practiced by certain individuals in each clan and is directed exclusively against enemy clans (Reay 1964: 242). Just as strength in warfare demonstrates the power of the clan, the power of its sorcery is also said to be a measure of its strength. Reay notes, "the natives equate the clan and the parish (territory) and speak of the latter as if it were composed of a pure agnatic descent group, with members' wives as the only people incorporated from other groups of the same order. . . . Whole spheres of corporate action have as their explicit purpose the welfare and continuance of the clan" (Reay 1959a: 51–52).

A group of clans with the tradition of common agnatic descent may be joined together as a single phratry. Though such clans are seen as descended from a single putative ancestor, this has no effect on present-day political relations since every phratry also contains clans that are traditional enemies to one another.

Positions of leadership exist on a number of levels of the segmentary system. Differentiation of these leadership positions is on the basis of the different activities associated with them. Below the level of the sub-subclan, informal leadership is present in the sublineages or the factions that make up the sub-subclan. The leader of the sub-subclan is called *kumna* or "the first." This position is primarily managerial in that "the first" organizes labor within the sub-subclan for work that has to be done, such as house building and clearing land for new gardens. He represents the members of his group when they are engaged in disputes with members of other sub-subclans within the subclan (Reay 1964: 244). The subclan leader is, at the same time, also a leader of his own sub-subclan. He has to be a skilled orator. Various actions on behalf of the subclan vis-à-vis other subclans requires stylized speech delivery. The role of the subclan leader—*kangab ro*—is translated as "rhetoric thumper." He adjudicates disputes within the subclan and speaks on behalf of members of the subclan involved in disputes with men of other subclans. Leadership on the clan level is operative only during the pig ceremony, which occurs once in a generation. During this time, a single ceremonial leader of the clan makes decisions regarding the timing of the various activities. He is a leader of one of the subclans, as well as a practicing sorcerer. The hawk's-wing headdress serves as an insignia of leadership. However, it is not used by all leaders on all occasions. The lower-level leaders wear it only in informal interactions with members of other clans. Only the ceremonial leader wears such a headdress on the occasion of the pig ceremony.

The Kuma ideal concerning succession to leadership is that the leader of the sub-subclan is succeeded by his eldest son. In actual fact, the data provided by Reay indicate that in 36 percent of the cases fathers are not succeeded by their sons but may be succeeded by brothers, patrilateral parallel cousins, or men who cannot trace genealogical relationship. In the 64 percent of the cases where fathers are succeeded by sons, there is no indication as to how many cases involve eldest sons. Not only is genealogical reckoning shallow but there is vagueness about the paternity of close collateral relatives. Reay presents an example of a case of succession to leadership where patrilateral parallel cousins are seen as brothers descended from one father, in justifying the line of succession. The classificatory use of the term father for men of the older generation of the subclan contributes to the vagueness in genealogical reckoning, making it possible to sustain the ideology of succession to authorized leadership from father to eldest son (Reay 1959a: 114–15, appendix).

Sorcery is associated with leadership, since "the practice of sorcery coincides fairly closely with the traditional positions of power" (Reay 1959a: 150). Most sub-subclan leaders are sorcerers, though there are sorcerers who are not leaders. Sorcery is inherited like leadership, though it is not necessarily an eldest son who inherits it. Sorcery may also be acquired through purchase via the trade network from outside sources. Sorcery is associated with relations between hostile groups when they are at war, as well as at other times. The practicing sorcerer has a special war-magic house in which weapons and magical materials are stored (Reay 1959a: 151). According to Aufenanger, who has described war-magic houses in the Banz area, rituals associated with warfare are held at these houses. Objects bespelled with war-magic are hung from the central pole of this house, and the bag containing them is taken down at the onset of fighting, to be carried into battle. Before and after battle, pigs are sacrificed at the war-magic house, where they are cooked in special ovens and eaten by the sorcerer and the warriors (Aufenanger 1959: 6–9). As will be discussed more fully below, "One of the most powerful sorcerers who was Rhetoric Thumper for his subclan is ceremonial leader for his clan. He is responsible for the conduct of the pig ceremony" (Reay 1959a: 151).

In addition to the position of authorized leader of the sub-subclan, there is also a secondary leader. The secondary leader may be someone who is in the line of succession by virtue of his genealogical position or he may have no traceable relationship with previous leaders but be a "spontaneous leader" who has achieved some wealth or renown. "When such spontaneous leaders attach themselves to authorized leaders the fiction grows that they have some vague claim to hereditary succession" (Reay 1959a: 116). The position of spontaneous leader is an avenue to power outside the ideology of hereditary succession to eldest son.

A spontaneous leader gains power by accumulating wealth. His wealth is used to put people in his debt and therefore to control them. The accumulation of wealth relates to polygamy, since having more wives to care for pigs enables a man to raise more pigs. "If a man has pigs to kill, and can command plumes and shells to present to others, he is able to press his claims to women—women to marry or to marry off to kinsmen" (Reay 1959a: 96). When a man gives a woman to another man he can claim a large share of the valuables from the return gift given in exchange for the marriage payment. A man may also help with the betrothal payment. It is repaid privately but places the recipient in a subordinate position to the wealthy man, who also gets a substantial gift from the bride's return payment. By manipulating exchanges, a man may gain wealth and eminence. A man who wishes renown must contribute lavishly to feasts and provide food for visitors. He needs to have gardens in all stages of production and to have sons and followers to exercise rights to cultivate land (Reay 1959b: 82). Power, therefore, relates to the extent to which a man controls the flow of valuables between his own group and other groups.

Marriage among the Kuma is conceptualized as an exchange. A man must always provide a woman in exchange for the bride he takes. An immediate exchange is preferable. "Sister exchange is the ideal, but generally the 'sisters' exchanged are the men's clan sisters" (Reay 1959a: 57). A man cannot activate a claim to a woman if the other subclan has already made a return. The clan is the exogamous unit. "A man is specifically prohibited from marrying close kin thus excluding his and his parents and children's primary relatives as well as his parallel and cross cousins" (Reay 1959a: 58). A man is forbidden to marry into his mother's subclan but he may marry into her clan. Though first cross-cousins may not marry, the children of first cousins can and do marry. A father obtains brides for his sons from his brothers-in-law so that ego may marry into the clan of his father's sister's husband or his mother's brother. Reay provides figures from the Kugika clan which indicate that most marriages are with these clans. "The rule is that if ego has not already claimed (for a clansman) a woman who is an actual cross-cousin, he may demand in marriage (for himself or his son) a female descendent of an actual cross-cousin, male or female. This is, of course, subject to his own clan having given the bride in the last marriage contracted between the two clans" (Reay 1959a: 64–65). The female cross-cousin of a man may be claimed in order to give her to someone else. This is a right sometimes exercised by wealthy men to gain followers. The term for cross-cousins is used for first cross-cousins as well as for their descendants, and the relationship is considered to continue, though in practice it grows weaker with succeeding generations. "It becomes so weak, in fact, that further intermarriage has to reaffirm it if it is continued at all and for this there is an established mechanism" (Reay 1959a: 64). This mechanism involves the marriage of descendants of cross-cousins and is called "taking one's road." The emphasis is upon clans that maintain a relationship by the exchange of women over successive generations. These are called "brother" clans (Reay 1959a: 61). The ties between clans established by marriage are not easily broken. A woman may be divorced from a particular husband but not divorced from his group (Reay 1967: 15). Elopements short circuit the exchanges and may be cause for war between subclans. Marriages do not occur between clans who are traditional enemies to one another. The Kuma place great emphasis on marriage as a form of exchange, and on continuing relations between clans by means of marriage. The actual units that exchange are subclans (Reay 1959a: 55). Though the marriage prohibitions prevent subclans from marrying in every generation, the larger units, the clans, are exchanging in every generation. The intermarriage between subclans marks their separation into clans. Polygamy is the aim of most men since extra wives help to provide the labor necessary to become wealthy and successful. In Kugika clan, 26 percent of the men had more than one wife and 38 percent had been polygamous at some time.

The kinship terminology of the Kuma is Iroquois, with bifurcate merging terminology in the first ascending generation. The same term, *abap*, is used for mother's brother and for sister's children. The term for cross-cousins, *bebe*, is extended to contemporaries of both sexes in mother's brother's entire clan but only to the subclan of father's sister's husband. The term is extended to any descendant of cross-cousin. The term *gulnan* is used for both types of brother-in-law.

We shall now proceed to analyze the exchange system of the Kuma. The exchanges at marriage begin with the betrothal. At that point there is a formal presentation of plumes and shells, together with a cooked pig, by the groom to be to the girl's relatives. The future groom keeps a record of the size of the pig to prove his claim to the girl. The boy himself provides the bulk of this payment. This payment is not reciprocated. The main marriage payment is an exchange between two clans, since some of the items are directly reciprocated in a return payment, and the bride's group must be given a woman in exchange (Reay 1959a: 99). A father helps his son with the payment, and other members of his sub-subclan also contribute. The woman is considered to have been bought by the sub-subclan, and therefore to belong to it. Members of the boy's clan who have married women of the clan of the in-marrying bride will also make a contribution. The marriage payment consists of ropes of cowrie shells, salt, plumes, and pigs. The girl's father decides how the balance of the marriage payment is to be distributed. This main marriage payment by the groom may be delayed until the birth of the first child. If such is the case, the payment is larger and there is no separate payment made for the child itself.

A payment is made at the birth of the first child to the wife's relatives, the mother's brother of the child. It should be as large as the marriage payment. Payment for subsequent children is much smaller. Payments for girls are usually overlooked. These latter payments ideally should be made but are usually delayed indefinitely, while the man makes small payments regularly.

At the death of the child born of the marriage, payments are made in the same direction. The deceased is addressed as son by his mother's clan. His mother's brother receives a payment of compensation for his death which is equivalent in size to a marriage payment. The maternal clan mourns the deceased with wailing and blames his agnatic group for their neglect that caused the death (Reay 1959a: 69). The payment is made with valuables collected largely from members of the deceased sub-subclan outside of his immediate family and from members of the deceased's subclan who have married women from his mother's clan. Most of the dead man's wealth is destroyed by his sons (Reay 1959a: 97). The maternal cross-cousins of the deceased lie with his wives and slaughter his pigs, reducing the herd inherited by his sons to one of small size (Reay 1959a: 96). Some of the valuables given in a death payment are returned in equivalent form by the mother's clan of the deceased. They in turn are distributed to the members of the subclan of the deceased who have contributed to the death payment. When an important man dies it is assumed that sorcery was involved and his maternal and affinal relatives undertake to discover the sorcerer.

Marriage establishes the relationship of brothers-in-law. Though they are distinguished terminologically from brothers, it is said that brothers-in-law should act toward one another as brothers should ideally. We have seen that in fact brothers do not come close to this ideal of mutual assistance and solidarity. However, brothers-in-law do come close to the ideal and assist one another with labor and food, and true friendship may develop between them. The wife's brother will side with his brother-in-law rather than with his sister when husband and wife quarrel. As noted above, a man will also turn to his brother-in-law when seeking a wife for his son and it is the duty of mother's brother to find a wife for his sister's son (Reay 1959a: 63). The mother's brother of the boy is thus part of the category of affines. He and his group are paid when that sister's son dies, in recognition of their loss. The cross-cousin relationship is a continuation of the affinal relationship. The further, generationally, the cross-cousin relationship is from the original affinal genera- tion, the more tenuous it becomes. Nevertheless, in warfare, a man must never fight members of his maternal clan. A man can fight the clan of his father's sister's husband but he must avoid injuring his patrilateral cross-cousin. One clan may stand as mother's brother's clan to the sub-subclan of another clan, its sister's child. This is because the maternal ancestress of that sub-subclan came from the mother's brother's clan. No warfare is allowed between the two groups.

The sharing of food has particular symbolic significance. Reay indicates that people may share food with affines, cog- nates, and members of their own clan. "As with the corpo- rate activities of political groups, the significant unit in the sharing of vegetable food is nominally the clan but in prac- tice the subclan" (Reay 1959a: 90). Not eating with others is a form of protection against sorcery. The fire-taboo system is the means by which conflict is inhibited and danger averted, by avoidance of food sharing. Men within the sub-subclan who quarrel, and their descendants, may not use one another's fires. A man who is practicing sorcery on behalf of his clan against outsiders is also subject to the fire taboo to protect those around him as well as himself. When a man shares food he is identified with that group. The ending of a relationship is brought about by instituting taboos that end the sharing of food and fire.

We will now go on to consider exchanges between groups. The large-scale vegetable distribution or *wubalt* ceremony is given by one clan to another. It is held in the dry season when the nuts are plentiful. "Wubalt festivals are given to demonstrate friendship between clans that have lived in peace with each other as long as their members can recall. An exchange may be initiated as a prelude to the exchange of women, or it may occur between clans that have already exchanged a few brides" (Reay 1959a: 89). *Wubalt* are never held between clans that are traditional enemies, since such clans never intermarry. Food can never be shared with enemy clans. Temporary enemies must exchange pigs before they can share food and intermarry. Though nominally the *wubalt* takes place between two clans, the donor clan and the recipient clan, other clans are involved. Some clans help the donor, and other clans, who will receive nuts from the recipient clan, help the latter by swelling their numbers in the dancing at the ceremony. The recipient clan must hold a return festival, which completes the exchange. This is held from three to five years later. A recipient clan cannot initiate a second exchange while it is in debt to a donor. Since the donor clan is assisted by members of clans with which it has established marriage ties, "brother" clans, the recipient clan is probably in the category of potential affine and the *wubalt* may signify the beginning of closer relations marked by more frequent intermarriage. The *wubalt* primarily involves vegetable food; in recent times groundnuts have replaced pandanus nuts, which grew only in the steeper side valleys. Sugar cane and bananas, which are grown by men, are included but never sweet potatoes, which are the staple diet and are grown by women. Game, if available, is included. Reay estimates the total amount in 1964 to be sixty thousand cubic feet of unshelled groundnuts. "Wubalt is unique in displaying the largest quantity of vegetable food ever gathered together. Apparently because vegetable food itself is not highly valued, its display for formal presentation has to be blatantly excessive if it is to acquire enough symbolic value for the transfer to establish new relationships" (Reay 1959a: 112).

Individuals gather the nut crop and form it into parcels. These are eventually placed in a large clearing accessible to all members of the clan. A small festival is held at which a "brother" clan makes a group contribution of a mass of food to the donor. The foodstuffs are kept in their original parcels so that the identity of the giver may be ascertained in order to avoid the possibility of members of enemy clans receiving indirectly by an individual gift, food grown and gathered by their enemies.

The actual ceremony includes dancing with spears which expresses in symbolic ritual the conflict with enemies. There is also transvestism, as men of the donor clan impersonate women and are successively seduced by other men of their own clan. This symbolizes the success of the donor clan with women. The excessive food display symbolizes the prosperity of the clan, and its strength. The recipients dance forward to encircle the heap of food, and make speeches praising the great amounts of food displayed.

The most important ceremonial exchange is the *konggol* (Kong Gar Gol). This climactic ritual at which great numbers of pigs are killed and pork distributed, which so dominates the life of the Kuma, is held approximately every fifteen years or every generation (Reay 1959a: 2, 170; Luzbetak 1954: 60). The *konggol* is a clan ritual. However, since the pig ceremonial is held on old burial grounds, a clan may frequently hold its *konggol* simultaneously in more than one festival ground. Reay and Luzbetak, in their descriptions, both give examples where three clans held their pig festivals simultaneously, though at a number of different festival grounds. The relationship between clans holding their festivals simultaneously is that of "brother" clans who intermarry and are close neighbors (Reay 1959a: 26). Reay indicates that affinal and maternal relatives must lend ceremonial display objects like plumes. Further, those who lend ceremonial plumes are recompensed with gifts of pork at the main and final distribution of meat which marks the completion of the ceremony (Reay 1959a: 104). This would seem to place affinal and maternal relatives in the category of guests and recipients of pork at the *konggol* ceremony.

The headmen of the various subclans of the clan decide when to hold the *konggol* ceremony. This is dependent upon how long it has been since the last ceremony and whether the clan has sufficient pigs for a *konggol*. Reay states that all of the activities of a clan associated with the pig ceremonial are coordinated by a single ceremonial leader. He is a leader of one of the constituent subclans, and one of the most powerful of the sorcerers. Luzbetak does not indicate that there is a single ceremonial leader, but speaks rather of headmen who coordinate activities, and of a number of hereditary statuses associated with particular tasks. These offices include: the summoner to the meeting to decide whether to hold a festival, the magician who smears the blood of the sacrificed pigs on digging sticks (which will be used to clear the festival ground), the official wood cutters for each subclan for building the ceremonial houses, the magician who embues magical power into the hand drums, the official wig makers for each subclan, and the man who locates ritual relics from the previous festival. Reay's account is somewhat different. She states, "Building the spirit's house is an hereditary task" (Reay 1959a: 152). Fifteen to twenty men help to find the sacred objects that were used in the previous *konggol*, and to guard the secrets.

The *konggol* is intimately tied to Kuma conceptualizations of the spirit world, since pigs are given to various categories of spirits, as well as to living men. Reay states that there are four categories of spirits—spirits of the recent dead, spirits of remote ancestors, bush spirits, and the two powerful and ubiquitous spirits known as Bolim and Geru. The Kuma conceive of the soul as having two aspects, the conscious aspect, which is extinguished soon after death, and the immortal aspect, which is the spirit or ghost-*kibe* (Reay 1959a: 132). The spirits of the recently dead are considered to be malevolent, and must be placated. Pigs that are sacrificed have a spiritual aspect, which is eaten by the spirits. Only spirits of relatives whom an individual knew can return to harm him, and they must be placated with the spirits of pigs sacrificed to them. In time, the spirits of the recent dead retire to the community of spirits of remote ancestors, when no living men remain who had known them. "These truly ancestral *kibe* are conceived, not as particular ancestors from whom descent can be traced, but as the collective ancestors of a particular clan. They are thought of as being essentially benevolent. They bless the crops and ensure bountiful harvest. They give their descendents and living clansmen strength and success in war" (Reay 1959a: 134).

Bolim and Geru are conceived of as dangerous spirits who must also be propitiated by being fed pigs. Bolim is the red spirit, concerned with human fertility and the fertility of crops. A special house is built for him, in which he is said to reside during the pig festival. A special dance is held for Bolim, during which he is impersonated by a man wearing pig's tusks. Geru is concerned with the fertility of pigs, as well as crops. Though he himself is not the spirit of a particular ancestor, Geru represents the essence of the ancestral spirits. "He can vent his anger by destroying a clan's entire supply of pigs, but will guard them from harm so long as the ancestors are honored and the ceremonies and symbolic sacrifices are properly enacted" (Reay 1959a: 140). The central purpose of the Konggol is to promote the fertility of the clan, its pigs and its gardens. Warefare is tied to this theme, in that the clan can increase and maintain its solidarity only by maintaining its traditional enmities (Reay 1959a: 290). Bolim and Geru, as well as the ancestor spirits, are honored by having pigs sacrificed to them, and in return the help of the spirits is sought in fertility and in warfare.

After the decision to hold the ceremony has been made, pigs are slaughtered at the various festival grounds as a sacrifice to the ancestors to insure a successful festival (Luzbetak 1954: 64). The ancestors are asked to make the pigs to be slaughtered in the upcoming festival fat. The next event involves the building of the Geru spirit house by each subclan. Many events of the *konggol* take place in the Geru house, which is taboo to women. The spirit flutes are kept here, and the initiation of boys at the end of the ceremony takes place here. There are several Geru houses at each festival ground because a number of subclans use the same ceremonial ground. After the building of the Geru houses, each man brings a pig to his Geru house. The pigs are killed and cooked, and after the ceremonial lighting of fire in the Geru house, the pork is given to members of other clans who are obliged to return valuables in the form of body ornaments to be used during the festival. Subsequently, an entire temporary village is built, with long houses, containing sitting rooms for guests, and private dwellings. Each subclan builds its own long house, and the other subclans assist them by bringing kunai grass, which they use to thatch the house during a ceremony. This village will be occupied for a number of months by subclans who normally live dispersed among their gardens. At this time, the men gather from the side of the road the "bombo," part of an edible plant which is placed on the tops of houses and near trails and roads as protective magic. This "bombo," which is said to have caught and preserved the black magic spells of the enemies, is thrown into the river. "Now all the black magic of the enemy has been cast into the river, all is safe; now no harm can befall the participants of the festival" (Luzbetak 1954: 69–70). Reay states that the ceremonial leader of the clan, who is chosen because of his power as a sorcerer, continues to practice sorcery against enemy clans during the entire pig ceremony (Reay 1959a: 151–52).

The several groups at different festival grounds which are coordinating their ceremonial activities visit back and forth. These visits are to foster friendship and intermarriage (Luzbetak 1954: 77). The guests receive vegetable food, which is reciprocated when hosts visit guests. The official wig makers (hereditary positions) for each subclan present the wigs they have manufactured. The wigs are woven from the hair of members of the subclan. At a feast, the wig makers receive a pig for their work and the relatives who have contributed hair receive a pig, pearl shell, hatchet, and plume. The wigs are worn beginning about two months before the great slaughter of pigs and are said to show that the killing of pigs is near (Luzbetak 1954: 80). The wigs are supposed to make the men sexually attractive for courting (Reay 1959a: 160). The wigs are removed on the day of the great slaughter of pigs.

The headmen of the various subclans then decide on the date for the climax of the festival, when the mass killing of pigs occurs. The guests who come from other parts of the Middle Waghi Valley are notified of the approximate date of the final slaughter of pigs. They are expected to bring the firewood and banana leaves for cooking the pigs, and sweet potatoes and sugar cane. At this point, each subclan sacrifices two or three pigs for the ancestors at different parts of the burial grounds and only the subclan members are allowed to eat this pork (Luzbetak 1954: 103).

The next stage of the ceremonial involves the building of the House of the Bolim Spirit. First, the relics of the house built for the last pig ceremonial are located and exhumed from the ground. Then the Bolim House is erected secretly in the center of the festival ground with the Geru Houses facing it. Luzbetak's description seems to indicate that there is a Bolim House at the center of each festival ground. Reay, in her description, indicates, "Each clan, however, has only one set of sacred objects for building the red spirit house and the group that uses them provides the most important ceremonial leader of the clan" (Reay 1959a: 151).

The next event is a fertility dance in honor of Geru spirit. The participants wear Geru boards on their heads. These boards are decorated with signs of fertility and are to honor the ancestors. They are worn by men and children in this ceremony. The dancers assemble and dress in the Geru House, where the Geru boards for this occasion were stored. During the course of the dance, "A man, taking his bow, shot an arrow toward Minj, 'where we have plenty enemies. By shooting an arrow in the direction of our enemies, our ancestors will be pleased; they will come to our assistance and will punish the Minj people' " (Luzbetak 1954: 107). The people of Minj are referred to by Luzbetak previously as the "friends" who were notified of the date of the festival climax (Luzbetak 1954: 102). The visitors at the climax of the festival would seem, therefore, to be in the category of "potential affines/potential enemies," rather than from "brother" clans holding their festival simultaneously.

The next days are devoted to bringing all the pigs to the festival grounds, where they are exhibited with pride as a sign of wealth. Firewood and stacks of banana leaves and other native vegetables to be used in the slaughter of the "small pigs," or spirit pigs, are then brought to the festival ground. These pigs are slaughtered in honor of departed relatives and ancestors. They are cooked at various family burial grounds in the area and the meat is distributed to relatives and friends (Luzbetak 1954: 108; Reay 1959a: 104 seems to disagree on this point and indicates that these pigs are not sacrificed to the ancestors). Luzbetak reports that on this occasion ninety-seven pigs were slaughtered at the Kombulno festival ground. At night the jaw bones of these spirit pigs are tied to the house of the Bolim spirit and the walls are smeared with pig grease. The long central pole of the Bolim house represents a penis. At this point, three diamond shaped pieces of wood with center holes, representing the female sex organ, known as the *tundus*, are placed by the ceremonial leader, over the central pole. The Bolim Bombo fertility rite is then held. People from "brother" clans holding the ceremony at other festival grounds come to join in the ceremony. Several hundred men and women take part. It is the most elaborate of the various performances. The women stand around the Bolim House with heaps of vegetable food and pork at their side, and vines of sweet potato on their heads. This action is said to represent the fertility aspect of the ceremony. A parade of men enters, first the warriors who charge with the spears, then the sorcerers doing a variety of symbolic acts of protective magic, and then the drummers. Among the sorcerers' acts are included symbolic intercourse, preventive fire magic, and the symbolic exchange of gold lip shells back and forth. One man, called "the pig Bolim," is driven about by his partner holding a stick. Several times, the warriors charge around the Bolim House. Speeches about the eating of the small pigs as a prelude to the great slaughter are then made from the top of the Bolim House by men who place the *tundus* over the central pole. Pork is then given by the women to the male dancers (Luzbetak 1954: 111). Reay has a somewhat different version. The ceremonial leader makes a speech from his special platform. Leaders of sub-subclans also make speeches. Then pork is hurled at the crowd from the roofs of the Bolim House and long houses, and from the ceremonial leader's platform while the crowd laughingly struggles to get pieces of meat (Reay 1959a: 155).

The next day, the large pigs are brought to the center of the festival ground. The slaughtering clubs have already been prepared. The women on this day only wear the costumes and body ornaments of men, including wigs and plumes. Then the slaughter begins. Luzbetak notes that at Kombulno about four hundred pigs were clubbed to death in three-quarters of an hour. After the pigs are killed water is poured over them by the women and new Geru boards are placed on the heads of many of the pigs. Both these acts are said to make the surviving pigs prolific. Reay adds that wigs are placed on the pigs and their faces are painted (Reay 1954: 156). The pigs are then arranged in lines like spokes from the Bolim House, which is the hub, and each spoke terminates at a Geru House. Each row of carcasses comprising a spoke belongs to the men of a single sub-subclan occupying that Geru House. The pigs are cut up and pork is cooked. Reay indicates that the cooking is done by the visitors after they have built great ovens on what formerly was the dancing field (Reay 1959a: 156). After the cooking, men climb on each Geru House and throw the cooked pork down in all directions, while everyone below scrambles for meat.

The final phase of the pig ceremony is the boys' initiation. Since this occurs at the same time as the pig ceremony, once every fifteen years, the boys range in age from about four to twenty and some of the latter may even be married. The boy's family must have sacrificed at least one pig at the ceremonial. The initiation is referred to as "seeing the flutes." The bamboo flutes are called birds and formerly were kept secret from women and uninitiated boys. The purpose of the initiation is to show the initiates the sacred flutes so that they may become fully fledged members of their subclan. Women and children are told that the birds drink the blood of the slaughtered pigs. Each subclan holds its own initiation rites in its Geru House. At this time the initiate is lectured by the old men of the subclan, who are called the fathers of the flutes, on traditions and proper behavior, such as fighting one's enemies and helping brothers. The initiates undergo a series of ordeals, endurance tests, long walks, rubbing of the tongue with nettles, and, in former times, the causing of the nose to bleed. Luzbetak notes, "The highlanders had the custom of rolling up a banana leaf and then spinning it inside the nostrils of the candidate till blood began to flow freely. . . . According to some interpreters, the purpose of letting blood was to rid the candidate of the bad blood he had received from his mother" (Luzbetak 1954: 120).

At the conclusion, the boys are dressed in their parents' finest ornaments and the parents of the boy cook pork, which they distribute to the old teachers of the initiates. Each boy has an older man who serves as his protector during the rites: this man will be the boy's father or a close agnate. The initiation ceremony lasts for several days and nights. The concluding event of the entire *konggol* ceremony is the burial of the *tundus* and the slaughtering clubs. Two years later, the parts of the Bolim House will be ceremonially buried and pigs killed and distributed on this occasion.

Each Kuma clan holds its *konggol* approximately every fifteen years. In the intervening years, other Kuma clans will hold their *konggol*. Reay indicates "The major ceremonial cycle, the Pig Ceremonial or Konggol, is celebrated by each clan in succession, in an approximate order to which no slavish adherence is required; each clan is free to celebrate its Pig Ceremonial whenever it is ready to do so" (Reay 1959a: 131). From the viewpoint of the region, the *konggol* serves to integrate a large number of Kuma clans into a single overall system.

Exchange relationships between trading partners are also present among the Kuma. The term for trading partner is *Na te nont*, which translates as "I together I-eat." Hospitality is an important aspect of the trade relationship. Trading partners are in particular places; for example, the Kugika men have their trading partners in the Jimi River region (Reay 1959a: 105). Groups of men, usually from one clan, make the trip to their trading partner's clan. The trading relationship is continued in the next generation. The trading that takes place does not involve haggling. The Kuma trade for items such as bird of paradise plumes, gold lip and bailer shells, salt, and stone axes. Sorcery spells have also come along the trade routes, in exchange for women (Reay 1959a: 149–50). Direct barter, outside of the trading relationship, also takes place. It consists of casual exchange. For example, after the pig ceremonial, men from other clans may come to trade piglets for plumes. New piglets are needed by men who have held the pig ceremonial to replenish their herds, and they will therefore pay plumes of great value which are no longer immediately needed in order to get the pigs.

The Kuma, like the Maring and Manga, have a segmentary lineage system. The structure of relationship between groups based on marriage is also very similar. There is a prohibition against marriage with first cross-cousin, and marriage between the children of cross-cousins is preferred. This is called "taking one's road." The Kuma emphasize reciprocity in the exchange of women between clans.

Leadership positions among the Kuma are inherited from father to son in most cases. The leader controls specialized ritual knowledge and sorcery as in the case of the Maring. This gives him control over a strategic resource, which he passes on to his son. He also plays a central role in production. Spontaneous leaders may arise but they must gain access in some way to this ritual knowledge, which is a requisite of leadership.

The *wubalt* vegetable distribution is distinct from the *konggol* pig festival. In this respect, the Kuma differ from the Maring-Manga though the latter have a large vegetable distribution as one of the stages of their pig festival. The separation between *wubalt* and *konggol* ceremonies would seem, however, to parallel the *walage* and *warabwa* of the Wogeo, though there is a reversal in that the *wubalt* is competitive since a return must be made while the *walage* is not, and the *warabwa* is competitive while the *konggol* is not.

The *konggol* pig festival is held to propitiate the ancestors with the sacrifice of pigs, and this together with the two themes of fertility and warfare make the Kuma pig festival very much like the pig festivals of the Maring-Manga. Like the Maring-Manga, the Kuma build a ceremonial village for the pig festival, with two separate ritual houses for Geru and Bolim which correspond to different levels of the segmentary structure. Though the Kuma have Bolim or the red spirit, he differs from the red spirits of the Maring-Manga in that he is not connected to ancestors who have died in war. The series of binary oppositions present in Maring-Manga are not evident in the Kuma material. The two spirits Geru and Bolim are both concerned with fertility, but Bolim with the fertility of humans and Geru with the fertility of pigs. There are two categories of ancestor spirits among the Kuma as in Maring-Manga, but the line of separation is different. In Kuma, immediate ancestors are malevolent and must be appeased with pig sacrifices while remote ancestors beyond living memory are benevolent. There is no separation of those who have died in war and those who have died of natural causes as in Maring-Manga. However, in the context of the pig festival live pigs are given to the dead ancestors and spirits, and cooked pork given to the living guests as in Maring-Manga. The initiation of boys occurs after the large-scale pig distribution as a final event. It is held in the Geru house where the sacred flutes are kept during the pig ceremony and is a matter with which the subclan is concerned.

Male initiation is not reported for the Maring or Manga. The *konggol* pig ceremony is jointly held by clans who are "brother" clans to one another. It is a unit that is structurally equivalent to the Manga phratry. Guests at the *konggol* are never traditional enemies but rather in the category of potential enemies/potential affines. Traditional enemies are prevented from eating together by the fire taboos that the Kuma share with the Maring-Manga. There seems to be a pattern of sequencing of pig festivals over a region present in Kuma which is not evident for Maring-Manga.

9   Chimbu

In the central Highlands of New Guinea, in the area between the Chimbu and Wahgi River valleys, live the twenty-one tribes that comprise the Chimbu. The total population of the Chimbu is some sixty thousand and their density is the highest of any nonurban area in Melanesia and New Guinea (Brookfield and Brown 1963: 4; Brown 1972: 52).

Among the Chimbu, the nuclear family is recognized as a social and economic unit. However, the residential pattern is such that a woman and her unmarried daughters and young sons live in one house on one of the husband's garden plots, while the husband resides with other males in a men's house nearby. In polygynous families, each wife and her children have a separate house on a different garden plot. Each man has a number of plots of land which may be located in several areas that are suitable for different kinds of crops. Women's houses are located near plots that are in current use or near pig forage areas, but there is no aggregation of women's dwellings. They may or may not be close to a men's house. The family as a unit usually clears the land. Each wife has her own plot or section of land which she plants and harvests. Harvesting occurs continually as sweet potatoes, the staple food, are removed by the women a few at a time when they are needed. Gardening of sweet potatoes is solely woman's work, while sugar cane and bananas are grown by men (Nilles 1950–51: 49). Food consumption is within the nuclear family, the man taking his afternoon meal with wife and children in the woman's house.

While houses of women and children are interspersed in the fields, groups of men live together in one house, close to the fields but on high ground in a defensible position. In the permanent state of enmity which exists between tribes, the men's house is frequently the focal point for attack. According to the figures given by Brown, the size of the men's house groups varies from one to sixteen men attached to the house, with a mean of 4.8. This does not include unmarried youths and boys (Brown and Brookfield 1959–60: 65). Brookfield and Brown note, "Each house is regarded as belonging to the subclan or sometimes the subclan section on whose land it stands. The men who use it regularly for sleeping, resting, informal social life, and storing personal goods form a core group" (Brookfield and Brown 1963: 97). A major proportion of the men in a men's house will be of the subclan that owns the house, but they may not be close agnates. At about the age of six, a boy moves into the men's house of his father. The figures presented by Brown and Brookfield indicate that there is a higher frequency of senior and junior agnates (fathers and sons, etc.) than of coeval agnates (brothers and patrilateral parallel cousins). According to the figures, most brothers tend not to live in the same men's house. Men have a number of residential options. They may live in any existing house owned by their subclan of which there may be several. They may choose to build an independent house on their own land. They also may choose to reside in the house of another subclan in their own clan section, if it is convenient to their land. A man may also go and reside in a men's house with his matrilateral of affinal kin. In this case he may be given land by them as a gift or a loan. If he remains there he will gradually lose his rights to his land in his group. Nine percent of the men in the sample of men's house residents were residing in this way. Access to garden land determines where a man will reside. Since he inherits land from his father he tends to remain in the men's

house of his father or in a men's house belonging to the same
subclan which is close by. In the former case, the result is a
core of closely related agnates which may be seen as a coher-
ent and persistent group. This unit tends to have its land-
holdings in a single block in different parts of the subclan
territory. The group moves from site to site following the
cultivation and fallow cycle. In the ideal picture that the
Chimbu have, the core group of the men's house is referred
to as "one blood." Brown refers to this unit as the subclan
section. A different situation exists when the land of individuals is more scattered over the territory of a subclan. In
both types of cases, the men's house group may also include
individuals residing temporarily or permanently by virtue of
matrilateral or affinal links. The Chimbu men's house represents an extreme in residential segregation yet it does not
have any of the ceremonial associations found in other New
Guinea societies. The men's house is not a center for ritual
activity. Brown and Brookfield note, "The interior of the
men's house is not sacred or taboo to women" (Brown and
Brookfield 1959–60: 9).

The men's house may include affinal and matrilateral relatives and its membership may fluctuate with shifts in residence. However, as Brown notes, "The Chimbu ideology of
group structure is agnatic—they call their main groups
'father-son' (*nem-agigil*)" (Brown 1967a: 40). Elsewhere
Brown states, "Thus a group which is regarded as composed
of the patrilineal descendants of a man is called *nem-angigl*,
meaning 'father-brother'; *nem-angigl* is used for groups of
various sizes—the sub-clan, clan, and phratry, but always to
connote common agnatic descent" (Brown 1960: 31). *Nem-
angigl* is the Chimbu term for a descent group. Descent
groups are hierarchically ordered into a segmentary system
with nesting characteristics. The groups at the different
levels are named. However, genealogical relationships between individuals who are members of the same group are
not known.

As we have noted above, the minimal social unit in the
segmentary structure, the subclan section, may be equated
with a men's house. Subclan sections will sometimes form
activity groups in pooling valuables for a distribution when

separation between sections has become more pronounced. They also own a pair of flutes in common. Subclan sections most frequently are referred to by locality names even when the subclan sections are genealogical units. Some may be referred to by the name of a leader (Brookfield and Brown 1963: 100).

The next more inclusive level in the segmentary system is the subclan, with a population of 50 to 250 persons. The subclan as a unit emerges in ceremonial activities where its members act as a unit vis-à-vis other such units. As will be seen in our discussion below, the subclan acts as a unit in the accumulation of the necessary goods for marriage and death payments. Each subclan has one or more cemetaries. The subclan as a unit also builds a house on a ceremonial ground for the pig feast. The subclan also owns forest land in common; however, land used for cultivation by the members of the subclan does not form a block of contiguous plots but rather is dispersed over the clan territory.

Subclans may also join together, forming clan sections. The clan section is part of the process of differentiation of units which occurs with segmentation. As clan sections move toward separate clan status, they become increasingly separate in ceremonial activities, and cease to support one another in fights.

Clans are named groups with an average population of six hundred to seven hundred. Clan names are taken from the putative founder, with the addition of a suffix meaning rope or line. The clan is the exogamous unit, and courting parties involve boys and girls of two different clans meeting as groups. The territory of a clan tends to be in a block so that each clan has its separate territory. When part of a clan moves off, this affects internal clan relations and marks a move toward segmentation. No permanent hostility within the clan is possible. When disputes arise, there is pressure by fellow clansmen to settle them. Regarding clan activities, Brown notes, "While the clan carries out some independent large food distributions and sometimes fought as a unit, it more often collaborates with some or all of the other clans in the tribes" (Brown 1967a: 48). It is the tribe that carries out the great pig feast; however, the clan dances in as a unit at the pig feast. The clan is the largest unit within which mutual assistance occurs. Outside the clan such relations are only with affines and with matrilateral kin.

A phratry is a group of from two to eight clans, linked by common descent. Clans within a phratry are always seen as descended from a group of brothers. Brown notes, "most phratries are more or less dispersed" (Brown 1960: 27). As a result, the largest social unit of the Chimbu is the tribe, which is a military alliance usually composed of phratries or parts of phratries which occupies a single territory but does not have the tradition of common agnatic descent. Tribes range in population from one thousand to four thousand and there are twenty-one Chimbu tribes. Relations between tribes are characterized, as Brown notes, "By a continuing state of inactive hostility or armed truce frequently broken by raids and warfare" (Brookfield and Brown 1963: 143). Frequently there is a no man's land separating two tribes. During peaceful interludes, encroachment and settlement in this area take place which lead to contact and friction over theft of pigs, bringing about renewed hostilities. During more peaceful times, the competition between tribes is expressed in large-scale ceremonial distributions, in particular the large-scale pig ceremonies. Both warfare and the large-scale distributions are the occasions for the expression of tribal solidarity in opposition to other tribes. Aufenanger reports the presence of war-magic houses in a number of locations in the Chimbu area. In these houses, sacred stones are hung and rites involving the slaughter of pigs take place in time of war (Aufenanger 1959: 18–24).

Leadership exists in various kinds of activities among the Chimbu; however, there are no fixed offices in which authority over a group rests, nor is there a special term for a leader, or special marks or insignia distinguishing leaders. Individuals have varying degrees of influence within their groups. The least influential are the "rubbish men," "most of whom have failed to keep a wife, but in any case they produce little and take only a small, if any, part in exchanges or distributions" (Brown 1972: 41). Ten percent of the Chimbu men could be so classified. The next category, ordinary men, constitute the bulk of the population who fulfill their obligations in exchanges satisfactorily and provide for their families. Some 20 percent are prominent men. "They are more active and productive than the average, initiate new gardening work, house buildings, fencing and such local activities, speak up in discussion, make speeches in subclan affairs and often have some dependants and followers attached to their household" (Brown 1972: 41–42). Still more influential is a smaller group of men, about 5 percent, "who are more than prominent, who make speeches at their clan prestations and meetings, when the main organizers are of a different subclan, who speak at tribal ceremonies, initiate important tribal and clan enterprises and whose disapproval is likely to stop any plan from being carried out. Big men are the largest participants in all exchange relationships: they engage in more frequent transactions than other men and their ties extend to more distant tribes" (Brown 1972: 42). A man becomes increasingly more influential as he contributes larger and larger amounts to marriage and funeral payments made by members of his group. This increases the prestige of the group in the eyes of other groups and his own influence within his group. In time, when return is made, he will get a larger share. This too increases his influence since he will now control more valuables and pork. To make such contributions, he needs labor in order to produce. This means that he needs to attract followers in addition to his immediate agnates. He attempts to attract sisters' husbands and wives' brothers, and to hold on to the core of agnates which forms his immediate group. "If land falls without heir, as occurred frequently in the past, it falls nominally into the claim of a prominent man. . . . [he] may retain the land, or may reallocate it to younger men of the subclan or kinsmen, and thus gain a following" (Brown and Brookfield 1959–60: 27). In addition to the land he allocates, his group's prestige increases in direct relation to the increase in his own prestige and this permits him to speak on behalf of successively more inclusive groups as his influence grows.

A number of personal characteristics are important. Managerial capacity involving coordination and foresight for planning agricultural activities and accumulation for large distributions, ability to represent the group forcefully (which involves possession of a good oratory style), the stance of a bold warrior, and certain aesthetic qualities required in displays and ceremony are all essential characteristics for a Big Man. The daring fighter is admired and important in time of war but he does not always attain a following (Brown 1967a: 46–47; 1972: 43–44). Prominent men or Big Men operate as leaders at various levels in the segmentary system. The degree of a man's prestige and importance is reflected in the size of the group on whose behalf he talks. The largest group for which a Big Man can speak is a tribe. His position is validated by his organization of the big pig ceremony, an intertribal occasion (Brown 1972: 95). The planning of prestations and displays is an important part of the Big Man's activities.

A man must be married in order to begin to try to achieve the position of Big Man. For a time after marriage, he is engaged in repaying the debts incurred by marriage and birth payments. As he reaches thirty and his children can be productive in terms of labor, he can increase his contributions and enhance his prestige. He must take a second wife to increase his agricultural productivity and pig-raising potential as well as his range of affinal connections. If he is ambitious, he will maintain an active claim to all of his own land and also assume custodianship over unclaimed and uninherited land in his subclan or subclan section. He then uses this land to attract followers—men of his subclan and others (Brookfield and Brown 1963: 130). These followers participate in his enterprises, "from house building to payments of pigs and valuables" (Brookfield and Brown 1963: 130). As a man ages, it becomes more and more difficult for him to maintain his position because of the vigorous activities required. Ambitious younger men move into the positions of men who speak for the group. A Big Man's son has certain initial advantages since he takes over the exchange relationships of his father. However, he will not become a Big Man unless he has the personal qualities to maintain the position.

The clan is the unit of exogamy, and marriages are seen as alliances between two groups. Not only is one not permitted to marry within his own clan but there is "a prohibition of marriage into the mother's subclan section" (Brown 1969: 81;

in her earlier publications [Brown and Brookfield 1959–60: 60; Brown 1962: 64], Brown presents the latter marriage prohibition as extending to mother's subclan). Nilles presents a somewhat more expanded set of marriage prohibitions in his discussion of the Upper Chimbu. He indicates that a man cannot marry a woman called *yongura* or cross-cousin (Nilles 1950–51: 44). He states, "The relatives on the father's side are not eligible as marriage partners because of clan or subclan exogamy. So too the in-laws from the father's mother's side up to the second generation. The same applies to the in-laws from the mother's side and as far as they can be traced to the third generation" (Nilles 1950–51: 30). Nilles's version of the marriage prohibition is more like the Crow-Omaha pattern of marriage prohibitions, extended to several groups. Every marriage sets up a series of relationships. It also results in prohibition of future marriages in the next generation, since cross-cousins cannot marry. Nilles's version of the prohibition is more explicit about the degree of extension of the marriage prohibition collaterally in mother's group, and also adds a two generation prohibition on father's mother's side.

The Chimbu emphasize exchange in marriage despite the fact that their marriage rules are phrased in terms of marriage prohibitions that prevent immediate exchange. Brown notes, "Marriage between groups is sometimes discussed as if it were a delayed exchange of women. That is, after a woman marries, her natal group expects to get a bride from her husband's group in the future. . . . The speeches made at a marriage always mention the state of the exchange between groups: it may be noted that several girls from one group have married into the other without any return or that this is a return after two or three in the other direction, or that the last married pair have long been dead" (Brown 1969: 82). Keeping within the marriage prohibitions, the units that tend to exchange women are subclan sections within different clans. However, the return bride may merely be from the same subclan, clan section, or clan. Geographical location is an important factor. Marriages are most frequently with neighboring clans and adjacent tribes. Tribes that exchange women may have been enemies who fought one another in the past, and may resume fighting in the future. When hostilities cease, marriages between these tribes are again arranged.

Polygyny was fairly common in the past. "The earliest census records and other evidence suggests that in the past fifty percent of men were bachelors and half the married men were polygynists" (Brown 1969: 92). After children are born, dissolution of the family through divorce is less common, since children are claimed by the father (Brown 1972: 52). After the death of the father, the widow is pressed to remarry someone in the same subclan but a determined widow may leave the group taking her children with her. The children will be pressed to return to their agnatic group at a later point.

The kinship terminology is provided by Nilles. In the parental generation the terms are bifurcate merging. Cross-cousins on either side are referred to as *yongura*. The term *kombona* is used for sister's child and her children, daughter's child, as well as matrilateral parallel cousins, and the children of father's brother's child. Father's brothers children are called by sibling terms. Son's children, brother's children, and the children of brother's children are referred to by the term *gwana*. The term *kera* refers to wife's brother and sister's husband.

We will now turn to an analysis of the exchange structure. A marriage establishes the category of affines and marks the beginning of a series of future exchanges. The marriage itself is formalized by the payment of valuables by the groom's group to the group of the bride. The contributions to make up the payment for a wife are sometimes assembled before the girl is found. Brown states, "In Chimbu, the largest contributors are the close agnates of the groom" (Brown 1969: 84). A Big Man of his subclan gives to the marriage payment about as much as a father or elder brother of the groom (Brown 1970: 111). The valuables presented include different kinds of shells, plumes, steel axes and knives, and pigs. Negotiations are carried out between a boy's close agnates and leading men of his subclan and the counterparts of a suitable girl. When agreement is reached about the payment, the day is set for the wedding. The girl's agnates must also accumulate valuables to be given as a countergift. The valuables they give amount to from one-quarter to one-half of the payment made by the boy's group, but the number of pigs returned is equal. The husband buys the wife with valuables. Brown notes, "pigs are exchanged to seal the contract" (Brown 1970: 110). The valuables received by the bride's group are allocated among her agnates and her mother's agnates by her father and the men who have contributed pigs to the return gift. Given the principle of exchange in marriage, it is likely that two groups participating in a marriage are already in the category of affines to one another as a result of previous marriages. "When the marriage was between subclans with few ties, members of both groups put out some valuables specifically to exchange—the goods were carefully matched and the transaction initiated the new relationship" (Brown 1970: 109).

At the birth of a child a formal gift is made to the infant's matrilateral group as part of the continuing series of exchanges with affines (Brown 1969: 90). Again, when a child begins to walk another gift is made to its matrilateral group (Brown 1961: 90). During childhood a ceremony is held at which nasal septum and ear lobes are pierced so that ornaments can be inserted. Piercing is carried out by the father or by a male agnate of the child. At the subsequent feast at which a pig is killed, meat, shells, and feathers are given to the mother's brother of the child. (Rosman and Rubel 1974: 37, 40, 41, 66, 71). This practice is no longer carried out by the Chimbu.

Initiation ceremonies, distinct from piercing of the septum and ear lobes, also occur among the Chimbu. They are not described in detail by Brown since the Central Chimbu whom she studied were no longer practicing these rites. Nilles, on the other hand, does provide a description of initiation for the Upper Chimbu indicating that two forms occur. The first type of initiation is a small affair involving only the subclan section (he called it a joint family). The second initiation, involving boys from an entire subclan or clan, occurs in conjunction with the pig ceremony, which is held every seven to ten years. Nilles describes the smaller of the two. The boys are secluded in the men's house and are shown the sacred flutes (koa), each initiate being shown the sacred flute belonging to his immediate family. Should women or children look upon the *koa*, it is said that their pigs would die and that their own bodies would waste away (Nilles 1950–51: 49). The next day the boys are taken into the bush where, one by one, they undergo the operation of rubbing the nasal septum until it bleeds profusely. Should a woman witness this, she would be killed. The next day a large amount of food is prepared and laid out with cooked pork and then distributed (Nilles 1950–51: 37–8). Nilles does not indicate whether mother's brothers or other matrilateral kinsmen are present or play any significant role or receive from the distribution.

After the initial nasal bleeding, which is part of initiation, men continue to induce nasal bleeding, especially before large-scale ceremonies at which dances are held. Father Schaefer indicates that the Chimbu explanation for the first nasal bleeding at initiation is that the boy's body, made of the blood of both mother and father, must be cleansed of mother's blood (personal communication, Father Nilles; see also Nilles 1940: 97). This explanation was substantiated by an aged ritual specialist (Rosman and Rubel 1974: 67, 71). The explanation provided for nasal bleeding before ceremonies subsequent to the initial bleeding at initiation is that bleeding makes the skin shiny and the face bright, so that women will be attracted to men at the dance. The latter explanation is currently used to explain initial blood letting as well.

The separation of women from initiation, the flutes, and the blood letting is only one aspect of the more general separation of men and women. Nilles points out, "The women's sex is considered by men as dangerous. . . . Menstruation blood is regarded as highly infectious to men but not to women" (Nilles 1950–51: 48). Menstruating women can, by stepping over something, defile it. At any social event, men and women always form separate groups.

Death is another important occasion for exchange and distribution with affines. When a man dies, his mother's brother, mother's brother's son, or other members of the matrilateral group receive payment from the deceased's agnates. When a married woman dies, her husband's group pays her agnatic group. During the first stage of the proceedings, immediately after the body has been buried, the close agnates of the deceased, the bereaved, receive groups of visitors. Representatives arrive as groups from other sections in the subclan, other subclans, and other clans or even tribes. The visitors bring gifts for the bereaved—valuables including shells, axes, knives, and money; sugar cane, bananas, and finally sweet potatoes to be used later in feeding the guests. "The names of the recipients of valuables and bags of sweet potatoes are called out, and they are privately told the identity of the individual donors" (Brown 1961: 80). At the same time, the bereaved agnates are also receiving live pigs from the matrilateral kin of the deceased.

The next stage in the death ceremonies involves the pooling and display of valuables and food received by the bereaved agnates. Many piles of food are made since every group present will receive at least one bundle of sugar cane and bananas. After speeches by the leaders of the bereaved group and the guests, the distribution takes place (Brown 1961: 81). The visitors then depart with their food and valuables.

Several days later, a distribution of pork takes place. As many as forty pigs may be killed and cooked. This takes place, if the number of pigs is large, on the ceremonial ground. Some of the pigs killed are those brought by matrilateral kin earlier; some are the deceased's. But most of the pigs have been donated by members of the deceased's subclan. Each donor takes charge of the cooking and distribution of the pig he has donated. Individuals from the deceased's matrilateral kin who brought pigs earlier as well as the individuals who contributed valuables and the men who carried the corpse to the cemetery must be paid in pork. Subclan leaders decide upon the recipients, and the amounts each group and each individual will receive. Prominent men act as recipients for groups. At the same time as subclan obligations are being fulfilled, individual donors of pork are discharging their obligations by repaying personal debts. Several months later, after the ghost of the deceased has left, there is a final distribution of pork to remove the widow's mourning. The close agnates of the deceased repay with their own pork the members of their own clan for the pigs and the valuables which they have contributed. At funerals of less important people, the events are telescoped, the scale is smaller, and distributions are only in terms of groups, with no individuals being singled out (Brown 1961: 84).

According to Brown, "The Chimbu say that the payment by the agnates of the deceased to his kin is the true purpose of the death observances, and that this is a formal requirement for all deaths. There is an additional sanction requiring payment to the kin of the dead person: if kin harbour a grievance they can supernaturally injure the survivors" (Brown 1961: 89). Though Brown emphasizes that the death payment goes to those who have nurtured the deceased in his childhood, she, in several other instances, stresses death payments as part of the continuing series of affinal payments. We have taken the latter perspective in our analysis of exchanges at death. It is more consistent with the sequence of exchanges through the life cycle, and further, the explanation of the payment in terms of nurturing seems inconsistent with the fact that the nurturing is done typically not by the matrilateral kin but rather by the virilocal nuclear family. In fact, the death of the last male offspring ends the exchanges begun by his mother's marriage. However, exchanges between the subclans will continue because there usually are other marriages between the groups in keeping with the ideal of ongoing exchange of women between groups.

Examination of the various exchanges connected with a death will show that the groups on the various levels of the segmentary system are defined and bounded by the exchanges. In the first event, the subclan section of the bereaved, as a group, receive visitors. The first to arrive is the other subclan section of their own subclan. They bring valuables and by their giving indicate their separateness. By the time other guests arrive the two subclan sections are seated together and a joint offering of valuables representing the subclan of the bereaved is evident. Though the major role of organization is in the hands of the subclan, the prestige derived goes to the clan. "Indeed death payments are one of the few opportunities to build clan reputation" (Brown 1961: 94). The subclan section of the bereaved are the receivers at this point. They receive live pigs, the giving of which sets off the matrilateral kin of the deceased. In the next stage, the be-reaved are distributing. Here the distribution is on behalf of the clan, and a leading man of the clan speaks on this occasion. The matrilateral kin are separated from other groups at this point by the receipt of valuables and large amounts of food destined for them which are placed at the head of the column. The receivers in this instance are not the individuals from the entire clan of the mother of the deceased, but rather the individuals in her subclan section which, as it will be remembered, is the unit into which the deceased could not marry. The remaining piles of food are given to the rest of those present who represent groups agnatically related to the deceased and his group. In the final distribution, pigs are donated primarily by the subclan of the deceased and the pork is distributed to matrilateral kin. When the mourning taboos are removed, members of the agnatic clan are given pork. In the distributions, Big Men appear to be the receivers (Brown 1961: 83). At the same time that groups are giving and receiving, the individuals representing those groups are said to be fulfilling their own obligations and repaying debts.

The large-scale vegetable distributions, the *mogena biri*, which are held every few years are "the collaborative affairs of a clan, subtribe or tribe and are presented to another clan, to a subtribe within or outside the tribe or intertribally" (Brown 1970: 104). The exchanges involved take place be-tween the larger-scale segments—clans and tribes. This dis-tribution tends to focus upon pandanus nuts and pandanus oil fruits. Pandanus nuts grow in forests and groves in altitudes above six thousand feet and pandanus oil fruits in lower-altitude gardens. Pandanus nuts come to fruit in large quantities at irregular intervals. If a large nut crop seems to be developing, a large distribution is planned and extra gar-dens for the needed food supplies are planted. Such planning is coordinated on the clan or subtribe level. While the food is being accumulated for the *mogena biri*, neighboring clans may make contributions of food. Such contributions may later be the basis for the giver to be seen as part of the host group (Brown and Brookfield 1959–60: 48). The food accumu-lated for the distribution includes the following items in ad-

dition to a large quantity of pandanus nuts: bananas, sugar
cane, sweet potatoes, taro, yams, other vegetables, chicken,
marsupial, and other items. A distinction is made between
ordinary crops such as sweet potato, and food grown for
feasts such as bananas, sugar cane, and pandanus (Brown
1972: 80). A huge pile, twenty to fifty yards in diameter, is
formed to display all the items. The only indication of where
the ceremonial distribution is held is that when a *mogena biri*
is held between two groups after hostilities have been ended
as a peace gesture it is held near the boundary between
donors and recipients (Brown and Brookfield 1959–60: 49).
"The recipients dance into the enclosure with spears in a
mock battle and the speeches on both sides are boastful and
insulting" (Brown and Brookfield 1959–60: 48). The speeches
also indicate the relations between the two groups (Brown
1972: 47). After the speeches, the pile is taken apart parcel by
parcel and distributed to individuals designated by each
donor. The pile of goods to be distributed represents a
group, either a tribe or a group of clans in a subtribe. The
recipients behave as a group, a subtribe or tribe. The men
who speak on behalf of their group as orators and who give
and receive are prominent or Big Men. In the two examples
provided by Brown and Brookfield, the host and guest tribes
at *mogena biri* are tribes who are neighbors to one another
and who intermarry with one another, as will be recalled
from our discussion of marriage (46 percent of marriages are
with neighboring tribes).

The competitive nature of the *mogena biri* emerges from the
speeches at the ceremony as well as from the need to reciprocate. Brown notes, "*Mogena biri* between tribes should
alternate every few years. A long delay in returning a *mogena
biri* is loudly criticised by the creditor tribe and the debtor
loses in prestige" (Brown 1970: 104). After a war, as compensation to allies or for injury, a distribution like a *mogena biri*
may be made from one group to another. "Such payments
may create or reestablish an intergroup relationship which is
followed by intermarriage" (Brown 1970: 104).

The pig ceremony or *bugla gende* is the largest ceremonial
distribution among the Chimbu, one in which several
thousand pigs are killed. The stated purpose, according to

the Chimbu, is to propitiate the ancestors and by this means to insure the welfare of the group and in particular the multiplication and fertility of their pigs (Brown 1961: 79; 1972: 52–53). Since the spirits of the dead are said to inhabit cemeteries, pigs are always killed there (Brown and Brookfield 1959–60: 47). In addition to the ancestor spirits, the two spirits Gerua and Koa are also involved in the *bugla gende*. Koa as represented by the bamboo flutes are the immaterial embodiment of the patrilineal group. The blowing of the Koa announce that a *bugla gende* will be held. The Gerua and the small decorated board which represents him are directly connected to the fertility of humans and pigs. The sacrificial killings of pigs on the burial ground and the making of the Gerua boards is done to propitiate both the ancestors and Gerua Spirit. This rite is an integral part of the *bugla gende* (Nilles 1950–51: 60). The *bugla gende* takes place at large ceremonial grounds, which adjoin cemeteries (Brown 1972: 49). Each tribe has several ceremonial grounds (*bugla yungu*).

The pig ceremonial is a tribal occasion. Several tribes may hold a pig ceremony more or less simultaneously; however, the coordination of activities occurs within a tribe. The final killing of pigs occurs on the same day at the various ceremonial grounds belonging to a single tribe (Rosman and Rubel 1974: 12). The ceremonial grounds are divided into sections where each subclan, or occasionally a subclan section, will build its men's house or Gerua house and several associated long houses for families and visitors. Each ceremonial ground is thus transformed into a temporary village, which is occupied by hosts and guests during the course of the pig ceremony.

Each tribe will hold its pig ceremony every six to ten years. This allows time for the herds to be replenished. If a group feels it does not have a sufficient number of pigs it will not join the other tribes of its set and will delay its pig ceremony (Brown 1970: 105). That tribe then remains in debt and loses prestige until it holds its ceremony. "The whole tribe, under the direction of its 'Big Men', must agree that its pigs are large and numerous enough to begin to prepare for a feast" (Brown 1970: 105). A year or two before the actual pig ceremony, a preparatory ceremony is held, normally by a sub-clan, on the ceremonial ground. At this time, the large-scale boy's initiation mentioned earlier takes place and nasal bleeding is induced for the first time. The boys are shown the flutes, which represent the patrilineal ancestors, and the playing of the flutes proclaims that a pig ceremony will be held (Brown 1970: 105; Nilles 1950–51: 41). Nilles indicates that a rite concerning the rapid increase of pigs also takes place (Nilles 1950–51: 41). New gardens to provide food for the guests are now begun.

In another year or two, the ceremonial grounds are cleared. At the ceremonial grounds, the temporary village of Gerua houses and long houses is constructed. After the houses are built, visiting groups of dancers from other ceremonial grounds of the same tribe and from neighboring tribes not hosting a pig ceremony will come to dance at the ceremonial ground. The dancers are decorated with plumes and carved Gerua head boards. The host groups also perform dances with spears at their ceremonial grounds. While the dances continue, the Bolum house, or sacred pig house, is built in the center of the ceremonial ground. Pieces for building the new Bolum house are retrieved from the secret place where they were placed when the Bolum house was dismantled after the last *bugla gende*. A ritual specialist supervises this activity. He has knowledge of magical spells inherited from his father and grandfather which are to induce affines to be generous with valuables to be donated and used as decorations by the hosts at the forthcoming *bugla gende*. He makes the special fire, embers of which are distributed to the people, and which are subsequently used to make fires in the houses of the ceremonial village in order to cook pigs referred to as spirit pigs. This takes place sometime before the final and much larger pig killing. The jaws of the spirit pigs are hung from the Bolum house. The smoke from the special fire "goes everywhere" and is said to bring feathers, shells, and valuables from affines to be used in the *bugla gende*. After the Bolum house is completed, the ritual specialist receives a small portion from every spirit pig killed (Rosman and Rubel 1974: 63–70). The remainder of the meat is distributed mainly within the tribe that is hosting the ceremony. At this point there is a discrepancy between the descriptions of Nilles and Brown. Nilles indicates that the spirit pigs are eaten only by the host group (Nilles 1950–51: 41). In contrast, Brown says that the meat may go to members of one's own subclan or to affines. Marriage payments may be made at this time as well as birth and death payments which have been delayed.

"The climax of the *bugla gende* is a mock attack on the ceremonial ground by male dancers and a fertility ritual which involves blessing sweet potato vines, women and pigs. Pigs are killed in a cemetery (which usually adjoins the ceremonial ground) as a sacrifice to the ancestors. They are then carried into the central ceremonial area and lined up so that each group's pigs can be displayed" (Brown 1972: 49). The lines of pigs radiate like the spokes of a wheel from the Bolum house, which stands at the center of the ceremonial ground. Each line of pigs or spoke represents one Gerua house, which is associated with one or more men's houses. Sometimes the line of pigs represents the several men's houses associated with one subclan. The lines of pigs belonging to particular groups are compared with one another and comparisons are made with recollections of the past performances of these groups. Groups gain and lose prestige by virtue of these comparisons. Within each line, the pigs belonging to the Big Man are at the head of the line closest to the Bolum house. Pigs of lesser Big Men are behind his, followed by the pigs of ordinary men (Rosman and Rubel 1974: 24, 30–33, 35, 96, 115, 120, 125, 129).

Those who are to receive the meat are members of other tribes who are also affines, maternal kin, and exchange partners of the donor. They help to butcher and cook the meat, and each receives a whole pig or half-side of pig. Brown provides a chart in which she lists the relationship, kinship, or friendship to the donors of 132 recipients of pork at several pig feasts (Brown 1964: 346). An analysis of the categories of relationship reveals the following. All the kinship categories are groups related to the donor by various marriages; no recipients are agnatic kinsmen. One category of recipients is termed "friends." Brown states, "It includes descendants of exchange partners who no longer recall the source of their relationship" (Brown 1964: 347). Our own field data are in accord with Brown in that affines, in the same categories as reported by Brown, are the recipients of most of the pork at a *bugla gende*. Friends may receive small pieces in contrast to the receipt of whole cooked pigs or half-sides of pork given to affines. Distributions of pork at the *bugla gende* seem to involve an element of reciprocity. This is supported by informants' statements. Though life-crises payments go only in one direction—to maternal kin—*bugla gende* distributions are reciprocated at a future *bugla gende* when the present recipient serves as host. The recipients of the whole pigs or half-sides of pork return home and distribute their pork among their agnates and affines, who similarly divide their portions and redistribute what they have received. Brookfield and Brown note, "the two or three thousand pigs killed by a large tribe may be consumed by as many as twenty thousand people" (Brookfield and Brown 1963: 63–64).

When one tribe holds a *bugla gende* the visitors who come to receive pork are the affines of the people in that tribe. Since most of the marriages not within the same tribe are with neighboring tribes, the people from those tribes come as guests to dance, to act as witnesses to the prestige of the hosts, and to receive pork. Neighboring tribes may compete and engage in warfare with one another, and affines from these tribes may have been recent enemies or may be enemies in the future. For example, the history of the relationship between the Kamaneku and Naregu tribes indicates that fighting and enmity alternated with intermarriage and attendance at one another's *bugla gende*. The *bugla gende*, like all ceremonial occasions, links groups in exchange but has the potentiality for the outbreak of hostilities. In fact, reports of outbreaks of fighting at *bugla gende* are not infrequent.

In addition to neighboring tribes that come en masse, individual affines from more remote tribes also attend the *bugla gende*. Where there are no current marriages with another Chimbu tribe, usually there will be no guests to represent that tribe. If marriages have taken place beyond the linguistic borders of Chimbu, with Banz or Minj, peoples of the Middle Wahgi, for example, these people will be in attendance at the *bugla gende*. Each Chimbu tribe invites to its *bugla gende* those tribes with which it has more dense affinal connections. These tribes are neighboring tribes, although not all neighboring tribes exchange women in this way.

Tribes that are contiguous will have slightly different circles of affinal connection with other tribes, and the guests attending their *bugla gende* will be different. At the regional level, one sees a series of overlapping circles, the centers of which are the tribes hosting their *bugla gende*. As noted above, each tribe holds the *bugla gende* roughly every six to ten years. An examination of the *bugla gende* on the regional level reveals that the various Chimbu tribes hold their *bugla gende* in a particular sequence. This diachronic sequence of *bugla gende* serves to integrate many contiguous groups through a series of circles of overlapping relationship. Groups which live in the center of the Chimbu linguistic area will have infrequent affinal connections beyond the Chimbu boundaries and therefore infrequent *bugla gende* relationships. Chimbu tribes at the periphery of the Chimbu area will have regular relationships with tribes beyond the Chimbu area and will invite them as groups to their *bugla gende* and likewise attend their pig ceremonies. Such relationships exist, for example, between Chimbu tribes and Sinasina, and Bomai.

Exchange partners are not a named category among the Chimbu, although Brown uses the term on numerous occasions. Brown refers to affinal and matrilateral kin who give to and receive from one another on various occasions as exchange partners. As we noted in the discussion of Big Men, a son takes over the exchange relationships of his father. It is apparent that what begins as an affinal relationship may continue as an exchange relationship handed down from father to son after the precise connection is forgotten. At a marriage ceremony individuals from the groups to be connected by the marriage who are not close relatives of the bride and groom may, by the exchange of goods, establish an exchange partnership (Brown 1969: 88–89).

Most of the valuables involved in the Chimbu exchanges—shells, plumes, and stone axes—come from outside the Chimbu area. They are traded for pigs, which are provided by the Chimbu. These non-Chimbu groups also exchange some women with neighboring Chimbu clans. Brown notes, "On the Wahgi-Sepik divide Chimbu have trade and marriage ties with the non-Chimbu peoples which bring valuables into the Chimbu area" (Brown 1970: 109). Travel in distant areas is fraught with danger; hence people travel only where there are friendly hosts—affines and exchange partners. Big Men have friends and exchange partners, perhaps developed through distant kinship and affinal ties, in far-off places, and transactions with them bring into Chimbu the shells, plumes, and other objects which form a most important part of the exchange system (Brown 1970: 112).

Among the Chimbu, not only do exchanges end hostility and cement alliances, but exchanges may be the cause of hostilities. We indicated earlier that a *mogena biri* type of distribution may be a peace gesture to end hostilities. This occurs only in the case of intratribal hostilities. In a table listing some causes of warfare among the Chimbu, Brown includes "pork debt, inadequate repayment." Elsewhere, attempts to secure return of a marriage payment after the wife has left and inadequate payments in exchange are listed as causes of fighting (Brown and Brookfield 1959–60: 40; Brookfield and Brown 1963: 79).

The segmentary structure of the Chimbu resembles that of the Kuma, except that the Chimbu have tribes, which are military alliances of clans not related by agnatic descent. Chimbu marriage prohibitions are more extensive than those of the Kuma. In addition to all first cousins, marriage is also prohibited with women of mother's subclan section, and father's mother's group up to two generations back. When a man dies, his mother's subclan section receives the payment of death dues in the form of valuables. The grandson of the deceased can renew the marriage tie with his father's father's mother's clan. Exchange of women between groups over generations is emphasized, though not as much as among the Kuma. The absence of a preferential marriage rule among the Chimbu means that there is no system of regular transgenerational ties through the exchange of women. However, there is continued intermarriage between neighboring clans and tribes, with whom there may also be conflict. These groups remember and keep an account of the state of the exchange of women.

Big Men act on behalf of their groups in exchanges, giving the goods and making speeches, as well as directing the action. The most important Big Men speak for groups of largest magnitude. There is no indication that leadership positions are inherited, in contrast to the Kuma. The important ritual role of the Kuma leader is not discussed for the Chimbu. Ritual specialists, whose knowledge of magic is inherited, do play a role in the Chimbu *bugla gende*.

The Chimbu have a large-scale vegetable distribution, the *mogena biri*, which is identical to the Kuma *wubalt*. It is competitive, given by a clan or tribe to its neighboring clan or tribe, and it must be reciprocated. Thus the ceremony has a two-sided organization. In both the *mogena biri* and the *wubalt*—in addition to pandanus nuts—sugar cane and bananas, which are male crops, are distributed.

The overall organization of the Chimbu *bugla gende* is identical to the Kuma *konggol,* though the ceremonies differ on a number of specific points. Initiation of boys among the Chimbu is held as part of a preparatory ceremony of the *bugla gende,* in conjunction with a rite to bring about the rapid increase of pigs. In contrast, Kuma initiation is held at the end of the *konggol.* Initiation of boys in both societies involves showing them the flutes and inducing bleeding of the nasal septum.

In both the Chimbu and the Kuma, a Bolum house is built which is associated with the entire group holding the pig festival at a ceremonial ground, while separate Gerua houses are built for each subclan. No information is provided about the symbolism of the Bolum spirit among the Chimbu, to enable comparison with Bolim among the Kuma, or the red spirits of Maring-Manga. The Geru spirit is associated with the fertility of both humans and pigs, while among the Kuma Geru is associated solely with fertility of pigs. In both Chimbu and Kuma pig festivals, the carcasses of pigs are displayed at the final distribution like the spokes of a wheel radiating out from the central hub, which is the Bolum house. The pigs forming a single spoke stand for the men occupying the Gerua house at the end of the spoke. The final distribution of cooked pork is somewhat different in that the Kuma throw the pork from the rooftop, while the Chimbu do not.

Among the Chimbu, the men of a tribe marry the women of surrounding tribes, with whom they may also have hostile relations. These are the people with whom they exchange ceremonial goods and pigs, and whom they invite to their *bugla gende*. There is no category of traditional enemies as among the Kuma. The sequencing of pig festivals noted for the Kuma is also present in Chimbu. Thus over a period of years one tribe after another in a general sequence holds its pig festival. The hosts at one pig festival will be guests at a number of other festivals in subsequent years. In both Chimbu and Kuma, this sequencing process serves to integrate a region. However, the region does not have sharp boundaries since Chimbu tribes on the boundaries of the linguistic area will include non-Chimbu tribes in their circle of relationships and exchanges. These tribes, who have ceremonies similar to the *bugla gende*, reciprocate by inviting their Chimbu affines to their pig ceremonies.

10 Melpa

The term Melpa refers to the several groups of people inhabiting the valleys around Mount Hagen in the western Highlands of New Guinea. These peoples speak Melpa and a closely related language, Gawigl. They have been variously referred to as Melpa, Mbowamb, or Hageners. In this chapter we will be drawing upon the works of the Stratherns, Vicedom and Tischner, Ross, Gitlow, and Strauss.

The settlement pattern is one of dispersed homesteads or hamlets. Homesteads may be made up of nuclear or polygynous families. The larger agglomerations of homesteads represent the families of agnatically related males (A. J. Strathern 1972a: 60–61). Though families may occupy a single house with separate rooms for males and females, more typically men sleep together in men's houses and each wife sleeps with her children and the pigs in a separate house. In larger settlements, the men's house is centrally located near the ceremonial ground and the women's houses are dispersed, located closer to gardening and grazing areas.

The residential separation of men and women is related to ideas about the polluting influence of women. As Strathern notes, "It is safer to have intercourse with a wife during the day, when her condition (menstrual or not) can be more readily ascertained, and at night to sleep separately from her along with one's kinsmen in the men's house" (A. M. Strathern 1972: 241, n. 4). In addition to the pollution of menstruating women, who must be secluded from men, the polluting influence of women extends to the act of intercourse itself. Frequent intercourse is considered harmful to men (A. M. Strathern 1972: 164). There is a taboo on sexual intercourse for men engaged in certain kinds of activities, such as making ceremonial wigs, making shields and spears, preparing to decorate for a dance before hunting, trapping fish, and making a new garden. Sexual intercourse is tabooed during the lactation period, two and one-half to three years, "lest the milk become contaminated with semen and destroy rather than nourish" (A. M. Strathern 1972: 168). This directly parallels the Melpa belief that mothers protect, while wives are dangerous (A. M. Strathern 1972: 172). For this reason milk, which represents the nurturant mother, must be kept separate from semen, which represents the copulating wife. Women are also seen as potentially dangerous because of the threat of their poisoning the food they prepare for their husbands. Wives, who always come from other groups, frequently minor enemy groups, must prepare food for their husbands, thus providing nourishment while at the same time being potentially dangerous poisoners. It is interesting to note that "sexual intercourse is also 'food' " (A. M. Strathern 1972: 167). The polluting influence of women is so strong that if a woman steps over the feathers being prepared for a dance, they are said to lose their brightness (Strathern and Strathern 1971: 28).

There is a sexual division of labor and the growing of particular crops is associated with either males or females. Men plant bananas, sugarcane, xanthosoma taro, and certain other vegetables, while women plant sweet potatoes, maize, most types of green vegetables, yams, and colocasia taro (Gitlow 1947: 64; A. M. Strathern 1972: 21). Men perform the heavier tasks associated with gardening such as clearing, fencing, and ditching, while the women do the planting, tending, and harvesting of the crops with which they are associated.

The husband and wife have mutual responsibilities for the production and provisioning of food and this serves to demarcate the nuclear family as an entity (A. M. Strathern 1972: 41). Men and boys may eat the food with the women, or it is sent by the latter to the men's house. Polygynous wives each provide meals for their husband and they may do this in rotation.

The Melpa have a segmentary structure with several levels of segmentation, including tribe pair, tribe, tribe section, clan pair, clan, clan section, subclan, sub-subclan, and lineage (A. J. Strathern 1972a: 9). There are two terms that may be used for groupings at any level of segmentation—*reklaep*, which means "row," and *tepam tenda*, meaning "one father." Several alternative ways exist by means of which the Melpa conceptualize the nature of the groups in the segmentary structure, group membership, and the relationships between groups. The descent idiom is used to express the continuity of relationship between group and territory over time and the links between groups which are phrased in terms of descent from a common ancestor. A second idiom refers to groups as "gardens" and the membership of individuals in such groups in terms of their being "planted and taking root." Still another idiom used by the Melpa refers to the units that operate in exchange as "men's house groups." These units revolve around Big Men who, by drawing to themselves groups of followers, create new units within the segmentary structure (A. M. Strathern 1972: 28; A. J. Strathern 1972a: 51). When these new units do not fit the descent idiom, the Melpa do not feel compelled to manipulate genealogies to bring about consistency.

The groupings at the different levels of segmentation differ in the activities and functions which they perform. The minimal unit is a lineage. "At any given time lineage mates are likely to live close to each other and to cooperate closely in garden work. . . .Lineage mates are the first to have a claim on garden lands" (A. J. Strathern 1971a: 28).

The lineage is conceptualized as a group of descendants of a named apical ancestor two generations back, referred to as a "father-son" group, or the "sons of" the named ancestor. According to the figures presented by Strathern, approxi-

mately one-third of the male population resides with nonagnates (A. J. Strathern 1972a: 104). Most of these men are
sisters' sons who have been incorporated into the lineages
from which their mothers came. Sisters' sons must be ac-
cepted if they should desire to join their mother's group.
They are considered as "planted" rather than "replanted"
men, since they have a "definite potential claim to the land"
(A. J. Strathern 1972a: 20). Though the lineage is described as
"one semen" group, an alternative categorization, *mema
tenda*, meaning one blood group, recognizes the presence of
cognates in the lineage group (A. J. Strathern 1971a: 34). In
addition to sisters' sons, a small percentage of husbands reside uxorilocally, if the wife's lineage mates agree to give the
husband land. The children of such a marriage may choose to
remain with matrilateral kin as "sisters' sons" or to return to
their own agnatic group. The choice is theirs. The lineage
may be identical to the sub-subclan or "small men's house"
which operates as a separate subdivision in ceremonial exchange in the receipt and consumption of pork.
Alternatively, this subdivision may be created merely for the
purpose of obtaining separate shares of ceremonial gifts for
each segment (A. J. Strathern 1971a: 26). The sub-subclan or
"small men's house," the group involved in ceremonial exchange, is not conceptualized in a descent idiom but in the
idiom of "men's house groups."

Above the sub-subclan is the level of the subclan or "one
men's house group." The men of the subclan may not live in
the same house but meet in a single men's house, which is
associated with a ceremonial ground, to discuss ceremonial
exchanges. Subclans of two different clans may make moka
exchanges with each other independent of other subclans in
their clans. Subclans of the same clan may exchange pork
based on reciprocal payments for mourning service (A. J.
Strathern 1971a: 26). Though outsiders may not know the
names of lineages or sub-subclans, they do know the subclan
names since these units operate in external exchange. If the
subclan is conceived of in descent terms, it is seen as made
up of the descendants of one of the wives of the polygynous
clan ancestor.

The next more inclusive unit is the clan. A clan usually

occupies a single territory and fights as a unit to defend that territory. Ideally, there should be no lethal fighting within the clan. The clan is the exogamous unit. Men of a clan organize moka exchanges as a group. There is a clan cemetery that is the location for sacrifices made to clan ancestral spirits. Clansmen are obliged to take blood revenge and must contribute to compensation paid to allies for men lost in warfare on their behalf. The clan operates as a unit at cult performances and dances as a unit at festivals. Clans stand toward one another as major or perpetual enemies or as minor enemies who can become allies. The clan will also have a major ceremonial ground (Vicedom and Tischner 1943–48: 2:9–10). In terms of descent dogma, "The clan is spoken of emphatically as *tepam tenda* = '(founded by a) single father', and this dogma is referred to as the basis for rules of exogamy, and cooperation in warfare and ceremonial exchange" (A. J. Strathern 1971a: 33).

Subclans that grow in size and begin to assume clan functions are referred to by the Stratherns as clan sections. There is no Melpa term for this type of unit. Men of two clan sections may marry each other's sister's daughters. (Reay reports the same procedure for the Kuma, stating that when two men in the same clan are turned into affines, this signifies that the lines of fission are becoming more pronounced.)

At the next highest level, clans may be grouped into tribal sections. A tribal section of several clans may constitute itself as a single exogamic unit, in which case there is usually no internal warfare. However, clans within a section may war against one another. Tribal sections are descended from the sons of the founder of the tribe.

The tribe as a unit is conceptualized as descended from a single founder who first appeared in a particular place. The origin myth of the tribe describes this appearance. The tribe may have its own ceremonial ground and is associated with a particular divination substance (*mi*), which is used by all its members. Tribes may be joined in pairs that are usually allied. Pairing may occur at any level, from the sub-subclan up to the tribe. Its presence indicates a special linkage between two groups. Above the clan level, this pairing is characterized by intermarriage and a tendency to assist one another in warfare. The competition between the paired clans or tribes fits the pattern of minor enemy relations as well (A. J. Strathern 1972a: 223). Tribes may be combined into a great tribe that links tribes in terms of a myth of common origin or association with a single mystical divination object.

The segmentary structure of the Melpa as described above consists of an elaborate series of hierarchical levels. Positions of leadership exist, but they do not have a one-to-one relationship to the levels of the segmentary structure. From an analysis of the material, it would appear that Big Men may act as leaders on behalf of groups up to and including the clan and perhaps even the tribe (A. J. Strathern 1966: 358; 1970a: 572–74). Strathern identifies major and minor Big Men as well as ordinary men and men of low status or "rubbish men." There is general agreement among the Melpa as to who the major Big Men are, and they tend to represent the higher level segments, such as clans. There is less agreement among Melpa on minor Big Men (A. J. Strathern 1971a: 140).

The position of Big Man does not involve a formal rule of succession. The characteristics required of Big Men are skill in oratory and the entreprenurial ability to manage exchanges successfully. In the absence of any rule of succession, it might appear that anyone with these characteristics may succeed in raising his status to that of a Big Man. This is in fact not the case. Strathern notes, "Major big men certainly do place value on the idea that at least one of their sons should take their place—the Melpa phrase is *kokl ile mukli* 'to be in the place where the father's house was before' " (A. J. Strathern 1971a: 212). Further, his analysis of statistics on Big Men indicates that of thirty-six major Big Men, the fathers of twenty-seven were also Big Men. In the case of minor Big Men, thirty-one out of sixty-one had fathers who are Big Men. Fathers who are Big Men may assist their sons to become Big Men in a number of ways (see Vicedom and Tischner 1943–48: 2:59). The father will give his son pigs as well as other valuables to launch him in moka exchanges. When the Big Man dies, his son will move into a certain number of his father's exchange partnerships, particularly the most important ones (A. J. Strathern 1971a: 211). If a sister's son has been raised by his mother's brother who is himself a Big Man, the sister's son may sometimes become a Big Man with the assistance of his mother's brother. In such a situation, a nonagnate has become the Big Man of the group (A. J. Strathern 1972a: 212).

All of the activities of major Big Men as leaders are concerned with their role in intergroup relations. "Symbolically, the big man, as 'head' of his clan, concentrates and holds together the strength of the clan" (A. J. Strathern 1971a: 190). Big Men are distinct from violent men as a type; the role they play in warfare is as planners, organizers, and orators who exhort their fellow clansmen, rather than as feared warriors. Their skills as orators can also enable them to influence others in the direction of peace. In the latter instance, they have the means to obtain the goods necessary for the payment of compensation to bring about the cessation of hostilities. Big Men may also act as mediators between other groups. Big Men stand in a pivotal position in the moka relations between clans. The Big Man of the clan prays on behalf of the clan to its ancestors on public occasions. The prayers concern requests for success in warfare and ceremonial exchanges. The Big Man holds the ropes of the pigs to be sacrificed on such an occasion. Big Men are involved in the organization of cult activity as well as the spread of some spirit cults.

Big Men may be distinguished from ordinary men in a number of ways. They have more wives, control more valuables, and own more pigs than ordinary men. Big Men, in Melpa eyes, are associated with their own ceremonial grounds (A. J. Strathern 1971a: 195). The most important Big Man has his pigs placed at the head of the ceremonial ground and "this is a mark that he is *wuɔ nyam mumuk,* 'a big man who holds the head of the moka' " (A. J. Strathern 1972a: 160). There are a number of status symbols which Big Men wear to record participation in moka. The length of the *omak* ornament indicates the number of sets of shells he has given away. The death of a Big Man is the occasion for special funeral rites. A "head house" is erected as a shrine to contain his exhumed head (A. J. Strathern 1971a: 189–92). The ghosts of Big Men become guardians of clan morality.

The Big Man is at the center of a circle of helpers, followers, and supporters. Young bachelors may attach themselves to a Big Man in hopes of obtaining bride wealth from him. Such help may or may not materialize, but in the interim they help him with labor, and his wives take care of their pigs, and feed the unmarried men. These men may be sisters' sons. Such men may get land and a wife and settle down after marriage in the Big Man's settlement and become his supporters. The Big Man's other supporters, adult men with wives, will come from his own agnatic group. There may be competition between major Big Men of a clan. They maneuver over the timing and location of the moka exchange so that each can extract the maximum prestige from the event.

The Melpa combine the use of marriage as alliance with an extensive series of marriage prohibitions. There are two marriage rules, both of which involve marriage prohibitions. Persons who share blood cognatically may not marry. This prohibition is in force for the three or four generations that the tie through blood is remembered. The prohibition also extends to individuals on the basis of the application of the kinship terminology (Strathern and Strathern 1969: 143). The second prohibition relates to marriages between *rapa* or "man's house groups." "Once, depending on context, a clan's or subclan's lower level units (sub-subclans, lineages) have each made a marriage with those of another subclan, no further unions can be contracted between the two groups" (A. M. Strathern 1972: 80). There is an earlier version of this prohibition which states, "*rapa* (sub-subclan or subclan) groups linked directly or indirectly by a remembered marriage may not contract further marriages" (Strathern and Strathern 1969: 140–41). This would seem to imply that a *rapa* of one clan can contract only a single marriage with each *rapa* of another clan. M. Strathern observes, "Marriages create the 'roads' (*nombokla mon*) which give an individual important connections with groups other than his own. . . . These are the roads pursued in making *moka*, attending feasts, visiting friends or collecting bridewealth. But once a marriage has established a road, further unions between those already closely linked by it are not possible" (A. M. Strathern 1972: 65).

The Stratherns reiterate at several points that sister exchange is not permitted (A. M. Strathern 1972: 65, 80; Strathern and Strathern 1969: 141). However, Vicedom notes that when a Ndika man marries a Mokae girl, then the Mokae marry a sister of the man who has gotten a woman, if he has one (Vicedom and Tischner 1943–48: 2:201). The Stratherns neither present nor discuss the information presented by Vicedom and Tischner on this point. If sister in the Vicedom data means clan sister, then there is no contradiction. The Stratherns and Vicedom and Tischner both stress the importance of the exchange of women between the larger entities of the segmentary system, such as clans. Clans that exchange women are never in the relationship of traditional enemies to one another. They are either allies or in a relationship of minor enemies to one another. Given the prohibition on sister exchange, when a woman is given in marriage by one *rapa* to a *rapa* in another clan, the return is made to a different *rapa* than the one that gave the woman. "The lower-level segments actually arrange marriages, but it is the clans that are said to exchange women" (Strathern and Strathern 1969: 156). Informants state that the exchange of women between clans is advantageous in maintaining the peace between them. Other men's sisters who come as wives can be the carriers of poison, but if one sends one's own classificatory sisters back to their group then this danger is neutralized. There is a native term that "refers to the way a reciprocating marriage retraces (literally, 'harvests') the footsteps taken at the first transaction" (A. M. Strathern 1972: 73). The Stratherns indicate that "there are no precisely reckoned debts in women existing between clans" (Strathern and Strathern 1969: 156). It would appear, however, that informants do keep track of numbers of women going back and forth. "A Hagener may enumerate the total number of women who have passed between two groups and add the balance of wives *not* exchanged for. Thus: 'We have sent them two and they sent us six' " (A. M. Strathern 1972: 75). The awareness of imbalance relates to the notion of superiority since the group that takes more wives from the other group gains in prestige. It seems quite clear that the notion of transgenerational alliance of two clans through intermarriage is important. It is advantageous when alliances are beginning for more than one marriage to be contracted within a generation, and women who marry into distant clans are anxious that other of their clanswomen shall also make marriages into their affinal clan. (A. J. Strathern 1972a: 132, 176). If the intensity of intermarriage becomes too high, then the two clans will cease intermarriage and henceforth regard each other as "brothers" who do not exchange women.

The data on the kinship terminology come from Vicedom and Tischner and Marilyn Strathern's work on women among the Melpa. In the latter instance, it is from the female point of view only. It is an Iroquois terminology with reference to the terms on the first ascending generation and the cousin terminology. Cross-cousin terms on both sides are identical and are distinct from those for parallel cousins, for whom sibling terms are used.

The structure of exchanges recapitulates the patterns of relationship through marriage between larger and smaller entities in the social structure we have described above. The larger units are involved in continuing moka exchange relationship, while smaller-scale units like lineages and sub-subclans tend to be involved in cycles of affinal relationship which commence with a marriage and end with the death of the offspring of that marriage.

The first marriage for boy or girl is usually arranged by the elders on both sides. After the preliminary agreement of both sides, the first stage in the bride-wealth transactions takes place. This is the solicitory gift of pearl shell and cooked meat which is carried by the girl, accompanied by her kin, to the boy's house and is intended to show good will. The meat is intended for those members of the boy's side who will contribute to the bride wealth in order to encourage their largesse. The pearl shell goes to the groom's father and a matching shell should later be returned as part of the bride wealth.

The next stage involves the public display of the bride wealth, consisting of shells, pigs, and money, to lineage mates and clansmen as well as to maternal relatives on both sides. The father of the boy, or the man who is in locus parenti to the boy as his sponsor, and close lineage mates contribute to the bride wealth. At a first marriage, the groom makes little or no contribution to the bride wealth. In acquiring additional wives, the groom himself provides the bulk of the bride-wealth contribution. At the public display, the bride's father will allocate portions of the bride wealth to agnates of the bride and to her maternal relatives, such as mother's brother, who have given the bride shells that she has worn. The relatives then leave with the portions of the bride wealth they have received.

Subsequent to this, the groom's kin kill and cook a number of pigs and carry the pork to the bride's father's house. The bride wealth is reassembled and again displayed, including what is to be returned. The groom's group takes the items given as a return and departs with the bride. The cooked meat the groom's group has brought is then divided among a wide range of the bride's kin. The sequence of giving pork on the part of the groom's kin (known as *mangal kng*) and return of pigs on the part of the bride's kin is repeated. Later, the bride receives a gift of several breeding pigs from her parents which she cares for. This becomes the basis of her husband's pig herd. Future gifts of pork (which come under the rubric of bride wealth) may be sent from the husband and his lineage brothers to their new affines in the next few months.

After the birth of a child, a payment is made that follows the same direction, from father of the child to maternal relatives of the child. This payment is made to "redeem" the child. The mother's brother of the child is also called upon to name it (Ross 1936: 359). Payments continue to be made in the same direction. There is the payment for mother's milk, payment when the child is weaned and when its hair is first cut. "Gifts to maternal kin continue when a person grows up, and a man takes them on himself, continuing his father's earlier payment on his behalf. Such gifts are called *mam-nga pulk kaklp ngond* 'I straighten my mother's root and give' " (A. J. Strathern 1971a: 93). These gifts are said to insure the goodwill of the maternal kin so that they will not send sickness and maternal ghosts will not harm the sister's son.

Generosity in the payment of bride wealth is also said to insure the health of future children of the marriage in the same way. There are now no initiation rites among the Melpa, though Vicedom and Tischner indicate that they were practiced in the past (Vicedom and Tischner 1943–48: 2:184–85).

The death payments, *kik kapa,* which are made to maternal kin "are in effect the final stage of *mam-nga pukl* payments" (A. J. Strathern 1971a: 93). There are several phases involved in the funerary rites. The body is first taken to the men's house, then publicly displayed and mourned while visitors come with food gifts for the mourners. The maternal kin may bring a small pig at this time. Then the body is buried. Several days later some pigs are killed and the visitors depart. The final stage, which marks the end of the mourning period, occurs several weeks or months afterward. At this point, a large number of pigs are killed and a feast is held. The visitors at the mourning, those who buried the corpse or reported the death, are now repaid. The death payments to maternal kin are made at this time, if they have not already been paid. If they did not attend the mourning rites, they do not receive death payments. Most of the deceased's pigs are killed for this funeral feast. Prior to the final feast, the deceased's head has been exhumed and placed in a "small ghost men's house" or "head house" if he was a Big Man. At the public mourning and the death feasts, guests are seated by clans (Vicedom and Tischner 1943–48: 5.2: 287, 295). If a child has died after the father of the child has made payments to the child's maternal relatives, the father may refuse to make *kik kapa* payments to the child's maternal relatives because they have not protected the child. The death payments for males and females seem to reflect a different kind of incorporation into kin groups; however, they are based on one general premise. For males, the bride wealth given for their mothers begins the payments to affines which, seeking to maintain their goodwill as protection against harmful supernatural forces, is continued until the male child of that marriage dies. For females, the marriage of their mothers sets up the relationship with affines which continues through the childhood of the girl but ceases with the marriage of that girl.

At her marriage, she joins her husband. If she dies after this point, death payment goes not to her maternal relatives but to her agnates, the affines of her husband. If she resides with her natal group, then her husband's group, as affines, receive the death payment. When an old lady whose ties with her own kin are cold, dies, the affines who receive are her daughter's husbands.

The Melpa have a vegetable distribution which is not described in detail. There is sometimes a First Fruits ceremony after the harvest of bananas, taro, yams and greens at which these vegetables are given from one clan to another (A. J. Strathern 1971a: 113; A. M. Strathern 1972: 29).

The major ceremonial exchange among the Melpa is the moka. Moka exchange is competitive and rivalrous and in that sense resembles warfare. The theme of fertility is not present in any aspect of the moka. The resemblance between moka and warfare may be seen in the similarity of decorations (Strathern and Strathern 1971: 105). Before embarking upon warfare or holding a moka exchange ceremony, a sacrifice of pigs will be made to the clan ancestors at the clan cemetery ". . . asking for success in warfare and ceremonial exchange" (A. J. Strathern 1970a: 573). When the sacrifice precedes warfare, the meat is eaten only by men of the warrior group (Strathern and Strathern 1971: 104). Before a moka ceremony, women are absent and the meat is given to affines who have lent decorations to the host group (Strathern and Strathern 1971: 132).

Strathern states that the Melpa use the term moka in two ways: "first, as a general word for the whole complex of their ceremonial exchange system apart from bridewealth [and a few other types of payments which I list below—payments to maternal kin]; and second more specifically to refer to all ceremonial gifts in which one partner makes a presentation which is greater in value than the simple debt which he owes. It is strictly this increment in excess of debt which is the moka element in the gift and which brings prestige to the giver" (A. J. Strathern 1971a: 93). In the first stage, one moka partner gives an initiatory gift. Six months to two years later a return is made in the second stage, with a main gift that is ideally four times larger than the initiatory gift (A. J. Strathern 1971a: 97). The person who gives the main gift is said to be "making moka" because he has given more to his partner than he himself has received. In the ongoing structure of moka partnerships, in the next sequence of exchanges, the giver of the main gift now begins by giving a solicitory gift that is returned by a much larger main gift. In the second sequence, the other partner now has a chance to "make moka."

There is an inherent element of competition in the moka exchange. One aspect of the competition is between the partners in the exchange. A man making moka will try to give an amount that will exceed the amount of the main moka prestation between the same partners on a previous occasion. There is also competition between groups, which will be discussed below.

Strathern defines two types of moka transactions on the basis of the kind of object being exchanged. Shell moka involves an initiatory gift of two pearl shells of unequal size plus a pig. The main gift returned is a unit of eight to ten pearl shells. The second type, pig moka, consists of an initiatory gift of cooked pork or pigs for which the return is a main gift of cooked pork or live pigs (A. J. Strathern 1971a: 97). Making shell moka entitles one to add a slat to his *omok*, while making moka with pigs does not. The *omok* is a standard symbol worn around the neck. The length of the series of slats of the *omok* indicates the number of times the wearer has made shell moka, and is a measure of his prestige. A moka prestation may involve the distribution of both pigs and shell.

The linkage between shell moka and the *omok* slats would seem to relate to the earlier scarcity of shells and the monopoly of trade routes by Big Men. (A. J. Strathern 1971a: 236). To acquire shells, one had to have outside trade partners and to be able to provide pigs in exchange. Men who were able to do this in the earlier period became Big Men and monopolized the symbols of prestige, the *omok*.

The sequence of events in a large-scale ceremonial moka exchange between groups is as follows: the first stage involves the presentation by one group of initiatory gifts of shells, pigs, and legs of pork to their exchange partners in another group. These gifts can be given privately or publicly. The recipients of the initiatory gifts begin to discuss the amount of shells and the number of pigs which they are planning to give. They set up stakes for the number of pigs they intend to give on their ceremonial ground. At this stage the Big Man, leader of the men at a ceremonial ground, will urge groupmates not to hold back their pigs. The next stage is the showing of the gifts by the donor group on the ceremonial ground. After the live pigs are lined up and tied to stakes, and the shells are arranged in the special shell display-house, the Big Men of the donor group step forward "and make formal speeches, explaining why the gift is the size it is and reiterating how this presentation relates to others in the past and to projected future occasions" (A. J. Strathern 1971a: 118). These speeches are delivered in a formal oratorical style. The recipients then remove their gifts, unless it is a large distribution, in which case removal is postponed for one day while additional pigs are killed and cooked for distribution to the guests. On the final day the donors and the recipients, using different kinds of decorations, adorn themselves for dancing and subsequent speech making. Decorations may be borrowed from the guests. Women elaborately decorated with feathers dance, and thereby "become like men" (Strathern and Strathern 1971: 148). The gifts are again brought out for formal display, and "the donors mark their achievement by racing up and down the row . . . [and] they perform a war-dance, kicking up their heels and twirling their axes" (A. J. Strathern 1971a: 120). If there are extra pigs to be given, in order to gain additional prestige, the donors rush out with them at this point. An orator counts the pigs and shells on behalf of the donors, and an important man among the recipients acknowledges their receipt on behalf of his group. The pig stakes are knocked down, except for those to which the extra pigs were tethered and a special stake marked with charcoal, which remains standing as a record that a moka has been held.

Payment of compensation for loss of life during warfare is structurally similar to the moka in that the side that has lost a man pays an initiatory gift, the *wu ombil*, which is re-

ciprocated by a main gift, the *wuə peng*. The structural similarity of these payments to moka makes it possible for war
compensation payment to be converted into a moka exchange relationship between the two groups if exchanges
between them continue to take place. In this case exchange of
pork, which characterizes war compensation, is transformed
into the moka exchange of pigs. The moka partners in this
instance are not likely to be related to one another. Compensation payments may not lead to a moka relationship and a
death payment may merely be made (A. J. Strathern 1971a:
95).

In similar fashion, the exchanges that take place at a marriage also resemble moka in that a solicitory gift on the part
of the bride's side is reciprocated with a much larger return
gift—the bride wealth. The affinal relationship may be used
as a basis for a moka relationship. When this occurs, "there
is always a distinction made between gifts which are for
bridewealth proper *(kuimo)* and those which are designed to
initiate moka partnerships between the affines" (A. J. Strathern 1971a: 93). Thus brothers-in-law often become moka
partners to one another, though this is not required of
affines. A wife, however, will try to encourage her husband
to become a moka partner of her brother, for it is in her
interest that these two men should have an ongoing exchange relationship. Since the pigs she brings with her upon
marriage are the basis for her husband's herd, she feels that
these should go as moka gifts to her family rather than
elsewhere. If a Big Man so chooses, he may make the growth
payments for his children a basis for moka exchange. The
payments made to one's own maternal kin may be utilized
by a Big Man as a basis for moka relationship. All payments
to maternal kin are one-sided. After the establishment of the
affinal connection through a marriage, payment is always to
the wife giver and it is not reciprocated. No details are provided by the Stratherns as to the way in which these gifts
may be made the basis of a moka relationship that is reciprocal and in which both sides give in turn. In order to
utilize maternal payments as a basis for moka, it would seem
necessary to clearly distinguish goods that go as the maternal
gift from the portion intended for moka exchange.

Affinal and maternal payments are one-sided, going from wife receivers to wife givers. The initiative in converting affinal maternal relationships into moka relationships comes from the wife receivers. They include goods for moka exchange as part of the payments they must make to wife givers. Their interest in initiating moka partnerships may be a way of attempting to rectify the basic inequality of the wife giver/wife receiver relationship. Though the initiative comes from the wife receivers, the wife givers must agree to the establishment of the moka exchange relationship. If a divorce occurs, the affinal relationship ends, and moka partnerships established on the basis of the marriage rarely persist (A. M. Strathern 1972: 236).

Moka partnerships may be inherited. A moka partnership between a man and his sister's husband may shift to one between the man and his sister's son. This occurs when the sister's husband grows old. It has the effect of transferring a partnership from father to son. The father does not initiate the transfer but rather his moka partner, his brother-in-law, does. When the mother's brother dies, his son may take over the partnership, which becomes one between cross-cousins (see A. J. Strathern 1971a: 144). A. M. Strathern notes that a man's relationship to his wife's brother does not descend to his wife's sister's son, indicating that "the tie between WBS and FZH is rarely used in moka" (A. M. Strathern 1972: 123). She also concludes that "The son thus succeeds to his father's moka partnerships on his mother's but not on his father's sister's side" (A. M. Strathern 1972: 124). The continuation of the moka relationship to the cross-cousin generation would seem to imply an inconsistency in portraying a relationship only with mother's brother but not with father's sister's side. If ego maintains a relationship with mother's brother's son, then that man is maintaining a relationship with his father's sister's son. In line with our earlier discussion, ego will take the initiative in seeking a moka partnership with his mother's brother's son; that man must then accept the responsibility of the relationship with father's sister's son.

Moka exchanges are the means by which aspiring Big Men advance themselves. Big Men have more moka partners than do ordinary men, and their network of moka partners is more widely spread. A higher percentage of their moka partners are unrelated to them, in contrast to ordinary men. Strathern observes that "big men expand their sets by using both their own classificatory and other men's immediate kin and affinal links, and . . . the shape of their sets thus comes to be different from that of ordinary men" (A. J. Strathern 1971a: 163). Whereas ordinary men will be more active in moka exchanges within an "alliance block," Big Men are the foci of moka exchanges between groups that have been traditional enemies to one another (A. J. Strathern 1971a: 122). The death of a Big Man results in "an objective crisis in his group's gift exchange ties with other groups, for many of these ties may to a considerable extent have depended on his personal partnerships and policies" (A. J. Strathern 1971a: 193). This crisis demonstrates that Big Men act not only as individuals, but also as representatives of their groups.

Though the exchange of moka valuables such as pigs and shells takes place between individual partners, the moka exchange is a group event. A. J. Strathern, in his discussion of the "events leading up to a moka," supports the picture of the moka as a group event. The planning and coordination of the activity, as well as the "concerted showing" of the gifts, and the comparison of this gift with other presentations given or received by the group in the past, all serve to emphasize that each individual gift is also part of the conglomerate offering of the entire group (A. J. Strathern 1971a: 115ff.). When groups in the category of former enemies to one another are involved in an exchange, donors contribute to a block gift that is handed from one group to the other, and then redistributed (A. J. Strathern 1971a: 98). Later on, in the development of the exchange relationship between these two groups, exchanges between Big Men, as well as ordinary men, who have become partners replace the block gift, though the ceremonial ritual continues to emphasize group relations.

Participation in the ceremonial activities accompanying moka exchange is the means by which membership in a group is publicly proclaimed (A. J. Strathern 1972a: 100). A man who does not reside with a group with which he identifies can demonstrate his membership with that group by contributing to its moka presentations and dancing and speaking as a member of that clan (A. J. Strathern 1972a: 97). Strathern describes a case of a Big Man residing with his mother's brother who has acquired supporters within that group and, aided by his supporters, proceeds to make moka to his own natal group. His identity in this case is with his mother's brother's group (A. J. Strathern 1972a: 150).

Both Stratherns refer to moka partnerships between men in the same clan (A. J. Strathern 1971a: 113; A. M. Strathern 1972: 97). The above case fits into this category. Here a man has moka partnerships with his own clansmen while identifying himself with his mother's group. However, this type of situation would seem to account for only a small proportion of the exchanges within a clan. From our analysis of the Strathern material, we have concluded that there are two kinds of exchange relationships which occur within the clan. These are based on the differences in status between giver and receiver. One type involves support given to a Big Man by his subordinate followers, which is reciprocated in some fashion. As Strathern notes, "He obtained a few 'extra' ones (pigs) also, and instead of cooking these he used them to pay back his 'little men'—supporters within his clan section—in order to retain their good will" (A. J. Strathern 1971a: 155). The other type involves two Big Men of the same clan, who assist one another in their moka exchanges outside the clan.

These exchanges of pigs within one's own group do not seem to us to be moka partnerships, if the term moka refers to the ceremonial exchange system between groups. We realize, however, that the Stratherns use the term moka to refer to partnerships within the clan, as well as between clans. An internal exchange between members of the same group is described by Strathern as part of the private display preceding a moka distribution. Ruk and Kot, two Big Men of the Eltimbo clan, were to distribute pigs they had received four days earlier. "Ruk's main difficulty was that he was due to settle some internal debts with Kot before distributing to his other partners" (A. J. Strathern 1971a: 173). Among the seventeen individuals to whom Ruk allocates pigs at this event, all of them his creditors, are three men of his own group, as well as members of various other groups. As Strathern points out, when a Big Man receives a large number of pigs in the moka, as Ruk had, his many creditors, in his group and in various other groups, flock to him to press their claims before he has given away his pigs. It would be pointless to arrive after the distribution to collect one's debt from the pigless Ruk. In discussing the subsequent group event, Strathern notes, "His (Kot's) clan, the Eltimbo, are few and scattered, and their continued corporate existence, as well as his own prestige, depends on their participation as a group in moka ceremonies. Ruk and Kot delayed allocating their pigs to recipients until 7 January; and on the same day the pigs were formally transferred on the Eltimbo ceremonial ground" (A. J. Strathern 1971a: 185, see also 128, 129). The case of Ruk and Kot illustrates the distinction between intra and inter-clan exchanges. Big Men must repay fellow clansmen to whom they owe pigs, just as they must return pigs to their moka partners outside the clan; however, the two types of repayment are very different in character and are distinguished from one another by the contexts in which each occurs, and by the accompanying behavior.

This contextual distinction is emphasized by Strathern in his discussion of the difference between public and private moka. He states, "Gifts are made either privately or publicly. Private gifts are offered by the donor in his own house. Public gifts also involve individual partners, but at these donors and recipients act as members of their respective clan groups. . . . Private moka may be made within the clan also, and men have a number of partners in other clans, with which his own may or may not be friendly" (A. J. Strathern 1972b: 788). Moka exchanges that are group events must, of necessity, be public moka. Descriptions of such events indicate that they are accompanied by ceremonial display, dancing, and feasting. Private moka, in which the donor gives in his own house to the recipient, would seem to be a contradiction in terms. How can the giver make moka and acquire prestige when there is no public witnessing of the event? Private moka does not represent group, but rather individual, exchange. It may occur between members of the same clan, or between members of different clans. These characteristics of private moka make it seem like the support that followers give to Big Men.

In former times, according to the accounts of Vicedom and Tischner, Big Men monopolized moka exchange relationships, and acted on behalf of other people (Vicedom and Tischner 1943–48: 2: 455). It is probable that contributions of pigs to the Big Man from his supporters played a more significant role in his accumulation of moka goods than at present, since ordinary men at that time did not act as independent moka exchangers. At the present time, the block gift between former enemy groups would seem to be a continuation of that earlier pattern. As Strathern notes, "In this moka, then, we see big men as major recipients, drawing in gifts of pigs and distributing these, chiefly to their own subclansmen, in specific preparation for a bigger moka which they are due to make" (A. J. Strathern 1971a: 138). The Big Men recipients of a block gift, for which the term *kng ende* is used, have need of supporters. The large influx of pigs which they receive cannot be cared for and fed through their own immediate resources, and therefore must be redistributed to supporters (A. J. Strathern 1971a: 132).

At the present time, many more ordinary men have moka partners in other clans with whom they exchange. Their relationship with the Big Men of their clan is somewhat different than in the past. Instead of the block gift, the Big Man now exhorts his fellow clansmen to stand with him as donors and to give their pigs to exchange partners in the clan to which a moka presentation is being made (A. J. Strathern 1971a: 116). Two Big Men in a subclan or clan may also compete with one another for followers in their group when each is exchanging with a partner in a different group. Vicedom and Tischner present the position of the Big Man at the time of contact as more highly developed and possessing greater power than the present-day account of the Big Man's position according to Strathern (A. J. Strathern 1971a: 207). The differences between the earlier and later accounts in the position of Big Man would seem to be in accord with our discussion above of the change in relationship between the Big Man and his supporters within his own clan. With the weakening of the support base for a Big Man within his clan, he is compelled to call upon extraclan partners for assistance in accumulating pigs and valuables in order to make a moka presentation on behalf of his clan to still another clan. Thus, moka exchanges today seem to place greater emphasis upon the individual aspects of transactions, rather than the group aspects.

The linkages between moka partners in different groups may be joined in a sequence to form a chain of moka exchanges. It is to the advantage of the Big Man "to select a set of links and define the beginning and the end of the chain for a particular sequence of transactions, and to elevate this arrangement to the level of intergroup relations" (A. J. Strathern 1969b: 56). In addition to the help from supporters in their own group, Big Men also use help from outside groups in order to amass goods for their major moka distribution. Strathern refers to this as "helping moka." "It is in this way that ropes of moka are created and attached to important chain sequences of gifts between allies" (A. J. Strathern 1971a: 131). The "helping moka" would seem to be structurally identical to the main chain of moka transactions. The moka chain itself is planned by the Big Men who are the major participants in the exchanges. The Big Man who participates in such a moka chain can immediately pass on the pigs he has received to his partner in still another group, without having to worry about feeding those pigs or redistributing them to his supporters so that they will care for them. He has therefore gained prestige by making moka, with a minimal outlay of resources on his part (A. J. Strathern 1969b: 58). The particular path that a moka chain will take at one point in time depends on negotiations between participants and the state of political relations between their groups at that time. Succeeding moka chain sequences need not follow that same pathway. "Hageners do not expressly say, as a generalization, that they make their moka in chains, in the way that the Enga make their *Tee* exchanges, although they do define and refer to particular chain sequences while these are in progress. They do, however, refer in general to the ropes of moka which run from group to group, and I have suggested that particular exchange sequences can be looked on as special arrangements of these ropes" (A. J. Strathern 1971a: 131).

As we have indicated in our discussion of the moka, pigs are sacrificed to ancestral ghosts before warfare and before moka. This also occurs after the building of a new men's house on the ceremonial ground. "A sacrificial cooking of pork for the ancestors of the men who use the pena (ceremonial ground) follows this ritual. Visiting kin, in-laws, and exchange partners are given portions of the leg and stomach, while the clansmen themselves take the heads and tail-pieces of pigs, cook them in a sacrificial hut at the back of the men's house and consume them privately. Prayers to the ancestors, to favor the ceremonial ground and insure that its owners will be wealthy are made at the same time" (A. J. Strathern 1971a: 38).

Ancestral spirits are but one category of spirits in the Melpa spirit world. The ghosts of the immediate dead become ancestors after pig has been sacrificed to them. The spirits of ancestors and the wild spirits comprise the class of earth spirits "people of earth," which contrast with the class of sky spirits "people of the sky." (In his article on Female and Male Spirit Cults, Strathern links the wild spirits to the sky people in contrast to the spirits that had once been human beings [A. J. Strathern 1970a: 573].) Ancestral ghosts can ensure the success of an enterprise and are solicited for their support. Ghosts of close relatives can also bring sickness and death (A. J. Strathern 1972a: 26–28). Ancestral spirits are conceptualized as being "planted" just like men and they live in close proximity to men, near where they are buried. Ancestral spirits intercede between men and wild spirits. The wild spirits live in the bush and own the fauna therein which are referred to as their "pigs," especially forest marsupials, cassowaries, and several other categories of wild things. Success in hunting the "pigs" of the wild spirits is attributed to the intercession of ancestral spirits with the wild spirits, which necessitates sacrificing a pig to the ancestors who will then give the meat to the wild spirit (Strathern and Strathern 1968: 190). There is an association of the forest, the bush, the wild things located there, hunting, an activity pursued there, strength, power, and men. Birds and cassowaries from the forest are particularly associated with men in that the elaborate decorations of plumage make men like birds and cassowary meat is to be eaten only by men (Strathern and Strathern 1968: 198, 196). Sexual intercourse is forbidden before and during hunting. The leaves of wild plants are used for decoration to make men strong (Strathern and Strathern 1971: 147). Forest seedlings planted on the ceremonial grounds ally these grounds to the wild domain. The maleness of the wild is in contrast to the femaleness of the domesticated area of pigs and women in their gardens.

The sky spirits are generally associated with growth and fertility. The spirits involved in the Female and Male Spirit Cults are sky spirits. These cults seek to promote the fertility of the clan and its well-being through ritual action. Since the sponsorship of cult performances involves the financing of the cult house and cult performances by a Big Man of the clan, this ritual activity also demonstrates the strength and prosperity of the clan. The Female Spirit Cult has as its central themes fertility and male purification. Women are excluded from all of its aspects. The myth of the origin of the Female Spirit separates her from ordinary women in that she lacks a vagina and therefore cannot menstruate, have intercourse, or produce children. She protects men from the dangers of their wives' menstrual blood. As part of the cult performance men eat, within the cult enclosure, a meal of forest herbs and pig kidney to protect them against menstrual blood. All the ritual action during the cult performance involves the separation of the men of the clan into what are two ritual moieties, labeled "the men's house" and "the women's house," thus symbolically recapitulating Melpa society with men only. These two groups sit on opposite ends of the cult site and father and son are usually in separate groups (A. J. Strathern 1970a: 576–77). Round cult stones are associated with the Female Spirit Cult. At one stage in the ritual they are shown to boys whose fathers have given them pigs to sacrifice, thereby initiating these boys into the cult secrets. The action of the cult ritual is led by ritual experts who are paid for their services and who are distinct from the Big Man who sponsors the performance. Several distributions take place in conjunction with the Female Spirit Cult. A sacrifice of pigs to the ancestors takes place so that the clan ancestors will not be jealous of the forthcoming sacrifices to the Female Spirit. This meat is distributed to the settlement including wives. Subsequent distributions that are directly associated with the Female Spirit Cult completely exclude women and are made to men of local clans who come as visitors to witness the cult performances. After the final performance, the distribution of pork is made from a high platform from which the meat is thrown upon the spears of the guests (A. J. Strathern 1970a: 578). White is the dominant color of the decorations used in the Female Spirit Cult, and its meaning is health, fertility, and attractiveness. The decorations worn contrast with those worn for moka and the Male Spirit Cult. These decorations emphasize the themes of the Female Spirit Cult, which are the purification of men from the polluting effects of females and menstruation and male fertility." . . . by excluding women, the men are asserting that their own male fertility is sufficient to perpetuate the clan" (Strathern and Strathern 1971: 161).

The Male Spirit Cult has as its main aim the health and fertility of women, children, men, pigs, and crops (A. J. Strathern 1970a: 582). Cult stones play a role in the Male Spirit Cult; however, rather than being rounded river stones, they are indented and often are prehistoric pestles and mortars. In a preliminary ceremony in which pigs are sacrificed by the ritual experts, the pestles are placed in mortars as a symbol of sexual intercourse and are wrapped in moss saturated with pigs' blood and buried under a tower in the cult enclosure (Strathern and Strathern 1971: 57). The moiety division, discussed in connection with the Female Spirit Cult, operates at the preliminary ceremony when male celebrants share a meal of sweet potatoes, pork, and marsupials. The marsupials have been trapped earlier and kept alive until sacrificed and eaten at this rite. Women are excluded from any aspects of the cult ritual. At one point in the ritual cycle flutes are blown to warn the women to keep away. However, women take part in climactic dancing and are symbolically represented in the cult stones. As a final stage, there is a pig display, killing, and cooking and finally a distribution to guests who are affines, and cross-relatives of the celebrants.

The symbolic emphasis in the Male Spirit Cult is on male phallicism as it relates to copulation, and fertility (A. J. Strathern 1970a: 583, 584). Here the interdependence of the sexes in procreation is recognized in contrast to the Female Spirit Cult's emphasis on the polluting aspects of women.

The segmentary structure of the Melpa has more levels of segmentation than any of the Highland societies we have thus far discussed. The marriage prohibitions are more extensive than in the other Highland societies. Larger units like clans exchange women and keep track of the exchanges. The extent of the prohibitions are such that once a marriage is contracted between two lineages no further marriages between those lineages are permitted. The return of a woman will be to another lineage in the clan. Vicedom and Tischner report the presence of sister exchange without indicating whether it is real or classificatory. The Stratherns report that the exchange of real sisters is precluded.

The affinal relationship is the basis for exchange partnerships in the moka exchange system. In the pig festival of the Maring-Manga, Kuma, and Chimbu, affines are also the recipients. However, among the Melpa moka partnerships are more formalized. They are named and inherited from father to son until the original affinal connection may be forgotten. A return must be made to one's moka partner.

Rivalry and competition characterize both moka exchange and warfare. Compensation after a death in warfare may be transformed into moka exchanges. Though the Melpa have "traditional enemies," these may be converted into moka partners. In Maring-Manga, Kuma, and Chimbu pig festivals, the major themes of warfare and fertility are both present, and pigs are sacrificed to the ancestors. The moka exchange ceremony does not have as its avowed purpose the sacrificing of pigs to the ancestors. However, pigs are sacrificed to the clan ancestors among the Melpa. This occurs on clan burial grounds on a number of occasions, such as: prior to warfare, before the final moka ceremony, after the erection of a new men's house, and in connection with holding spirit cult rituals. The pigs are sacrificed to the ancestors to elicit their help in each of these different endeavors. The moka is totally different from the pig festival of the Maring-Manga,

Kuma, and Chimbu, though pigs are sacrificed to the ancestors in all of them. In the other pig festivals, live pigs are given to the ancestors and cooked pork is the primary item of distribution to the affinal guests. In contrast, in the moka live pigs are the primary items given to moka exchange partners. In the moka, pigs are sacrificed to the ancestors explicitly to gain their help in ensuring success in the forthcoming moka exchange. Pigs are sacrificed to the ancestors in the other societies to thank the ancestors for previous help in warfare, and to promote the general well-being and fertility of the group in the future.

No mention of fertility is made in connection with the moka or with sacrifices to clan ancestors. The theme of fertility appears only in the Male and Female Spirit Cults. The Female Spirit Cult has as its two main themes the purification of men from the polluting influence of menstruating women, and the fertility of men apart from women. The general theme of the polluting effects of women, the dangers of sexual intercourse, and the need to keep the sexes apart is also present in the Melpa. The Male Spirit Cult emphasizes fertility through the phallic aggressiveness of men, and intercourse between the sexes.

11 Enga

The Enga people occupy Enga district of the western Highlands of New Guinea. The Central Enga, numbering about fifty thousand, are themselves divided into eastern or Laiapu(Raiapu)-Syaka and the western or Mae-Yandapu groups. We will be utilizing the material of Meggitt, Elkin, and Bus on the Mae, and the material of Waddell on the Raiapu-Syaka. Since the Kyaka, an Enga-speaking group further east, are part of the Te ceremonial exchange cycle of the Enga, we will include Bulmer's material in our discussion of the Te. The population density "averages more than 90 per square mile and in some localities along the upper Lai River is as much as 350 to 400 per square mile" (Meggitt 1967: 24).

Despite the density of population, the settlement pattern is a dispersed one with no nucleated centers. Individuals usually reside close to their gardens. The basic gardening unit is a man, his wife, and unmarried dependants. The wives of a polygamous man constitute separate gardening units. Husbands and wives live in separate houses. The wife lives with her unmarried daughters, and sons under eight years of age. The wife's house usually contains stalls for the pigs belonging to the family. The husband and sons over eight live in a men's house with other men and boys of their patrilineage. The men's house will also contain boars belonging to these men. Ideally, the men's house should be composed of closely related agnates from one patrilineage. However, men's houses frequently contain men of parallel patrilineages and subclans who have moved there to be closer to their gardening land, and also nonagnates who may have shifted their residence. In a sample of fifty-seven men's houses, the average number of inhabitants was 5.4, with a range of two to sixteen (Meggitt 1965a: 22). The Laiapu-Syaka men's houses contain fewer men and many of them are occupied by only one man. More young Laiapu-Syaka boys live in men's houses than among the Mae, since boys remain longer with their mothers among the Mae. Meggitt indicates that this is because the Laiapu place less stress on the polluting effect of women, including one's mother. Waddell on the Laiapu notes, "It is the hearth or eating group which provides the most tangible expression of the basic unit of production, the household. Those who work their gardens in common invariably eat together, wherever they may sleep" (Waddell 1972a: 122). The Mae Enga appear to differ in this respect: "Food preparation occurs in both husband's and wife's houses, depending on the type of food involved. Among the Mae Enga, in particular, a husband may eat apart from his wife for days at a time, cooking the food himself that she brings him each evening" (Meggitt 1957–58: 275–76).

Waddell describes the Laiapu agricultural system as having two subsystems. The first, the open-field subsystem involves the cultivation of sweet potatoes, the main staple diet and the primary food for pigs, which is almost exclusively the concern of women. The second is the mixed garden system in which the yam cultivation is largely the concern of the men while the cultivation of other crops therein are the concern of the women. "This distinction within the mixed gardens accords with the designation of certain crops (principally yams) as 'male' and others as 'female'" (Waddell 1972a: 98). Sugar cane and bananas are also male crops planted and tended by males. "Moreover, the gardens as a whole are considered 'male,' in contrast to the 'female' open fields, and menstruating women are not allowed to enter them for fear of polluting the 'male' yams. These sexual distinctions reflect something of the different values attached to the several crops where the 'male' ones, in particular the yams, are of considerable social significance, cooked in earth ovens and consumed primarily when exchange partners visit or at the food distributions associated with life crises" (Waddell 1972a: 51). Among the Mae, Meggitt does not delineate two clearly separate agricultural subsystems. However, he does distinguish between cultivation methods related to sweet potatoes, the staple crop, and those related to other kinds of crops. Men are concerned with the preparation of the soil and the fencing of the sweet potato gardens, while women do the planting, weeding, and harvesting. Sugar cane and ginger are cultivated exclusively by men and taro cultivation is predominantly a male concern. The Mae also classify crops into male and female categories. A menstruating woman, who remains in seclusion, is considered polluting to male crops. "She can collect food at night, but may harvest only mature 'female' crops such as sweet potato, setaria or crucifera, those which women normally cultivate. Should she enter plots containing 'male' (-tended) plants such as taro, ginger or sugar cane, those would die. . . . She may feed pigs, for these are usually in her care and are therefore 'female,' but not dogs or cassowaries as these are male and would lose their condition" (Meggitt 1964a: 208).

Gardening land and groves of planted trees are owned by individual families. Such land is under the control of the father, who is the head of the family. He is expected to preserve it for his sons. Each son receives a share of the land at the time of his marriage. The land is divided equally among the sons irrespective of their birth order or the seniority of their mothers (Meggitt 1965a: 248). The father retains only enough land for his own use. If a man should die before his sons marry, the sons may cultivate the land as a group. As each marries he will take a portion. Affines and cognates may sometimes be granted usufructory rights and residential privileges. These rights are usually temporary and may be terminated at any time. An affine who takes up residence with his wife's clan or a sister's son who takes up residence with his mother's brother's clan is expected to give political support to the group with which he is residing and to contribute to its exchanges and distributions. However, such people usually continue to maintain ties with their natal groups. An affine who moves to live uxorilocally is always an affine even if he is buried in the land of his wife's clan. His rights to land of his wife's clan are usufructory rights only. His son is a sister's son, whether born on his mother's clan land or not, and he receives land at the will of the members of his mother's lineage. But only the sons of those sisters' sons who have been born on the clan land of their mothers are regarded as "clan agnates" (Meggitt 1965a: 36 refers to them as quasi-agnates). This conversion of affines into agnates is reflected in Meggitt's analysis of his genealogical data, where recognition of nonagnates declines with generational distance.

A number of families comprise a patrilineage. The patrilineage, which may be called "one penis," "a small line of men," or "the people of one blood," comprises the agnatic descendants going back to a common great-grandfather, the founder of the patrilineage (Meggitt 1965a: 16). Its members believe they can trace their precise genealogical connections. The founder gives his name to the patrilineage. A founder more rarely is a "daughter's husband" of the subclan founder. "As the men (the oldest living men of the patrilineage) die, the patrilineage name changes informally or by default to that of a putative and significant son of the previous founder i.e. this is the point in the system where there is constant cleavage with associated 'structural amnesia' " (Meggitt 1957–58: 266).

Arranging marriages is one of the activities of the patrilineage. Members contribute the bulk of the bride price when one of their male lineage mates marries. When a daughter of the lineage marries the latter receives the bulk of the bride price. Members of the patrilineage also help to pay death and illness compensation. Most of the labor in house building comes from one's lineage mates, as does assistance in gardening tasks requiring additional labor. The patrilineage has full title to its territory, which comprises the estates of its members, in opposition to parallel patrilineages. Its territory may form a block but more frequently it lies interspersed with that of other patrilineages. However, the lineage does not possess a cult house or enclosure (Meggitt 1965a: 235).

Several lineages make up a subclan. The subclan takes its name from its putative founder, who may be a son of the clan founder or an in-marrying daughter's husband of the clan founder. The subclan lands and residences ideally should be discreet; however, in actuality, there is frequently inter-penetration with the garden lands of other subclans (Meggitt 1965a: 15–16). When subclans become very populous they may segment, with their component patrilineages assuming the functions of subclans while subunits within the new subclans assume patrilineage functions. The activities considered to be the province of subclans are: assistance in major gardening projects, payment of death compensation and the holding of mortuary feasts, and the organization of the purificatory rituals for bachelors. The bachelors of each subclan own forest enclosures and houses and when the purificatory rites are performed nonagnatic bachelors residing in subclans may participate in these rituals (Meggitt 1964a: 223). Subclans also own separate dance grounds.

Several subclans, from two to eight, are combined within a clan. "The clan is . . . a 'line of men', begotten by 'the one penis' of the clan founder" (Meggitt 1965a: 8) The clan founder is also the putative son of the phratry founder. The clan bears the name of its founder and ranges in size from 100 to 1,000 members with a mean size of 350. The clan as a unit owns a discrete territory that is compact in shape and averages between one and two square miles. The name of the clan territory, which is different from that of the clan, is the same as that of its main dance ground. Each clan has a myth that validates its rights to the land it occupies (Meggitt 1965a: 52). Each clan founder bequeathed ghost placatory rituals and magic spells concerned with ritual purity (Meggitt 1965b: 124). Sometimes a clan will have branches in separate, noncontiguous territories. Arable land is owned by the individual families. However, certain areas are owned in common by the clan. These include forest, swampland, and sections of streams and rivers. These areas are used for hunting, fishing, and the gathering of firewood. In addition to the dance ground, the clan also possesses stones or small pools where its ancestors are said to reside, and the cult house and ritual paraphernalia used for clan rituals, which are set in a fenced-in acre of overgrown land.

Clans with smaller populations and surplus land may invite affines or nonagnates to reside permanently with them to augment numbers for defense purposes. Defense of territory is one of the central functions of the clan; it is the unit that carries out independent military actions. The attempted seizure of land by a neighboring clan was the most frequent cause of warfare. Other causes included theft of pigs, avenging a homicide, and abduction or rape of women. Another function of the clan is the payment of compensation in homicides. The clan is the exogamic unit. The clan ancestral stones are said to be the locus of the clan ancestral ghosts. "Calamities affecting the entire clan are ascribed to the malevolence of the totality of ancestral ghosts" (Meggitt 1965a: 233). The important ritual of "bespelling the clan stones" must then be held on behalf of the entire clan. The clan as a whole is also involved in the ceremonies of the emergence of bachelors from ritual seclusion (Meggitt 1965a: 232). The clan as a unit participates in the large ceremonial exchange cycle known as the *te*. Each of these will be discussed in detail below.

Clans are grouped into phratries. This is the largest agnatic group recognized as descended from an eponymous phratry founder. A phratry usually occupies a continuous area along a valley. New phratries are usually formed when the original phratry covers too great a geographical distance for there to be contact between the clans on opposite peripheries (Meggitt 1965a: 65). The ancestor of the phratry is said to have come from the sky people and to have brought ritual knowledge and paraphernalia which he bequeathed to his sons who were the clan founders. He also laid claim to an area that he divided amongst his sons, these divisions becoming the clan territories. Hence, when clan ancestor rituals are carried out members of other clans of the phratry have the right to be present. Sometimes clans in a phratry share ancestral stones, or the largest clan of a phratry will have stones regarded as the parents of those of its fraternal clans. In these cases, which represent different stages of the segmentation process, clans will attend one another's rituals. Warfare for land should only be directed against clans of other phratries. In interphratry fighting, all the clans of the respective phratries were seldom mobilized. However, a form of ritualized fighting which did engage whole phratry against whole phratry sometimes occurred. Such an event lasted a week, resulted in very few deaths, and was concluded by formal ceremonial exchanges. Its purpose was to enhance the military prestige of the phratry (Meggitt 1957–58: 257).

The data on political leadership, primarily from Meggitt, reveals that leaders are ranged hierarchically to match the levels of the segmentary system, up through, and including, the clan. There is no rule of hereditary succession to leadership positions. There is a Mae term for leader or Big Man, *kamunggo.* "The Mae terminology distinguishes between the 'really' Big Man, (*kamunggo erete, kamunggo andaiki*) and the 'mere' Big Man (*mekamunggo, kamunggo kori*) that is, between the acknowledged and powerful leader and the aspiring or potential leader, between the clan leader and the subclan or patrilineage leader. It is the former who is *sauwu pinggi,* the first in order or the first in the line" (Meggitt 1967: 34, n. 7). Each family has its male head. The most powerful, influential family head in the patrilineage is the head of the patrilineage. Within the subclan, the most powerful patrilineage head is the head of the subclan. Within the clan, the most powerful subclan head is acknowledged as leader. Leadership at any level is always in the hands of agnates. This is because it is necessary for leaders to have secure title to their land, which coresident affines or sister's sons do not have.

Waddell indicates that the Big Man must have a large work force at his disposal. It consists of women who tend the sweet potato fields and the pigs and who are part of his household as wives, attached widows, or spinsters; and bachelors or unattached men who contribute labor in return for the services provided by women of the Big Man's household (Waddell 1972a: 110). The unattached males may be agnates whose field resources are limited and who therefore have little chance of obtaining wives. The wives of the Big Man will tend to the pigs and sweet potatoes of the unattached man, in return for the latter's support in the form of directing surplus production to him and assisting in various menial tasks (Waddell 1972a: 190).

With his surplus of goods, the incipient Big Man makes larger contributions to the bride price and death and illness payments made by the members of his patrilineage. He may build them a dance ground on land he donates in order to enhance his prestige. He will also be overgenerous in returns. He hopes by this to challenge the position of the present patrilineage leader. A patrilineage leader who aspires to become a subclan leader will contribute to the bride price payments of men in parallel patrilineages and volunteer help to persuade the people of his suitability as a leader. Similarly, the Big Man of a subclan may involve himself in the exchange of a parallel subclan to announce his intention of trying to become clan leader (Meggitt 1967: 30). The position of Big Man is a transitory one, tied to the life cycle of a man. In order to eventually become Big Man of a clan, a man must first have been a successful patrilineage and then a subclan leader. With increasing old age and illness, a Big Man will find it difficult to maintain his position and he will become more and more vulnerable to the challenge of a rising Big Man. The declining Big Man is not usually replaced by a close agnate. Positions of leadership tend to oscillate between constituent segments (Meggitt 1967: 30).

The Big Man speaks on behalf of the group he heads, and he organizes and coordinates the activities appropriate to that group. For example, the patrilineage leader will coordinate the activities involved in marriage prestations; the Big Man of the subclan will coordinate the activities involved in funerary distribution and the ritual of clan stones. The clan Big Man will coordinate the activities of the clan when they are hosts for the *te* ceremony. In Meggitt's view "What is significant among the Mae is the way in which the segmentary lineage system can function to pre-define the personnel of the groups of followers even before they possess leaders. That is to say, 'followers' (who are largely allocated in agnatic terms) are the constant; it is they who demand and create leaders" (Meggitt 1967: 23).

There is one hereditary position among the Mae, that of

the ritual expert at the clan bespelling ritual. His knowledge is inherited within his patrilineage (Meggitt 1965b: 114). However, the ritual expert is rarely a Big Man. Warriors may occasionally be referred to as *kamunggo,* but "Such men are rarely the true *kamunggo,* who plan military strategy and direct tactics from behind the lines" (Meggitt 1967: 34, n.5).

Marriage prohibitions are phrased in terms of clan and subclan, while the lineage is the unit involved in the various payments made when a marriage is contracted. Postmarital residence is patrivirilocal. Polygamous marriages occur (Meggitt 1957–58: 308). Meggitt presents what he calls the "kin-based marriage prohibitions from the viewpoint of a Mae man. He should not marry:

i.   Any woman of his clan;
ii.   Any female descendant of any living or dead woman of his clan, a category that for lack of precise genealogical knowledge rarely includes more than second cousins;
iii.   Any woman of the subclans of the husbands of women of his own subclan;
iv.   Any woman of the subclan of his father's mother, mother's mother, and mother's father;
v.   Any woman of the subclans of his mother's husband and mother's sister's husbands;
vi.   Any woman of the subclans of his wife's mother and wife's father;
vii.   Any woman of the subclan of his father's wife;
viii.   Any woman of the subclans of wives of living men of his patrilineage;
ix.   Any widow of a relative not of his own generation level."

(Meggitt 1965a: 93; these marriage prohibitions are also presented with some variations in Meggitt 1957–58: 276–77; 1964b: 191–192; 1969:9)

Meggitt then notes that the people explain the prohibitions as a result of two different categories of disqualification. One category is women with whom sexual intercourse is regarded as incestuous, and the other category is women with whom marriage would be inexpedient for socioeconomic reasons (Meggitt 1965a: 94). Prohibition iii would eliminate the possibility of sister exchange (see also Elkin 1952–53: 176).

In another publication where Meggitt discusses marriage

prohibitions he phrases them somewhat differently from the list above.

A man may not marry into his patrilineage nor may he marry any woman known to be a descendant of his patrilineage founder. Since few details are known of women marrying into or out of the lineage before the generation of ego's grandmothers, the prohibition does not as a rule extend beyond a man's second cousins and their lineages. . . . It is also extended to cover all clanswomen and the known daughters and granddaughters of living or dead clanswomen as far back as ego's father's father's generation level. Absence of genealogical knowledge prevents as a rule any further extension of this prohibition. A man should not marry into the patrilineages of his mother and mother's brother's wives (also called mother), or of his father's sister's husbands and mother's sister's husbands (who are called father). In practice, this prohibition usually extends to these men's own subclans, although not to the other subclans of their clans. These bans are often explained in terms of belief that one's parallel and cross-cousins are "the same as" one's siblings (Meggitt 1957–58: 277).

Meggitt's presentation of the prohibitions regarding own clanswomen is from two points of view. On the one hand he indicates that all descendants of women of the lineage, for two generations, are prohibited as wives, while on the other hand he notes that one cannot marry into the patrilineage of father's sister's husband. (He notes the overlap between categories ii and iii in the 1965 presentation.) The second categorization rules out whole lineages or subclans as the prohibition is extended to them. The first categorization rules out individuals; however, given the weakness of genealogical reckoning especially through women (for example father's sister's daughter's daughter) it would seem to be difficult to sustain. Further, the exchange relationships that follow marriage do not appear in any way to link ego's lineage and members of the lineage into which his father's sister's daughter marries. Another discrepancy is that though women of mother's brother's wife's lineage are mentioned as prohibited in the 1957–58 version, they do not fit into any of the categories in the 1965 version. In the 1965 version, Meggitt refers to prohibition of marriage with women of father's mother, mother's mother, and mother's father subclans. Of these three, only the third, mother's father's subclan, is mentioned and referred to as patrilineage of mother in the 1957–58 version. The other two do not appear, though they do appear in versions after 1965.

It is apparent from Meggitt's data that all first cousins, cross and parallel, are forbidden as marriage partners. Some second cousins are specifically forbidden as marriage partners, the women of the subclans of father's mother, mother's mother, and mother's father. The daughters of women of these clans, who are also second cousins, are possible mates. Because of the shallowness of genealogical reckoning, all third cousins would seem to be possible mates. "Very few men can, for instance, recall the personal names or clan affiliations of wives possessed by their paternal great-grandfathers, while many are unsure of the identities of their paternal grandmothers" (Meggitt 1965a: 158).

Meggitt presents data to show the direct relationship between marriage and propinquity of clans. Sixty-one percent of the marriages in his sample were between clans whose territories were contiguous (Meggitt 1965a: 102). In a number of different contexts, Meggitt points to the relationship between warfare and marriage. He notes, "Marriages are not contracted at random within a cultural grouping. The geographical origins of spouses form a definite pattern in relation to a given clan, and the Mae recognize this when they assert 'We marry the people we fight!' In fact they tend most often to marry and to fight those who live near them" (Meggitt 1965a: 191; see also Elkin 1952–53: 170; Meggitt 1957–58: 278; 1964a: 218).

It would appear that the prohibitions presented by Meggitt, if looked at diachronically, are only part of the picture. Given the frequency of intermarriage between neighboring clans, the Mae statements about marriage with neighbors, and finally the important exchange relationships that develop from the affinal relationship, we hypothesize that connections between clans will be renewed by marriage when the ties grow cold, that is after two generations have passed.

Since marriage sets up a continuing set of exchanges between the two groups, divorce is disapproved of and is rare (Meggitt 1965a: 149–50). When it does occur, the woman may remain with her husband's patrilineage and be passed on to another man who recompenses the husband, or she may be sent back to her agnates who then return part of the bride price, or she may be passed on to another clan as a wife in exchange for bride wealth (Meggitt 1965a: 145–47). Her children normally remain with their father's clan, as is usually the case with the children of a widow. (Waddell's material on the Laiapu Enga indicates a high frequency of divorce, in contrast to the Mae [Waddell 1972a: 25].)

The kinship terminology of the Mae Enga is characterized by Iroquois cousin terms and bifurcate merging terminology in the first ascending generation. An interesting feature of the terminology is that children of male cross-cousins are called by the same terms as ego's children; children of female cross-cousins are called by the term for sister's children, which is also the term used for mother's brother.

We will now begin our analysis of the exchange system of the Mae Enga. A marriage initiates the exchanges between affines. The first stage in a marriage is the payment of a betrothal gift. This gift is provided primarily by the young man himself and consists of as little as a shell headband or as much as several pearlshells, headbands, axes, and pieces of pork. It is given to the girl with no formality and she gives it to her father or her elder brother. This is seen as an advance donation of the bride price. The betrothal gift establishes an exchange relationship between the suitor and the girl's father, since the latter will return this initiatory gift at the next stage of the great ceremonial exchange cycle. On the basis of the betrothal gift, men from the suitor's subclan may also find exchange partners in the girl's subclan (Meggitt 1965a: 107). The close agnates of both suitor and girl discuss the size of the bride price and agree on an amount. The men of the patrilineage of the suitor and other agnates from his subclan or clan and other close relatives such as maternal kin decide what they will contribute to the bride price. Maternal kin and affines may contribute in small amounts (Meggitt 1965a: 125). The size of a bride price is larger if it is a first marriage for the groom. When the bride price contributions are ready, the wives of the suitor's close agnates go to the girl's house and bring her back to the groom's house. The bride price is then exhibited. The people who will share in the bride price, close and some more distant agnates of the bride and her maternal uncles, are present. They will be contributing to the return gift. After the bride publicly accepts her future husband in marriage, the bride wealth is formally transferred to her kin group. In the ensuing ceremonies, the bride's group will give an indication of the minimum size of the return gift to be made. If wealthy, the group may even give one or two pigs as a return gift at this time. After all the installments of the bride price have been given to the bride's kin group, the date is set for the presentation of the return gift pigs at the house of the bride's mother. This transfer occurs with no ceremony. From the data that Meggitt presents the bride price is considerably larger than the return gift.

According to the Mae theory of conception, the father's semen is the means by which the foetus acquires its spirit, which is an emanation of the ancestral ghosts of the father's clan, while from the mother, the foetus acquires skin, flesh, and blood. Since the flesh and blood are seen as coming from the mother, her clan has the right to demand compensation when blood is shed, or when sickness or injury befalls the child. Such injuries are believed to be caused by the ghosts of the dead agnates of the child. The first haircut for the child after he is weaned is seen as such as injury. The child's hair is cut by the mother's brother who also bestows a name on the child. The mother's brother is then compensated for this with a pig, a pearlshell, or axes by the father of the child. A man will have these services performed for the first and second children of each wife; however, if he is wealthy, he will perform it for all children and even divide the naming and haircutting into separate occasions (Meggitt 1965a: 168).

After this initial transaction, whenever an injury or illness occurs a sacrifice of pigs is held in an attempt to placate the ghost who is believed to be responsible. Most frequently the ghost is of a close agnate but ghosts of the mother can also be malevolent (Meggitt 1965b: 112). Part of the pork from this sacrifice is given to the maternal kinsmen as "payment for the skin" of the sick man (Meggitt 1965a: 175). The rest of the meat is eaten by the sick man's agnates. "Sometimes sisters' sons or fathers' sisters' sons of the victim are asked to share the agnates' pork. As children of female agnates they are regarded as a sort of agnate who may later be approached to contribute towards the extra compensation that the sick man gives his maternal kin" (Meggitt 1965a: 175). The compensation given to maternal kin is also shared. "The mother's sisters of the injured or deceased and their children may also be involved. The women are here treated as nominal members of their natal patrilineages and share in the compensation. Their sons may receive a portion on account of their consanguineal link with the victim through the mother's agnates" (Meggitt 1965a: 169).

The death of a person marks the culmination of payments made to matrilateral kin. Immediately after the death, there is a period of initial mourning attended by male agnates, their wives, and a few maternal kin of the deceased. Some of the closest kin of the deceased cut off finger joints. Burial, which takes place the next day, is carried out by several close relatives not of the immediate family. When an important man dies his body is decked with ornaments appropriate for his status and displayed on the main dance ground of clan or subclan so that his exchange partners from other clans can come to mourn him (Meggitt 1965a: 186). During the mourning period of two or three weeks the immediate family does no work. Close agnates attend to all necessary tasks and for this they will later be repaid.

The "house of death feast" is the first large-scale event of the death rites which involves the interaction and exchange of pork between the agnatic kin group of the deceased and his mother's kin group. Additional contributions are made to the accumulations of both agnatic and maternal kin groups of the deceased (see Meggitt 1965a: 193–94, 201). Other clans, besides the two involved in the exchange, witness the event sitting in groups by clan. The agnatic group of the deceased assembles near their clan or subclan dance ground and marches in an impressive array to their dance ground, where they set out sides of pork and valuables in a row with each donor behind his own contribution (Meggitt 1965a: 195). The mother's brother's clan of the deceased is joined by other clans containing mother's sister's sons who have made contributions to their accumulation at the border of the deceased's clan. They enter it in a phalanx, destroying property as they go toward the dance ground. If the destruction gets out of hand, a brawl results and the feast must be postponed. "The visitors place their pork and valuables in a row along the sides of the dance ground opposite to that occupied by the agnates. Each matrilateral clan or subclan forms a section of the row" (Meggitt 1965a: 196). Individuals of the agnate side exchange pork and valuables with particular individuals of the matrilateral side. The agnates must never return what they have received. Each side in the exchange has kept aside some sides of pork and other food. This is then cut up and distributed to the onlookers. What each side has actually received in the exchange is also distributed. Those who comprised the burial party, those who contributed food and services to the bereaved family, and those who visited the mourning house also receive gifts of meat from the agnates of the deceased. Whatever is then left over is distributed by the agnates in small portions to friends, relatives, and exchange partners. The matrilateral relatives also share out what they received from the agnates.

The payment of compensation to maternal kin that follows every death should ideally occur before the mourning feast, but usually occurs after (Meggitt 1965a: 204). Sisters' sons and husbands, father's sister's sons, and wives' brothers of the dead man contribute to the payment. People from parallel patrilineages and subclans may also contribute. Each visitor spends the night in the house of the man who will give him pigs. "Individual donors and recipients are not named; the transactions ostensibly involve agnatic groups" (Meggitt 1965a: 207). The next day, the pigs and valuables are taken to the dance ground. Long lines of stakes are driven into the ground, and "each line is divided into sections that represent pigs to go to particular clans and subclans" (Meggitt 1965a: 207). The pigs are tethered to the stakes. The man Meggitt identifies as "the elder" counts the wealth and announces the share of each visiting group which is then called upon to take the articles away (Meggitt 1965a: 208).

When a married woman dies after only a few years of marriage, the payment goes to her maternal kin and is made by her own agnates, helped by her husband's clan. If she dies after long residence with her husband's agnates, the latter pay her matrilateral relatives or her sons-in-law (Meggitt 1965a: 204).

The series of payments that mark the death of a person would seem to involve the two sides linked by a marriage in the previous generation. At marriage, there is series of exchanges between wife givers and wife receivers with the preponderance going to wife givers. At the birth of a child, the wife receiver pays once again. Each time the child is injured or insulted, wife receivers must give wife givers compensation.

In addition to affinal exchanges there are other large-scale ceremonial distributions and exchanges that express the relationships between groups.

When there has been an exceptionally larger harvest of certain prestige crops such as taro, sugar cane, or pandanus nuts, a distribution will take place. ". . . a clan or subclan may mount a feast at which this food is distributed, to the accompaniment of boastful and aggressive speeches, to visiting clans" (Meggitt 1971: 199).

Enga ideas concerning the polluting effect of females underlie the ceremony of the *sanggai*. Mae Enga men believe that women are intrinsically unclean. They are especially dangerous when they menstruate and must seclude themselves. The act of copulation itself is detrimental to well-being and married men must protect themselves by the use of spells (Meggitt 1964a: 210). Young bachelors periodically go through the *sanggai* purification rite of seclusion to protect themselves from the pollution of women. At the age of fourteen or fifteen a boy ceases to be a minor and enters the bachelors cult of his subclan. Periodically, he joins with the other bachelors of his subclan in retiring to the seclusion of their bachelors' house in the forest where for four days they perform a number of purificatory ceremonies. They must observe a number of prohibitions beyond merely separating themselves from women, such as not setting eyes on anything that a woman has looked at. Meggitt notes, "Pork is forbidden them, for women have tended the pigs; the only food permitted comprises tubers harvested at night and game and pandanus nuts taken from the forest" (Meggitt 1964a: 219). There is a pool located near the bachelors' house where they bathe repeatedly. As part of the ritual, they rub the leaf of the bog iris which is called *sanggai* against their hair and skin. Each clan has its own bog iris plants, which have come down to them from the clan ancestors.

Though each subclan has its own seclusion house, the emergence of the bachelors from seclusion is a clan affair. The bachelors have earlier gone in subclan groups to neighboring clans to invite girls whom they know or to whom they are betrothed to come to the festival of their emergence. The bachelors of the clan finally emerge from seclusion brandishing weapons and dressed in fine decorations to make themselves attractive. They enter the dance ground where the visiting bachelors are singing in clan groups. The girls in song and dance do the aggressive courting. Prior to the emergence, the families in each subclan of the host group have accumulated many bags of cooked vegetables including taro and pandanus nuts, items "normally eaten in small quantities" (Meggitt 1965a: 233), which are distributed by the Big Men on the dance ground (Meggitt 1964a: 216). While older men drift away, groups of visiting bachelors compete with those who have emerged from seclusion in singing aggressive songs. Fighting may break out.

Since the first ritual seclusion and emergence marks the majority for a boy, this ceremony is the equivalent of male initiation for the Enga. It is directly connected with courting and marriage. The girls of neighboring clans who are invited are potential and future wives of the secluded bachelors. The young men of the girls' clans with whom competitive singing takes place are the future brothers-in-law of the bachelors. It should be noted that the food distributed in connection with the emergence ceremony is vegetable food only. Pork is not cooked or distributed and there is no sacrifice of pigs to the ancestors in connection with the *sanggai* ritual. Though the young bachelors may eat game, which is associated with maleness, they may not eat pork, which is associated with women.

The Mae Enga distinguish between sky people, ancestral ghosts, and demons. The latter inhabit the forest and are essentially malevolent toward humans but there are not rituals associated with them or sacrifices made to them. The sky people control meteorological phenomena and the fate of man, but the Enga believe they have no way of influencing the decisions of the sky people. Ghosts of the dead are essentially malevolent particularly to their close agnates. Most injuries, illnesses, and deaths are attributed to them. The ghost of the dead person wanders around clan territory. Once he kills someone he is driven off by the ghost of his victim and joins the undifferentiated category of clan ancestral ghosts (Meggitt 1965b: 110–11). These clan ancestral spirits can also cause harm to the clan. They must be placated by sacrifices of pigs. The immaterial spirit of the pigs is consumed by the ancestors.

When various types of calamities affect the clan, their cause is ascribed to the anger of clan ancestral ghosts. Their anger may be attributed to various human failures and delinquencies or "simply to the fact that the ancestors hunger for pork and wish to force the clansmen to kill pigs for them" (Meggitt 1965b: 114). A ritual and a great feast are then planned to placate the clan ghosts. In the past this occurred only once or twice in a decade. On the initiative of the Big Man of the clan, the clansmen announce the date of the ritual to neighboring clansmen who should now remain at peace with them. In particular, they invite other clans of their own phratry. A ritual expert who may be of another clan is asked to officiate. The special knowledge he possesses is inherited within his patrilineage (Meggitt 1965b: 114). The women harvest vegetable food and no new gardens may be prepared. The men call in their debts to have enough pigs and other goods for the ceremony. The cult house is renovated and the same day the visitors from other clans arrive in groups, armed and adorned with marsupials they have brought for exchange. They are met by the host clan whose men are adorned with shells and plumes and whose women bear all the food they have cooked and items such as salt, shells, oil, fiber, and net bags for exchange. The food is distributed and the commodities exchanged for the game.

The following day, pigs are killed and cooked along with the marsupials that have been received and more vegetables are also prepared. Several marsupials are kept aside to be used in the cult ritual. This food is distributed at the dance ground to the visitors. While the visitors eat, the men of the host clan retire to the cult house with the ritual expert. He will perform a ceremony involving the bespelling of sacred stones from which the power of the clan ancestral ghosts is said to emanate. Some of the clan stones are natural stones, while others are ancient artifacts such as mortars and pestles. They take the marsupials (possums) that have been set aside, and the pigs to be dedicated to the ancestors, to the cult house. "Sometimes, as they set off, they bury a large black possum alive in a swampy garden as a gift to the ancestors and to make the land fertile" (Meggitt 1965b: 117). At the cult house, they club the pigs they have brought with them and dedicate them to the ancestors. "The clansmen separate, on a subclan basis, into two groups and each cooks half the pigs in a long trench in front of the house. Then, while the pork cooks, the groups throw possums to each other, back and forth over the cult house, as a subsidiary gift to the ancestors" (Meggitt 1965b: 117). The possums are then cooked and eaten. The clan stones are smeared with pork fat, tree oil, and red ocher. After the clansmen in turn inhale smoking pork fat, they eat the pork they have cooked from the pigs dedicated to the ancestors. The ritual expert is then given his fee, consisting of minor valuables and several joints of pork. Men must not copulate with their wives or make new gardens for a month or two after this ceremony, in order not to antagonize the ancestors, and to give them time to revitalize the clan and its land. The division of the clan men into two halves by subclan at the cult house is the only mention of any possible moiety division in Meggitt's material. It is interesting to note that Goodenough in his brief ethnographic notes on the Mae, presents the moiety division for two different sibs (clans). This moiety division orders the seating on the ceremonial ground for ritual occasions. However, Goodenough does not discuss the ritual of the bespelling of clan ancestral stones (Goodenough 1953: 35).

The last exchange complex to be discussed is the *te* cycle.

(The Kyaka Enga, a fringe Enga group, use the terms *te* or *moka* to refer to the exchange cycle. *Moka* is used by the Melpa, their immediate neighbors to the east, to refer to pig exchanges. These are not part of the *te* cycle.) Before discussing the operation of this ceremonial exchange cycle, it is necessary to discuss the institution of exchange partnership among the Enga. Exchange partnerships are built upon the affinal relationships, established as a result of marriage. These affinal relationships may be used by men further removed from the marriage, members of parallel lineages or subclans, as a basis for establishing new exchange partnerships. The more important a man is, the more likely he is to use the establishment of such an affinal connection to create a new exchange partnership and thus to have many more exchange partners than the average man. These exchange partners should be in as many different kin groups as possible. Exchanges between affines at life-crises rites provide the occasion to exchange with the partners in that affinal group. The marriage prohibitions prevent the renewal of marriage ties between groups in successive generations. However, exchange partnerships are passed on from father to son so that the relationship continues from generation to generation (Meggitt 1974: 184). Bulmer also refers specifically to the inheritance of *te* partners among the Kyaka (Bulmer 1960–61: 9). Thus, the structure of affinal relationship between groups may be continued in the next generation through the mechanism of the exchange relationship. As we hypothesized that marriage relations between groups are renewed after they grow cold, so it would seem that exchange relationships are the means by which older affinal connections are sustained until a new marriage can take place. Meggitt further notes, "Finally, I should remark that not only do the various obligations that exist between un-related *Te* partners (for instance, those of hospitality and of military and economic aid) resemble those holding between relatives; they also operate to convert the former partners into affines. Mae are well aware that such *Te* partners especially the Big Men, are happy to see their children marry so that the exchange connections with their complicated balances of debts and credits are further reinforced and may be extended into the next generation"

(Meggitt 1974: 189). Long-distance trade partnerships may also lead to marriages and thus are analogous to exchange partnerships (Meggitt 1965a: 103; Waddell 1972a: 111).

The discussions of *te* partnerships in all of the sources (Bulmer, Meggitt, and Elkin) emphasize the importance of affinal links as a basis for *te* exchange partnerships. For example, Bulmer notes, "The most frequent Moka partnership outside the clan is between brothers-in-law or father-in-law and son-in-law, though these are often carried over into the succeeding generation so that they then occur between mother's brother and sister's son and between cross-cousins. Maternal parallel cousins are also frequent partners. However, not only in terms of frequency, but of content, the partnerships between affines tend to be the most significant" (Bulmer 1960–61: 10). Elkin's data would also indicate that the majority of *te* partners are affines. He points to the fact that one Big Man, with seven wives, distributed pigs to men characterized as brothers-in-law who lived in eight different places. Elkin's material mentions agnates as *te* partners. However, closer scrutiny of his description reveals that in the instances where agnates received pigs as *te* partners, the givers were not residing with their natal groups (Elkin 1952–53: 194). Meggitt presents a table analyzing the categories of relationship between *te* partners. Fifty-seven percent are affines, 16 percent are unrelated, and 27 percent are categorized as own clansmen. Meggitt does not present any discussion or explanation of the last category, which would seem to contrast with his emphasis on the *te* as facilitating "The flow of economically important commodities (pork, salt, axes etc.) whose disposition is also critical in establishing and supporting intergroup relation, whether marital, economic, or military" (Meggitt 1974: 200–201). This emphasis on intergroup relations in the *te* is supported by all of the descriptions. Distributions to members of one's own clan as regular *te* partners is inconsistent with this picture. We would suggest that Meggitt's category of *te* partners who are one's own clansmen reflects the frequency of shifts in residence, where individuals leave their natal group. It might also reflect potential clan fission or the process by which Big Men amass goods from clan followers. Bulmer also notes that intraclan exchange takes place among the Kyaka Enga but it occurs several days prior to the main *te* distribution (Bulmer 1960–61: 6). The intraclan exchanges seem to be the means by which Big Men amass goods. They involve little formal ceremony. The main *te* distribution is accompanied by formal ceremony and involves Big Men who give to their *te* partners in other clans (Bulmer 1960: 367).

Exchanges which are transacted as part of the *te* cycle follow a particular set of rules. The *te* exchange links exchange partners and their groups in a chain such that A gives to B, B gives to C, C gives to D, and so on. The *te* exchange cycle involves a large number of people in a number of different contiguous linguistic groups. Goods move consistently in one direction until they reach the last group. Then different goods move in the opposite direction. There are three phases to each cycle. Initiatory gifts given in the first phase consist of valuables such as small pigs, pork, salt, axes, shells, plumes, and, more recently, money. They are given privately or as part of a public payment of an affinal obligation. The individual nature of these gifts makes them appear like the other kinds of exchanges, which take place between partners outside of the *te*. Items are passed from exchange partner to exchange partner. It takes a period of two to three years for the first phase to reach the end of the *te* route (Meggitt 1974: 176). Eventually, the givers of the initiatory gift begin to demand repayment in live pigs. The clans at the far end return pigs plus some cassowaries and pearl shells, to their adjacent *te* exchange partners, at formal ceremonial distributions. The recipients, in turn, hold their distribution ceremony and so on down the line, as clan after clan successively hold the *te* ceremony. The pigs move in one direction to the end of the route. When this phase is completed, the clans at the other end begin to ask for pork. Those who received pigs last kill roughly half of the pigs they have gotten and cooked pork is returned to the givers of the pigs and so on along the route (Meggitt 1974: 177). The passage of pork takes from six to nine months to the end of the chain. The givers of the pork then begin asking for a return payment, which will initiate another cycle. Each complete cycle takes approximately four years, which allows sufficient time for the pig population to be replenished. This is an idealized version of the operation of the *te*. In actuality, when a clan holds its distribution, exchange partners from a number of different clans are present. The result is not a single stream of goods flowing from east to west, or from west to east, but rather a process by which goods move in those directions but along an intricate series of pathways.

Most accounts of the *te* concern the main distribution of pigs in the second phase. Men of clans who are about to receive in the *te* carry out a number of rites. Bus states that they do not speak, and they observe food restrictions, the most important of which is a taboo against eating sweet potatoes. The Big Men of the host clan will each kill a pig to make the spirits favorable so that their distribution is a success (Bus 1951: 820).

In the *te* distributions, Big Men act on behalf of their kin groups; the focus is on the relationship between groups. Followers of a Big Man do not act independently in the *te,* but channel their pigs to their Big Man (Waddell 1972a: 191). "The performance of the leaders of the clan in the Moka is also seen by its members as a performance of the whole group" (Bulmer 1960–61: 8). Only Elkin provides details of the actual distribution of pigs. Stakes are placed in lines and a pig is tethered to each stake. Each line of stakes represents a donor or several men acting together as a donor, either father and sons, brothers, or mother's brother and sister's son who resides with him (Elkin 1952–53: 186). Where two generations cooperate as a donor, the younger of the two will inherit the *te* partnership when the older dies.

Elkin observed three *te* distributions. The number of lines in the first case was twelve, with 443 pigs being distributed and two thousand people present (Elkin 1952–53: 179). In the second case, there were ten lines with 183 pigs distributed. In the third case, there were eight lines and 306 pigs distributed. The number of pigs in each of the lines varies. The lines would seem to represent the patrilineages of the clan. The range of eight to twelve fits Meggitt's figures for patrilineages per clan. It would seem that the Big Men who are donors vary in their status, since the number of pigs in each line varies, sometimes widely. Some Big Men head only lineages; more important Big Men head subclans as well. The most important Big Man heads the clan. Elkin specifically notes that the longest line of pigs belongs to the person who heads the *te* at that place (Elkin 1952–53: 191). He is the head of the clan that is hosting the *te*. The pigs are formally counted and then distributed. This is followed by a parade of Big Men and their followers who bring in bags of shells for distribution. Each Big Man has his own bag of shells. The Big Man who is giving the shells calls out the name of the recipient but the Big Man of the clan who heads the *te* directly hands out the shells. (Elkin 1952–53: 184; see also Bulmer 1960–61: 6). (Meggitt's discussion of the shells distributed indicates an important distinction between the Mae and the Laiapu. The latter place great emphasis on the shells as validating the distribution of the pigs, while the former see the shells as merely an accompaniment to the *te* [Meggitt 1974: 177 n. 23]). The important Big Men of the various invited clans will receive the greatest numbers of pigs, from different lines representing several lineages within the host clan. To enhance their own prestige, they will take all the pigs they have received from the various lines and arrange them in a separate line in order to display them (Elkin 1952–53: 187). The prestige of both givers and receivers is established in a public setting in the *te*. The several thousand people serve as witnesses to the enhancement of the prestige of the host group.

The third phase of the *te* cycle, the large-scale distribution of cooked pork, has not been described in the various published accounts of the *te*. As we had the opportunity to observe this phase of the cycle we will briefly describe it. (These observations were made during the course of field work in the Enga district in the summer of 1974.) The *te* distribution took place at Lenke (Lengge) on the Mae-Laiapu border. We attended this distribution with a Big Man from the Tsak (Syaka) Valley who had come to receive pigs from his *te* partner there, and hence our description is from the perspective of a recipient. The day before the scheduled distribution took place at Lenke, a smaller pork distribution had taken place at Lakamunda, at which the Lenke people had received sides of pork. The hosts at the Lenke distribution were of the Langgape clan of the Yakane phratry of the Mae Enga. Early on the morning of the distribution, smoke could be seen coming from the men's houses in various parts of the valley and slopes surrounding the ceremonial ground at Lenke. At each men's house, groups of men were butchering pigs and preparing and cooking the pork. Several cows were also butchered and cooked. Exchange partners of the hosts from more distant places had spent the night in the various men's houses in expectation of receiving pork the next day. In addition to the immediate partners of the hosts, some partners of those partners from still more distant places were also present.

A long wooden platform had been erected on the ceremonial ground where the sides of pork were to be displayed. The platform was about eighty feet long, about five feet wide, and about four and one-half feet from the ground. Guests began to arrive in the late morning, seating themselves not randomly but in particular locations depending upon their clan association and exchange partnerships. Those in groups receiving from Lenke, geographically to the east, sat on the left side facing the platform, to the east. Those groups who had given to Lenke and lived to the west and who had come as observers sat on the right facing the platform geographically to the west. At the peak of activity, people in attendance numbered over one thousand. Shortly after noon, men and women from the various men's house groups began to arrive carrying cooked sides of pork and vegetables. Ninety-four sides of pork representing forty-seven pigs, and the meat from two cows, were displayed. Four live pigs were tethered in front of the platform and were also subsequently distributed.

As the platform was being filled with sides of pork, those Big Men whose groups had already placed their pork on the platform stood on the platform with faces blackened, some of them decorated with fur and feathers, and delivered speeches about their importance and role in the *te*. Nine men's house groups or patrilineages were represented on the platform though the numbers of pigs displayed by each group varied, sometimes greatly. The distribution began with the live pigs. On hearing his name called, the recipient ran up to the platform where the donor stood holding the tethering rope of the pig. The recipient executed a circle around the donor and then took the pig. This is the normal procedure followed in the distribution of live pigs which occurs in the second phase of the *te*. The sides of pork were then distributed, several men calling out the names of recipients and giving sides of pork at the same time. When a man's name was called he would run up to the platform, the side of pork would be placed on his shoulders by the giver, and he would stagger back to his place under the weight of a hundred or more pounds of pork. Sons and younger brothers of Big Men shared the honor of distributing by assisting on the platform. Sometimes a son was delegated by an aged Big Man to go up to the platform to receive in his place. Quarters of the cows were similarly distributed at this time. Smaller packets of vegetables and innards were given with the sides of pork. When only a few sides of pork remained on the platform, these were cut into smaller pieces, which were then distributed along with some vegetables until the platform was bare.

Amongst those who received in the audience, sitting in the eastern area of the ceremonial ground, some received many sides of pork, as did the Big Man whom we accompanied to the ceremony. Others received single sides while many more received small packets of food. In addition to the distribution from the platform, many of those who received redistributed what they had received when they returned to their places. For example, our Big Man friend immediately redistributed four of the seven sides he received as well as pieces of meat and packages of vegetables to his exchange partners who had accompanied him. In fact, at the center of one group of recipients, we observed a man who had a notebook in which he was keeping track of those individuals to whom he was redistributing what he himself had just received.

Earlier, we indicated that a man's son inherited his father's exchange partnerships. This was confirmed by what we observed in connection with the distribution described above. Our Big Man friend had not redistributed three sides of pork that he had received. The day following the *te* distribution, these three sides were delivered to the son of a *te* partner of his who had just died. This was done in the presence of assembled mourners who acted as witnesses. The giving of this pork confirmed that the son was now his *te* partner.

Our Big Man from Tsak came to Lenke to receive pigs. He returned to the Tsak Valley empty-handed but in the course of the distribution and redistribution his status as a Big Man was enhanced. He received many sides of pork and he redistributed them to many of his partners. He also reaffirmed an exchange relationship with the next generation upon the death of an exchange partner. It was now his turn to kill many pigs and make a large-scale ceremonial distribution in concert with the other men's house groups of his clan to his *te* partners further east.

It is important to note that though Enga clans that border each other are frequently engaged in hostile actions with one another, they also intermarry and therefore are *te* partners to one another. Meggitt observes, "neighboring clans participating in the Te should mute hostilities during the second and third phases when clans have to act as corporate units. But sometimes the fighting (especially if it is over land) gets out of hand and Big Men simply have to postpone their clan's public distributions until they can negotiate a truce. In these circumstances, men of clans that are awaiting pigs or pork may try to intervene as peace makers" (Meggitt 1974: 178–79; see also Elkin 1952–53: 199; Bulmer 1960–61: 11).

Since *te* is a time of truce, it seems reasonable that it should be associated with the ceremonial payment of homicide compensation. Both Elkin and Meggitt state that *te* is the term for homicide compensation. Meggitt notes that, among the Laiapu, homicide compensation is always an accompaniment of the *te* whereas, among the Mae, homicide compensation may be part of the *te* as a matter of convenience but it may be paid independently of the *te* (Meggitt 1974: 174 n. 15; see also Elkin 1952–53: 200). In Elkin's description of three *te* ceremonies, homicide compensation was paid at each ceremony (See Elkin 1952–53: 184, 187). Thus there is the identification once again of enemies, with whom one fights, and to whom one pays homicide compensation; neighbors and affines; and *te* partners. Sometimes, dissatisfaction with the *te* payments received is a source of quarrel and dispute, which may escalate (Meggitt 1974: 181 n. 30; Elkin 1952–53: 164, 199).

From our information, the route of the Te generally conforms to Bus's description in his 1951 account as well as to that of Meggitt. Bus indicates that "Time and again rumors had it that they had started at Kore, but it was always denied again" (Bus 1951: 816). Bus identifies Kore with Kaugel. Our own informants twenty-three years later consistently spoke of waiting for the *te* to come from this area, which is in fact non-Enga-speaking. In general, the *te* moves along the river valleys, but frequently the connection between two river valleys will be across a range of mountains. For example, Tambul in the Kaugel Valley is joined to Walya on a branch of the Lai River and to the Tsak (Syaka) Valley, in both instances over ranges of mountains. The *te* therefore joins contiguous groups who compete over land, as well as groups separated by mountain ranges. The Kyaka Enga in the Baiyer River area, a fringe Enga group immediately adjacent to the Melpa, are involved in the *te* exchange cycle and the moka exchange of the Melpa, a different system of exchange. Mae Enga groups in the western part of the Enga district are not involved in the *te*.

Groups on the fringes of the *te* area, both Mae and others, as affines to Mae clans in the *te*, are connected to them as exchange partners. Though they do not actually participate in the *te*, they may be sources of goods used by their affinal connections in the *te* exchange (See Meggitt 1974: 173–74; Waddell 1972a: 86). They also may ultimately be receivers of *te* goods that are siphoned out of the *te* flow, in instances where *te* valuables are used to pay affinal obligations and debts. Since men are aware of the links in the exchange chain, their partner's partner and several links beyond, such siphoning off of valuables may result in disputes if individuals anticipated receiving particular objects they fancied.

In our discussion of the *te* cycle above, the timing of the various phases of the *te* was presented in a rather mechanical fashion. In reality, the timing of the phases is subject to great variation. A particular phase may not follow the full length of the *te* paths before it is reversed. Variation in the *te* cycle will also be introduced if people in a particular place refuse to take pigs when they are offered by exchange partners. They remove themselves from that particular *te* cycle while the flow of pigs will continue along other paths. This occurred during the famine of 1972 when partners refused to accept pigs because of the difficulty in feeding them. Thus, the geographical route followed during a particular *te* cycle varies. The timing of sequential distributions may be speeded up or delayed as well. For example, Elkin observed *te* distributions of live pigs by three different clans whose members were linked as exchange partners at three locations on three successive days. Like Elkin we also observed *te* pork distributions on successive days.

One of the structural implications of the *te* exchange cycle is uncertainty and doubt on the part of the participants. As Elkin long ago noted, the exchanges in the *te* are delayed exchanges. The organization of the *te* is such that A gives to B and B gives to C. A does not receive back from B until the cycle has reversed itself. When A does receive from B, he will receive goods of a different type than he has given. If A gave B an initiatory gift of shells and axes, he will be receiving live pigs in exchange at a much later date. A is never certain when, or how much, or even if he will receive a return from B. The delayed aspect of the exchange which characterizes systems of generalized exchange involving chains of exchange partners creates a greater degree of uncertainty than that which characterizes reciprocal exchange (A gives to B; B repays A). Since generalized exchange systems involve chains of partners exchanging, A depends not only on B but on successive partners down the line, C, D, E, and F, also repaying in order for A eventually to receive. If D refuses to accept live pigs from F during a time of famine, this act ultimately effects the receipt of pigs on the part of A. The uncertainty regarding returns, discussed above, relates to other aspects of the relationship between exchange partners. *Te* exchange partners are typically affines. Since the Enga marry the people they fight, *te* partnerships are between people who are potentially hostile to one another. This adds another dimension to the uncertainty of future repayment of goods given in the *te*.

The activities of the *te* distribution necessitate cooperation and coordination at the lineage and clan level. The overall pattern of the *te* cycle necessitates coordination between clans up and down the line. The *te* must take place in a time of peace. In order to have *te* presentations, fighting must cease and homicide compensations must be paid. The inter-relationship between homicide compensation and *te* exchanges is thus clarified. The *te* exchange cycle integrates a large number of groups, Enga and non-Enga, in a single system of generalized exchange. This represents a more inclusive level of structure than the individual Enga clans protecting their own interests, more inclusive even than Enga culture.

The Enga have an elaborate segmentary structure with several levels of segmentation. There are leaders at every level and their activity is situationally determined. The position is achieved and is not connected to ritual practice or the control of special knowledge. The Enga have the most extensive marriage prohibitions of the societies we have considered. Sister exchange is expressly forbidden. Though there is no mention of keeping track of exchanges of women by clans over time, in fact the tendency of neighboring clans to intermarry would lead to continuing relationships through the exchange of women. The exchanges of women take place with the same clans with whom they engage in warfare. The Enga say, "We marry the people we fight."

As in some of the other societies we have considered, there is a sharp separation between men and women. Women are considered to be polluting and intercourse with them is dangerous. Meggitt suggests that this is connected to the fact that wives come from enemy groups. A married man will use magical spells to protect himself, while bachelors practice the *sanggai* purification ritual to accomplish the same aim. Only vegetable food and marsupials play a role. Pigs, which are identified with females, are not involved. The bog iris, a wild plant, is identified with the clan and inherited from generation to generation like the *mi* among the Melpa. The ceremony does not involve blood letting, but emphasizes purification through bathing and the rubbing of the bog iris on the skin.

The clan bespelling ceremony is a dedication of pigs and

marsupials to the ancestors in order to insure the well-being and fertility of the clan and its gardens. Ritual experts involved in the ceremony are not the clan Big Men but the Big Man acts as a sponsor. The sacred stones of the clan are involved.

Ritual is minimal in the *te,* although there is sacrifice of a pig to the spirits at the start to make the ceremonial distribution a success. The theme of fertility is not mentioned. However, there is a connection between warfare and *te. Te* partners are affines with whom one may have a hostile relationship and the word *te* itself means compensation for a homicide. Sometimes compensation is given at the same time as one of the stages of the *te* distribution. Warfare and *te* are like two sides of the same coin. When the *te* is in progress, compensation is paid and peace and regional integration are emphasized. Warfare on the other hand emphasizes hostility and the fragmentation of the region.

Kin Groups and Kinship Terminology

With this chapter, we embark on a comparative study of the material we have presented in chapters 2–11. There has been considerable debate regarding the nature of kin groups in New Guinea and we think it is important for us to present our own perspective on this matter. We begin our comparative analysis with a discussion of this topic but this is not because we give residential and descent groups a logical priority. Instead, our approach is one that focuses upon the nature of relationships between groups with particular emphasis upon exchanges as manifestations of relationship and upon the hierarchical ordering into successively more inclusive groupings. Relationships of exchange characterize groupings at all levels of the hierarchy. These relationships involve warfare, homicide compensation, exchange of women, and exchange of ceremonial goods. Particularly striking in the New Guinea societies with segmentary systems but also evident in the others is the characteristic that external relations on a lower level of the hierarchy become internal relations on a higher level.

The first attempt at a comparative analysis of New Guinea kin units was part of a larger consideration of local groups in Melanesia by Hogbin and Wedgewood (1952–53). They set up a conceptual framework using a range of quasi-botanical terms which encompassed the variations in sociopolitical organization found in Melanesia. Their framework was concerned with the intersections of local political and residential units and the kinship structure. This theme of the relationship between residential units and the nature of the kinship and descent system has continued to be the concern of subsequent analysts of New Guinea social structure, but the terminology proposed by Hogbin and Wedgewood has not been adopted.

Beginning in the 1950s, ethnographic accounts of societies in Highland New Guinea started to appear and the segmentary character of these patrilineal societies prompted anthropologists such as Salisbury (1956) to suggest the applicability of the segmentary lineage model developed for African societies to Highland New Guinea. Though Salisbury made note of the fact that there were some differences between the structure of African societies and Highland New Guinea societies, such as importance of genealogies, it was Barnes (1962) who called into question the applicability of African models to New Guinea. In classical descent-group theorizing, focus is upon the nature of the units and their composition rather than upon the relationships between units. Barnes therefore dwelled upon the problem of recruitment to group membership and the fact that, in the Highlands, descent is not the principal mode of recruitment to groups. He was concerned that a sizeable proportion of nonagnates are present in what have been characterized as descent groups. However, the rights of these individuals are not equal to the rights of agnates until they have been assimilated into the descent groups, which usually takes several generations. He placed greater emphasis upon individual ties and relationships than upon intergroup ties. Ceremonial exchange was seen by Barnes in terms of individual transactions rather than as the way in which groups are both linked and opposed to one another. In similar fashion he viewed relationships through marriage on an individual basis rather than in terms of alliances between groups. Finally he noted that in Highland New Guinea societies, long genealogies of agnatic ancestors which elsewhere serve as a charter for group membership are not maintained, nor are there ceremonies that bring all agnatic relatives together. Barnes did not recognize a distinction between descent as an ideological construct and descent as the means of recruitment to corporate groups.

M. de Leprevanche (1967–68), in a later article, emphasized the importance of the local group as a focus of a wide range of activities including warfare, ceremonial exchange, and marital relationships. Residence and participation in the activities of the local group serves to identify individuals as members of the group. Individuals may be recruited to the group in a variety of ways. Agnatic descent is the idiom used to characterize the local group and to refer to intergroup relations. De Leprevanche echoes the general point made by Sahlins (1965) that descent provides an ideological framework separate and apart from its operation as a mode of recruitment. This position that descent or kinship operates as symbol system used to represent social relations is carried forward in a discussion of descent in New Guinea by La Fontaine (1973). Strathern in his discussion also emphasizes the importance of descent as a dogma. He notes that agnatic relationships especially fit the emphasis in the Highlands on male strength, cooperation, and superiority over women (A. J. Strathern 1969a: 39).

Aside from Hogbin and Wedgewood, all of the previous authors have been concerned only with the Highlands. Kaberry (1967) reiterates the optative nature of recruitment to groups in the Highlands and then proceeds to demonstrate its applicability to her own field materials on the Northern Abelam. Agnatic descent is present as an ideological principle of organization in the Northern Abelam though they do not have a segmentary system.

Like Kaberry, we see profit in considering the Highlands and Lowlands of New Guinea as a single area within which various types of comparisons can be made. In all of the societies we have considered, postmarital residence is virilocal. There is a difference in settlement pattern in which Highland societies contrast with Lowland societies. In the Lowlands, there is a pattern of nucleated settlement with several hamlets close together comprising a village, or a single village center with dispersed hamlets used at various times during the agricultural year. In the Highlands, which has a higher density of population, there are no nucleated centers of populations except for the temporary ceremonial villages built for the pig festivals. There is also a difference in the number of levels of segmentation between the societies in the two areas. There are many more levels of segmentation in the Highlands ranging from three to six levels. Among the Lowland societies we have considered, the range is from one to three.

Tor exhibits the simplest type in which a core of men form the stable component of a village though there is no ideology of agnatic descent. The village, which is equivalent to the tribe, is the unit that is territorially defined, controls land, and acts as a unit in warfare and feasting.

In the other Lowland societies we have examined there is more than one level. The form that characterizes Arapesh and Abelam is ideally a single clan hamlet owning land and with an ideology of patrilineal descent which is paired in an exchange relationship with another patriclan hamlet. The village is composed of several such patriclan hamlets on opposite sides of a moiety division, one of each pair ranged on the opposite side. The Iatmul do not have clan hamlets, but only large, compact, multiclan villages. The village or locality which is the most inclusive solidary unit engages in some activities with other villages or localities such as marriage exchanges, warfare, and large-scale feasting associated with ceremonial activities such as interlocality initiation rites. Only at the clan level is there a linkage between clan and ancestors, totemic associations, and names comprising an ideology of agnation. The Banaro represent a variation of this pattern in which each hamlet is in turn subdivided into two parts, each one a distinct kin group, which may not intermarry but which have a special exchange relationship. However, the two parts of a village believe themselves to be descended from a common ancestor. Like the others, a hamlet is paired with another hamlet, several making up a village. In Wogeo, two patrilineal kin groups, unrelated to one another, comprise the two parts of what Hogbin calls a single village. In many respects, the paired halves of the Wogeo village are like the paired clan hamlets discussed above and the districts are the equivalent of localities. Among the Keraki, the tribe is composed of several villages and seems to be the equivalent of the locality. Each village ideally consists of men of one side of the moiety division. Ceremonial activity, such as initiation, which requires both moieties involves the villages of the tribe which sort themselves on either side of the moiety division.

Though patrilineal ideology characterizes units at the lowest level in the societies we have examined with the exception of Tor, actual composition of these kin units seems to include varying proportions of nonagnates. The combination of optative recruitment coupled with an agnatic ideology recognized by Kaberry as applicable to the Northern Abelam clan is also recognized as applicable to the Wogeo patrilineage by Hogbin (1970a). In Lowland societies, the ideology of agnatic descent as an organizing principle characterizes only a single level of segmentation (clan) with units at the next more inclusive level of segmentation, the locality, tribe, or village being defined on the basis of common residence and participation in a number of activities as a unit.

For the Highlands, the three to six levels of segmentation of the descent system were seen as a segmentary lineage structure, which then led to the comparison with African societies. The segmentary structure of the Highlands is hierarchically ordered so that minimal groupings—men's houses, sublineages, or sub-subclans—are ordered into subclans, which are ordered into clans, which are ordered into phratries or tribes. The Highland societies we have examined vary in that there may be fewer levels or more levels of segmentation than the schematic form we have presented. A clear distinction must be made between the principles by which individuals become members of a group and the ideology that is used to characterize the unity of the group. In all of these Highland societies, individuals may become members of minimal residential units through some claim other than agnation. One of the ways in which nonagnates may come to be included is as followers of a Big Man. They may also come as war refugees, or as sons of sisters who have been divorced. For the most part these minimal residential groups seem to be characterized in terms of an ideology of agnatic descent, regardless of the means by which individuals may have come to be members. In some cases, like Melpa and Chimbu, an alternative conceptualization exists for this minimal group which recognizes that its members in actual fact have varying origins. Among the Melpa, the contrast is between the agnatic conceptualization of "one blood" as applied to the minimal unit and the conceptualization of the men residing in the men's house as a unit on the same level.

In all of the Highland societies, there is a single native term that can be applied to groups at any level of segmentation. This term usually has the connotation of a line of men.[1] Though there is one term that is used to refer to groups at all levels of segmentation in terms of an ideology of agnation, the degree to which these groups are united in a single genealogical charter varies among these societies. In some societies like Enga, Melpa, Chimbu, and Kuma, there seems to be a more or less stable genealogical charter that links groups at the subclan levels as separate groups descending from the sons of the clan founder and groups at the clan level as sons of the founder of the phratry. Meggitt also indicates that, more rarely, founders on the clan or subclan level may be sons-in-law who have married in and whose descendants are referred to as nephews, but they operate toward one

1. The specific terms and their glosses in each of the societies we have considered are as follows:

> Maring: *kai* or *yu kai*, meaning root or root of men (Rappaport 1968: 17, 18)
>
> Manga: *ka*, meaning rope or line (Cook 1967: 257)
>
> Kuma: *doogum*, meaning line, used with adjectives denoting bigness and smallness (Reay 1959a: 41)
>
> Chimbu: *nem-angigl*, meaning father-brother, used for groups of various sizes (Brown 1960: 31)
>
> Melpa: several terms are provided, each of which can be used for groups at the various levels of segmentation such as *mbo tenda*, meaning one stock; *mbi tenda, reklaep tenda*, meaning one name, one line (A. J. Strathern 1972a: 18)
>
> Enga: Meggitt refers to the conceptualization of a line of men from one penis for phratry, clan, and patrilineage (Meggitt 1965a: ch. 2)

another for practical purposes as agnates (Meggitt 1965a: 14). The groups at these levels are linked in terms of the genealogical relationships of their putative founders. In general, actual genealogical reckoning is very shallow, particularly for the Kuma and the Enga. In fact, Reay notes that it is expedient for the Kuma to be uninterested in genealogies since the lack of strict reckoning facilitates assimilation into agnatic descent groups of nonagnatic kin (Reay 1959a: 34). The units at the various levels of segmentation in Manga and Maring are characterized by agnatic descent ideology. However, no genealogical charter such as described above seems to link the units at the different levels of segmentation. Another variation is presented in Chimbu where, at the most inclusive level of segmentation, the tribe, a political alliance between clans not agnatically related, is at the same level as the Chimbu phratry. While the phratry is conceptualized agnatically, the tribe is a territorial and political entity.

Mention should be made of the variations in kinship terminology in the societies we have examined. In the Highlands all six societies have Iroquois terminology. Four of the Lowland societies, Abelam, Wogeo, Banaro, and probably Keraki also have Iroquois terminology. Among the Tor, the intertribal variations in kinship terminology make it impossible to characterize it in a general way. Among the Highland societies, the kinship terminology is applied so that the children of nonagnates residing in the same place are referred to as son and daughter. The terminology therefore facilitates the absorption of nonagnates into agnatic kin groups. Two of the Lowland societies, Arapesh and Iatmul, have Omaha terminologies. In the case of the Arapesh, the terminology is clearly linked to the separation of lineages into wife givers and wife takers in several generations above ego so that marriage prohibitions with these lineages may be observed. This is an instance where a Crow-Omaha marriage structure, as described by Lévi-Strauss, correlates with Omaha kinship terminology. The Omaha terminology of the Iatmul also serves to separate the lines of wife givers and wife takers. In this case it is related not to a negative marriage rule but to a positive marriage rule of preference for marriage with second matrilateral cross-cousin.

In summary, the kinship and descent systems of all of the societies we have considered share a number of characteristics. In all of these societies postmarital residence is virilocal. They uniformly have descent groups based upon a patrilineal ideology of descent, with the exception of the Tor, who are cognatic and have no descent groups. Nonagnates are regularly incorporated into residential kin groups, and after several generations their descendants become regular members of the patrilineal descent group. There are also important differences, which serve to contrast the Highlands with the Lowlands. The settlement pattern of the Lowlands is primarily that of nucleated villages, with two hierarchical levels of grouping: the patriclan hamlet and the village consisting of unrelated clans. In contrast, in the Highlands, with dispersed settlement, up to five levels of hierarchy are linked into a segmentary structure. A common ideology of patrilineal descent unifies the groupings at the different levels.

13 Marriage Rules and Structure of Affinal Relationship

The marriage practices of New Guinea societies have been seen as almost infinite in their variety. In actual fact, as we shall demonstrate, the marriage patterns in our sample can be reduced to several basic patterns of marriage structure. Further, these patterns represent a series of transformations. We will consider the structure of marriage in terms of three variables. The series of transformations we will present represent permutations of these variables. The first variable is the exchange of women between two groups. In some societies, the exchange is of real sisters; in others it is of classificatory sisters. Immediate exchange of women is emphasized in some cases, and delayed exchange in others. The second variable is the preference for renewing the tie created by a previous marriage. Sometimes, the emphasis is upon immediately renewing the tie created by a marriage in the next generation. In other instances, the tie cannot be renewed for one or more generations. This latter point is related to our third variable, the extent to which one marriage generates prohibitions on a series of future marriages.

Direct sister exchange, as exemplified by the Tor, Keraki, and Banaro, is the simplest and most basic form of marriage in the societies under consideration. Among the Tor, a man can marry only if he has a sister, or a female substitute, to give in exchange. The Tor say, "When you have no sister, you cannot marry." Several possible alternatives to direct sister exchange are mentioned. If a man has not been given a wife in exchange for his sister, he has a claim over his sister's daughter. Though he cannot marry his SiDa himself, he can use her to exchange for a wife for himself. Marriage with bilateral cross cousin is permitted. This marriage structure creates a dual organization; however, there is no formal moiety system. In terms of the variables, direct exchange of women emphasizes real sisters, though the exchange need not be simultaneous. The exchange usually takes place within a single generation; however, a man giving his sister has a claim upon her daughter, if the exchange has not been completed in the previous generation. There is no prohibition created by a previous marriage, and the tie would seem to be renewed in the next generation.

Like the Tor, the Keraki emphasize the exchange of true sisters. If a man does not have a true sister, he may exchange a classificatory sister for a wife. He is then under an obligation to return a woman in the future to the kinsman who gave him a "sister." He may also acquire a woman of his own moiety by purchase, and use her as a "sister" to exchange for a wife. The exchange may be simultaneous or deferred. The two categories of women with whom marriage is permitted are bilateral cross-cousin, and SiDa, and in both cases marriage with the classificatory rather than the actual relative is the more common. The preference for bilateral cross-cousin marriage is an indication that sister exchange can occur in successive generations. The dual organization exemplified by Keraki marriage structure is also manifested in their moiety system. Among the Keraki, the variables operate in the following manner: ideally there is an exchange of true sisters, though classificatory sisters may be substituted. The exchange is usually completed in the same generation. If the exchange has not been completed, a man may take his SiDa as a wife. The completion of the exchange in this manner constitutes an oblique marriage. The presence of bilateral cross-cousin marriage indicates that the ties should be renewed in every generation. There are no prohibitions created by a previous marriage.

Among the Banaro, the marriage pattern is one of sister exchange, as strictly observed as possible. The exchange of sisters takes place between "the left" clan in one hamlet and its corresponding "left" clan in another hamlet. When a pair of marriages is negotiated, the second clan in each hamlet will also immediately negotiate a marriage exchange. Bilateral cross-cousins can marry in every generation. In Banaro, there are two sets of cross-cutting divisions encompassing two hamlets (see figure 9). Two clans in the same hamlet, the "left" and the "right," are on opposite sides of a moiety division and they exchange ceremonial services as *mundu* with one another including sexual intercourse in ceremonial contexts, but they cannot exchange women in marriage. The pairs of clans of the two hamlets which intermarry form the other cross-cutting dual division, which is based upon the exchange of sisters. The ties between a pair of intermarrying clans are renewed in every generation. This can be through the marriage of bilateral cross-cousins or through the marriage exchange of other families in the appropriate clan. The Banaro case may be seen to be the result of the interaction of two variables: the exchange of women between two groups and the preference for renewing the tie created by a previous marriage. In the Banaro case, the exchange of women is the exchange of real sisters. The Banaro prefer to renew the tie created by a marriage in the succeeding generation so that

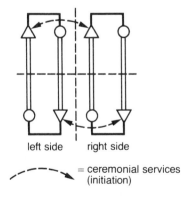

left side   right side

= ceremonial services
(initiation)

Fig. 9.   Banaro

the sides of the dual organization continue to remain affines to one another in every generation. A marriage does not create prohibitions on future marriages.

The societies we shall now discuss all share a prohibition against marriage with first cousins. This prohibition significantly alters the basic structure of dual organization, sister exchange, and bilateral cross-cousin marriage which characterizes the three societies we have just considered.

The island of Wogeo has exogamous localized patrilineages and exogamous matrimoieties. Though first cross-cousins may not be married, there is a preference for marriage between the children of cross-cousins. The ideal marriage is for a man to marry his FaFaSiSoDa. A headman usually gives land as part of the dowry of his eldest daughter. Given the prohibition against marriage between first cousins, the preferred marriage rule is the means by which dowry land given two generations earlier is returned to its original owners.

In the Wogeo case, exchange of women is very important, but not immediate exchange. Though actual sister exchange does occur, it is of minor importance. It is delayed exchange that is significant here. The return may occur in the next generation. However, in that instance a girl is returned but to another family in the village from which her mother came, since marriage with first cousins is prohibited. The preferred return is made two generations after the original marriage, when a girl and the original dowry land is returned (see figure 10). In this instance, a girl returns to the family from which her own grandmother came. Ties between groups through affinal links are renewed but in every other generation rather than in every generation. If the return is made in the next generation, then classificatory rather than actual relatives are involved. In this case we encounter prohibitions created by a marriage. The prohibition against marrying first cross-cousins is of this kind. This prohibition taken together with the presence of a preference for marriage with second cross-cousins, localized exogamous patrilineages, and non-localized exogamous matrimoieties suggests the possibility that Wogeo may be seen as an eight-class section system.

Preference for marriage with second cross-cousin, spe-

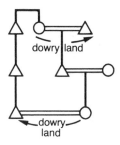

Fig. 10.   Wogeo—FaFaSiSoDa Marriage

cifically father's father's sister's son's daughter, in conjunction with sister exchange also occurs in the Highlands of New Guinea in Maring, Manga, and Kuma societies. After describing each, we shall analyze them as a unit. Among the Maring, sister exchange is said to be the ideal way to obtain a wife. A number of marriage prohibitions are present. The patrilineal clan is exogamous. When men of a clan give or receive women from other clans, the next generation is prohibited from giving or receiving women from those clans. All first cousins as a result are therefore prohibited spouses. The Maring have one prescriptive marriage rule, which states that a man should marry his FaFaSiSoDa. In Maring eyes, a woman's granddaughter should marry back into her own subclan, and they refer to this as "returning the planting material." This marriage is a means of renewing ties between groups in alternate generations. Clans that renew their ties through marriage in this way are said to form a "pig-woman road." Reference to women as "planting material" also occurs when women are exchanged between formerly warring groups as a peacemaking gesture.

The Manga have the same set of preferences and prohibitions as the neighboring Maring. Sister exchange is the most frequent way of obtaining a wife. Actual as well as classificatory sisters are exchanged. In addition to clan exogamy, once a marriage has taken place between two clan moieties from different clans, no other marriages may take place for a generation (see figure 11). All first cousins are prohibited as spouses, but second cousins who live elsewhere and are not categorized as relatives may be married. The prescriptive rule for marriage with FaFaSiSoDa requires that a man give his daughter to his mother's lineage. If he does not return his daughter to the lineage that provided his mother, then his mother's spirit is said to become angry. When clans continue to exchange women they are said to be joined by "roads."

The Kuma are similar to Maring and Manga. Exchange marriage is the basic form. This is phrased in terms of exchange of sisters, but more frequently classificatory rather than real sisters are exchanged. An immediate return is preferred. The Kuma clan is exogamous. The other marriage prohibitions encompass all close kin including first cousins and forbid marrying into one's mother's subclan. When ties between affinally linked groups grow weak, then it is desirable to reaffirm such ties through the marriage of children of cross cousins. This is referred to by the Kuma as "taking one's road." Most marriages renew such affinal ties. Reay explicitly indicates that if the return has not been completed within the same generation then it is completed two genera-

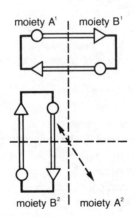

Fig. 11.   Manga

tions later when a man may demand a second cross-cousin in exchange for the woman given two generations earlier. Thus, two alternatives are present among the Kuma, either immediate return in the form of sister exchange or delayed exchange in which, because of prohibition against first cross-cousin marriage, the return must be made two generations later. Since what is occurring in the second generation is a return rather than an exchange, it is not simply the marriage of second cross-cousins but specifically marriage with patrilateral second cross-cousin. This is the only second cross-cousin marriage that can constitute a return. Marriage with second matrilateral cross-cousin is not a return because women in this case only move in one direction.

In these three Highland societies, the Maring, Manga, and Kuma, there are great similarities of marriage structure. The variables we have considered operate in a similar fashion in all three societies. Sister exchange is an ideal in all three, real sisters if possible, but otherwise classificatory sisters. This type of direct exchange is preferred. However, in the absence of direct exchange, delayed exchange is necessary. In all three societies if the exchange is not completed in the same generation, there is a rule that allows a man to claim a second cross-cousin as a return for the girl's grandmother. In the native terminology, this is conceived of as "following one's road" or 'returning the planting material," thus conceptually linking the two marriages. Regarding renewal of affinal links in succeeding generations, there seems to be a preference for such renewal among all three societies. This renewal can be achieved through a new exchange of sisters. If there is a return of a girl as a wife to her grandmother's group, this constitutes a continuation of the tie. In all three societies, the prohibition against marriage with any first cross-cousin is present.

In his analysis of the Manga marriage system, Cook offers a model in which he tries to incorporate the three features of sister exchange, prohibition on marriage with first cross-cousin, and preference for marriage with second cross-cousin. While it is possible to present a model that incorporates the three features, there seems to us to be a logical contradiction. If direct sister exchange is practiced, there would seem to be no reason for the continued existence of a claim to be exercised two generations later. Prior to his discussion of the model, Cook presents the two marriage forms as alternative methods for acquiring a wife. In that case, they would represent complementary patterns and would not operate simultaneously. Reay also presents these two patterns as complementary for the Kuma. Taking sister exchange by itself, the exchange is accomplished in one generation, not to be renewed in the next generation because of the prohibition on first cross-cousin marriage, but possibly renewed anytime thereafter. Given that the preference is for renewal of the marriage tie as soon as possible through sister exchange again, the outcome is a model requiring four groups which is in fact Cook's model (see figure 12). In this instance, male egos are marrying second bilateral cross-cousins. The prospective marriage partner would be MoMoBrDaDa, who is also FaMoBrSoDa, who is also MoFaSiDaDa, who is also FaFaSiSoDa. Cook's model represents this system rather than the Manga preference for only FaFaSiSoDa. With the preference for marriage with FaFaSiSoDa and an absence of sister exchange, the result is a model with a minimum of eight groups. We are inclined to see these four societies, Kuma, Maring, Manga, as well as Wogeo, as societies in which two complementary marriage patterns, sister exchange and de-

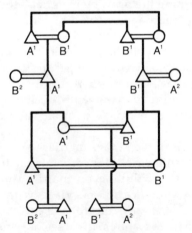

Fig. 12.   Cook's Model for the Manga

layed exchange over two generations (marriage with
FaFaSiSoDa), coexist. In Wogeo, there seems to be greater
emphasis upon preference for marriage with FaFaSiSoDa
than upon sister exchange. The intersection of exogamous
patrilineages and matrimoieties makes it possible to fit
Wogeo to the model of FaFaSiSoDa marriage with its
minimum of eight groups. Cook in fact "creates" Wogeo
when he suggests that "In order to analytically exclude the
remaining two male second cousin types (as marriage
partners), it would be necessary to construct an eight section
system and perhaps matrilineal 'ghost moieties' " (Cook
1969: 11, n. 4). The Highland societies—Kuma, Maring, and
Manga—place equal emphasis on sister exchange and marriage with FaFaSiSoDa. We see these as alternative marriage
patterns that are the expression of two different, though related, exchange structures.

The characteristics that define marriage among the Kuma,
Maring, and Manga are also found in Northern Abelam, but
to a lesser extent. Though there are no prescriptive marriage
rules, statements of marriage preference are presented by
Kaberry. The clan is exogamous. Real sister exchange occurs;
however, the exchange of women between clans is more
common, and is favored. Sometimes the exchange is immediate, at other times the return is delayed until the next
generation. Marriage between first cross-cousins is regarded
as incestuous. However, marriage between the children of
first cross-cousins is said to be desirable because it encour-
ages cooperation between their groups. In terms of our analytic variables, the Northern Abelam exchange women,
more usually clan sisters, rather than real sisters. The return
may be immediate, or it may be completed in the next generation. A marriage creates a prohibition against renewal of the
tie in the next generation, since first cross-cousins are forbidden as mates. Renewal of ties between groups is favored
in the second generation after a marriage. The model that
combines sister exchange and second bilateral cross-cousin
marriage would also seem to be applicable to the Northern
Abelam. There is no mention of second patrilateral cross-
cousin marriage, as occurs in the Highlands or Wogeo. The
emphasis here is on renewing the tie in alternate generations

by the exchange of women rather than the return of a woman in the second generation for a woman given two generations earlier.

As in the Highland societies, Kuma, Maring, and Manga, in Iatmul there are two different marriage rules that are in complementary distribution. The complementarity of the two rules is clearly established by the ethnographer, quoting native informants who state that one either marries according to one rule or according to the other but that both rules may not operate simultaneously.

The first marriage rule is that sisters should be exchanged. The exchange of women need not involve real sisters, but may involve women of the same clan or of the same village who are considered classificatory sisters for the purposes of the exchange. Real sister exchange in the next generation is not possible since the Iatmul prohibit marriage with the first cross-cousin. This relationship between two clans based upon the exchange of "sisters" is continued over time. Two clans in such a relationship have a special reciprocal term for one another, and assist one another.

The second Iatmul marriage rule is for marriage with FaMoBrSoDa, who is called *iai*. Marriage with *iai* creates a structure of generalized exchange in which each group gives women to two other groups, and receives women from two other groups. Wife givers and wife takers are always separate, and no return is ever made for a woman received. *Iai* marriage seems to be the pattern that is reflected in Iatmul kinship terminology. Bateson long ago pointed out that ego's group was related to four other groups and a separate term existed for each of them.

The Iatmul, like Wogeo, Kuma, Maring, and Manga, practice a form of second cross-cousin marriage. Both bilateral second cross-cousin marriage and marriage with FaFaSiSoDa involve exchange of women between groups. Marriage with FaMoBrSoDa, the form found among the Iatmul, does not. The Iatmul are aware of the absence of a return since they say that "a woman should climb the same ladder that her father's father's sister climbed," meaning that she should marry into the same family that her father's father's sister did. This contrasts with the Maring idiom of "returning the planting material" in which they describe FaFaSiSoDa marriage as a return of a woman for a woman given two generations earlier.

In terms of our three diagnostic variables, the two alternative marriage structures of the Iatmul, sister exchange and *iai* marriage, operate in very different ways. The first is characterized by the exchange of women, while the second is not. With regard to the second variable, renewal of the marriage tie in succeeding generations, clans which exchange women through sister exchange continue to do so through the generations. In *iai* marriage affinal links are also renewed, but through women going in the same direction. The third variable operates in both Iatmul marriage forms, since a marriage creates a prohibition on future marriages, marriages with first cross-cousins being prohibited. These two marriage structures cannot be collapsed into one another, or combined into a single structure.

The next group of societies in our sample is differentiated from those we have already considered by the expansion of the scope of their marriage prohibitions. Emphasis upon exchange of women continues to be important; however, the exchanges take a different form.

The Chimbu, a Highland society, exemplify this combination of more extensive prohibitions, coupled with an emphasis on the exchange of women. Nilles's account of the marriage prohibitions indicate that first and second bilateral cross-cousins are prohibited as mates as well as third cousins who are members of mother's clan.

The Chimbu emphasize exchange in marriage. Though the smaller scale units—the subclan sections—negotiate marriages, it is at the level of the larger scale units—the clans—that an account is kept of the state of the exchange. Simultaneous exchange of women between two groups does not take place. Rather, the return may be delayed sometimes into the next generation. In fact, several women may go in one direction before women go in the opposite direction. The state of the exchange between the two clans is usually commented upon at the marriage ceremony.

Though exchange of women is emphasized among the Chimbu, the return is delayed rather than immediate. Nevertheless, continuing exchange over generations seems to be important. The extent of the prohibitions would seem to necessitate spreading affinal connections in such a way that a subclan must intermarry with several subclans in one or several other clans. The emphasis on continuing exchange would imply that ties are continually renewed, especially between clans and tribes.

Among the Arapesh, marriage prohibitions are further extended. If one's own lineage either gives a woman to or takes a woman from another lineage, no marriage can take place with that lineage for at least three and possibly four generations. All first and second cross-cousins and possibly third cross-cousins are prohibited as spouses in addition to the prohibition on females in one's own group. Sister exchange is mentioned as a positive preference in marriage. True sister exchange occurs, but is not very common. More usually two clans or two localities are involved in a continuing exchange of classificatory "sisters" over time.

In terms of our analytic variables, the extent of prohibitions is greater than among the societies we have considered so far, extending through the third generation. If a renewal of the tie is to take place, it cannot occur before the fourth generation, given the prohibitions. However, renewal of ties does seem to be of significance in the relations between localities. Localities, made up of a number of clans, become entities in such exchanges and keep track of the state of the exchange. Exchange of women between groups is heavily stressed by the Arapesh and an effort is made to see each marriage as either a return for a previous marriage or as the incursion of a new debt. The effect of the extensive prohibitions taken together with the other features results in a system in which a particular clan will be exchanging women with a wide range of other clans in their own locality and in a few other localities.

The Melpa, a Highland society, have as extensive a set of prohibitions as the Arapesh. No marriage is possible if blood relationship is remembered. Since genealogical reckoning is shallow, this is usually for three or four generations. Seen in group terms, once a marriage is contracted between two men's houses, no further marriages are possible as long as the tie is remembered. This series of prohibitions would seem to preclude the possibility of true sister exchange and in fact the Stratherns indicate that direct sister exchange does not take place. However, the Melpa place great emphasis upon the desirability of the exchange of women between clans, thus classificatory clan sisters can be exchanged. Clans keep track of the state of the exchange. Several marriages between two clans within a single generation are advantageous to strengthen the ties between them. However, if too many marriages take place intermarriage ceases because the ties are too close. The combination of the desirability of exchange of women and ties through marriage, coupled with the extensive series of prohibitions, produces a pattern of relationship wherein the minimal units—the men's houses—are compelled to maintain a spread of affinal links with different men's houses. However, because of the continuing relationships between clans, these ties between men's houses tend to cluster in a limited number of clans. At the clan level, this results in an optimal density of marriages between two clans, with each of them concerned with the balance of the flow of women.

The Melpa place emphasis on exchange of women. However, clan sisters rather than true sisters are exchanged. One marriage creates an extensive series of prohibitions. The men's house units have a wide spread of affinal ties as a result of these prohibitions. However, renewal of ties between clans in successive generations is stressed.

The Mae Enga have as extensive a set of marriage prohibitions as the Chimbu, Arapesh, and Melpa. What is most striking about the Enga is the absence of any emphasis on the exchange of women. Real sister exchange is prohibited and there is no conceptualization of exchange of classificatory sisters between groups. Meggitt presents a complex series of prohibitions which indicates that all first cousins, cross and parallel, are forbidden as mates. Some second cousins including the women of the subclans of father's mother, mother's mother, and mother's father are prohibited as spouses. The daughters of female cousins in these clans, who are second cousins, may be married. The shallowness of genealogical reckoning noted by Meggitt would seem to permit the possibility of marriage with third cousin.

It would appear that the prohibitions presented by Meggitt are only part of the picture. Given the frequency of inter-marriage between neighboring clans, the Mae statements about marriage with neighbors, and finally the important exchange relationships that develop from the affinal relationship, we hypothesize that connections between clans will be renewed by marriage when the ties grow cold, that is after two generations have passed.

Of all the societies we have considered, the Mae Enga stand out by the absence of any mention of exchange of women. Similarly, there are no statements about the desirability of renewal of ties created by earlier marriages. Renewal can only be inferred from the tendency of individuals from neighboring clans to intermarry over the generations. The only statements that are presented comprise an elaborate set of prohibitions on future marriages which have been created by previous marriages. These would seem to have the effect of spreading affinal ties very widely, which is in keeping with the nature of the integration of their exchange system.

The societies whose marriage patterns we have considered here can be represented as a series of transformations from the Tor to the Enga. Each of the societies represents a particular combination of the variables. The transformations represent changes in these variables. Exchange of women is present in every society of the series except the Enga. True or classificatory sisters may be exchanged. What constitutes a classificatory "sister" varies in relation to the size of entities exchanging women. Among the Tor, family lines exchange women, and a classificatory "sister" given in marriage must be a close agnatic relative. In Arapesh, localities exchange women, and a classificatory "sister" is a member of one's locality. In Chimbu, clans keep track of the exchange, and a classificatory "sister" is a clan "sister." The exchange may be simultaneous, as among the Banaro where a woman is returned as part of the same ceremony, or the return may be delayed a few years or into the next generation. With societies having a prohibition on marriage with first cross-cousin like Wogeo, the return may not come until two generations later. Either the return is made in the same generation or it is delayed two generations. These represent complementary alternatives. In none of these societies is the delayed return the only possible marriage.

In terms of prohibitions, the societies may be ranged from minimal prohibitions as among the Tor, Keraki, and Banaro, through a series of societies prohibiting first cross-cousin marriage, to those societies characterized by a wide-range series of multiple prohibitions extending over several generations. The more extensive the prohibitions, the larger the scale of grouping which is engaged in the exchange of women. All of the societies seem to renew ties created by previous marriages and all, with the exception of Enga, see this as desirable. The metaphor of "roads" is frequently used to refer to the connections made by previous marriages which should be continued through new marriages.

Tor and Keraki represent the basic structure of which the others are transformations. This structure is one based on sister exchange in which two sides exchange sisters in every generation. Bilateral cross-cousin marriage is the preferred form, with exchanges being completed in the same generation. In both of these societies, however, rights over sister's daughter are an indication that delay can sometimes occur. This is a precursor of one of the transformations from this basic structure. The dual organization of this basic structure is formally manifested in the moiety structure of the Keraki. The Banaro marriage structure represents a transformation from the basic structure which entails an internal division of each hamlet into a left and right side which cannot intermarry. A moiety division within the hamlet cross-cuts the dual organization created by sister exchange, which is the basic structure. This produces a four-part system; however, one group intermarries only with one other group.

There are several lines of development from Banaro structure, each of them involving different transformations. In several of the societies there are alternative marriage structures, which involve different transformations that we will treat separately.

The Manga sister exchange model represents one type of transformation from the Banaro. The Manga have a moiety division that divides exogamous clans into two groups, which exchange ceremonial services but cannot intermarry. This may be likened to the *mundu* relationship of the Banaro, a feature of Banaro structure which the Manga therefore retain. The sister exchange model, in which simultaneous sister exchange and bilateral second cross-cousin marriage are combined, depends upon the following transformation: the Banaro exchange sisters in every generation. The shift to a prohibition on first cross-cousin marriage among the Manga prevents a recapitulation of the Banaro structure. The resulting Manga system is one in which sisters are exchanged with two other groups in alternate generations, requiring a minimum of four groups or two clans split by a moiety division, in other words, Cook's model (see figures 11 and 12). In the four-part system of the Banaro, one group only intermarried with one other group. In the Manga case, each group marries with two other groups in the four-part structure, each clan moiety marrying into the two clan moieties of the opposite clan. Kuma and Maring represent a transformation from the basic structure similar to the Manga in that the prohibition on first cross-cousin marriage produces sister exchange in alternate generations; however, they have no moieties.

The transformation from Banaro which produces Abelam is like that discussed for the Manga. The pairs of clans which exchange across *ara* lines may be likened to the *mundu* relationship, in that ceremonial exchange is important but exchange of women is not involved. This, taken together with sister exchange and prohibition of first cross-cousin marriage, makes Abelam structure look much like that of the Manga, Maring, and Kuma sister exchange structure. It too is a four-part structure (see figure 11).

The alternative model for the Manga, Maring, and Kuma, which stresses a preference for marriage with FaFaSiSoDa and an absence of simultaneous sister exchange, also characterizes Wogeo. This model derives from the previous Manga sister exchange model, through the following transformation. An exchange of women in one generation becomes a delayed exchange. The prohibition of first cross-cousin marriage results in the delay of the return of a woman until the second generation. In the idiom of these societies, this marriage preference is conceptualized as the return of a woman for one given two generations earlier. This structure requires a minimum of eight groups.

The Iatmul have two alternative marriage patterns and in this case there is a clear statement that marriages contracted between groups must conform to one type or the other. One of the Iatmul marriage patterns is sister exchange and, given the prohibition on marriage to first cross-cousin, the resulting structure is identical to that discussed above for the Manga, Maring, and Kuma. The second marriage pattern is radically different and involves a transformation of the exchange variable such that a return of a woman is never made. This marriage pattern, *iai* marriage or marriage with FaMoBrSoDa, involves a transformation from reciprocal exchange, which is characteristic of all the other societies in our sample except the Enga, to generalized exchange. Given the prohibition on first cross-cousin marriage, one must marry one's second matrilateral cross-cousin.

The remaining societies are characterized by an expansion of the scope of the marriage prohibitions and a corresponding loss of specificity regarding the structure of relationships between groups brought about by the exchanges of women. The Arapesh have a ceremonial exchange relationship, the *buanyin* relationship, which is like that of the relationship across *ara* lines in Abelam. It is clear that affinal links do not parallel but are complementary to links between *buanyin*. The extension of marriage prohibitions to include third cousins serves to link a group by marriage with a range of other groups. Since the state of the exchange of women is important, it would seem that larger entities like localities are the groups that are exchanging.

The Chimbu resemble the Arapesh. They also emphasize exchange of women between groups and the state of the exchange. In this instance, the subclans carry out the exchanges and the clans keep track of the balance of the exchanges between them. The Melpa resemble the Chimbu and the Arapesh. They have a wide range of marriage prohibitions, but emphasize continuing exchange of women between groups. The large-scale units, clans, keep track of the flow of women, but the men's house groups cannot exchange directly because of the prohibitions. The Enga, with the most extensive set of prohibitions, are not reported as being concerned with the state of exchange of women between groups. The structure is based solely on prohibitions. This has the negative effect of compelling groups to marry widely, which is in accord with their exchange system.

In this chapter we have dealt with but one aspect of the relationship between groups, that brought about by their exchange of women. The structure of that relationship in these societies may be represented by a transformational series. In the next chapter, we will examine the exchanges of goods which follow the same lines as the exchanges of women.

14 Affinal Exchanges at Rites de Passage

In the societies we have examined, marriage creates a relationship between two groups which continues over several generations. These groups are by and large a core of males linked by a patrilineal ideology whose wives reside virilocally after marriage. Varying percentages of nonagnates are included in this core in all of these societies.

A single pattern characterizes the relationship between groups created by a marriage. A marriage involves a woman going in one direction, and bride price going in the opposite direction. For the next two generations, goods will continue to go in the same direction as the bride price. The marriage creates a relationship between men who are brothers-in-law. When a child is born of that marriage there is additionally a relationship between MoBr and SiSo. The various rites de passage of the sister's child, starting with birth, are occasions for continuing payments that parallel the initial bride price. These payments sometimes may be given in exchange for services the MoBr has performed at these various rites. After the MoBr dies, his place is taken by his son, the MoBrSo, who continues to receive payments as representative of the maternal patrilineage. When the SiSo dies, his son makes the final payment to the maternal patrilineage of the deceased, which, at this point in time, may be represented by MoBrSoSo. In other words, this final payment will be between second cross-cousins.

The ethnographers have made a separation between affinal relationships and bride-wealth payments on the one hand, and maternal relationships and payments to mother's lineage on the other. From our discussion of the marriage patterns above, it can be seen that this is an artificial separation. From the perspective of the groups, the same relationship continues for three generations, though the actual wife receiver is portrayed as involved in an affinal relationship, and his son as involved in a maternal relationship. The relationship is asymmetrical in that a woman goes in one direction and goods go in the opposite direction. The goods continue to flow in that same direction, to the wife givers, until the child of the marriage dies. Even in societies with sister exchange, real or classificatory, the same general pattern is present. When groups A and B exchange sisters, A stands as mother's brother to B's children and A's group receives all of the payments due the mother's group. At the same time, B is mother's brother to the children of group A and receives the payments due them as mother's brother. Though women have been exchanged, this does not cancel the payments that flow from wife receivers to wife givers.

The societies with the possibility of direct sister exchange in every generation, Tor, Keraki, and Banaro, vary from this pattern. There are no reported payments of bride wealth, though there may be small gifts of food. In these societies, the ties are being renewed in every generation, while in the other societies we have examined the tie is maintained by the series of affinal payments. There are no regular payments to the maternal lineage in these societies; however, MoBr plays an important ritual role in the rites de passage of his SiSo.

Since affinal payments begin with the payment of bride wealth, the nature of the affinal relationship must begin with a discussion of the relationship between husbands and wives. Women in general, and wives in particular, are considered to be polluting in many of the societies we have analyzed, though there is some variation in this regard. The polluting influence is particularly associated with the act of

sexual intercourse, and with menstruation. Sexual abstinence is usually practiced in conjunction with ritual ceremonies to prevent the contamination of the participants
through their sexual intercourse with women. This occurs
before the Tor flute feast, in conjunction with the Abelam
and Arapesh yam cults, when the spirits are called forth in
Wogeo, and during the Maring and Manga pig festivals.
Male purificatory rites, which are necessary to remove the
effects of contamination which have resulted from contact
with women, also occur in a number of societies. The
Arapesh, Abelam, and Wogeo all practice periodic incising
of the penis. Resultant letting of blood cleanses men after
contact with women, particularly through sexual intercourse.
Both the Kuma and the Chimbu induce nasal bleeding.
Among the Chimbu, this is said to make the face shiny and
attractive, and is not described as a purificatory rite. The
Melpa and the Enga have purificatory rites for males which
involve seclusion but do not involve letting of blood. This is
done to purify them from previous contact with women in
sexual intercourse, and to protect them in future contacts.

In all of the societies we have considered, wives come from
potentially hostile groups. Wives are taken from groups that
have been enemies in the past and may again become
enemies in the future. The actual structure of affinal relationships as seen in exchanges is very similar in all these
societies. However, the manner in which the affinal relationship is conceptualized is different. The Enga, for
example, say that they marry the people whom they fight,
and characterize the groups from which their affines come as
their enemies, though they carry out the same kinds of affinal
exchanges as the other societies and use the affinal relationship as the basis for *te* partnerships. In Wogeo, marriages are made between what are characterized as enemy
districts, whose headmen are *bag* (exchange partners) to one
another. In Abelam also, a sizeable proportion of marriages
are between traditional enemy villages. In these three
societies, intercourse with women is seen as polluting. This
connection has been discussed by Meggitt (1964a) for Highland societies. On the other hand, Kuma and Melpa distinguish between traditional enemies whose women they can-

not marry, and groups that are minor enemies and with whom hostility can break out but whose women they marry. The Chimbu, Maring, and Manga recognize that groups that are currently their enemies have been their affines in the past and may be their affines in the future if enmities are ended through peacemaking ceremonies. Though there are variations in whether affines are conceived of as outright enemies, they usually are potentially hostile, if not at the time of marriage then at some point in the future. This is reflected in the conceptualization of wives as dangerous, both in the realm of food, which they must provide for their husbands, and in the realm of sex, in which they are a polluting influence. Indeed, sex and food are related, as we shall discuss in detail below.

Though the relationships between affinally linked groups may be potentially hostile, normative statements about behavior between brothers-in-law usually stress their need to cooperate with one another. Among Maring and Manga they are the source of allies in warfare. The potentially hostile side of the relationship is recognized, for example, in Abelam and Arapesh, where brothers-in-law who quarrel are exhorted to make peace by exchanging rings, or among the Manga where, in the case of open warfare, they must avoid killing each other. The relationship overall is an ambivalent one with emphasis on the need to cooperate and continue the relationship paralleled by potential hostility. Both allies and enemies are affines in many of these societies.

With the birth of children, the affinal relationship continues into the next generation. Underlying the continuing affinal payments between groups are the conceptualizations of what the child receives from mother and father, respectively. Information is not provided on this subject for all of the societies in our sample. Among the Iatmul, the mother contributes the blood and flesh of the child, while the father contributes its bones. The Arapesh child is conceptualized as a combination of the father's semen and the mother's blood, in equal proportions (Mead 1940: 350). Abelam belief differs from that of the Arapesh. Kaberry notes, "The Mamu (Abelam of Kalabu village cluster) believe that female blood is cold, and that male blood is hot. If the child is a male, then he receives his blood from his father; if the child is female, then she receives her blood from her mother" (Kaberry 1940–41: 245). Hogbin observes, for the Wogeo, that "maternal and paternal kin are sometimes distinguished as 'blood' (*dara*) and 'water' (*dan*), a euphemism, as is admitted, for semen" (Hogbin 1942–43: 287). Semen and the female secretion form the embryo, which is nourished by menstrual blood until birth. The Chimbu believe that the child is formed of blood from both mother and father (Nilles 1940: 97). According to Strathern, writing about the Melpa, "A child is thus thought to be physically formed by the conjunction of its father's semen and its mother's blood, and in some sense metaphysically quickened by its soul, which is bestowed upon it by ancestral ghosts" (A. J. Strathern 1972a: 10). The Enga believe that the mother provides the skin, flesh, and blood, while the father provides the spirit, which is an emanation of his ancestral ghosts, through his semen. For the societies for which information is available, by and large there is an association of mother with the blood of the child.

The mother's contribution of the blood to the child represents the link of the child to her patrilineal group. This is in contrast to the child's link with his own agnatic group, which is frequently symbolized by another substance. This link to mother's group may become the basis for his membership as a nonagnate in that group, since in most of these societies a widow or divorcee may return with her children to her own group, or sister's son may reside with his mother's brother and his children become incorporated into mother's group.

The societies we have analyzed attempt to sever this connection with the maternal group in a number of ways. Payment of child price is an assertion of the claim of the agnatic group over the child vis-à-vis the maternal group, but at the same time this payment can be seen as a recognition of the link of the child to his maternal group. In the Manga case, the final bride-wealth payment is often made with the child payment, and the symbolic capture of the wife and child by the husband's group signifies their incorporation into his group. If the husband should die before the payment, the wife and child would return to her natal group. Among the Maring, if a child payment is not made for a girl, her mother's brother retains the right to receive a portion of her bride price. The Manga and Maring make a single child price payment, as do the Kuma. More common is a series of payments made in conjunction with events in the child's developmental cycle such as when the child first walks (Chimbu), weaning (Melpa), first haircut (Melpa, Enga), girl's menarche (Arapesh), ear and nose piercing (Chimbu, Arapesh).

These multiple payments are associated among the Arapesh, Abelam, Chimbu, and Melpa with the fear that if such payments are not made, the child will be cursed by the ghosts of his mother's lineage and harm and sickness will come to him. The Enga are slightly different in that payments to mother's lineage during the developmental cycle of the child are present but are not associated with the fear of mother's curse if such payments are not made. In the Enga, the maternal relatives do not protect, but if injury should come to a sister's child or his blood should be shed, they are angry that their sister's child has not been protected and they must be paid compensation. Though the Arapesh make payments to maternal relatives to protect the child, as noted above, maternal relatives themselves such as mother's brother and mother's sister do shed the blood of the child in rites de passage such as piercing ears and nose and the scarification of a girl. If the child's blood is shed by someone else, as in initiation for a boy, or by accident, then the maternal relatives must be paid.

Initiation is a rite de passage in which maternal relatives are typically involved and often play important roles but where the initiator is someone else, not a maternal relative. There are no rites which can be explicitly identified as initiatory rites in Maring, Manga, Melpa, or Enga. In the other societies of our sample, initiation involves successive rites that emphasize a boy's becoming a man and being separated from the category of women. Generally speaking, the mother's brother plays a nurturant role like that of a male mother. Though the sister's son goes through ordeals, these are not inflicted upon him by his mother's brother. In five of the societies, initiation specifically involves the letting of blood from the penis, nose, or tongue. In Chimbu and Kuma, the avowed purpose of blood letting is to rid the child of his mother's blood, which is bad. The Arapesh boy lets out the female blood through the penis and drinks good male blood to identify him with the men of the locality (Mead 1940: 349). In Wogeo, the tongue of the initiate is cut to remove the pollution brought about from drinking mother's milk. Initiation in these societies involves ridding the child of the female element, which links him to his mother and to her group. As one would imagine, since the purpose of this blood letting is to rid the child of mother's influence, the blood letting is not performed by the mother's brother or anyone from that maternal group. In the case of the Chimbu and Kuma, the blood letting is done by more distantly related members of the boy's agnatic group. In Abelam and Wogeo, the incising of the penis is done by a man from the opposite moiety. The mother's brother in Wogeo who is in the same matrimoiety as the boy provides pigs at initiation. In Abelam, the mother's brother shields the initiate and is given rings in return, while the *tshambəra*, the initiator and the father's exchange partner, is given pigs for his service. In Arapesh, the initiator is the "cassowary," a member of a clan that hereditarily has this right. The mother's brother must be given a postinitiatory *balagasi* feast. The Banaro resemble Wogeo and Abelam in that a member of the opposite moiety, the *mundu*, the father's exchange partner, forces the initiate to go through ordeals including the insertion of barbed grass into the urethra while the mother's brother acts as the boy's protector. In the Iatmul case, there is the same sorting of personnel. The man from the opposite moiety scarifies back and breast, while mother's brother plays a protective role. After the initiation, as after other significant events in the child's life, mother's brother makes a *naven* at which he gives pigs to the initiate and gets shells in return. In both Tor and Keraki, the mother's brother plays a central role in initiation. Tor initiation involves seclusion but not ordeals. The mother's brother imparts mythic knowledge and songs necessary for hunting. When the boy emerges he takes his place in the men's house. The Keraki initiation does involve ordeals. The initiate is sodomized by males of the opposite moiety, but of his own generation, who have previously been initiated. The mother's brother who is in the senior generation of the opposite moiety gives the initiate his penis sheath at the end of the initiation. The Keraki are the only society where mother's brother does not perform a nurturant role at initiation.

The first menstruation for a girl is marked by rites in only three of the societies, Banaro, Arapesh, and Wogeo. In these societies, the rites for a first menstruation involve seclusion and lead directly into betrothal or marriage. The mother's brother plays a role only in Arapesh, where he scarifies the sister's daughter and is feasted in return.

In many of the societies of our sample, the maternal relatives receive a payment at the death of sister's child which constitutes the final affinal payment. In some of the societies this payment is in return for burial services, which the dead man's maternal lineage performs. In other societies, the maternal relatives may be the chief mourners but do not perform the specific service of burying the deceased. All of the Highland societies of our sample fall into the latter category. In Enga, Chimbu, and Kuma, the mourning payment constitutes compensation to the maternal relatives of the deceased for their loss. This payment constitutes a recognition of the link through blood of the deceased to his maternal kin. With the death, the link is terminated and relationship between groups which has lasted for three generations is ended. Among the Kuma and Enga, the deceased's maternal group expresses anger at the funerary rites that the agnates of the deceased have not protected their sister's son and have allowed him to die. The Arapesh are similar to the Highland societies in that maternal kin do not perform funerary service but receive shell rings, the characteristic affinal payment. For Abelam and Keraki, maternal relatives perform burial service, digging the grave. They then receive rings in the case of Abelam and a feast in Keraki. In Keraki, the maternal relatives are in the opposite moiety. In Banaro and Wogeo, the major part of the funerary rites is performed by the members of the moiety opposite to that of the deceased. The nature of the marriage structure among the Iatmul sets up continuing links between an ego's lineage and those of sister's son and mother's brother (*iai* marriage form). In mortuary rites, both of the lineages perform services, playing the flutes at different points in the ceremony. There are no final payments to maternal relatives in keeping with the ongoing nature of the affinal relationships between groups in this society.

The typical pattern in the societies we have analyzed is that mother's brother performs some ritual service for sister's son and is recompensed for it. In one of the societies, Iatmul, there is a reversal and sister's son provides a variety of ritual services for the mother's brother. The *naven* ceremony, sponsored by the mother's brother, is held in conjunction with the significant rites de passage of sister's son. This is the only instance in which mother's brother sponsors a ceremony for sister's son. The exchanges that accompany the *naven* are interesting in that sister's son receives pigs from mother's brother and mother's brother gets shells in return. Shells to mother's brother parallels the payment of bride price to wife givers as in other Sepik societies such as Arapesh and Abelam. The giving of pigs to sister's son does not occur in these other societies. Shells there mean affines, in contrast to pigs, which are given to exchange partners and define that relationship. In the Highlands, affinal payments also include shells but are accompanied there by pork or pigs, and affines and exchange partners are identical and the shells and pigs define the relationship.

The affinal relationship grows out of a link between two groups established by a marriage. In many societies in the world, with the payment of bride wealth the claim of her natal group upon a woman and her children ceases. However, in New Guinea, the bride wealth payment is but the first of successive payments by wife takers to wife givers which will continue to be made for two more generations in the same direction.

Affinal payments represent both a connection and a separation at the same time. The affinal relationship itself is an ambivalent one. The woman as wife who is the tangible expression of the affinal relationship represents ambivalence, potentially hostile since she is a woman and polluting and she comes from a potentially hostile group, and at the same time the nurturant mother of a member of the wife-receiving group. Her brother is potentially an ally or friend with whom one cooperates in hunting and gardening, or potentially an

enemy whom one fights in war. The mother contributes the
blood to the formation of the child which is necessary to his
existence, but at the same time that blood must be removed
in some of the societies in order for him to become identified
as a mature member of his group of coresident males, a line
of men linked through semen, the male substance, which
contrasts with blood. The conceptualization of links through
blood is tied to the meaning of affinal payments. In those
societies in which initiation involves the shedding of blood,
a dialectic relationship can be perceived in which the patrilineal element tries to rid the child of the mother's blood
but this can never really be accomplished since the child is
always tied to the maternal group through his entire life. The
final mortuary payment to mother's group is a recognition of
this. Even in societies where initiation does not involve
bleeding, this dialectic operates. This also explains why
mother's group is angry when the child is hurt or, as in some
cases, is paid when the child's blood is spilled. Mother's
brother's curse operates when the connection is denied and
the affinal payments are not forthcoming. The affinal payments involve a dialectic of their own. They are said to be
payment in full for the wife, for blood of the child, or for
nurturance of the child. The affinal and child payments made
by the wife takers do not satisfy the debt. The payments that
are an attempt to sever the tie, to pay for the blood, serve to
emphasize and mark the connection. In fact, the tie to
mother's group may frequently be used as a basis to shift
residence to mother's group. It is interesting to note that in
such cases a reverse process takes place in that the tie of a
child to his father's group is not extinguished until the generation of his child or grandchild.

15 Ceremonial Exchange

Large-scale ceremonial distributions of food or valuables are found in all of the societies we have analyzed. Relations between groups are manifested through these distributions. The distributions are carried out according to culturally defined rules so that they bring about the desired culturally defined goal or value. The rules regarding who the recipients are, when the distribution takes place, what should be the nature of the return, the occasion upon which the distribution should take place and its location vary in the different societies. However, all these societies share an emphasis upon the importance of making as large a display as possible. In all of them, prestige derives from the size of the display. Rules regarding the exchanges of goods define structures in the same way as rules regarding the exchange of women. As will be seen, the societies we have analyzed exhibit four types of structures. Two of the structures are clearly forms of restricted exchange; the other two have characteristics of both restricted and generalized exchange.

Both Tor and Keraki have rules that taboo the eating of one's own pigs (pigs that one has raised). This prohibition is the basis for the first rule of exchange. You cannot eat your own pigs but must give them to someone else. The recipient cannot eat his own pigs and gives them in return for the pigs he has received, creating a reciprocal exchange relationship. Reciprocity is therefore the first rule of exchange here. This rule is like the incest taboo. You must give your sister to someone else in exchange for a wife, and you must give your pigs to someone else in exchange for his pigs. In its simplest form restricted exchange produces dual organization, and the Keraki do have a moiety organization. The Keraki have feasts on rite de passage occasions. The guests at these feasts are affines who have performed ritual services as members of the opposite moiety. Cooked pork and vegetables are consumed by the guests, but the major feature of the ceremonial distribution involves the giving away of great quantities of raw yams and uncooked pork. The yams are displayed prior to distribution on a specially constructed platform and the butchered pig to be distributed is also displayed. Exact tallies are kept of the amounts distributed. This is because a reciprocal return of equal size must be made in the future. Prestige accrues to the group in accordance with the quantities amassed and distributed; however, the aim is strict reciprocity.

The major occasion for feasting among the Tor is the building of a men's ceremonial house (*faareh* feast). Large quantities of sago and pork are provided as food for the guests, and the feast lasts as long as there is food. The jaws of the pigs that have been consumed at the *faareh* feast are displayed on the roof of the men's house. When the feast is reciprocated the guests who become hosts must distribute at least as much as they have received.

The Tor and Keraki represent the simplest form of restricted exchange in both their exchanges of women and their exchanges of goods. Both of them have explicit rules that forbid a man to eat his own pig and impel him to exchange it with his affines. Thus the structure of dual organization is manifested both in their marriage and in their ceremonial exchange. The recipients in both cases return an equivalent of what they have gotten. The exchange is reciprocal. In addition, the two sides perform ceremonial services for each other. Among the Keraki, the more that is accumulated and distributed, the greater the prestige accruing to the host and the greater the amount that must be returned in the future. This is revealing of the competitive and hostile aspects of the distribution. Among the Keraki, disputes may be channeled into competitive food displays rather than warfare. Exchanges may also be used to resolve conflict.

The next category of societies, Banaro, Arapesh, Abelam, Iatmul, and Wogeo, exemplifies a restricted exchange structure, coupled with other complementary structures involving the exchange of women. These societies also have the prohibition against eating one's own pig. The ceremonial exchanges are channeled through named exchange partners. Restricted exchange between exchange partners produces dual organization, which in these societies is also manifested in moiety structures. Exchange partners are always in opposite moieties.

The Arapesh provide extensive information about how the exchange of goods serves to sustain a dual organization. The Arapesh unequivocally state that eating one's own pigs or long ceremonial yams is equivalent to incest. Game that is hunted, including the kangaroo, cassowary, and wild pig, must also be exchanged.

The things an Arapesh may not eat are given to his exchange partner or *buanyin*. *Buanyin*, on opposite sides of the moiety division, which is expressed spatially in village organization, are typically Big Men in their clans and channel exchange relations between their two groups. The relationship between *buanyin* is inherited and continues in succeeding generations, sustaining the *buanyin* relationship as a transgenerational relationship between their groups. Exact returns are expected from one's *buanyin*. The *buanyin* relationship is competitive and giving to one's *buanyin* represents a challenge to him which compels him to return the equivalent. When *buanyin* exchange feasts, neither of them eats. They distribute the food to the members of their respective groups. The *abullu* yam ceremony is also tendered to one's *buanyin*.

Buanyin on opposite sides of the moiety division of a village assist one another when one of them is the representative of the village in a ceremonial exchange relationship with another village, the representatives of the two villages being *gabunyan* or intervillage exchange partners to one another. Thus dual organization is present on two hierarchically ordered levels, between *buanyin* within the village and between *gabunyan* in two different villages. Interlocality feasts involve the exchange of pigs, coconuts, and yams between *gabunyan* in different localities.

The dual organization of goods exchanged between *buanyin* within the village is unrelated to the structure of relationships between groups based on exchange of women in marriage. This is in contrast to the simple dual organization of Tor and Keraki. The marriage pattern in Arapesh which combines an extensive series of prohibitions with sister exchange between clans and localities would seem to relate only to interlocality exchanges of goods focused on the *gabunyan*. There is an emphasis on equality in the exchanges of women between localities and equality in the exchanges of goods between *gabunyan*.

The Northern Abelam also have named ceremonial exchange partners, *tshambara*, who are on opposite sides of a moiety division, the *ara*, in each village. In Abelam, one cannot eat pigs one has raised or the uncooked meat of wild pig or cassowary one has hunted. One must exchange them with one's *tshambara*. The relationship between *tshambara* is inherited from father to son. *Tshambara* are Big Men who represent their groups, usually clan hamlets in a single village, in paired exchange relationships that are maintained transgenerationally.

Tshambara perform initiatory service for each other's sons. The most important aspect of the relationship between *tshambara* involves the ceremonial exchange of long yams. The growing and exchange of yams are surrounded by complex taboos. The large yams to be exchanged are elaborately decorated and displayed. Tallies are kept of the length and thickness of the yams. At least an equivalent is expected in return. However, a Big Man and his group try to return more than they had been given on a previous occasion, as an assertion of their superiority.

The *tshambara* relationship is an intravillage relationship. During a truce between traditional enemy villages, exchanges of pigs and long yams will take place. This parallels the *gabunyan* relationship among the Arapesh. Such exchanges are not carried out between friendly or allied Abelam villages. Exchanges of women with both allied and enemy villages take place.

As is the case among the Arapesh, dual organization among the Abelam is maintained by the exchange of goods, and has nothing to do with marriage and the exchange of women.

In Wogeo, as in the other societies so far considered, there is an injunction against eating one's own pig. Exchange partners, referred to as *bag,* are present. Headmen who are *bag* to one another must be in different districts. This makes the *bag* relationship different from the *buanyin* of the Arapesh and the *tshambɔra* of the Abelam. *Bag* must also be in opposite matrilineal moieties. Since the moieties cross-cut the localized patrilineages, they do not have a spatial expression. Exchange partnerships are inherited from father to son, so that in the succeeding generation the moieties of the individuals are reversed.

The *warabwa,* a large interdistrict food distribution, must be held by a *kokwal* in order to commemorate the appointment of an official heir, the construction of a new men's house, or the settlement of a dispute. The recipient of a *warabwa* is a man who is *bag* to the host from an enemy or a neutral district. Since that which is given at a *warabwa* must be returned with exact equivalence, and no prestige accompanies the return, the invitation constitutes a challenge. It cannot be refused. At the final stage of the *warabwa,* a large platform in the shape of an outrigger canoe is built to display the tons of taro, almonds, bananas, coconuts, areca nuts, and betel pepper. The pigs to be given are attached to it. No feasting or eating of cooked food takes place at the *warabwa,* and the guests depart with the uncooked food that they have received. The exact return is made without any display or ceremony, and the pigs are considered "alive" until the return.

In the *warabwa,* the principal donor and recipients are *kokwals* in opposite moieties. Their groups of followers comprise individuals of both moieties. But those followers in both groups who are exchanging are *bag* to one another and in opposite moieties. The result is a two-sided structure in the sense that giving is across moiety lines. The *warabwa* is between two patrilineages acting as groups. Though the leaders are on opposite sides of the moiety division, their followers are from both sides.

The other large-scale food distribution in Wogeo is the *walage*. This is a vegetable distribution of tree or bush crops, in which pigs are absent. Since the distribution takes place between the villages of a single district, *bag* are not involved. The *walage* is held to commemorate lesser rites de passage.

The size of the displays of food at the ceremonial distributions directly reflects upon the importance and the prestige of the *kokwal* and his group who are acting as hosts, and people derive aesthetic pleasure from carrying out and gazing at the display.

In contrast to Arapesh and Abelam where exchange partners are not affines, in Wogeo *bag* are likely to be affines since their children frequently marry. In this society the two kinds of exchange relationships are not incompatible with one another. The presence of exogamous matrimoieties cross-cutting patrilineages appears to relate to this.

Both the Iatmul and Banaro have named exchange partners, *tshambela* in the case of the Iatmul, and *mundu* for the Banaro. The *mundu* in Banaro are on opposite sides of a moiety division that bisects every hamlet and is spatially represented in the men's house. Exchanges of women between these divisions cannot take place so that the children of *mundu* cannot marry. There is detailed information about how *mundu* exchange a range of ceremonial services, but no information about how exchanges of goods also relate to the maintenance of this dual organization. The *tshambela* relationship among the Iatmul involves the exchange of goods as well as services. Among the Iatmul, one cannot eat one's own pig or cassowary or wild pig hunted in the bush. A recipient for such meat is one's *tshambela*. Clans that are *tshambela* to one another live in different parts of the village. The *tshambela* relationship is inherited from father to son. Among the reciprocal services provided by *tshambela* to each other are building of a house or men's house, particular services at initiation and after warfare when a skull is taken.

Tshambela feast each other and give each other long yams, bananas, shells, pigs, and cassowaries in exchange for the services. There is no indication that exchanges between *tshambela* involve competition or hostility, since giving is in exchange for services. Initiatory moieties are present in Iatmul, and from our analysis *tshambela* would appear to be on opposite sides of this moiety division.

The next category of societies includes the Maring, Manga, Kuma, and Chimbu, all of them Highland societies. These societies have patrilineal segmentary structures, no explicitly named moieties cross-cutting the entire society, and no named exchange partners. Their ceremonial exchange structure centers upon the large-scale pig distribution, which is held at intervals of from seven to fifteen years. In some of these societies, vegetable distributions, separate from the pig festival, are also held.

In these societies there is no prohibition against eating one's own pig, as was found in the previously discussed societies. Instead, different cultural rules apply to sort the pigs into those eaten by oneself and one's own group, and those one distributes to others. The two categories of pigs are treated differently, and labeled with distinct terms, which separate them conceptually. The Maring make a separation between pigs sacrificed to the Fight Ancestor Spirits, which are eaten by members of the host's agnatic group, and pigs sacrificed to the Ordinary Ancestor Spirits, which are distributed to the guests. The Manga, Kuma, and Chimbu make a similar kind of separation.

The pig festival is lengthy, lasting over a year and consisting of several stages. Different levels of the segmentary lineage structure come into play at these different stages. As the festival progresses, units at the more inclusive levels of the segmentary structure become more involved. This culminates in the final distribution of pigs, when the highest level unit acts as an entity.

The recipients at the pig festival are other groups of equivalent magnitude, linked to the host group through marriage. A number of guest groups, all of them affines of the host group, are present and receive pork. In the Maring and Manga cases the pig festival is specifically linked to previous warfare, in that affines who attend as guests are receiving pork in exchange for their earlier assistance in warfare. There is no direct evidence of competition between guests and hosts in these distributions. There is indication that the host group expects a return in the future, when each of the guest groups holds it own pig festival. The prestige of the host group is generally tied to the number of pigs killed and the amount of pork distributed.

In these four societies, live pigs are never distributed. Only cooked pork is presented to the guests. The final massive distribution consists only of pork, and no vegetables, and is not accompanied by feasting.

Boy's initiation occurs in conjunction with the pig festival among the Kuma and the Chimbu. The Maring and the Manga do not have male initiation rites.

Among the Kuma and the Chimbu, pig festivals are held consecutively by successive host groups, who have been guests at previous pig festivals. This sequencing may also be present among the Maring and the Manga; however, the linkage between pig festivals and the occurrence of warfare makes the pattern less evident.

Both the Kuma and Chimbu have large-scale vegetable food exchanges that are almost identical. The basic item distributed is pandanus nuts. Sugar cane, bananas, and game are also included. One clan, or tribe in the case of the Chimbu, tenders the vegetable distribution to another. The guest group is linked affinally to the host group. The distribution involves a large display of the uncooked food that has been accumulated and will be distributed. The guest group must subsequently make a return distribution in both societies. Delaying a return among the Chimbu results in a loss of prestige. The food distribution does not seem to be accompanied by feasting in either society. A vegetable distribution occurs at a particular stage of the Maring pig festival at which visitors come to dance, and they take home quantities of vegetable food that has been displayed on the dance ground.

The next two societies, Melpa and Enga, represent a transformation in the direction of generalized exchange structure.

The moka ceremonial exchange system of the Melpa is

based upon individual moka partnerships. Moka partnerships develop from affinal relationships, but affinal ties do not necessarily turn into moka partnerships. A son frequently inherits his father's moka partnerships. Moka partnerships of Big Men are the basis of the exchange relationships between their groups. The objects exchanged in the moka are shells, cooked pork, or live pigs. The tendency is to exchange like for like. When shells are predominant in the initial gift, shells predominate in the return gift.

The moka exchange takes the form of a solicitory gift, and the larger main gift that constitutes the return. In the next exchange, the man who has made moka gives the solicitory gift, and his partner gives the main gift and "makes moka." Competition exists in that a man making moka will try to give a larger main gift than the main gift he previously received from his partner.

Before the main gift is transferred from one partner to another, all of the men of the same group who are making moka will make a ceremonial display of the things that will be given to their moka partners. The prestige of the entire group is dependent upon this joint display.

Moka partnerships between groups represent a multiplicity of dyadic relationships. Sometimes, particularly when live pigs are involved in the exchange, a series of dyadic partnerships linking groups may be joined into a chain. Future moka chain sequences are likely to involve a different arrangement of the dyadic relationships.

Vegetable exchanges between Melpa clans also occur. In addition, distributions of pork are held in conjunction with the Male and Female spirit cults. One of the stages of the Female Spirit Cult involves the sacrifice of pigs to the ancestors, and the meat of these pigs is eaten by the group itself. Both of these cult rituals culminate in the distribution of pork to affines.

Moka exchange among the Melpa differs from exchange in all of the previous societies we have considered. The difference is in the sequencing of exchanges. In the other societies where restricted exchange operates, once a return is made, there are no rules regarding which of the exchange partners initiates the next round of exchanges. Among the

Melpa, the giver of the main gift, the man who makes moka, is required to make the initiatory gift in the next round. His partner may request it of him, in order to enable the partner to make moka (A. J. Strathern 1971a: 115).

Te exchange among the Enga represents a form of generalized exchange. In the *te* exchange cycle, Big Men, acting on behalf of their groups, exchange with their *te* partners who are Big Men of other groups. Affinal links between groups are utilized by Big Men of those groups as the basis for *te* partnerships. *Te* partnerships are also inherited from father to son. In the overall structure of the *te* individual partnerships are links in a long chain, so that A gives to B, B gives to C, C gives to D, and so on. Each complete *te* cycle consists of three phases. In phase one, initiatory gifts consisting of small pigs, pork, salt, axes, shells, and plumes move consistently in one direction along the chain. In phase two live pigs, cassowaries, and bags of pearl shells move in the opposite direction. In phase three, those who have received live pigs last kill pigs and present sides of cooked pork which move in the opposite direction to the live pigs of phase two. Each three-phase *te* cycle takes roughly four years to complete. A new cycle begins when those who have given pork ask for a return in the form of initiatory gifts. In the following cycle, the three categories of goods go in the opposite direction from the previous cycle. The distribution of live pigs in phase two and pork in phase three takes the form of a large-scale display witnessed by many people other than the actual receivers. The size of the display relates to the prestige of the group.

The structure of exchange in the *te* cycle is that of generalized exchange. In one cycle, live pigs will go, by means of a series of exchanges, from clan to clan moving from east to west. In the next cycle, which is a generation of pigs later, live pigs go in a chain of exchanges from west to east. The relationship between groups which is brought about by these exchanges is the same as that produced by patrilateral cross-cousin marriage. Chains of groups are linked to one another by *te* partnerships of their Big Men. The direction of giving is uniformly consistent at one point in time and reverses a generation of pigs later. Unlike restricted exchange, generalized exchange requires a certain degree of trust. There is a delay in the return and a dependence upon individuals further along in the chain. *Te* partners are in potentially hostile clans, but the *te* as a structure is external to these sets of relationships. The dependency upon trust created by the generalized exchange structure of the *te* produces a means by which these hostilities are muted.

After an unusual harvest of taro, sugar cane, or pandanus nuts, an Enga clan will host a vegetable distribution to several other clans. The distribution is accompanied by boastful and aggressive speeches. The *sanggai* ceremony for bachelors is also accompanied by the distribution of cooked vegetables, which have been accumulated on the ceremonial ground. At the ceremony to placate clan ghosts, guests are invited and fed pork cooked with vegetables and marsupials. At a final stage of the ceremony, pigs are sacrificed to the ancestors. The meat from these pigs is eaten by the host group itself.

We have grouped the exchange structures of the societies we have analyzed into four categories. The restricted exchange structure exemplified by Tor and Keraki represents the simplest structure. The other categories represent elaborations and transformations of this structure. This structure has the following characteristics. Rules are present compelling one to exchange one's sister, as well as one's pigs and game. One must give one's sister and one's pigs to another man, who reciprocates by returning his sister and his pigs. This creates a dual organization in which like is exchanged for like. There is an emphasis on exact equivalence, and tallies are kept of the precise amounts given so that it can be assured that the return measures up to what has been given. However, there is challenge and competition as each side attempts to outdo the other. This results in a dialectic between equivalence in exchange, which indicates equality between participants, and competition, which represents an attempt to demonstrate superiority.

Category two, consisting of Arapesh, Abelam, Wogeo, Iatmul, and Banaro, forms one type of transformation. There is a development of two separate structures of exchange, one for women and one for goods. The structure of exchange of goods is exactly the same as in the previous structure but more formalized. Partners who exchange only goods are designated by a separate term and are completely set apart from affines (except in Wogeo). The goods exchanged by exchange partners are different from the goods involved in affinal exchange. The dual organization is formalized in named moieties with exchange partners in opposite moieties. In other respects the structure of restricted exchange in category two societies operates in the same manner as in the earlier structure. One cannot eat one's own pigs or wild game hunted, or the long yams raised for exchange. The emphasis on exact equivalence and tallies is present with more elaborate mnemonic devices for keeping track of distributions. The challenge and competitive aspect present in the earlier structure is also found here. In fact, hostility is often channeled into exchanges between exchange partners. Exchange partners are frequently Big Men who represent their groups, and the exchange relationship that is transgenerational is a group-to-group relationship. Exchange of women in these societies takes a variety of forms. Direct sister exchange is present in the Banaro, producing cross-cutting moieties. In the remaining societies in this category, sister exchange continues to be present but it is not across moiety lines and is coupled in each society with a complementary marriage pattern.

The societies in category three, Kuma, Chimbu, Maring, and Manga, represent a different transformation from the structure of restricted exchange. In all four of these societies, the basic exchange structure involves a large-scale pig festival and distribution of pork, which a clan or tribe will host every seven to fifteen years. One clan or tribe acts as host to a number of other clans or tribes. The host group is in a dyadic exchange relationship with each of the guest groups present. The guest groups are the neighboring groups that surround the host group's territory. The structure of the pig festival is the summation of the dyadic relationships between host and guest groups, and takes the form of a star formation with the hosts at the center. The structure of marriage parallels the structure of exchange of pork, in that these neighboring groups are at the same time the affines of the host group.

Marriage in these societies is based upon a series of prohibitions that compel the spread of marriages among a
number of groups. Sister exchange is present, but it occurs
among larger-scale groups.

The structure of exchange for these societies seems to develop out of the simplest structure. Like the societies in category one, the structure of ceremonial exchange of goods follows along the same lines as exchange of women. In category
one, the two-part dual organization ranges pairs of groups
on opposite sides of the moiety division. In category three
societies, there is no moiety division on opposite sides of
which groups are ranged for the exchange of goods and
women. Instead, each host group is distributing to, and
eventually exchanging with, a circle of guest groups. This
structure retains a characteristic of the structure of category
one—restricted exchange—in that pairs of groups in a dyadic
relationship are exchanging like for like, women for women,
pigs for pigs. It is a transformation away from restricted exchange in that the dyadic relationships are joined into a star
formation centered around the host group. This is in the
direction of generalized exchange because each group is
linked in exchange to a number of other groups resulting in
an exchange system that serves to link large numbers of
groups within a region.

Moka exchange among the Melpa represents a further development in the direction of generalized exchange. It is like
category three in that the exchange relationship is based
upon an affinal connection. Since not all affines are involved
in moka exchange with one another, moka partnerships are
distinguished from the larger category of affines who carry
out regular affinal exchanges. Moka partnerships therefore
resemble the exchange partnerships in category two in that
they are inherited from father to son, and are the basis for
ordered exchange relationships between groups. They are
similar to all of the previously discussed societies in that like
is exchanged for like, which is a characteristic of restricted
exchange. However, they differ in that each exchange involves an initial gift and a much larger return. Only the giver
of the larger gift is "making moka." The sequencing of exchanges between partners is such that a man will give to his

partner twice in succession, and his partner will then give to him twice in succession. Each thereby makes moka in turn. This prescribed order of sequencing differs from the order of exchanges in the previously described societies. Moka exchange takes the form of a series of dyadic relationships, but when these are formed into chains the overall structure is different. When moka chains are formed, there is no longer direct reciprocation. The return can only come when pigs move back along the chain, and moka then becomes similar to *te*.

The structure of the *te* exchange of the Enga is an example of generalized exchange structurally identical to patrilateral cross-cousin marriage. *Te* exchange partnerships are formed in the same manner as moka partnerships among the Melpa. The three-phase *te* cycle does not involve direct exchange of like for like. One type of goods moves from *te* partner to *te* partner in a chain sequence. In the next phase, the goods are different and the direction is reversed. As a result, the return to one's partner is different from what was given, and the return is delayed. In the *te*, the situationally formed moka chains become more permanent, and the two-stage exchange of the moka, solicitory gift and main gift, becomes a three-stage cycle. In the latter, no *te* partner gives twice in succession.

16 Big Men and Exchange Systems

The key to understanding the position of Big Men in these societies lies in understanding their role in exchange. Big Men constitute the nodes of exchange systems. By examining the participation of Big Men in exchange, we intend to illuminate the way in which Big Men come to power, maintain themselves while in power, and compete with other Big Men until eventually their importance declines.

The term Big Man implies the presence of social differentiation within a group. Where there are Big Men, there are also ordinary men, and rubbish men. Around the Big Man there is a constellation of followers who belong to the other two categories. The Big Man and his followers have constituted the unit of analysis for economic anthropologists interested in redistributive economic systems. Associated with this perspective is the concern with problems such as the rise of the Big Man to power, how the Big Man intially attracts followers, how the Big Man sustains his following and continues to reward them for their support. This perspective, which involves the composition of the group, constitutes what we call the internal structure of the unit comprising the Big Man and his followers.

The external structure of this unit involves the exchanges made by Big Men to other Big Men. These exchanges involve competition for prestige and are the means by which Big Men may be ranked vis-à-vis other Big Men. The exchanges between Big Men symbolize the structure of relationship between groups. Internal structure and external structure are analytic concepts with analogs in other disciplines. These concepts are consonant with the conceptualization of hierarchical levels in that the external structure of a lower level becomes the internal structure of a higher level. The nature of the interrelationship between internal and external structure is one of the themes of this chapter.

The first important distinction to be made is between those societies that have segmentary lineage structures and those that do not have such structures. As we have noted in chapter 12, the Highland societies in our sample all have segmentary lineage structures, though there is variation in the number of levels of segmentation. In contrast, the Lowland societies in our sample, such as the Arapesh, Abelam, Tor, Keraki, Wogeo, Iatmul, and Banaro, have partriclan hamlets organized into villages, with no higher levels of segmentation. This distinction relates to the structure of social groups and also has important implications for the position of Big Man, since he acts on behalf of a group vis-à-vis other groups.

The position of Big Men may be linked to the exclusive possession of special knowledge and expertise. This special knowledge may consist of sorcery or of magical spells connected with growing crops or with warfare. Among the Abelam, the role of the Big Man is integrally involved with knowledge of special magic required for the growing of large yams, which are the basis of the yam cult. Sorcery and war magic are the special province of the Kuma and Maring Big Men. In contrast, among the Enga and the Chimbu, the position of ritual expert is distinct from that of the Big Man. Aside from these few situations where the Big Man controls special ritual knowledge, it is common for Big Men to act on behalf of their groups in communicating with ancestral spirits (Melpa, Chimbu, Manga, Maring, Kuma). His position as Big Man requires that he act as a leader in certain ritual acts as intermediary between his group and the spirit world.

Certain important personal characteristics are stressed in the different societies as typically possessed by men who become Big Men. For example, among the Chimbu, aesthetic qualities required in displays and ceremonies are essential characteristics for a Big Man. Skill in carving and painting the front of the Abelam *tamberan* is greatly valued in a Big Man. Oratorical skill is always a requirement in any aspirant to Big Man Status. This skill is important since the Big Man speaks on behalf of his group, and negotiates for them vis-à-vis other groups.

Big Men play an important role in warfare, but the ethnographers emphasize that their skills and activities involve the organizational and planning aspects rather than prowess in fighting. Many examples are given of prominent warriors who could not attract and hold followers and therefore did not become Big Men.

The most important personal quality essential to attain the position of Big Man in most of the societies we have analyzed is the ability to organize, plan, and manage both production and exchange. Only among the Maring and the Manga is the Big Man not a central figure in the organization of production. These skills lie at the heart of the role of Big Man. It is this ability to manage and organize which enables the Big Man to attract followers and build a constituency. The internal structure of the group comprises the Big Man and his followers. The Man who aspires to be a Big Man must be able to gain access to increasing amounts of land within the territory belonging to his agnatic kin group, which he then puts into production. He must be married, for his wife is essential in production. As he builds a surplus of goods and valuables, he can take another wife, thereby increasing his productive capacity. He may then begin to attract single male followers who become part of his household. These bachelors, in exchange for being fed by his wife, become part of his labor force. Their pigs are cared for by the Big Man's wife. They hope for his assistance in contributing to their bride prices. These single men may be members of his own agnatic group or nonagnates, attracted to him from other groups. This means holding on to younger brothers and subsequently sons who form the agnatic core of his group, and enticing brothers-in-law and sisters' sons from other groups. As the Big Man's position becomes more important, he may gain access to and control over clan land, which he then allocates to followers not part of his household for their own use in exchange for their support. With the surplus from his enlarged productive capacity, he will make contributions to the bride price of followers, placing them further in his debt. The knowledge of his generosity is a factor in his being able to attract still other followers. He will assist his followers with gifts to enable them to make other kinds of ceremonial payments such as the various payments to mother's group through the life cycle, including death payments, which are characteristic of these societies. Nonagnates seem always to be included as part of the following of a Big Man, though the proportion varies from one society to another. Despite this, the Big Man and his following are conceptualized within the descent system as a patrilineage.

It is apparent that the position of the Big Man is an achieved status. However, the son of a Big Man has considerable initial advantage over the son of an ordinary man in embarking on the path toward becoming a Big Man. Indeed, the Melpa say that at least one of the sons of a Big Man should take his place, "to be in the place where the father's house was" (A. J. Strathern 1971a: 212). The Big Man will provide his son with one or more wives; this gives the son increased productive capacity and the resulting advantage of having more resources to utilize in his operations. In most of these societies, when a Big Man dies a son inherits his father's exchange partnerships (see chapter 15). This thrusts him into a series of exchange relationships with men of other agnatic kin groups. If, through his own abilities, he makes himself into a Big Man, then these inherited exchange partnerships will come to represent intergroup relationships. As this represents external structure, it will be discussed in more detail below. The son of a Big Man may not become a Big Man in his own right if he lacks the necessary ability. Initial advantages can be dissipated, or can become the basis of success. On this point Strathern's figures on the Melpa show that, despite the absence of a formal rule of succession, twenty-seven out of thirty-six major Big Men had fathers who also were Big Men (A. J. Strathern 1971a: 209). The Kuma are similar to the Melpa in this respect. Reay reports that the ideal is that the eldest son should succeed his father as the leader of the sub-subclan. Despite the statement of this ideal of succession from father to son, there appears to be no formal installation ceremony at which the son succeeds to the position of his father. Reay also points out that a process exists whereby a "spontaneous leader," who has achieved wealth and renown, can assume the position of secondary leader, eventually to assume the authorized position of leadership. This is also true of the Keraki, who have a rule of succession, though there is no ceremony of installation and the headman has only vaguely defined authority, according to Williams.

This contrasts with the situation in Wogeo, where there is a formal rule of succession, and where the assumption of leadership by the successor occurs as part of a public ceremony involving a large-scale distribution (Hogbin 1940–41).

Among the Maring where, it will be recalled, the Big Men are associated with the control of special kinds of magic and sorcery, these powers are usually passed on from a father to his biological son. Therefore, as Lowman-Vayda indicates, the position of Big Man passes from father to son (Lowman-Vayda 1971: 339). In this respect, the Maring resemble the Kuma.

In the segmentary lineage system of Highland societies, the Big Man and his followers constitute the minimal unit on the lowest level. In contrast to minor Big Men, whose range of leadership is restricted to the minimal units they head, major Big Men speak on behalf of groupings of larger magnitude at the most important occasions. There is a degree of correspondence between the levels of leadership and groupings in the segmentary lineage structure.

A Big Man who is a leader of a minimal unit can aspire to the leadership of a grouping of larger magnitude, since leadership at that level is always achieved, even among the Kuma. The various levels of the segmentary structure are operative on different occasions. More important Big Men are distinguished by virtue of the fact that they speak on behalf of the larger groupings operative on these occasions and organize the activities involved. In the same manner that a Big Man attracts followers to him by contributing to bride price and to other ceremonial payments that his followers are required to make, an ambitious Big Man will also contribute to payments made by more distant agnates in collateral groups. This places them in his debt, and entitles him to a share in what they will subsequently receive. It also enhances his reputation, and enables him to speak for larger-level groupings on the more important occasions. In exchange terms, the internal structure of the higher-level groupings in the segmentary lineage structure recapitulates the internal structure of the lower-level groupings.

In the Lowlands, where segmentary lineage structures are absent, villages are made up of clan hamlets, and the Big Man and his followers constitute such a clan hamlet. There is no formal position of Big Man of the village, though some of the Big Men of the different clan hamlets may be more important than others.

Competition assumes a certain form in the internal structure. It occurs between Big Men within the agnatic group for followers, at various levels of the segmentary system. In his analysis of the Mae Enga, Meggit (1967) states that this type of competition is observable in times of peace, when an ambitious Big Man who aspires to be more important will compete with the current Big Man for support. A front of group solidarity is presented in times of external stress. Among the Kuma, the "spontaneous leader" represents a possible source of rivalry and factionalism, which can come to a head and result in the "spontaneous leader" and his faction splitting off to form their own group. As will be seen below, this kind of competition between Big Men in the internal structure is different from that competition which characterizes Big Men as exchange partners in the external structure.

It is apparent that the career of a Big Man is integrally tied to his life cycle. As a young man, his energies and abilities, which are at their maximum, are channeled into the various activities associated with accumulating followers, and meeting an increasing number of necessary obligations. At the height of his career, he is a vigorous adult, with experience, resources, and following. As he ages, his energy and activity decline, and he is no longer able to fulfill his commitments and to retain his following in the face of competition from younger men rising to power. He will ultimately be replaced by someone else who will speak and act on behalf of his group. As the career of a future Big Man unfolds, the factors involved in the process spelled out above are interrelated in such a way as to make it almost impossible to assign causality to one factor over another. The two exceptions seem to be Banaro, where Thurnwald describes a "gerontocracy" in power due to the magical knowledge of the old men, and Wogeo, where there is formal succession and the authority of the headman does not decline.

We turn now to a discussion of the position of Big Men in the external structure. Relationships between groups, which represent the external structure, take the form of either hostile relations or exchange relations, the latter involving exchanges of goods and exchanges of women.

In all of the societies in our sample, hostile relations between groups can erupt into warfare. Neighboring groups that fight one another may also be involved in the exchange of women or goods or both. Fighting and exchange are two sides of the same coin, expressing the same relationship. Big Men are invariably the planners and organizers of warfare, and are the pivotal figures in bringing about peace. Big Men take the initiative, using their influence and oratorical skills to stop the fighting. They can arrange for compensation payment by drawing upon their own resources as well as upon the resources of other members of their group. These payments may then become the basis for continuing exchange relationships.

Exchange partnerships involving the ceremonial exchange of goods are present in all of these societies and serve to link individuals of different groups. As we have noted, theoretically, all adult men may have exchange partners, but in actuality only the exchange partnerships of Big Men serve as the foci of intergroup relations.

Big Men coordinate and organize the various activities associated with the large-scale ceremonial pig exchanges and distributions which take place in category three societies in the Highlands. The major Big Men of the host group collectively decide when the event will occur. This is an important political decision, since, once the decision is made, all members of the group must participate, whether or not they have sufficient numbers of pigs to distribute. A number of tribes or clans may hold the ceremony simultaneously, requiring still further coordination on the part of their Big Men. Under the supervision of the Big Men, a temporary village is built on the ceremonial ground.

For the Chimbu and the Kuma, the climax of this ceremony is the large-scale killing of pigs and the distribution of pork. Each subgroup of the host group arranges and displays its own slaughtered pigs in a line. The number of pigs displayed by each individual reflects status difference within the group. The slaughtered pigs of the Big Man are most numerous, and they are at the head of the line representing his group. After the display, members of the host groups distribute the pork to their individual exchange partners in the different guest groups. Since Big Men have more exchange partners, they will be distributing more meat to a greater number of individuals.

In the *te* exchange cycle, the political role of Big Men is expressed as they act on behalf of groups of different magnitude. The activities involved in phase two illustrate the way in which group relations and individual interactions are interwoven. At the outset, Big Men of the host clan will kill pigs so that the spirits will make their distribution a success. At the distribution itself, the pigs are tethered to stakes placed in rows, each row representing a patrilineage. The followers of a Big Man do not act independently in the *te*, but give their pigs to the Big Man whom they support. He lines them up in his row, and then passes them on to his exchange partners. The most important Big Man of the clan has the longest line of stakes, since he accumulates more pigs and distributes them to a greater number of exchange partners than anyone else. Bags of shells are also distributed in this phase of the *te*. Though each Big Man has his own bag of shells to distribute, and publicly names the recipient, the Big

Man of the clan directly hands out the shells in each case. Big Men of the host clan, by their actions, gain prestige for themselves and for their entire clan. At the same time, the prestige of the Big Men who have received pigs is enhanced by the display of the number of pigs received.

The structure of external exchange among the Melpa, moka exchange, shows great similarities to the *te* of the Enga, though there are differences of scale and complexity (Strathern 1969b, 1971a; Vicedom and Tischner 1943–48). According to the ethnographic accounts of Vicedom and Tischner, Big Men formerly monopolized moka exchanges, carried out moka transactions using pigs from their followers, and acted on behalf of their groups. In more recently gathered Melpa material, the Strathern indicate that many more ordinary men have moka partners in other clans. Instead of contributing their pigs to the Big Man for distribution to his moka partners, they stand alongside him as independent givers while he exhorts them not to hold back their pigs. The size of their combined presentation reflects on the prestige of the entire group.

Though in the Lowland societies in our sample there is no segmentary lineage structure, hierarchy is present in the form of clan hamlets, which make up villages. Organized exchanges are much more frequent between clan hamlets than between villages, but at both levels Big Men serve as leaders in the various activities. Clan hamlets are arranged in pairs in opposite sides of a moiety structure. The Big Man of each clan has as his ceremonial exchange partner (*tshambəra* in Abelam, *buanyin* in Arapesh) the Big Man of the opposite clan. Among the Abelam, there may be more than one Big Man in a clan, but all exchanges between the Big Men of paired clans occur on the same day. Abelam Big Men exchange long yams they have grown with the assistance of their followers. Arapesh Big Men who are exchange partners to one another give each other meat and live pigs, and hold feasts for each other's groups.

In exchanges between villages, the biggest men, assisted by other Big Men in their own village, represent the village unit. Among the Arapesh, intervillage exchange has its focus in the ceremonial exchange partnership linking *gabunyan*, who are Big Men of the two villages. Each *gabunyan* is helped by his *buanyin* in his own village.

The *kokwal* of Wogeo is the most formalized of the Big Man statuses we have considered. The Wogeo *kokwal* as head of his partrilineage is exchanging with a *bag*, exchange partner, not in his own village or district but in another district.

Generosity to one's followers and display of what one Big Man and his group will give to another Big Man and his group are central aspects of the Big Man role in many of the societies we have considered. These features would seem to characterize the role of the Big Man in societies where Big Men have a degree of control over labor and production. The generosity to one's followers is part of the internal structure and operates in attracting followers and in redistributing what the Big Man has received in external exchanges. The display by a Big Man of what he gives to another Big Man and his group is a measure of his own importance and the prestige of the entire group.

We have focused attention on the way in which the Big Man operates as a node in the exchange system, both within his group and between groups. We have labeled the former "internal structure" and the latter "external structure." A comparison of the nature of exchanges in these two types of structures reveals the following points. Exchanges within the internal structure take the form of help and support, and emphasize inequality between giver and receiver. The contributions of a Big Man to the ceremonial payments of his followers, and the contributions of followers when the Big Man feasts or distributes to his exchange partners, mark the superior status of the Big Man. Exchanges in the external structure stress relative equality in rank. When Big Men, who represent their groups, exchange with other Big Men, it is exchange between equals. Another distinction is that only exchanges in the external structure are set in a ceremonial context accompanied by ritual. The giving of help in the internal structure involves contributions to ceremonial payments, and the subsequent sharing out of ceremonial payments, while the exchanges in the external structure involve the transfer of ceremonial payments themselves. Competition is present in both internal and external structure, but takes different forms. Internally, competition involves factionalism and vying for followers, but ideally can never lead to bloodshed. Such competition is overridden by solidarity at times of stress. In the external structure, competition is freely expressed in ritual form. Either exact equivalence of exchanges is stressed, or partners take turns in having an advantage. Though competition is always present, there is no external ranking. Competition between groups in the external structure can escalate into hostilities and warfare. Likewise, overt hostilities can be transformed into competition in the exchange of goods.

This analysis of the role of Big Men in a number of New Guinea societies suggests several modifications of some of the ideas expressed in Sahlins's paper on Big Men in Melanesia. Sahlins makes an important distinction between the role of the Big Man in societies with segmentary lineage systems, and those without. He notes "the greater the self-regulation of the political process through a lineage system, the less function that remains to big-men, and the less significant their political authority" (Sahlins 1963: 289). We have found that where Big Men speak on behalf of units in a segmentary lineage system, their role in decision making and their political authority are comparable to situations where segmentary lineage systems are absent. In both instances, the external exchange relationships of Big Men represent the political relationships between groups. Sahlins holds the view that the Big Man achieves his position solely through his own efforts. Our conclusions point to the fact that, where special knowledge of sorcery and magic is associated with the position of the Big Man, there is a tendency for such knowledge to be passed on from father to son, and for the position to be inherited. Furthermore, the son of a Big Man has certain advantages that he may build upon to become a Big Man in his own right, or squander. Sahlins sees the limits of the Melanesian Big Man structure as increasing extraction from followers without reciprocation in order to give to other Big Men to spread the giver's renown. The New Guinea material does not seem to support this process of extraction, as it occurs among the Siuai. Sahlins's point about extraction results from the fact that, though he rec-

17   The Symbolism of Exchange

The kinds of things that are exchanged in this group of societies cover a wide range of items including women, pigs, cultigens, wild plants and game, shells, plumes, and stone axes. All of these things differ in their symbolic significance and meaning in the various societies. Sometimes two categories of things, like pigs and shells or pigs and women have the same meaning in exchange terms in that they are given to the same category of people or are interchangeable. Sometimes a single category of things such as pigs may be differentiated in terms of meaning into two categories when they are used differently in exchange. In this chapter, we shall explore the relationship between the contrastive, culturally determined meanings assigned to the objects exchanged, the processes by which things are exchanged, and the structure of relationship of the exchangers. The meanings of the things exchanged and the kinds of social relationship between the exchangers are like two sides of a coin.

There are a number of kinds of cultural sortings of things exchanged. Not all these types of sorting are utilized in all of the societies we have analyzed. The distinction between wild and cultivated has importance in several of the societies. Among the Melpa, wild plants and animals are associated with the forest zone, with masculinity, and with strength and growth, in contrast to the domesticated zone and pigs, which are associated with women. In Wogeo, there is a separation between village and bush, which bears some relationship to the wild-domesticated distinction. Village spirits are associated with pigs and coconuts, and bush spirits with bananas, areca nuts, and Tahitian chestnuts. The appropriate spirits are called out to taboo these things before ceremonial distributions. The crops associated with the bush spirits are not wild crops, however. They are orchard crops. The only wild plant that is important in cermonial distributions in Wogeo is the giant taro, which is identified with maleness. The wild-cultivated distinction seems to have significance in exchanges only among the Maring and the Manga. In these societies, eels, marsupials, and cassowaries are hunted, cooked, and eaten by the agnatic group itself. They are not distributed to affines. Pigs, on the other hand, are divided into those given to agnates and those distributed to affines. Game, particularly marsupials, is distributed in connection with the clan-bespelling ceremony of the Enga and the Male Spirit Cult ceremony of the Melpa, but plays no role in connection with *te* or moka. It would appear that the distinction between wild and domesticated is not particularly significant in distinguishing categories of exchange though it has relevance as a dimension in separating other cultural domains and ultimately has relevance to the male-female distinction.

The second kind of distinction in the sorting of things exchanged is between male and female categories of things. This distinction is particularly important with respect to crops. The Highland societies in our sample are consistent in associating certain crops with men and other crops with women. All the Highland societies we have considered associate males with sugar cane and bananas. In addition, the Enga add taro, ginger, and yams to the male category; Melpa add one species of taro; the Kuma add maize, pandanus, and other tree crops; the Maring add pit-pit; and Manga add tobacco. In all the Highland societies, sweet potatoes and greens, which are the staples, are female crops. The Manga also include in the female category yams, taro, and cassava, and the Melpa maize, yams, and a species of taro (different from the "male" species). Where there are large-scale vegetable distributions in the Highlands among the Chimbu, Kuma, and Enga, in addition to the pandanus nuts, these vegetable distributions focus upon male crops, not female crops. In the Lowlands, the distinction between male and female crops does not occur as a regular pattern. Among the Arapesh and Abelam, however, the long yams that occupy the central position in exchanges are identified with males and any contact with them is taboo to women.

The male-female distinction also operates in the animal world. In all of the societies pigs are associated with women, and cassowaries are clearly associated with men in several of the societies (Melpa, Enga, and Manga). Mead notes that the Arapesh consider some species of bird to be male, and others to be female (Mead 1940a: 341).

The third type of distinction is based upon whether the goods distributed are live, raw or uncooked, or cooked. The basis of the distinction between live and the other two categories is that things that are distributed live can reproduce. These distinctions cross-cut both plant and animal domains. Ceremonial exchanges of plant and tree crops in all of these societies are of things that can be characterized as live, since what is distributed can be propagated by the recipient. Bananas that are distributed are the only exception. When pigs are distributed, they are either alive or cooked and distributed in the form of pork. Butchered chunks of uncooked pigs do not seem to appear in any of the distributions. Game is distributed either in the cooked form, or butchered, but is never distributed alive, except for cassowaries. Among the Enga, cassowaries are treated like pigs in the *te*.

A distinction must also be made at this point between feasting, the actual consumption of food on a ceremonial occasion, and ceremonial distributions of goods, where the things received are taken home by the recipients rather than consumed on the spot. In many instances, the ceremonial exchange is not accompanied by feasting. This is the case in the *te* of the Enga, and in the *warabwa* of Wogeo. When feasting does accompany ceremonial exchange, it is a separate activity since different kinds of foodstuffs are involved.

For example, in the Abelam yam exchange long yams are exchanged, while short yams and coconut soup with greens are eaten.

There is still another dimension, which creates a separation between things one has produced and can consume oneself and things one has produced and must exchange. The existence of a category of things that cannot be consumed by the producers means that an incest taboo is being applied to this category which demands that they be exchanged. This "incest taboo" applies to women in all of the societies, to pigs and game, in societies of categories one and two (see chapter 15), and to yams in the Abelam and Arapesh in category two. Thus game, pigs, yams, and women in Arapesh and Abelam are equivalents in that they must be exchanged. This distinction is based solely upon a feature deriving from exchange, in contrast to the distinctions discussed up to now where other attributes used to differentiate classes of objects were coupled with exchange features.

The next distinction in the categories of goods is based upon differentiations in the categories of receivers. Among the Abelam and the Arapesh, exchange partners and affines represent different kinds of social relationships. Pigs and yams are given to exchange partners, and women and shells are given to affines. As noted above, these are all equivalents in the sense that they all must be exchanged and cannot be consumed by those who produced them. However, the categories of recipients serve to differentiate the items exchanged. There is an association between the social relationship and the goods exchanged as an expression of that relationship. Exchange partners are associated with pigs and yams, and the competitive hostility that accompanies the exchanges of those items. Affines are associated with the exchange of shells as well as women, in a relationship that is culturally defined as cooperative. An Abelam man recognizes this identification by referring to his brother-in-law as "my ring."

When affines and exchange partners are not different social relationships, but are equivalents, as among societies in category three and category four and in Wogeo, then pigs, shells, and women are not differentiated since they are given to the same category of people.

Sometimes different categories of receivers will be given the same kind of object. However, the distinction between the different kinds of receivers will impose a category differentiation upon the item. In category three societies, pigs given to affines are differentiated from pigs eaten by agnates. Beyond this distinction, the Maring make further distinctions, which are superimposed upon this first distinction. Live pigs are given to the spirits, while cooked pork is given to men—both agnates and affines. There are two categories of spirit receivers, Fight Ancestor Spirits and Ordinary Ancestor Spirits. The meat from the pigs dedicated to the Fight Ancestor Spirits is given to the agnates, while the meat from the pigs dedicated to Ordinary Ancestor Spirits is given to the affines.

In Melpa and in Enga, exchange partnerships in the moka and in the *te* are based upon affinal relationships, but not all affines are exchange partners. The same kinds of goods, pigs, pork, and shells, are involved in both kinds of exchanges. Only ceremonial context serves to differentiate the goods in these two kinds of exchanges.

Up to this point we have been attempting to determine the meanings of the things exchanged by examining them in terms of several principles of classification such as wild-cultivated, male-female, live-raw-cooked. We have demonstrated how sortings along these dimensions are related to sorting according to exchange characteristics. We turn now to an examination of the principles underlying exchange in these societies, and their relationship to the distinctions that differentiate the categories of things exchanged.

In all of these societies, exchange is exclusively a male sphere of activity. Men are concerned with exchange, and women are concerned with production and reproduction. Among the Arapesh, men who do not exchange are relegated to the position of male women (Mead 1940: 352). Men must be separated from women in order to exchange particularly those things associated with males, but the ways in which this separation is brought about varies in these societies.

Separation from women can occur during the planting and growth period of crops that are exchanged. This involves abstinence from sexual intercourse by the male cultivators for the entire growth period, during which time women are prevented from coming into any contact with the crop. Women may be separated from the cultivator and from the crop during the harvest period. Women may be prevented from being present at and observing the exchange of crops or of any other item, or they may be allowed to be present but the exchangers are required to observe sexual abstinence before and during the exchange. The Abelam represent the extreme in that they perform all of these actions in connection with their yam cult. Among the Arapesh, women may be present at the exchange of yams at an *abullu,* but in all other respects Arapesh exchange of yams is like the yam cult of the Abelam. Sexual abstinence is also practiced by Arapesh men when carrying out rites to insure the success of pig exchanges, and before fastening pigs to be carried for exchange. Women are not separated from any aspect of crop cultivation in Tor. However, sexual abstinence must be practiced during the period of preparation for feasts. Women are present at the *faareh* feast to inaugurate a new men's house, but are kept apart from any activity associated with the flute feast.

In the Highlands, women are not excluded from any of the ceremonial distributions. Among the Chimbu and Kuma, women participate actively in the dancing as part of the ceremonies just prior to the final distribution and, interestingly enough, on this occasion they are dressed and decorated just like men. Sexual abstinence is practiced by the Manga during the entire length of the pig festival, and the taboo is lifted prior to the final distribution of pigs. Abstinence from sexual intercourse occurs only during the trapping of marsupials and eels in the Maring *kaiko.* The Melpa practice sexual abstinence in connection with making ceremonial wigs and prior to decorating for a dance, and both of these are associated with ceremonial exchange. Some of the Enga behavior associated with the growing of "male" yams is reminiscent of the Abelam and Arapesh of the Lowlands, in that menstruating women are not permitted to enter the gardens where the yams grow. Sweet potatoes, which are associated with women, in turn, may not be eaten by men who are about to engage in *te* exchanges. All of these activities, such as the observance of sexual abstinence or the avoidance of crops associated with women, serve symbolically to separate men from women when men engage in exchange.

Boys who are identified with their mothers are transformed through initiation rites into men who can exchange, in most of these societies.

When crops are the focal point of exchange ceremonies, they are always male crops rather than female crops and fall into the live rather than cooked category. This includes the yam cults of the Abelam and the Arapesh, the *wubalt* of the Kuma, the *mogena biri* of the Chimbu, and the vegetable distribution of the Enga.

Men also exchange things produced by women as well as women themselves. Women impregnated by men produce daughters for exchange. Women also rear pigs that are exchanged. Women produce the staple crops that provide food as well as the food that is used to feast guests when this occurs in conjunction with exchange. In the Highlands, the primary responsibility for rearing pigs is in the hands of women. The pigs live in the same houses with women, separate from where men live. Women nurse pigs and rear them like their children. There are explicit statements in Enga, Melpa, and Manga provided by the ethnographers which identify women with pigs. Despite the primary importance of women in rearing pigs, it is men who exchange them. In the same way, the decision about whom a daughter will marry is in the hands of the men of the group. Pigs and women are further identified in that they both are used by males to make links with other groups of males. The Manga refer to women metaphorically as "pigs" to be exchanged. Pigs, women, and staple crops are female and are in diametric opposition to the male crops, which are exchanged. The structure of exchange of women and pigs as well as shells contrasts to the structure of exchange of male crops in both Highlands and Lowlands. In the Highlands, the exchange of male crops is a competitive form of restricted exchange which involves two sides. The exchange of women and pigs by men involves a different structure than that involving male crops. In category three societies, the structure of exchange of both pigs and women involves the same star formation as described in chapter 15.

In the Lowlands, among the Abelam and Arapesh, the close identification between pigs and women such as is found in the Highlands is not present. Men and women are both identified with pigs. In Arapesh, the owners of pigs are called their parents. The "fastening" that prepares the pigs for exchange separates the pigs from women and enables them to be exchanged like male crops. Men must abstain from intercourse to "fasten" pigs. The structure of exchange of pigs is the same as the structure of exchange of male crops. It involves restricted exchange between exchange partners, *buanyin*, or *tshambara* on opposite sides of a dual division. It is also competitive in nature. In contrast, the structure of exchange of women and shells is a quite different pattern shaped by prohibitions. Shell rings, which are the equivalent of women, symbolize peace in contrast to the competitiveness of yam and pig exchange. In Tor and Keraki, there are no separate categories of male and female crops, nor a strong association between pigs and women. Neither the Tor nor the Keraki have domesticated pigs but men capture wild pigs to rear them for exchange. Consequently, there is only a single dual structure of exchange, with two sides exchanging the whole range of items.

Male-male relations may involve another kind of relationship that is the obverse of exchange. That is the relationship between enemies. The nature and meaning of the enemy relationship illuminate the meaning of the exchange relationship. In each of the societies we have considered, there is a category called enemy, with whom one engages in warfare periodically. Which groups are in the category of enemy changes over time, except for the Kuma and Abelam, who refer to "traditional" enemies, but even in these societies it seems likely that change would occur over long spans of time. One does not exchange with groups with whom active hostilities are taking place. In some of these societies, Maring, Manga, and Kuma, one is also forbidden to eat with people who have been in contact with one's enemy. This takes the form of a fire taboo where one may not eat food cooked over the same fire as food which one's enemy has eaten, or eat with someone who has been in contact with one's enemy. (Bateson indicates the same association among the Iatmul, "fire and food being closely analogous in Iatmul thought [Bateson 1936: 83].) The exchange relationship is competitive and potentially hostile and men can move from being exchangers to being enemies and from enemies to exchangers. The most frequently cited reasons for warfare in these societies are fights over pigs and women. Groups that exchange women and pigs may become enemies as a result of fights during the exchanges, or because promises made in regard to the exchanges have not been met, or through the inability to control the objects of exchange—women and pigs. In the Lowlands, if reciprocity is not adhered to, sometimes there will be attempts to break off the relationship. The Arapesh relationship between *ano'in* is the negation of exchange relationship in that it involves competition, comparison, but no exchange. In Abelam and Wogeo, exchanges take place with what are characterized as enemy groups. In Abelam, enemy villages are given long yams and pigs like *tshambɔra* but they are not so labeled nor is the exchange on a regular basis. Marriages also take place with women of these "enemy villages." These behaviors would obviously not coincide with periods of open hostility. In Wogeo, *bag* or exchange partners can come from enemy as well as neutral or friendly districts. The large-scale ceremonial distribution, the *warabwa*, is directed toward a *bag* in an enemy or neutral district. In fact, Hogbin records how a participant referred to the *warabwa* as a substitute for fighting with spears. Throughout the area, the transformation of enemies into nonenemies is accomplished through exchange. Peace is established among the Manga, first by the exchange of shoots and then the exchange of women. Former Kuma enemies exchange pigs first and then women before the fire taboos can be lifted so that former enemies may eat together. The payment of homicide compensation between former enemies can be the basis for ongoing Moka exchange among the Melpa. Finally, among the Enga, the word *te* means homicide compensation and in fact the payment of homicide compensation regularly occurs during the *te* in certain Enga areas, indicating that groups of *te* partners in the period just prior to the *te* had been at war. The relationship between neighboring groups fluctuates between periods of open hostility and periods of comparative calm when exchange that expresses linkage as well as competition takes place. Exchange can be the cause of conflict and open hostility but it is at the same time the way of ending conflict and hostility.

Men also exchange with spirits as well as with other men. We have information on its occurrence in only some of the societies we have analyzed. In the Highlands the pigs sacrificed to the ancestors constitute an exchange between men and spirits. Mauss long ago recognized sacrifice as an exchange between men and the gods. In all of the category three societies, live pigs are sacrificed to the spirits. The killing of the pigs releases their spiritual aspect to be consumed by the spirits while their corporeal aspect is cooked and used in man-man exchanges. Sometimes, in the case of the Maring, spirits have given their "pigs," the marsupials and eels, in exchange. Pigs sacrificed to spirits serve a twofold purpose, exchanges with men and exchanges with spirits. None of the other objects exchanged in these societies have this twofold capacity, that is, live and given to spirits, killed and cooked and given to men. Besides their own "pigs" the spirits also give to men the fertility of their women to make the strength of their clans increase, and fertility of pigs and crops. The sphere of pigs and reproduction is a female sphere. Giving pigs to the spirits is designed to influence the spirits to promote the productivity of the female sphere. Among the Enga and the Melpa, these exchanges with spirits occur at special clan ceremonies that are not related to the *te* and moka exchange cycles. These special clan ceremonies rather than the *te* and moka resemble the pig festivals of the societies in category three. In these special clan ceremonies, as in category three society pig festivals, spirits get pigs and men get cooked pork; however, in *te* and moka, men get either live pigs or pork.

In the Lowlands, there are few examples of specific sacrifices to spirits. The two occurrences in the Lowland societies we have examined do involve pigs—the flute feast of the Tor and the *warabwa* of Wogeo. The Tor flute feast involves the hunting of a special flute pig in the forest which is sacrificed to the flutes that represent spirits, in exchange for the maintenance of the natural order of things. The flute is actually fed the food, which is then eaten by the men of the group (Oosterwall 1961: 239). A man cannot kill a pig that he has domesticated and reared. The flute pigs for sacrificial purposes must be specially obtained through hunting. In Wogeo, before the *warabwa,* the *nibek,* represented by the flutes that are considered to be the voices of the spirits, are summoned in order to taboo the slaughter of pigs or use of crops that will later be exchanged. At the end of the *warabwa,* the *nibek* are said to have eaten the pigs and are told to return to their homes. The pigs in actuality have been given to the *bag,* exchange partner, of the host. It is interesting to note that among the Chimbu there is reference to the fact that women who are forbidden to see the flutes are told that the flutes, during the initiation phase of the pig festival, drink the blood of the pigs sacrificed. In the Lowlands, in contrast to the Highlands, with the two exceptions we have discussed which do not involve ancestor spirits, pigs do not seem to be sacrificed to spirits. This seems to be related to what we have referred to above as the "incest taboo" against killing and eating one's own pigs. This taboo is absent in the Highlands, where pigs are sacrificed to ancestor and other spirits and are consumed by one's own groups and one's affines. The exchange of pigs with spirits in the form of sacrifice also sheds light on the live-raw-cooked distinction discussed earlier.

As we have noted, an important distinction is made between the exchange of those things identified with men and the exchange by men of those things identified with women. This relates to the separation in mode of production between the crops and animals identified as male and the crops and animals identified as female. This is a reflection of one of the most important general themes in all the societies we have examined—that is the separation of men and women. There is a feeling that women in general are contaminating; however, it is much stronger in some societies than in others. Sexual intercourse is felt to be polluting even in the case of Wogeo where the ethnographer reports that it is considered to be a pleasurable act. In Arapesh, Abelam, and Wogeo men practice periodic penis bleeding in order to purify themselves of the culmulative pollution resulting from sexual intercourse. The other forms of purificatory rites practiced by the Kuma, Chimbu, Melpa, and Enga are said to achieve the same effect. The Highland pattern is one of residential separation and eating separation though men and women are not forbidden to have contact with one another, either in residences or at meals. In the societies in category three, the special ceremonial house erected in connection with the pig festival contains objects that are obviously male and female symbols. Men and women are involved in rituals manipulating these symbols, which are related to fertility.

In the Lowlands, men and women occupy the same residences but there is a separate ceremonial house associated with spirits where flutes are kept and to which only men have access. Men and women also seem to eat together in these societies. Though men live and eat together in the Lowland societies, the rites of purification in Arapesh, Abelam, and Wogeo by periodic bleeding of the penis are the most pronounced. The bleeding is connected to female menstruation in that both are seen as the means by which males and females purify themselves from contact with the other sex.

The symbolism of exchange in the New Guinea societies we have considered is the product of the interaction of three fundamental characteristics. The first of these is that exchange, which is entirely in the hands of men and controlled by them, takes place at exchange ceremonies that constitute total social phenomena, in the Maussian sense, and express the relationships between groups. The second characteristic is the basic dichotomy between males and females in these societies. Their insignificance in the public sphere and the symbolic statements about women are but one indication of where women are located culturally in these societies. The third characteristic is that women are central to the reproduction of society and the production of pigs and staple crops, which are necessary to feed pigs and people.

Given these three characteristics, exchanges take the following forms. There are two separate structures of exchange—one in which men exchange things produced by men alone and another in which men exchange things produced by women. The latter involves the exchange of daughters and the ensuing affinal exchanges that are included in this category. When men exchange things produced by women, men assert their right of control and disposal. Sexual intercourse between men and women is necessary to produce children, particularly daughters to exchange in marriage. However, given the separation between men and women, when sexual intercourse occurs in order to produce children, both sexes must be purified from the contamination resulting from intercourse. Similarly, a child receives elements from both mother and father, but in order to become a man, a boy must be cleansed of the maternal element. Even after maturity, the tie between a man and his maternal relatives is characterized by a dialectic between termination and maintenance, between protection and harm. In the Highland societies, the fertility of women and pigs and staple crops, the things in which women play a central role, is in the hands of the spirits, particularly male ancestor spirits of the husband's agnatic group. Males in these societies are exchanging with male spirits to promote the fertility of things associated with women. Exchanges between men of things associated with women are generally not competitive or hostile. Sexual abstinence, which is one of the ways of separating men and women prior to exchange ceremonies, is not an important element of the pig festivals of the Highlands and is not associated with pig distributions to affines at these festivals.

The structure of exchange in which men are exchanging male things is contrastive with the structure of exchange of things associated with females. The exchange of "male" things is an exchange of things produced by males without females as a demonstration of the male capacity for fertility without females. Women must be kept from contact with these crops. Further, the producers of these crops must separate from women even to the extent of practicing sexual abstinence during the growing of these crops. This is in contrast to the intercourse that is necessary in order to produce daughters for exchange. The Yam cult of the Abelam and Arapesh most clearly embodies these features. In fact, among

18 Transformations in New Guinea Societies

The New Guinea societies we have analyzed place great emphasis upon ceremonial accumulation, distribution, and exchange. As several Wogeo men observed to Hogbin, "We have food both for display and to eat. . . We like to see it all spread out before us. . . . That is why we take so much trouble with it. . . . Food is the most important thing here in Wogeo and must be treated with respect" (Hogbin 1938–39: 324–25). The things most prized are accumulated, displayed for all to see, only to be given away. Those who have received subsequently become accumulators, displayers, and givers because of the need to return what one has received. The great emphasis in New Guinea societies which is placed upon ceremonial distribution and exchange made it logical to focus upon exchange as a central theoretical concept in the analysis of these societies. We have considered a number of New Guinea societies in terms of several variables. Our initial concern was with the nature of the units carrying out exchange. We turned then to the way in which the political power dimension of exchanges, through leadership, structures units internally and externally. Next we considered all of the things exchanged, including women, the various contexts in which exchanges take place, and finally the meanings of the things exchanged as these relate to other symbolic structures.

Each of the societies represents a particular configuration of these variables and constitutes a system. However, as our analysis of these societies has revealed, a particular manifestation of one variable may be coupled in different societies with different forms of another variable. Thus the rule that one must exchange sisters, which is present in a number of societies, is coupled with different forms of ceremonial exchange. Any one particular configuration is not inevitable. Within a society, a variable may undergo transformation resulting in a different system.

Our initial hypothesis was that our analysis would reveal that a single structure of exchange underlay all the exchanges that took place in a society. Thus we anticipated that the ceremonial exchanges of valuables, pigs, and yams would be identical to the structure of exchange of women such as we found in our earlier work on the Northwest Coast (Rosman and Rubel 1971). While in some of the societies—in the New Guinea Highlands—this hypothesis was confirmed, in others, notably Arapesh and Abelam, we found two separate structures of exchange—one between named exchange partners and the other between affines who exchanged women. Whether there is a relationship between these two structures of exchange and the nature of the relationship, if such exist, was the next question we explored. Further analysis revealed for example in the case of the Abelam that the two structures of exchange represented homologous structures that dealt with the same themes of fertility and competition but in different ways. The two are related through a series of transformations. These two structures coexist in the case of the Abelam so that the transformational relationship between them is a synchronic one. Models of these two structures are isomorphic with one another such that the elements of one are systematically transformed into the elements of the other. This represents a different use of the term transformation from the sense to which we referred when we discussed the possibility of changes in variables. In this earlier usage, we were dealing with changes in variables through time or diachronic transformations. The change in one variable also implies some sort of change in the other variables so that the system changes over time. This is different from the synchronic usage of transformation discussed above. The synchronic and diachronic usages of transformation are related to one another in that the synchronic is the result of the diachronic. At any single point in time, homologous structures within a single society which are related to one another through a transformation, are the result of a diachronic transformation from a single structure. This follows Jakobson's dictum that diachrony is contained within synchrony (see our discussion in the Introduction, p. 3).

The second stage of our analysis concerned a comparison and sorting of the data from all of the societies in our sample in terms of certain aspects of our central variables. We first examined the units engaged in exchanges, the principles of kinship and residence according to which they were organized, and the hierarchical nature of the ordering especially in the societies with segmentary structures. We then focused our attention upon the way in which the most valuable of commodities, women, were exchanged. This led in turn to an examination of the pattern of affinal exchanges which started with marriage and, in most of the societies we analyzed, continued until the death of the children of that marriage. We then focused on nonaffinal exchanges of valuables and things other than women in the chapter on ceremonial exchanges. The units exchanging, the context of the exchanges, and frequently the things exchanged were contrastive with affinal exchanges. In the chapter on Big Men we explored the way in which political power and leadership related to exchanges. With the exception of Wogeo, the pattern in the other societies is very similar except for difference in scale and degree. Finally, we examined the meanings of exchange and how these related to other domains, such as male-female relations, concern with fertility, and mode of production.

The resultant sortings formed the basis for the development of four categories. A consideration of the structural models resulting from the comparisons indicated to us that the ceremonial exchange structures were the dominant structures for these societies. The structure that underlies ceremonial exchange is the same structure underlying other cultural domains. In cases where there were separate structures for the exchange of women and ceremonial goods, the structure of ceremonial exchange was still the dominant structure. Ceremonial and ritual are the crystallization of the cognitive themes of the society. Behavior, dress, and verbal statements express the meanings of the ritual. Performance of the ceremonies reinforces and gives strength to the cognitive orientation. The structure of ceremonial exchange also organizes behavior in other cultural domains, which is why it can be singled out as the dominant structure.

The four categories were therefore based upon the sortings related to ceremonial exchange structures. These categories and the nature of their relationship to each other will be discussed in detail in the succeeding pages of this chapter. They can be ranged in terms of degrees of complexity from the two-sided moiety structure of Keraki exchange to the *te* exchange system of the Enga which links many groups and thousands of individuals. The relationships between the four categories will be presented as a series of transformations. They do not form a simple linear series but rather a multilinear series. The basis of this multilinear series is a hypothesized prototypical structure.

The Prototypical Structure

The prototype to be described here was arrived at by a process of triangulation from the four categories developed as a result of our analysis. We shall show how, from this structure, the structures of the societies in each of the categories could have developed by means of a series of transformations. Even though significant transformations may have occurred in some of the societies resulting in great structural divergence from the prototype, it will be seen that they still retain specific features of the prototype.

The prototype has the following characteristics:

a. Postmarital residence pattern of virilocality, but with the possible option of living with affines; husbands and wives reside together.

b. A weakly developed ideology of patrilineal descent characterizing residential units resulting from virilocality.

c. Politically autonomous residential units, hamlets formed into villages that are small in scale and in population, which either war or exchange with similarly composed neighboring units.

d. Sister exchange, which is continued transgenerationally as bilateral cross-cousin marriage.

e. Sister exchange may take place within the autonomous group, or between two autonomous groups. The structure of affinal relationships is identical in the internal and external forms of sister exchange, but the two forms have different implications for group relations. The internal form serves to divide the groups into two parts, while the external form serves to relate two autonomous groups in alliance and exchange.

f. Affinal exchanges between groups at the rites de passage of a child born of a marriage serve to continue the relationship established through the initial exchange of women until the death of that child.

g. Bifurcate merging kinship terminology and Iroquois cousin terms.

h. Women make the major contribution of labor to food production.

i. Presence of rules making it obligatory to exchange: "Your own pigs, your own yams that you have piled up, you may not eat" (Mead 1935: 83). This is analogous to the incest taboo and the necessity to exchange women between groups.

j. Though women may produce the things exchanged, the control of exchanges is entirely in the hands of men.

k. Large-scale ceremonial distributions of cooked and uncooked food are hosted by the autonomous groups. These distributions are competitive since group prestige depends upon the size of the display and the amounts distributed. Groups receiving have the obligation to reciprocate. The structure of ceremonial exchange recapitulates the structure of exchange of women, so that affinally linked groups are recipients at ceremonial distributions. Distributions internal to the autonomous group will be characterized by a

two-sided structure of exchange. Distributions
between autonomous groups will be two-sided, or
star-shaped in form, depending on the character of
external marital alliances. The magnitude of the
ceremonial distribution will vary with the structural
level of the host group, so that the largest distributions
are hosted by the politically autonomous village or
tribe.

l. Political leadership involves a central role in exchange
as well as some special access to ritual knowledge.
Political leadership is of the Big Man type, since
preparation for the accumulation of goods, their
display, and their distribution at ceremonial exchanges
is organized by the Big Man. Big Men represent their
groups in exchanges.

m. Though women are central to the reproduction of
society through childbearing and central to the
production of crops, fertility is symbolically controlled
by the actions of men. This is accomplished through
rituals enlisting the assistance of the spirit world.
Flutes, which are associated with spirits and with men,
and are forbidden to women, play a central role.
Sacrifices and the feeding of the flutes may form a part
of these rituals.

n. Ritual separation of men and women. Sacred objects,
mainly flutes, are kept from women in a ritual house,
which women cannot enter. When men are in a ritual
state they must abstain from sexual intercourse with
women, or from contact with them. However,
ceremonial sexual intercourse takes place on certain
ritual occasions to promote growth and fertility.

o. Importance of male initiation ceremonies. Boys are
separated from their mothers, secluded, and taught the
secrets of male ceremonialism and of the flutes.
Initiation rites are carried out within the autonomous
group, which is divided into two sides. The opposite
side acts as initiator, mother's brother performing this
role if there are no ordeals, or a surrogate in the
opposite moiety if ordeals are involved. Thus at
initiation the two sides are exchanging ritual services.
The culmination of initiation is a ceremonial
distribution by the host group to other politically
autonomous groups.

p. A structure of dual organization which is manifested in the following features: sister exchange, which divides the autonomous group into two parts which are spatially separated; other exchanges of ritual services at various rites de passage including death between the two parts of the structure; male ceremonialism including initiation involves a two-part structure; reflections of dual organization in the systems of classification of the natural and supernatural worlds.

q. A star-shaped structure characterizes external marriage alliances between the politically autonomous group and its neighbors, and large-scale ceremonial distributions to those neighboring groups.

Category One: Tor and Keraki

Tor and Keraki are structurally closest to the prototype. They exhibit most of its characteristics, though in specific respects each has undergone some changes. Like the prototype, they are small in scale, with sparse populations. They retain the pattern of sister exchange practiced transgenerationally which produces the two-sided structure. In both, marriages are predominantly within the autonomous group, which is thus divided into two intermarrying segments. Some sister exchange marriages also take place between autonomous groups. Affinal exchanges as well as ritual exchange of services follow these two patterns. Neighboring autonomous groups are either allies or enemies. Large-scale ceremonial feasting and distribution controlled by men is hosted by the autonomous group for surrounding and more distant groups with whom they are not currently at war. The pattern for such distributions is star-shaped. These groups are also the autonomous groups with whom marriage is contracted. As is the case in the prototype, a rule is present in both Tor and Keraki forbidding the eating of one's own pigs, which in both societies refers to piglets captured in the bush and raised to maturity. In both societies, women are kept separate from male ritual objects, such as flutes and bull-roarers, and male rites. However, ceremonial sexual intercourse occurs. Among the Tor, sexual intercourse occurs between men and women in connection with fertility rites, and among the Keraki male sodomy occurs as part of initiation. The Big Men structure of Tor and Keraki is like that of the prototype.

Tor differs from the prototype in several respects. One series of transformations concerns the nature of the units involved in exchanges. Unlike the prototype, Tor have no ideology of patrilineal descent as an organizing basis for units engaged in exchanges. The basic unit in the single level of their structural hierarchy is the residential unit, which is at one and the same time a village and a tribe. Most marriages take place within this unit. For such endogamous marriages there is no definitive rule of postmarital residence. Marriages outside the tribe are bilocal. In addition to the lines of fathers and sons exchanging sisters, lines of mother's brothers and sister's sons own the sacred flutes. Thus two vague moiety divisions cross-cut each other though in neither case are the moieties named. This represents a transformation from the prototype in that the explicit patrilineal father-son line of the prototype has been transformed into a father-son line exchanging women and mother's brother/sister's son line owning flutes. Tor kinship terminology varies and is not strictly Iroquois. Some Tor tribes also permit parallel cousin marriage. Aside from these characteristics involving the structure of the units exchanging, the Tor are identical to the prototype. Women make the major contribution to food production in the society in their harvest and preparation of sago. However, men symbolically control the fertility of women and crops through their exclusive possession of myths, magic, the flutes, and *faarah* ceremonial house. These symbols and rites control the fertility and growth of crops and children. Tor myths state that women once owned the flutes and the *faarah* house and the curative magical snakefat, but men at some point obtained them and must keep women from them to maintain their power.

The Keraki are much like the protostructure particularly in respect to the units exchanging. They have exogamous patrilineal moieties; however, these exhibit an anomaly in that one of the moieties consists of two named parts but operates as a single moiety. The politically autonomous unit is a tribe consisting of several villages. Typically men of one moiety reside in a village and exchange women with men of another

village of the opposite moiety in either the same or a neighboring tribe. Thus the hierarchy here consists of two levels of
structure—the village and the tribe. It is not clear that women
are the major food producers among the Keraki since both
men and women produce yams and taitu. It would appear,
however, that women make the major contribution to every-
day subsistence production. However, men and women harvest, sort and store the yams, retaining the largest for exchange. Though men capture piglets in the forest, women
feed and care for them. The fertility of crops is controlled by
men through the performance of rites at the beginning and at
the end of the gardening cycle. Bullroarers, the male symbols, which are kept separate from women, are sounded at
these rites.

Category Two: Banaro, Abelam, Arapesh, Iatmul, and Wogeo

The societies in category two represent a transformation of
the prototype, in the direction of elaborations of dual organization. These are combined with transformations of marriage
rules away from the simple restricted exchange marriage of
the prototype. The Banaro represent a transition from the
prototype to category two; Wogeo, while sharing most of the
characteristics of category two societies, also evidences some
of the features of category three.

A number of characteristics of the prototype are retained.
Moieties are present in these societies, and are always the
basis for boy's initiation. Dual organization is sometimes
elaborated resulting in more than one moiety structure in a
society. Postmarital residence is virilocal. An ideology of patrilineal descent forms a basis of clan organization, and the
clan is associated with symbolic representations such as
totem or ancestral carvings. Multiclan villages are present,
and clan hamlets are sometimes paired within these villages.
Units are thus organized into a two-level hierarchy. Sister
exchange continues to be important, but it is usually classificatory sisters who are exchanged. The pattern of affinal
exchanges is the same as in the prototype, though the marriage rules vary significantly from the prototype. Women are
the major contributors of production for subsistence, while

men control exchange. As in the prototype, there are rules
obligating one to exchange. Pigs one has raised and frequently yams one has grown may not be eaten, and must be
exchanged. The structure of political leadership is as described for the prototype, except for Wogeo. Paralleling the
two-level structure of hamlet and village, some Big Men are
more important than others and represent the village vis-à-
vis other villages.

A major transformation in category two societies from the
prototype is the separation of exchange partners from affines,
producing two separate structures of exchange, one of goods
and one of women. Wogeo is the exception in this. The moiety structure of the prototype is continued in that the exchange of goods is between exchange partners in different
moieties. The exchange of women is based upon rules that
do not relate to the moiety structure. All except Banaro prohibit marriage with first cross-cousins, and Arapesh extend
this prohibition to second and third cousins. A variety of
preferential marriage rules are present, all emphasizing reciprocity or deferred exchange, except for Iatmul. Kinship
terminologies vary with the marriage rules. As in the prototype, men and women are ritually separated, but ceremonial sexual intercourse is not carried out. Ideas about ritual
separation are elaborated into ideas about the polluting effects upon men of contact with women. Men cleanse themselves by letting blood. There seems to be an absence of
ritual directly relating to the fertility of women and crops.
What are present in category two societies are male rites
producing symbolic forms of fertility at which women are
not present, and indeed female fertility is not even
mentioned. The ceremonial sexual intercourse to promote
fertility in the prototype is transformed into its opposite—
the avoidance of all contact with females due to their polluting effects in order to promote male symbolic fertility.

For these societies, the structure of large-scale ceremonial
exchanges is that of dual organization, on both levels of the
political hierarchy. There is no indication of the star-shaped
structure that is present in the prototype.

Though the Banaro share many of the features of category
one societies, Tor and Keraki, exchange partners and affines
are separated, resulting in two structures of exchange. They

thus represent a transformation from the prototype and are a transition to category two. The relationship between the halves of a hamlet is transformed into the *mundu* relationship, which is characterized by the exchange of ceremonial services but no exchange of women. The *mundu* relationship is like the moiety structure of exchange partners in the other societies of category two. The marriage structure is identical to the prototype in that the Banaro have direct exchange of real sisters which continues over generations, resulting in a dual structure of marriage linking two halves of two different hamlets. There are therefore two separate forms of dual organization, producing cross-cutting moieties. The Banaro are like the Tor and Keraki of category one in that ceremonial intercourse occurs in the men's house, before the flutes, between men and the wives of their exchange partners. The polluting effects of women which characterize other category two societies are not present among the Banaro.

The Arapesh, Abelam, and Iatmul typify the societies of category two. In the prototype, one side of the dual structure exchanged women, pigs, and yams with the other side. The relationship between the two sides was an ambivalent one, involving both cooperation and competition. Each side initiated the boys of the opposite side. The transformation from the prototype to category two societies involves a transformation from a single dual structure of exchange into two separate structures. Exchange partners exchange pigs and yams in a competitive form of exchange. Exact measures of what is given are kept and reciprocity is demanded. The one type of yam, which in the prototype is used for subsistence and for exchange, is transformed into two distinct types. One produced by women is for subsistence; the other produced by men is for exchange. Women are excluded from most or all of the phases of the growth cycle, harvesting, and display of exchange yams. This may include all contact with women including sexual intercourse. Before pigs are fastened for exchange among the Arapesh there can be no sexual intercourse. Initiation of boys also involves the structure of exchange partners. The structure of exchange partners and the activities characterizing this structure represent a continuity with only certain aspects of the prototype. The remaining aspects are continued in a transformed state in the structure of exchange of women. Sister exchange, usually classificatory, takes place but it is coupled with a series of marriage prohibitions and alternative marriage rules. Goods given to affines contrast with goods exchanged with exchange partners. The different meanings of these two categories of goods symbolize the difference in the two kinds of relationships. Yams exchanged between exchange partners symbolize the competition between them while the shells given to affines symbolize peace and harmony which characterize the emphasis on cooperation in this relationship. In the transformation to category two societies, the ambivalence of the relationship between the two sides of the prototype becomes the competition overtly expressed between exchange partners and the cooperation stressed between affines. These are the formal expression of these two relationships though ambivalence may still underlie these relationships. Rituals concerning the fertility of women and crops are not associated with affinal relationship, and further there are no rituals to promote this type of fertility. Rather they are transformed into ideas relating to male fertility and productivity which are associated with the solely male structure of exchange partners. The yams produced in the Abelam yam cult are an example of such a symbolic form of fertility involving only men. Exchange of these long yams between exchange partners is a transformation of the affinal relationship, which combines competition and fertility. Similarly, Iatmul headhunting, which involves solely males, is a way of promoting fertility, and recapitulates the connection between aggressive male-to-male activities and fertility. Activities of the strictly male Tamberan cult of the Arapesh also promote fertility.

Wogeo represents a transformation from the prototype, but somewhat different from that of the other societies of category two. Wogeo has exchange partners, known as *bag*, who are on opposite sides of a moiety division. However, the structure is different since the moieties are matrilineal and cross-cut the localized patrilineal descent groups. There are three structural levels in the political hierarchy. The matrimoieties operate at male initiation, burial, and the large-scale competitive food distributions that take place between *bag* of enemy or neutral districts. In contrast to other category two societies, where moieties line up patrilineal descent groups on either side of a dual structure, the matrimoieties that cross-cut patrilineal descent groups in Wogeo are categories and not groups. This structurally resembles Tor, where matrilineal flute-owning groups cross-cut the local descent lines. The marriage structure of Wogeo is characterized by a prohibition on first cousin marriage, and a preference for marriage with FaFaSiSoDa. Alternate generations whose members are identical in terms of matrimoiety membership are identified with one another by this marriage rule. This seems to explain why, in Wogeo, in contrast with other category two societies, the children of exchange partners may marry. Initiation, which in all the societies in category two is carried out by exchange partners on opposite sides of the moiety structure, is carried out in Wogeo by the father's matrimoiety for his own son, thus altering the roles of father and mother's brother vis-à-vis the boy at initiation. Wogeo has been included in category two because the large-scale ceremonial distributions—*warabwa*—which take place between *bag* have the structure of dual organization that characterizes all category two societies. However, since the children of exchange partners marry there are not two separate structures of exchange in Wogeo as in other category two societies. The ideas about the polluting influence of women and male menstruation practices are present in Wogeo as in other category two societies. Male rites involving flutes and bullroarers are also present but they do not seem to involve fertility and productivity but only the tabooing of particular crops or pigs prior to ceremonial distribution. However, the playing of flutes by men is seen as equivalent to women bearing children. Magic promoting growth of crops in Wogeo is inherited and in the hands of the hereditary headmen.

Category Three: Maring, Manga, Kuma, and Chimbu

Category three societies represent an independent transformation from the prototype. They exemplify an expansion in scale and in density of population, with a concomitant loss of many of the features of dual organization. Though their large-scale ceremonial distributions are of much greater magnitude and link many more groups in a more or less regular cycle of ceremonial distributions, the star-shaped form that the distributions take is already present in the prototype.

The societies of category three all have segmentary lineage structures, with an ideology of patrilineal descent. Postmarital residence is virilocal, though shifting of residence sometimes occurs and nonagnates become part of the residential unit. The kinship terminology facilitates their descendents becoming absorbed into the agnatic group. The residential pattern represents a transformation from the prototype in that men reside apart from their wives in a separate men's house. This men's house provides sleeping quarters, and is not the center of ritual activity. The population is dispersed and there are no permanent nucleated settlements. The weakly developed ideology of patrilineal descent of the prototype becomes more formalized as the ideology of the segmentary lineage structure. The two-level hierarchy of the prototype is transformed into a multileveled hierarchy of the segmentary structure in which the most inclusive level carries out the large-scale ceremonial distribution at the pig festivals. The largest political entity, which we shall call tribe here, is surrounded by neighboring groups of the same type, who are either enemies with whom they war, or allies with whom they exchange both goods and women.

Sister exchange marriage, which characterizes the prototype, is continued in category three societies. As in the prototype, marriages take place within the tribe and between tribes. Marriages within the tribe do not produce a dual structure because of the presence of prohibitions on marriage with first cross-cousins in all the societies. There are preferential marriage rules that in Maring and Manga stipulate a preference for marriage with FaFaSiSoDa and in Kuma for bilateral second cross-cousin. Among the Chimbu the prohibitions are more extensive and there is no stated preference.

The pattern of affinal exchange continues to be the same as in the prototype. As in the prototype the structure of exchange at large-scale ceremonial distributions recapitulates the structure of exchange of women and is the dominant structure. Ties established between autonomous groups through the exchange of women are continued through the exchange of goods by exchange partners. These large ceremonial distributions primarily of pork, hosted by politically autonomous groups, follow the star shape. The host is the center and the invited groups of guests who are affines are the periphery since the pattern of external marriages of an autonomous group with neighboring groups also takes the star-shaped form. The Manga clan moieties that exchange ritual service but cannot exchange women are one of the few examples of dual structure. The other manifestation is the large-scale vegetable distribution of the Kuma and Chimbu which involves reciprocal exchange of vegetable crops between two groups. The distribution involves crops associated with men and, like the prototype, is competitive. Unlike the prototype there are no obligatory rules requiring exchange. In these societies, you can eat your own pigs. As in the prototype, women contribute the major share of labor to the production of food crops and pigs. Men control all the exchanges. Big Men organize and direct the large-scale exchanges, which are not competitive. Big Men of varying degrees of importance direct the activities of groupings at various levels of the hierarchy, representing those groups in exchanges. In several of these societies, the position of Big Man is associated with ritual knowledge. Among the Kuma the Big Man controls sorcery and war magic, and among the Maring the Big Man controls access to ancestor spirits through his ritual knowledge.

Category three societies are characterized by a structure of exchange with the spirit world which represents a transformation from the prototype. The feeding of the flutes that represent spirits in the prototype is transformed into a complex structure of exchange with the spirit world. For these societies the spirit world includes the spirits of ancestors, and more generalized spirits. Both categories of spirits are concerned with the fertility of the women and the pigs of the group, and with the group's success in warfare. Men sacrifice pigs to the spirits in exchange for assistance in promoting fertility and success in warfare. Thus there are two structures of exchange—one with men, with whom one exchanges women and pork, and a second with the spirit world.

In the prototype men are separated from women when they are in a ritual state. In category three societies there is a division between rites associated with fertility and rites associated with preparation for warfare. Ritual separation of men from women occurs only in connection with rituals of warfare. Initiation rites (among the Kuma and the Chimbu) and the period of maturation for a boy in which his growing masculinity is emphasized (among the Maring) involve separation from women. The ceremonial intercourse that promotes fertility in the prototype is transformed into rituals that symbolize sexual intercourse and involve both men and women. These rituals promote fertility of women and crops, and are part of the climax of the pig festival. In these societies women and sexuality are considered to be polluting, except among the Kuma. In this respect the societies of category three resemble category two societies.

The large-scale pig festivals of category three societies represent total social phenomena, in the Maussian sense of the term. The two structures of exchange with men and with spirits are played out during this cyle of events. Male initiation, if it does take place, is held in conjunction with this festival. Rites involving success in fertility and in warfare are central to the festival. Its star-shaped structure is therefore the dominant mode for category three societies.

Category Four: Melpa and Enga

The societies in Category Four represent a branching off from the development of the prototype into Category Three. The pig festival as a total phenomenon in category three becomes separated into clan rituals involving the spirits, and the *te* and moka exchanges. The clan rituals perpetuate those aspects of the pig festival which are concerned with fertility, success, and well-being of the group through sacrificial exchanges with the spirits. The structure that characterizes *te* and moka exchange perpetuates the competitive ceremonial distributions of the prototype. However, the dual structures of the prototype are transformed into chains that evolve in Enga into a system of generalized exchange. This is one of the reasons why category four though related is not a direct transformation of category three. We have therefore postulated an intermediary prototype that gave rise to both categories three and four.

The characteristics of this intermediary prototype are: segmentary lineage structure; exogamous clans as the autonmous political units; neighboring clans exchange women and goods so that affines equal exchange partners; neighboring clans may also war with one another so that affines are potential enemies; a variety of clan-hosted ceremonies celebrating the themes of warfare, fertility and initiation through exchange relations with spirits; the structure of exchange is a star-shaped pattern; the periphery consists of affines and different groups of affines are present as recipients at the different ceremonies; those groups which receive eventually make a return.

This intermediary prototype evolves into category three by means of several transformations. The various clan-hosted ceremonies become a multipurpose pig festival hosted by a politically autonomous unit that is larger than the clan-tribe or clan-cluster. The pig festival does not involve competition, through the theme of success and assistance in warfare is present. All the affinally linked groups on the periphery receive at the same ceremony, and the need to reciprocate becomes a sequencing of pig festivals. The clan continues to be the exogamous unit, while a higher level entity hosts the pig festival. There are therefore affines within the host groups, as well as affines in groups on the periphery, and only the latter receive at the pig festivals.

Category four involves a different set of transformations from the intermediary prototype. While retaining many of the characteristics of the intermediary prototype, in category four some affines are selected to become named exchange partners, while others are simply present as recipients at the various clan ceremonies that involve the star-shaped structure. The exchange partnership is then inherited separately from affinal connection. The structure of named exchange partners which ties together groups is no longer star-shaped but assumes the following form. The moka of the Melpa constitutes stage one of the transformation. The moka partnerships of the men of one group to the men of a range of other groups constitute the "ropes of moka." This is a selection out of the periphery of men in particular groups who become moka partners. In moka, like is exchanged for like and therefore each cycle is completed. The nature of the return does not necessitate that one cycle follow upon another. Chains of moka giving develop when a recipient passes on goods to a third partner before making a return. Moka chains are situational in that goods may not follow the same chain of partners in every cycle. Chains when they develop turn concentric dualism into triadism. The ceremonial context of moka exchange is limited to external relations between groups, and of the themes in the clan ceremonies of the intermediary prototype only warfare is relevant in that payment of homicide compensation can develop into moka, and is structurally identical to it.

Stage two in the development of generalized exchange in category four is represented by the *te*. Like is now directly exchanged for unlike resulting in the tying together of the phases into a longer cycle. Just as there is no direct exchange of women in marriage, there is no exchange of like for like in the *te*. The triadic structure is the underlying structure of the *te*, since *te* partners of any group are always divided into goods givers or goods receivers, the essential criterion of generalized exchange. In category four, there is direct competition between exchangers and a connection between *te* and moka and the payment of homicide compensation after warfare. As in the prototype so in *te* and moka an exact accounting is kept of what is given in order to evaluate what is a proper return. This contrasts with the pig festivals of category three in which reciprocity may operate over time but is not an integral part of the exchange.

In both Melpa and Enga, there is no exchange of sisters, and marriage prohibitions are extensive resulting in a wide spread of marriage ties among the neighboring autonomous groups. Though there is an absence of sister exchange, neighboring clans exchange women over time and keep track of the state of the exchanges among the Melpa. Among the

Enga, this is not the case and therefore there are no vestiges of the dual organization of the structure of marriage found in the prototype.

The vegetable distributions of "male" crops which are present in category four societies are like distributions in the prototype, and category three in that they are competitive. However, there is an absence of information on whether reciprocation is required.

The polluting effects of women are characteristic of these societies. Women are kept separate from weapons in both. The Female Spirit Cult of the Melpa, and the *sanggai* ritual of the Enga, from which women are ritually separate, both involve the purification of men from the polluting effects of women. The Female Spirit Cult of the Melpa also emphasizes male fertility. There are no specific initiatory rites for boys in these societies. However, boys are initiated into the secrets of the Female Spirit Cult and into the *sanggai* ritual. This ritual separation of men and women derives from the prototype, but unlike the formal initiation of the prototype, category four societies introduce boys to the secrets of male purification but do not have initiatory ordeals. Additionally there is a Male Spirit Cult among the Melpa which involves the separation of women from men in most activities except a climactic dance, but which involves symbolic intercourse and a theme of the fertility of women and the interdependence of both sexes in procreation. In this it resembles the fertility aspects of the pig festivals of category three where males and females are present. The significant distinction between category three and category four societies is that though the structure of exchange with men is the same in that affines and exchange partners are identical, the ceremonials involving fertility, prosperity, and well-being of the group are separate from the exchange ceremonies in category four societies. The latter are competitive and related to warfare and thus we have derived them directly from the prototype rather than from category three. The clan rituals and the Male Spirit Cult are the equivalent of the fertility aspects of the pig festivals. The pig festival of category three encompassed both the structure of exchange with men and the structure of exchange with spirits. In category four societies the *te* and moka exchanges do not involve a structure of exchange with spirits.

Conclusions

We have presented a series of transformations that relate the societies in our sample. Our results have a number of theoretical implications. Our analysis has revealed the importance of dual organization, as a principle of organization in its own right, and as a basis for transformations into more complex forms of dualism or into other kinds of structures. The major theoretical discussion of dualism in recent years has been by Lévi-Strauss. The presentation of his ideas has prompted discussion by Maybury-Lewis (1960) and Ortiz (1969). In *Elementary Structures of Kinship*, Lévi-Strauss argues that the principle of reciprocity itself is more basic than dualism. He sees dual organization as capable of widely varying, and more or less elaborate applications (Lévi-Strauss 1969: 75). Lévi-Strauss also links exogamy, bilateral cross-cousin marriage, and dual organization. We too see the principle of reciprocity underlying dualism, but in the New Guinea societies we have considered, the native model emphasizes sister exchange rather than bilateral cross-cousin marriage. In the prototype and in category one societies, since sister exchange can be repeated in successive generations, it occurs together with bilateral cross-cousin marriage. Sister exchange continues as a preferred marriage form in categories two and three, despite the transformations of the marriage rules in these societies prohibiting bilateral first cross-cousin marriage. The two-sided dualism that is associated with sister exchange continues to be present but is no longer the dominant form since it is now associated with more extended prohibitions and sometimes preferences. The coexistence of varying expressions of dualism noted by Lévi-Strauss are manifested particularly in category two societies where moieties created by the exchange of goods and ritual services create a dual structure that is different from the marriage structure.

Lévi-Strauss (1963) distinguished between diametric and concentric dualism. The star form to which we have referred earlier is an example of what Lévi-Strauss defines as concentric dualism since it is comprised of a center and periphery. In the prototype and category one societies, marriages and exchanges of goods within the autonomous political group take the form of diametric dualism while marriages and exchanges external to the group take the form of concentric dualism. These two forms of dualism in the prototype are separately elaborated and transformed in categories two, three, and four, though both continue to coexist. In category two societies, diametric dualism is the dominant form as manifested in the moiety structure of the exchange of goods and ritual services, though concentric dualism continues to be present in the spread of marriage ties through the exchange of classificatory sisters. In category three societies, the star-shaped pattern of concentric dualism is the dominant form in the pattern of the exchange of women and the ceremonial distribution of the pig festival, while diametric dualism is present but of lesser importance being represented in the vegetable exchanges and in the exchange of ritual services in the Manga clan moieties. In category four societies, diametric dualism, as represented in the divisions within clans which exchange ritual services during certain rituals, and concentric dualism, represented in the clan rituals to ancestors, are overshadowed by a new dominant structure of generalized exchange which is triadic. The only other example of triadic structure in our sample is the generalized exchange of women practiced in the *iai* marriage of the Iatmul.

Our models also have implications for the distinction between restricted and generalized exchange. The dual structure of exchange is restricted exchange in which there is direct reciprocity of like for like. The most direct form of restricted exchange in marriage is sister exchange. Restricted exchange also characterizes the exchanges between exchange partners in category two societies. Delayed exchange occurs in marriage and goods-exchange structures. The marriage with sister's daughter among the Keraki and the return of a sister's daughter for sister who is then used to obtain a wife among the Tor are examples of delayed exchange. The preference for marriage with father's sister's daughter, which is also delayed exchange, is not present in our sample. What is present is return in the second generation in the form of FaFaSiSoDa marriage among the Maring, Wogeo, and Manga. This represents delayed exchange given the prohibition on first cross-cousin marriage. In category three societies, especially the Chimbu and Kuma, the obligation of a group to hold a pig festival means that what is given will eventually be returned at a future time; thus the pig festival in these societies can also be seen as a form of delayed exchange. Delayed exchange, of both women and goods, means that one group must be tied to several other groups in exchange relationships. If reciprocity does not operate in the same generation, as through sister exchange, then a wife giving group must get its wives from groups other than the wife takers which results in a triadic structure. Regularity of return in delayed exchange will produce chains. The *te* and the moka exchanges of category four from the perspective of one group are also forms of delayed exchange. The presence of chains, which are formalized in the case of the Enga *te*, makes the structure of relationships between groups like that of patrilateral cross-cousin marriage and represents generalized exchange since the structure of relationships between groups is perpetuated from one exchange cycle to the next. The only form of the matrilateral variant of generalized exchange in our sample is to be found in the second matrilateral cross-cousin or *iai* marriage form, among the Iatmul. In this marriage structure, women move in one direction, and no return of a woman is ever made to a wife-giving lineage. In our sample, there are no examples of such a structure of generalized exchange characterizing the exchange of goods. However, the *kula* exchange among the Trobriand Islanders is an example of this structure. In this case, givers of arm-shells (the female element) are always separate from receivers of arm-shells, in the same way that wife givers are separate from wife takers in matrilateral cross-cousin marriage.

The relationship between reciprocity and hierarchy is another problem treated by Lévi-Strauss and others. Lévi-Strauss long ago pointed out in his analysis of the Bororo how a moiety structure could express not only reciprocity but hierarchy as well. He states, "But, even in these relations of subordination, the principle of reciprocity is at work; for the subordination itself is reciprocal: the priority which is gained by one moiety on one level is lost to the opposite moiety on the other" (Lévi-Strauss 1944: 267–68). This relationship between reciprocity and hierarchy is exemplified in Ortiz's (1969) analysis of the Tewa. However, in this case there is an alternation of subordination through time. What is hierarchical synchronically becomes reciprocal diachronically. None of the societies in our sample manifesting some form of moiety organization exhibits hierarchies in its moieties. The Keraki represent an anomalous case in that a three-fold division operates as a moiety structure, with two parts standing in opposition to the third. Despite this asymmetry, the two halves operate reciprocally and symmetrically in relation to one another.

In contrast to the lack of hierarchy of dual organization found in the social structures, there are examples of hierarchy in the symbolic structure. A number of the societies have symbolic oppositional categories of male and female objects. Interaction at initiation between these two moieties is associated with male and female and involves the men of one side sodomizing the boys of the opposite side and vice versa. Thus the hierarchy of the symbol system is reversed in that the female side sodomizes the male side. Even the seeming hierarchy of male and female among the Keraki is flattened by the reciprocity. The male-female symbolic opposition between crops is present in all Highland societies. It is asymmetric and hierarchical in that female crops are the staple while male crops such as sugar and pandanus are usually luxury crops used primarily for exchange ceremonies. In the case of the Maring and Melpa, the symbolic distinction extends to other categories as well. The Maring-Manga set of binary oppositions represents a dual structure that is underlaid by this basic male-female opposition. This distinction is clearly hierarchical in a literal sense in that high versus low is hierarchical, and in a symbolic sense since males are superior to females. Once again this symbolic hierarchy is symbolically flattened by the structure of exchange of men with spirits of both of the categories in the dual structure.

The star-shape form to which we have referred many times

is an example of concentric dualism that is inherently asymmetrical since it always involves a center and a periphery that outnumbers the center. However, even this asymmetry is symmetrical on another level. If what is given by the center needs at some point to be reciprocated by those in the periphery, then each point on the periphery becomes successively through time a center. Once again synchronic hierarchy is resolved into diachronic reciprocity and symmetry in these forms of concentric dualism. In category three societies, concentric dualism, which is the structure of ceremonial exchange, provides regional integration, when seen from a more inclusive analytical level.

Lévi-Strauss has argued that concentric dualism is dynamic (and contains an implicit triadism) whereas diametric dualism is static and its transformations give rise to the same sort of dualism (Lévi-Strauss 1963: 151). The latter process has been observed in category two societies, with their multiplication of cross-cutting moieties. The possibilities in concentric dualism are seen in the development of the prototype into category three. The concentric dualism of category three represents an expansion in magnitude and in scale, and a formalization of the demand to reciprocate resulting in a sequencing of pig festivals and a higher order of integration. In order to understand how the generalized exchange systems of category four developed, it was necessary to postulate an intermediary prototype from which both categories three and four have developed. For, although category three represents simply an expansion in scale of concentric dualism, category four exemplifies a transformation into true generalized exchange.

Throughout this discussion we have seen that diametric dualism is a characteristic of the internal structure of politically autonomous groups, while concentric dualism is always a characteristic of the external structure of such groups as they relate to other groups of the same kind. The triadic structure of the *te* is also exclusively external. The star-shaped pattern of concentric dualism which characterizes external structure represents a more inclusive level of groupings in the hierarchical structure. The sequence of pig festivals in category three societies, and the moka and *te* in category four, represent structures of external relations which produce regional integration. The concentric dualism of the prototype and in category one represents an external structure in which regional integration is only sporadically present.

Structures play themselves out in different ways in their particular ecological settings. Generally speaking, the Highlands have a greater population density and a higher level of productivity than the Lowlands, and these factors are related to the more complex exchange systems in the Highlands. The Highlands, characterized by concentric dualism and by generalized exchange in some cases, have much larger pig populations and a higher ratio of pig population to human population than the Lowlands. A contrast may be seen in the continuum of pig husbandry, which ranges from Lowland societies where wild piglets are captured and raised to those Highland societies where boars are kept and pigs are bred. In the Highlands, a certain proportion of agricultural production is set aside to feed pigs. This is not done in the Lowlands. The Highlands have more advanced agricultural techniques and depend on a different staple crop—the sweet potato. These characteristics form an interrelated complex that serves to differentiate the Highlands from the Lowlands in terms of production.

The postulated evolutionary sequence of transformations set forth here may be compared with the archeological evidence and hypotheses about agricultural evolution which have been presented primarily for the Highlands. The debate between archeologists, ecological anthropologists, and cultural geographers concerning the role of the sweet potato in the agricultural evolution of the Highlands is relevant here.

In 1964, the Bulmers summarized the archeology of the Highlands in terms of three phases (Bulmer and Bulmer 1964). The first is a Pre-Neolithic phase of hunting and gathering, with the possibility of limited horticulture. The second phase is an indigenous development of agriculture, characterized by the introduction of new crops—taro, bananas, yams, sugar cane, and *pueraria*. This phase represents a continuity of population occupying the Highlands, rather than a migration from without. The third and last phase is marked by the introduction of intensive sweet potato cultivation, which in their view does not mark a discontinuity with the previous phase.

The following year, Watson (1965) offered a theory that suggested that the Highlands were occupied by small patrilocal bands of hunters or intermittent gardeners until three centuries ago. The introduction of the sweet potato at that time produced explosive changes, according to Watson, including rapid increase of population density and the development of intensive agricultural techniques for cultivation of sweet potatoes. He sees the presence of pigs as a measure of sedentarization, and believes that they were relatively unimportant until the introduction of the sweet potato.

Clark (1966), a geographer, analyzes a series of present-day agricultural systems, which he ranges along a continuum from simple, extensive forest fallow cultivation to a more elaborate, intensive grass fallow cultivation in which food production is increased. Without recourse to the archeological evidence, he views this continuum as representing "both a possible historic succession and a process of development" (Clarke 1966: 347). This succession is seen as a gradual one, with no abrupt change in technique or in crops.

Watson's hypotheses were considered at an interdisciplinary seminar in 1967, and the results were published by Brookfield and White (1968). Their conclusions, based on various kinds of evidence, some not available to Watson at the time that he advanced his ideas, are that there was no revolution in the Highlands with the introduction of the sweet potato. They see, instead, a long evolutionary sequence of agricultural development. Pigs are found in the Highlands at least 5,000 years B.P., long before the introduction of the sweet potato. There is archeological evidence of complex horticultural techniques as early as 2,300 years ago, which would have required stable and concentrated populations. They suggest that such a system could have been used for taro cultivation. Brookfield and White propose that the shift to sweet potato cultivation occurred because it offered a higher return for comparable inputs of land and labor (Brookfield and White 1968: 49). The sweet potato also permitted the expansion of agriculture into higher altitudes.

Watson (1977) has recently responded to his critics with a defense of what he calls the ipomean revolution brought about by the introduction of the sweet potato. He accuses Brookfield and White of emphasizing the efficiency of sweet potato production when compared to earlier crops, while ignoring the nonmaterial factors. According to Watson, the use of the sweet potato as fodder for pigs provided the impetus for conversion to sweet potatoes as the staple crop. The desire to increase the numbers of pigs was not to meet dietary demands but due to the need for pigs for exchange. The increases in production of sweet potatoes and pigs reinforce each other.

The only one in this discussion of agricultural evolution in the Highlands to concern himself with both Highlands and Lowlands is Waddell (1972b). His approach is primarily a synchronic one, in which individual agricultural systems are equated to stages along a continuum of agricultural evolution. The Lowlands and Highland fringe areas are characterized by simple shifting cultivation and nucleated settlements, which he suggests represent the earliest evolutionary stage. There is less evidence of dependence on a single staple, and hunting and gathering are important. The number of pigs is not great, and they depend primarily on forage. Population density is low. The core Highland area at the other end of the evolutionary continuum is characterized by intensive agricultural techniques, high population density, and greater number of pigs per human population. Both the Chimbu and Enga are in Waddell's core area. However, the Chimbu do not have the dual agricultural system of the Enga in which sweet potatoes are intensively cultivated in an open-field system and other crops in separate mixed gardens. Paralleling this difference, the Chimbu have a lower proportion of pig population to human population than do the Enga.

In comparing our postulated evolutionary sequence to the debate we have just summarized, the following points may be noted. In our view, the exchange system makes demands on the system of production in a society. Exchange systems evolve in terms of the limits of their environments to produce what those exchange systems demand. This position reflects agreement with Watson. However, we are interested in the transformations of exchange systems, while Watson simply takes them as given. Nor is he interested in the different forms of exchange systems in the Highlands, and their different operations within their environments. With respect to the rapidity of change in the Highlands, we do not see the introduction of the sweet potato as bringing about a revolution, in the way in which Watson does. We are more in agreement with Brookfield and White. The synchronic analyses of agricultural systems of both Clarke and Waddell also support this perspective. Our proposed series of transformations shows preexisting structures adapting and transforming themselves in response to new situations, rather than the rapid appearance of completely new structures after the introduction of the sweet potato.

Most of the people whose ideas about agricultural evolution in the New Guinea Highlands we have discussed above deal solely with the Highlands. Only Waddell has concerned himself with agricultural systems in both the Highlands and the Lowlands, which we feel is a more productive approach. The evolution of agricultural systems in the Highlands must obviously be seen as part of a larger picture of agricultural evolution in New Guinea as a whole. Diametric dualism as the dominant structure of exchange characterizing the societies in our categories one and two seems to reach its limits in the Lowlands, where shifting agriculture is practiced and the number of pigs per human population is low. Concentric dualism becomes dominant in the Highlands, where more intensive agricultural techniques result in a higher productive capacity. Though concentric dualism is present in our prototype, as well as in the Lowland societies of category one in an incipient form, in the Highlands it becomes systematized as the dominant structure producing regional integration. This type of concentric dualism characterizes our category three societies, where sweet potatoes are used as the human staple and for pig fodder, and the pig population is generally higher than in the Lowlands. In these societies there are no special agricultural techniques associated with sweet potato cultivation as are found among the Enga in category four.

The most intensive form of sweet potato production is correlated with the *te*, which makes the greatest demands upon production of the various systems of exchange which we have examined. The *te* probably evolved out of ceremonial payments of homicide compensation, when greatly increased sweet potato production permitted expansion in the number of pigs. The situational chains of moka exchange among the Melpa became fixed and systematized as they evolved into the *te* of the Enga. With the expansion of sweet potato production, older crops, now grown in mixed gardens, become associated with men as male crops. These crops continue to be exchanged in vegetable distributions in categories three and four, according to an older pattern of diametric dualism. In contrast, sweet potatoes and pigs both become associated with women. The introduction and expansion of sweet potato production made the women's contribution to agricultural production and to pig raising even more significant, but their ideological position remained very similar to that in Lowland societies—they continued to be polluting.

We began this book by posing the question: "Why doesn't everyone eat his own pigs?" The answer to this question would seem to be that, by giving one's pigs to other men, links between men are created and structures of social organization evolve.

Bibliography

Allen, M. R.

1967   *Male cults and secret initiations in Melanesia.*
      Melbourne: Melbourne University Press.

Aufenanger, H.

1959   "The war-magic houses in the Wahgi Valley
      and adjacent areas (New Guinea)." *An-*
      thropos 54: 1–26.

Barnes, J. A.

1962   "African models in the New Guinea high-
      lands." *Man* 62: 5–9.

Bateson, G.

1931–32 "Social structure of the Iatmul people of the
      Sepik River." *Oceania* 2:245–91, 401–54.
1936   *Naven: A survey of the problems suggested by a*
      composite picture of the culture of a New
      Guinea tribe, drawn from three points of view.
      Cambridge: Cambridge University Press.

Berndt, R., and Lawrence, P.

1971   *Politics in New Guinea.* Nedlands, Western
      Australia: University of Western Australia
      Press.

Brookfield, H. C.

1964   "The ecology of highland settlement: Some
      suggestions." *New Guinea: The Central High-*
      lands, ed. J. B. Watson, *American An-*
347   *thropologist* 66, no. 4, pt. 2: 20–38.

Brookfield, H. C., and Brown, P.

1963   *Struggle for land: Agriculture and group ter-ritories among the Chimbu of the New Guinea highlands.* Melbourne: Oxford University Press, in association with the Australian National University.

Brookfield, H. C., and White, J. P.

1968   "Revolution or evolution in the prehistory of the New Guinea highlands." *Ethnology* 7: 43–52.

Brown, P.

1960   "Chimbu tribes: Political organization in the eastern highlands of New Guinea." *Southwestern Journal of Anthropology* 16, no. 1:22–35.

1961   "Chimbu death payments." *Journal of the Royal Anthropological Institute* 91:77–96.

1962   "Non-agnates among the patrilineal Chimbu." *Journal of the Polynesian Society* 71:57–69.

1963   "From anarchy to satrapy." *American Anthropologist* 65:1–15.

1964   "Enemies and affines." *Ethnology* 3, no. 3:335–56.

1967a   "The Chimbu political system." *Anthropological Forum* 2, no. 1.

1967b   "Kondom." *Journal of the Papua and New Guinea Society* 1, no. 2:3–11.

1969   "Marriage in Chimbu." In *Pigs, pearlshells and women,* ed. R. M. Glasse and M. J. Meggitt. Englewood Cliffs, N.J.: Prentice Hall.

1970   "Chimbu transactions." *Man* 5, no. 1:99–117.

1972   *The Chimbu: A study of change in the New Guinea highlands.* Cambridge, Mass.: Schenkman Publishing Co.

Brown, P., and Brookfield, H. C.

1959–60 "Chimbu land and society." *Oceania* 30, no. 1:1–75.

Brown, P., and Buchbinder, G., eds.

1976   *Man and woman in the New Guinea highlands.*
              American Anthropological Association Spe-
              cial Publication No. 8.

Brown, P., and Podolefsky, A.

1976   "Population density, agricultural intensity,
              land tenure and group size in the New
              Guinea highlands." *Ethnology* 15, no. 3:211–
              38.

Bulmer, R. N. H.

1960   "Leadership and social structure among the
              Kyaka people of the Western Highlands Dis-
              trict of New Guinea." Canberra, Australian
              National University, Ph.D. thesis.
1960–61   "Political aspects of the Moka ceremonial ex-
              change system among the Kyaka people of
              the Western Highlands of New Guinea."
              Oceania 31:1–13.

Bulmer, S., and Bulmer, R.

1964   "The prehistory of the Australian New
              Guinea highlands." *New Guinea: The Central
              Highlands,* ed. J. B. Watson. *American An-
              thropologist* (Special Publication) 66, no.
              4(2):39–76.

Bus, G. A. M.

1951   "The Te festival or gift exchange in Enga
              (Central Highlands of New Guinea)." *An-
              thropos* 46:813–24.

Clarke, W. C.

1966   "From extensive to intensive shifting cultiva-
              tion in New Guinea." *Ethnology* 5:347–59.

Cook, E. A.

1967   "Manga social organization." New Haven,
              Conn., Yale University, Ph.D. thesis.
1969   "Marriage among the Manga." In *Pigs,
              pearlshells and women,* ed. R. M. Glasse and

M. J. Meggitt. Englewood Cliffs, N.J.: Prentice Hall.

1970 "On the conversion of non-agnates into agnates among the Manga, Jimi River, Western Highlands District, New Guinea." *Southwestern Journal of Anthropology* 26:190–95.

Elkin, A. P.

1952–53 "Delayed exchange in Wabag Sub-District, Central Highlands of New Guinea, with notes on the social organization." *Oceania* 23:161–201.

Forge, A.

1966 "Art and environment in the Sepik." *Proceedings of the Royal Anthropological Institute for 1965* (London), pp. 23–32.

1970a "Learning to see in New Guinea." In *Socialization: The approach from social anthropology*, ed. P. Mayer, ASA Monograph No. 8, London: Tavistock Publications.

1970b "Prestige, influence and sorcery: A New Guinea example." In *Witchcraft confessions and accusations*, ed. M. Douglas, ASA Monograph no. 9. London: Tavistock Publications.

1971 "Marriage and exchange in the Sepik: Comments on Francis Korn's analysis of Iatmul's society." In *Rethinking kinship and marriage*, ed. R. Needham, ASA Monograph No. 11. London: Tavistock Publications.

1973 "Style and meaning in Sepik art." In *Primitive art and society*, ed. A. Forge. London: Oxford University Press.

Fortune, R. F.

1939 "Arapesh warfare." *American Anthropologist* 41:22–41.

1942 *Arapesh*. New York: J. J. Augustin.

Gitlow, A. L.

1947 *Economics of the Mount Hagen tribes, New Guinea*. New York: J. J. Augustin.

Glasse, R., and Meggitt, M. J.

1969   *Pigs, pearlshells and women.* Englewood Cliffs, N.J.: Prentice Hall.

Goodenough, W. H.

1953   "Ethnographic notes on the Mae people of New Guinea's Western Highlands." *Southwestern Journal of Anthropology* 9, no. 1:29–44.

Hogbin, H. I.

1934–35a   "Native culture of Wogeo: Report of fieldwork in New Guinea." *Oceania* 5:308–37.

1934–35b   "Trading expeditions in Northern New Guinea." *Oceania* 5:375–407.

1935–36   "Sorcery and administration." *Oceania* 6:1–32.

1938   "Social reaction to crime: Law and morals in the Schouten Islands, New Guinea." *Journal of the Royal Anthropological Institute* 68:223–62.

1938–39   "Tillage and collection: A New Guinea economy." *Oceania* 9:127–51, 286–325.

1939–40   "Native land tenure in New Guinea." *Oceania* 10:113–65.

1940–41   The father chooses his heir: A family dispute over succession in Wogeo, New Guinea." *Oceania* 11:1–40.

1942–43   "A New Guinea infancy: From conception to weaning in Wogeo." *Oceania* 13:285–309.

1944–45   "Marriage in Wogeo, New Guinea." *Oceania* 15:324–52.

1952–53   "Sorcery and succession in Wogeo." *Oceania* 23:133–36.

1970a   *The island of menstruating men.* Scranton Pa.: Chandler Publishing Co.

1970b   "Food festivals and politics in Wogeo." *Oceania* 40:304–28.

Hogbin, H. I., and Wedgewood, C. N.

1952–53   "Local groupings in Melanesia." *Oceania* 23:58–76, 241–78.

Jakobson, R.

1970   *Main trends in the science of language.* New
               York: Harper and Row.

Kaberry, P. M.

1940–41   "The Abelam Tribe, Sepik District, New
               Guinea: A preliminary report." *Oceania*
               21:233–58, 345–67.
1941–42   "Law and political organization of the
               Abelam Tribe, New Guinea." *Oceania*
               12:79–95, 209–25, 331–63.
1966   "Political organisation among the Northern
               Abelam." *Anthropological Forum* 1, nos. 3, 4.
1967   "The plasticity of New Guinea kinship." In
               *Social organisation: Essays presented to
               Raymond Firth,* ed. M. Freeman. London:
               Frank Cass and Co.

Korn, F.

1971   "A question of preferences: The Iatmul
               case." In *Rethinking kinship and marriage,* ed.
               R. Needham, ASA Monograph No. 11. Lon-
               don: Tavistock Publications.

La Fontaine, J.

1973   "Descent in New Guinea: An Africanist
               view." In *The character of kinship,* ed. J.
               Goody. Cambridge: Cambridge University
               Press.

Langness, L. L.

1964   "Some problems in the conceptualization of
               Highlands social structure." In *New Guinea:
               The Central Highlands,* ed. J. B. Watson. *Amer-
               ican Anthropologist* 66, no. 4, pt. 2:162–82.

Lawrence, P., and Meggitt, M. J.

1965   *Gods, ghosts and men in Melanesia.* Mel-
               bourne: Oxford University Press.

Laycock, D. C.

1973   *Sepik languages—checklist and preliminary
               classification,* Pacific Linguistics, Series B,

No. 25, Dept. of Linguistics, Research School of Pacific Studies, Australian National University.

Lea, D. A.

1965 "The Abelam: A study of local differentiations." *Pacific Viewpoint* 6:191–214.

Leach, E.

1961 *Rethinking Anthropology*, London School of Economics Monographs on Social Anthropology No. 22. London: University of London, Athlone Press.

1976 *Culture and communication: The logic by which symbols are connected.* Cambridge: Cambridge University Press.

Leprevanche, M. de

1967–68 "Descent, residence and leadership in the New Guinea Highlands." *Oceania* 38:134–58, 163–89.

Lévi-Strauss, C.

1944 "Reciprocity and hierarchy." *American Anthropologist* 46:266–68.

1963 *Structural anthropology.* New York and London: Basic Books.

1969 *The elementary structures of kinship.*, rev. ed., trans. J. H. Bell, J. R. von Sturner, and R. Needham. London: Eyre and Spottiswoode; Boston: Beacon Press (originally published 1949).

Lowman-Vayda, C.

1971 "Maring Big Men." In *Politics in New Guinea,* ed. R. Berndt and P. Lawrence. Nedlands, Western Australia: University of Western Australia Press.

Luzbetak, L.

1954 "The socio-religious significance of a New Guinea pig festival." *Anthropological Quarterly* (N.S.), ii.

1956   "Worship of the dead in Middle Wahgi." *Anthropos* 51: 81–96.

Malinowski, B.

1915   "The natives of Mailu: Preliminary results of the Robert Mond research work in British New Guinea." *Transactions and Proceedings of the Royal Society of Southern Australia* 39:494–706.

Mauss, M.

1954   *The gift,* trans. Ian Cunnison. London: Cohen and West Ltd. (originally published 1925).

Maybury-Lewis, D.

1960   "The analysis of dual organisations: A methodological critique." *Bijdragen tot de Taal-, Land-, en Volkenkunde* 116:2–44.

Mead, M.

1933–34   "The Marsalai cult among the Arapesh, with special reference to the rainbow serpent beliefs of the Australian aborigines." *Oceania* 4:37–53.

1935   *Sex and temperament in three primitive societies.* London: G. Routledge and Sons.

1937   "The Arapesh of New Guinea." In *Cooperation and competition among primitive peoples,* ed. M. Mead. New York: McGraw-Hill.

1938   "The Mountain Arapesh I. An importing culture." *Anthropological Papers of the American Museum of Natural History* 36, pt. 3:130–349.

1940   "The Mountain Arapesh II. Supernaturalism." *Anthropological Papers of the American Museum of Natural History* 37, pt. 3:317–451.

1947   "The Mountain Arapesh III. Socio-economic life; IV. Diary of events in Alitoa." *Anthropological Papers of the American Museum of Natural History* 40, pt. 3:159–420.

Meggitt, M. J.

1957–58   "The Enga of the New Guinea Highlands:
           Some preliminary observations." *Oceania*
           28:253–330.
1964a   "Male-female relationships in the Highlands
           of Australian New Guinea." In *New Guinea:
           The Central Highlands*, special publication, ed.
           J. B. Watson. *American Anthropologist* 66, no.
           4, pt. 2:204–24.
1964b   "The kinship terminology of the Mae-Enga
           of New Guinea." *Oceania* 34:191–200.
1965a   *The lineage system of the Mae-Enga of New
           Guinea*. Edinburgh: Oliver and Boyd.
1965b   "The Mae Enga of the Western Highlands."
           In *Gods, ghosts and men in Melanesia*, ed. P.
           Lawrence and M. J. Meggitt. Melbourne: Ox-
           ford University Press.
1967   "The pattern of leadership among the Mae-
           Enga." *Anthropological Forum* 2, no. 1:20–35.
1969   "Introduction." In *Pigs, pearlshells and
           women*, ed. R. M. Glasse and M. J. Meggitt.
           Englewood Cliffs, N.J.: Prentice Hall.
1971   "From tribesmen to peasants: The case of the
           Mae-Enga of New Guinea." In *Anthropology
           in Oceania*, ed. L. R. Hiatt and C.
           Jayawardena.   Sydney: Angus   and
           Robertson.
1972   "System and subsystem: The Te exchange
           cycle among the Mae-Enga" (shortened ver-
           sion of "Pigs are our hearts!"). *Human Ecol-
           ogy* 1, no. 2.
1974   " 'Pigs are our hearts!' The Te exchange cycle
           among the Mae-Enga of New Guinea."
           Oceania 44:165–203.
1977   *Blood is their argument: Warfare among the
           Mae-Enga tribesmen of the New Guinea High-
           lands*. Palo Alto, Cal.: Mayfield Publishing
           Co.

Nilles, J.

1940   "Eine   Knaben-Jugendweihe   bei   den
           östlichen   Waugla   im   Bismarckgebirge

Neuguineas." *Internationales Archiv für Ethnographie* 38: 93–98.

1950–51   "The Kuman of the Chimbu Region, Central Highlands, New Guinea." *Oceania* 21:25–65.

1953–54   "The Kuman people: A study of cultural change in a primitive society in the Central Highlands of New Guinea." *Oceania* 24:1–27, 119–31.

Oosterwal, G.

1959   "The position of the bachelor in the Upper Tor Territory." *American Anthropologist* 61:829–38.

1961   *People of the Tor: A cultural anthropological study on the tribes of the Tor Territory (northern Netherlands New Guinea).* Assen, Netherlands: Royal Van Corcum.

Ortiz, A.

1969   *The Tewa world—space, time, being, and becoming in a Pueblo society.* Chicago and London: University of Chicago Press.

Rappaport, R.

1967   "Ritual regulation of environmental relations among a New Guinea people." *Ethnology* 6:17–30.

1968   *Pigs for the ancestors: Ritual in the ecology of a New Guinea people.* New Haven, Conn., and London: Yale University Press.

1969   "Marriage among the Maring." In *Pigs, pearlshells and women,* ed. R. M. Glasse and M. J. Meggitt. Englewood Clifs, N.J.: Prentice Hall.

Reay, M.

1958–59   "Two kinds of ritual conflict." *Oceania* 29:290–96.

1959a   *The Kuma: Freedom and conformity in the New Guinea Highlands.* Melbourne: Melbourne University Press on behalf of the Australian National University.

1959b   "Individual ownership and transfer of land among the Kuma." *Man* 59:78–82.

1964   "Present-day politics in the New Guinea
             Highlands." In *New Guinea: The Central High-
             lands,* ed. J. B. Watson. *American An-
             thropologist* (Special Publication) 66, no. 4,
             pt. 2:240–56.
1967   "Structural co-variants of land shortage
             among patrilineal peoples." *Anthropological
             Forum* 2, no. 1:4–19.

Rosman, A., and Rubel, P.

1971   *Feasting with mine enemy.* New York: Colum-
             bia University Press.
1974   Field notes.

Ross, Father W. A.

1936   "Ethnological notes on Mt. Hagen tribes
             (mandated territory of New Guinea)." *An-
             thropos* 31:341–63.

Sahlins, M.

1963   "Poor man, rich man, big-man, chief." *Com-
             parative Studies in Society and History* 5:283–
             300.
1965   "On the ideology and composition of descent
             groups." *Man* 65:104–7.

Salisbury, R. F.

1956   "Unilineal descent groups in the New
             Guinea Highlands." *Man* 56:2–7.
1964   "New Guinea Highland models and descent
             theory." *Man* 64:168–71.

Saussure, F. de

1966   *Course in general linguistics.* New York:
             McGraw-Hill (originally published in 1915).

Seligman, C. G.

1910   *The Melanesians of British New Guinea.* Cam-
             bridge: Cambridge University Press.

Strathern, A. J.

1966   "Despots and directors in the New Guinea
             Highlands." *Man* 1:356–67.

1969a   "Descent and alliance in the New Guinea Highlands: Some problems of comparison." *Proceedings of the Royal Anthropological Institute for 1968,* pp. 37–52.

1969b   "Finance and production: Two strategies in New Guinea Highlands exchange systems." *Oceania* 40:42–67.

1970a   "The female and male spirit cults in Mount Hagen." *Man* (N.S.) 5:571–85.

1970b   "Male initiation in New Guinea Highland societies." *Ethnology* 9, no. 4:373–79.

1971a   *The rope of Moka: Big-men and ceremonial exchange in Mount Hagen.* Cambridge: Cambridge University Press.

1971b   "Pig complex and cattle complex: Some comparisons and counterpoints." *Mankind* 8:129–37.

1972a   *One father, one blood: Descent and group structure among the Melpa people.* London: Tavistock Publications.

1972b   "Moka." In *Encyclopedia of Papua and New Guinea,* 3 vols., gen ed. P. Ryan. Melbourne: Melbourne University Press.

1972c   "The entrepreneurial model of social change: From Norway to New Guinea." *Ethnology* 11, no. 4:368–79.

Strathern, A. J., and Strathern, A. M.

1968   "Marsupials and magic: A study of spell symbolism among the Mbowamb." In *Dialectic in practical religion,* ed. E. R. Leach, Cambridge Papers in Social Anthropology No. 5, Cambridge: Cambridge University Press.

1969   "Marriage in Melpa." In *Pigs, pearlshells and women,* ed. R. M. Glasse and M. J. Meggitt. Englewood Cliffs, N.J.: Prentice Hall.

1971   *Self-decoration in Mount Hagen.* London: Gerald Duckworth.

Strathern, A. M.

1972   *Women in between, female roles in a male world: Mount Hagen, New Guinea.* London: Seminar Press.

Strauss, H., and Tischner, H.

1962   *Die Mi-Kultur der Hagenberg-Stämme im Östlichen Zental-Neuguinea.* Hamburg: Cram, de Gruyter und Co.

Thurnwald, R.

1916   "Banaro society: Social organisation and kinship system of a tribe in the interior of New Guinea." *American Anthropological Association Memoirs* 3:253–391.

Vayda, A. P.

1975   "War and peace in New Guinea." In *Cultural and social anthropology,* ed. P. B. Hammond. New York: Macmillan.

Vicedom, G. F., and Tischner, H.

1943–48   *Die Mbowamb.* Hamburg: Cram, de Gruyter und Co.

Waddell, E.

1972a   *The mound builders.* Seattle and London: University of Washington Press.
1972b   "Agricultural evolution in the New Guinea Highlands." *Pacific Viewpoint* 13:18–29.

Wagner, R.

1974   "Are there social groups in the New Guinea Highlands?" In *Frontiers of anthropology,* ed. M. J. Leaf. New York: D. Van Nostrand Co.

Watson, J. B.

1965   "From hunting to horticulture in the New Guinea Highlands." *Ethnology* 4:285–307.
1977   "Pigs, fodder, and the Jones effect in post-ipomoean New Guinea." *Ethnology* 16:57–70.

Williams, F. E.

1936   *Papuans of the Trans-Fly. Territory of Papua, Anthropology Report,* No. 15. Oxford: Clarendon Press.

Index